Praise for

ROGER MARIS

Named one of "The Best Baseball Books of 2010" by Baseball America

"A wonderful book. . . . It makes me happy because Roger was such a nice guy and fine ballplayer—he deserves to be written about."

—*New York Daily News*

"This is one of the best portrayals of a famous athlete that I've ever read."

—Ken Davidoff, *Newsday* (New York)

"The definitive biography of an enigmatic and woefully misunderstood man."

—*The Philadelphia Inquirer*

"A first-rate biography, thoroughly researched and stylishly written."

—*Florida Times-Union*

"A compelling portrait of a good man and a great baseball player."

—*Spitball Magazine*

"One of the best players of his era has finally gotten the fair and accurate biography he deserves, and possibly more."

—*Sacramento Book Review*

"The details the authors present of Roger's life leave the reader wondering at times if Clavin and Peary had followed him around from his birth. It is a well-researched take on a misunderstood man."

—*Deseret News* (Salt Lake City)

"Hopefully this book will serve to restore some of the recognition that Maris failed to obtain in his lifetime."

—*Dayton Daily News*

"An important biography of one of the game's most misunderstood heroes."

—*Trenton Times*

"I've been hoping for a long time that the complexity of that honorable, serious, accomplished man would be captured and plumbed in a book worthy of his memory. Here it is."

—Robert Lipsyte, *East Hampton Star*

"Without question an entertaining book for baseball fans, but general readers of biography may also enjoy understanding the life of one who achieved greatness despite adversity."

—*Library Journal*

"No doubt, the book will spark conversations about restoring Maris's presteroid home-run record (something the family wishes) and considering him for the Hall of Fame."

—*Publishers Weekly*

"This is a wonderful, definitive biography. What an extraordinary, misunderstood life of a true American hero who didn't want to be one. This is a remarkable work that belongs in every baseball fan's house."

—Larry King

"The authors paint a splendid portrait of the Roger Maris I knew very well and the Roger Maris I wish I knew better."

—Tim McCarver

"The amazing thing about the man who broke Babe Ruth's record was how little he resembled Babe Ruth. Introverted, troubled, shy, Roger Maris was more like a next-door neighbor than any home-run king, any Sultan of Swat. His struggles to wear the heavy overcoat of fame and notoriety are fascinating. Tom Clavin and Danny Peary show us why it didn't fit. Terrific work."

—Leigh Montville, author of the national bestseller
The Big Bam: The Life and Times of Babe Ruth

"Roger Maris remains the authentic single-season home-run king. Perhaps too little, certainly too late in recent years, he has been venerated and vindicated. Better yet, in these pages, he is appreciated."

—Bob Costas

"Here, finally, is the book that Roger Maris deserved. With deep and dogged reporting, Tom Clavin and Danny Peary have done more than rescue his reputation. In this definitive portrait, Maris acquires a meaning beyond the home-run record. He's forced to straddle a fault line in American culture, one that separates the stoic from the glib, and authentic heroes from those merely famous. This is fine and fascinating stuff."

—Mark Kriegel, columnist for FOXSports.com,
author of *Pistol: The Life of Pete Maravich*

AUTHORS' BOOKS

TOM CLAVIN'S BOOKS

Last Men Out: The True Story of America's Heroic Final Hours in Vietnam (with Bob Drury)

One for the Ages: Jack Nicklaus and the 1986 Masters

That Old Black Magic: Louis Prima, Keely Smith, and the Golden Age of Las Vegas

The Last Stand of Fox Company (with Bob Drury)

Halsey's Typhoon (with Bob Drury)

Dark Noon

Sir Walter: Walter Hagen and the Invention of Professional Golf

The Ryder Cup (with Bob Bubka)

The Power of Soul (with Drs. Darlene and Derek Hopson)

Fatal Analysis (with Dr. Martin Obler)

We're Not Normal (with Bridget LeRoy)

Juba This and Juba That (with Drs. Darlene and Derek Hopson)

Raising the Rainbow Generation (with Drs. Darlene and Derek Hopson)

DANNY PEARY'S BOOKS

Tim McCarver's Diamond Gems (with Tim McCarver and Jim Moskovitz)

Great Golf (with Allen Richardson)

Baseball Forever (with Ralph Kiner)

1,001 Reasons to Love Baseball (with Mary Tiegreen)

Raising a Team Player (with Harry Sheehy)

The Perfect Season (with Tim McCarver)

Tim McCarver's Baseball for Brain Surgeons and Other Fans (with Tim McCarver)

Super Bowl: The Game of Their Lives

We Played the Game

Alternate Oscars

Cult Movie Stars

Cult Baseball Players

How to Buy, Trade, and Invest in Baseball Cards & Collectibles (with Bruce Chadwick)

Cult Movies 3

Omni's ScreenFlights/ScreenFantasies

Guide for the Film Fanatic

Cult Movies 2

Cult Movies

The American Animated Cartoon: A Critical Anthology (with Gerald Peary)

Close-Ups: The Movie Star Book

ROGER MARIS

BASEBALL'S RELUCTANT HERO

TOM CLAVIN

AND

DANNY PEARY

A TOUCHSTONE BOOK

Published by Simon & Schuster

New York London Toronto Sydney

Touchstone
A Division of Simon & Schuster, Inc.
1230 Avenue of the Americas
New York, NY 10020

First Touchstone trade paperback edition May 2011

TOUCHSTONE and colophon are registered trademarks of Simon & Schuster, Inc.

For information about special discounts for bulk purchases,
please contact Simon & Schuster Special Sales at
1-866-506-1949 or business@simonandschuster.com.

The Simon & Schuster Speakers Bureau can bring authors to your live event.
For more information or to book an event contact the Simon & Schuster Speakers Bureau
at 1-866-248-3049 or visit our website at www.simonspeakers.com.

Designed by Joy O'Meara

Manufactured in the United States of America

1   3   5   7   9   10   8   6   4   2

The Library of Congress has cataloged the hardcover edition as follows:
Clavin, Thomas.
Roger Maris : baseball's reluctant hero / by Tom Clavin
and Danny Peary.—1st Touchstone hardcover ed.
p.   cm.
"A Touchstone Book."
Includes bibliographical references and index.
1. Maris, Roger, 1934–1985.   2. Baseball players—United States—Biography.
3. New York Yankees (Baseball team)   I. Peary, Danny, 1949–   II. Title.
GV865.M274C53   2010
796.357092—dc22
[B]   2009039722

ISBN 978-1-4165-8928-0
ISBN 978-1-4165-8929-7 (pbk)
ISBN 978-1-4165-9682-0 (ebook)

In memory of my father, Joseph Clavin, for all those golden after-noons at Yankee Stadium where a little boy could be with Roger, Mickey, Yogi, Whitey, and all his other heroes.

—Tom Clavin

In memory of my mother, Laura Peary, who knew the names of only eight baseball players—Babe Ruth, Lou Gehrig (who died soon after she arrived in America), Mickey Mantle, Yogi Berra, Vic Power, Tim McCarver, Ralph Kiner, and, finally, Roger Maris.

And in memory of several dear friends who passed away since we began this book—Ruth Simring (our chief researcher), Sheila Lukins, Mary Ann Muro, Lynn Strong, Celeste Sturcken, and Virginia Suglia. And the lovely Karen Schmeer.

—Danny Peary

In memory of our close friend and golf buddy, Fred Baum, and several individuals who were interviewed for this book—Maury Allen, Johnny Blanchard, Bobby Bragan, Violet Marich Cortese, Ryne Duren, Merle Harmon, Ernie Harwell, George Kissell, Cal McLish, George Stickland, Tom Sturdivant, Tom Tresh, and Hal Woodeshick.

—Tom Clavin and Danny Peary

The mockery made him feel an outsider; and feeling an outsider he behaved like one, which increased the prejudice against him. . . . Which in turn increased his sense of being alien and alone. A chronic fear of being slighted made him avoid his equals, made him stand, where his inferiors were concerned, self-consciously on his dignity.

—ALDOUS HUXLEY, *Brave New World*

CONTENTS

PROLOGUE

OCTOBER 1, 1961

THE SAVVIEST PHOTOGRAPHERS GOT the two money shots.

The first, taken from behind and near the Yankee dugout, was of Roger Maris making solid contact over the plate on a 2-0 fastball by Tracy Stallard. The left-handed pull hitter is exhibiting his much praised swing with extended bat and arms parallel to the ground, his left hand turning over, his right leg straight and left leg flexed, his right foot pointing toward third base and his left one perpendicular to the ground, his muscles in his face, neck, and upper arms tense, and his hips rotating.

The second picture, taken from the front, was of Maris one breath later. With, surprisingly, still-seated fans behind him, he is completing his pivot, releasing the bat with his left hand, and watching with hopeful eyes the flight of his historic home run into Yankee Stadium's packed right-field stands.

But even the award winners among them missed something quite extraordinary that took place seconds later. Fortunately, one of the greatest, if most neglected, visual metaphors in sports history would be preserved on celluloid.

Having completed what his bedridden Yankee teammate Mickey Mantle always called the "greatest sports feat I ever saw," the new single-season home-run champion dropped his bat and ran down the baseline. He rounded first at the same time nineteen-year-old Sal Durante held up the 61st home-run ball in his right hand; another ecstatic young male fan leaped onto the field; and the clearly dejected Red Sox pitcher concocted an upbeat post-game response to the media ("I'll now make some money on the banquet circuit!").

As he neared second base, Maris suddenly escaped dark shadows and moved into the bright, warm sunlight. Just like that, he had finally found a slice of heaven after a long season he'd sum up as "sheer hell."

In Roger Maris's version of hell, he was the prey in a daily media feeding frenzy, lost his privacy, shed some hair, received hate mail by the bundle, experienced vicious heckling from even home fans, and, having arrived in New York from Kansas City only twenty-two months before, was treated by the Yankees organization like an outsider, an ugly duckling in a pond of swans. His blow on the last day of the season was a telling response to all that nonsense.

Maris ran as he always did after a home run—head down and at a measured pace, exhibiting nothing offensively ostentatious or celebratory, nothing to indicate he was circling the bases one time more in a season than anyone else in history. He was pounded on the back by joyous third-base coach Frank Crosetti as he came down the homestretch. Crossing home plate, he was greeted by on-deck batter Yogi Berra, then batboy Frank Prudenti, and, finally, the anonymous Zelig-like fan. Then he made his way into the dugout—at least he tried to. Several Yankees formed a barricade and turned Maris around and pushed him upward so he could acknowledge the standing ovation.

He reluctantly inched back up the steps, stretching his neck as if he were a turtle warily emerging from its shell. He dutifully waved his cap and gave his teammates a pleading look, hoping they would agree that he had been out there too long already. They urged him to stay put and allow the fans to shower him with the adulation that had been missing all year. So he waved his hat some more and smiled sheepishly.

The television camera zoomed in, and everyone could see that during his sunlit jaunt around the bases, he had, amazingly, been tranformed. With the burden of unreasonable expectations suddenly lifted and the knowledge that not one more dopey reporter would ask, "Are you going to break Babe Ruth's record, Rog?" the strain in his face and haunted look in his eyes had vanished. He no longer looked double his twenty-seven years and on the verge of a meltdown.

Baseball fans would, in their mind's eye, freeze-frame forever this image of the young, cheery innocent with the trademark blond crewcut who had just claimed sports' most revered record. For that one moment Maris believed all the bad stuff was behind him. For that one brief moment, he felt free. In reality, it was the calm before an even more vicious storm. He couldn't know that the press would not back off and the fickle, media-manipulated fans who had rooted against his breaking the record in 1961 would boo him in 1962 for not breaking it again.

Having come from a small town where privacy was cherished and celebrity was nonexistent, Maris was mystified that the media and the fans actually wanted to know anything about him. As Jim Murray of the *Los Angeles Times* observed, "Roger Maris was about as well equipped for fame as a forest ranger." It was true to form that he revealed far less about himself in *Roger Maris At Bat*, the autobiographical book he wrote with veteran reporter Jim Ogle after the '61 season, than in *Slugger in Right*, an obscure, semiautobiographical novel they wrote the following year about a troubled young Yankee right fielder named Billy Mack.

By all accounts, through 1961 Maris was considerate of reporters who needed copy and was regarded by teammates and opponents alike as one of the most quiet, shy, and decent people they had ever met. So it was all the more unjust that *he* would have the dubious distinction of being the first ballplayer that a large segment of the press went after, almost as savagely as the white press had attacked African-American heavyweight boxing champion Jack Johnson half a century before. Unprotected by the Yankees, he was the guinea pig for a new breed of hip, no-holds-barred reporters who wanted to flex their muscles and show they had the power to destroy a star player's reputation and his psyche.

That he accepted the brutally negative and often untruthful things written about him in 1961 and later years, rather than trying to make peace with the press in exchange for favorable coverage, eventually stripped him of his enthusiasm for baseball and cost him a legitimate shot at being selected to the Hall of Fame. He was too stubborn, too self-destructive, and too true to himself—and a bit too self-righteous—to compromise when he believed he was wronged. "When I think I am right," he declared in *Roger Maris At Bat*, "there is no man who is going to tell me that I am wrong unless he can PROVE IT to me. As long as I know I am right I'm going to put up an argument regardless of the consequences."

"The fact is," said his wife, Pat Maris, "that his combination of shyness and outspokenness confuses people who do not know him very well."

How did Roger Maris get that way? Surely he was the product of both family and the part of the country where he was raised. Yet even there he stood apart.

CHAPTER ONE

THE MARASES AND MARICHES

AMONG THOSE ROOTING FOR Roger Maris as he closed in on Babe Ruth's record in September of 1961 was a folksinger whose nascent career took off that month in New York City thanks to a rave in the *Times* and his first studio work. Although he wasn't much of a sports fan, Bob Dylan felt pride when he learned that the ballplayer making national headlines also hailed from Hibbing, Minnesota.

Dylan was born in Duluth and didn't arrive in Hibbing until he was seven and had nothing good to say or sing about it after he left and didn't look back. So it's ironic that he became the town's favorite son, while Maris, who was born in Hibbing, was consigned to outsider status. The reason is that Dylan at least acknowledged he was from there. "It still burns me up that Roger claimed he was born in Fargo, North Dakota," says Bill Starcevic, his childhood playmate in Minnesota. Roger didn't care if the record books or trading cards got his birthplace wrong or if no one knew he'd changed his name to Maris from Maras in 1954, infuriating the many Marases of Hibbing. If he thought something was trivial—or personal—he was surprised when others made a big deal of it.

His parents, Rudy and Connie, taught him and his older brother, Rudy Jr.—called Buddy by Roger and others—to be silent about private matters. Or maybe they learned that on their own. Roger was willing to be called bland rather than let on that he had a colorful background, with a family tree that had many intriguing, intertwined limbs. His tree included the names Maris, Maras (pronounced like Morris), Marich, Barich, and March. There was an overabundance of Rudys, Nicks, and Mikes as well as numerous variations on Mary, Ann, and Katherine. Roger's mother and grandmother each had four last names.

The Marases came from a mountainous area of southern Croatia, along the coastline of the Adriatic Sea, where their equally poor ancestors from, perhaps, Greece, Turkey, or even ancient Persia settled centuries before. Males fished along pebble beaches, females tended sheep, and everyone met in Catholic churches. Roger's great-grandparents John (Ivan) and Mary Dosen Maras, had six children: Mike (Mata or Mate), born in 1881; Paul (Pava), born in 1883; Roger's grandfather Steve (Stifan), born in 1885; Joseph (Jaso), born in 1893; Peter, born in 1895; and Anna, born in 1899.

They lived in Yugoslavia before it existed, so on their immigration papers they put down vast Austria-Hungary, making their exact point of origin uncertain. Most of the brothers told officials that their birthplace was Karlobag (which they wrote as Carlo Bag), but on one document Steve listed the smaller southern town of Kruscica, and on another he cited Gospic, to the east. Mike's grandson Bill Maras says his father, "Big Nick" Maras, told him he grew up in Lukova Sugarje. It is known that the Maras family lived near Barić Draga, an inlet village named after its most prominent (though not wealthy) family, because three of Roger's four granduncles married a Barich. (Anna married a Barich, too, but he wasn't related.)

Spurred by depressing economic and political situations in their homelands, more than 2 million Slavs—Croats, Serbs, and Slovenes—left for America between 1893 and the beginning of the war in Europe, including all five Maras brothers. Steve arrived in Baltimore on March 13, 1903, having just turned eighteen. He stood 5'9", weighed 180 pounds, and had brown hair, blue-gray eyes, and a scar on the left side of his forehead. He may have gone directly to Chicago, where Paul had settled the year before.

Paul, who was educated by monks in a mountain monastery, arrived in America at the age of seventeen, determined to be a successful barman, as he'd been in Germany. He spent several years in Chicago, which had a large Croat population, working in a saloon, improving his English, assimilating into the culture, and learning about capitalism in theory and practice. Exemplifying the spirit of the immigrant, Paul believed he'd have success in this land of opportunity if he became his own boss, so in 1906 he trekked to Hibbing, a bustling mining town in northeast Minnesota. Steve followed.

Founded in 1893, Hibbing was a melting pot, attracting immigrants from more than thirty nations, with the majority working in the underground and open-pit mines until most shut down during the ferocious winters; or as loggers, earning the same $40 a month. Because some mines were within walking distance, many men lived in Hibbing proper. Others resided in "locations," residential enclaves on mining-company land that often had the same names as the excavation sites they were next to. Essentially, Hibbing was comprised of the locations it gobbled up as the biggest iron-ore mines stretched out. Hull Rust Mahoning Open Pit Mine would become so large—3.5 miles long, 2 miles wide, and 535 feet deep—that tourists came to know it as the "Grand Canyon of the North."

On the north side of this thirsty community, Paul opened a small saloon with living quarters above, with Steve working for him. Satisfied he could make a good living in Hibbing, Paul sent for Eva Barich. She told her mother that she was going to America to marry Paul, and as the family legend goes, her mother fainted and Eva stepped over her body and walked out the door. Paul married Eva in Hibbing on June 22, 1907. On October 21, 1908, also in Hibbing, Steve wed Katharina Verderbar. Roger's grandmother had arrived in New York a few years earlier from Germany. It's likely she met Steve in Chicago, where her brother John decades later operated a popular ballroom featuring the big bands Roger adored.

Joseph Maras came to Hibbing with Eva and worked with Steve at Paul's saloon and boarded above it. Soon Mike joined them. He first set foot in America between 1902 and 1905, initially going to St. Louis, but he repeatedly returned to Croatia to court Eva's cousin Masha Barich. They married there in 1907, but Mike, an imposing, barrel-chested man with a gruff demeanor, returned to America without her. He probably was reluctant to work for a younger brother, but he needed money for his trips back home.

Steve and Katharina had five children. Rudy, Roger and Rudy Jr.'s father, was born on April 17, 1911, followed by four girls: Paulina in 1913, Josephine in 1914, Katherine in 1916, and Sofia in 1920.

Paul and Eva, an illiterate, Old World woman whose life was her family, had kids like clockwork: Frederick in 1908, Mary in 1909, Julia in 1911, Anna in 1912, John-Paul (called Jack) in 1913, Louise in 1914, Matilda (called Tilly) in 1916, and Pauline in 1925. Louise died of dysentery during a flu epidemic.

Masha bore Mike three children in Croatia: Nick (later called Big Nick) in 1909, Mary in 1912, and Katie in 1913. She would likely have had more kids if the World War didn't prevent Mike from continuing his conjugal visits.

On Mike's last voyage back to America, in 1913, eighteen-year-old Peter Maras accompanied him. For the first time, the five Maras brothers were in Hibbing. "Eventually, all the brothers learned English," says Paul's daughter Tilly Sanborn, who turned ninety-three in 2009. "They weren't fluent but they managed."

Steve, Mike, and Joseph continued to work for Paul when he became the proprietor of the Ryan Hotel, a classy establishment on Pine Street that attracted clients not only with clean rooms and a popular bar but also a buffet, soft drinks, fancy candies, and a three-lane bowling alley in the basement. Steve worked as a bartender and confectioner, Mike as a bartender and hotel clerk, and Joseph as a chauffeur.

"Everybody knew Grandpa Paul because he was a wonderful barman with a dynamic personality, and also he helped a lot of the Croats," says Peggy Sanborn, Tilly's daughter. "He got them jobs, did their banking, and wrote their letters. He organized a Croatian social and arranged marriages in the Catholic church and huge receptions at the Croatian Hall." Adding to his earnings, Paul worked as an interpreter for the Oliver Mining Company and started a shuttle service to transport miners to and from the various locations. He even went back to Croatia to recruit miners, which helps explain how five families of unrelated Marases ended up in Hibbing. (Some related Marases settled in Oklahoma and Washington.)

In 1917, Steve went into business for himself, opening a confectionery store with a small bar on the border of the Morton and Leetonia locations. It was attached to the small house where he and Katharina raised their children.

Meanwhile, Pete was with the U.S. combat forces in Europe. "I think he enlisted," his grandnephew Bill Maras says, "because when he got out, he became the first brother to become an American citizen." It annoyed Mike that the younger Pete was granted his citizenship while he got turned down repeatedly (until 1942), but he wanted his own bar and needed a partner with legal status.

Mike received advance word that the entire town of Hibbing was moving to the south—over nine years, 180 buildings and 20 businesses were relocated at the extraordinary cost of $16 million—due to the discovery of a large deposit of hematite iron ore under town streets. (The vacated area would become an extension of the Hull Rust Mahoning mine.) So he and Pete put up a building at 2213 First Avenue in the new Hibbing, which really was South Hibbing. Mike's intention was to open a tavern, with one entrance leading to a large bar and the other to the hotel. There is no evidence Paul helped Mike financially, but that might explain why they feuded years later, seemingly over money.

Unfortunately, Mike and Pete's timing wasn't the best. On January 16, 1920, the Eighteenth Amendment went into effect, banning the sale, manufacture, and transportation of alcohol for consumption in all forty-eight states. With booze illegal, the two brothers made money by letting rooms, renting out space for a movie theater and a pharmacy owned by a Homer Webster, running a speakeasy with liquor from their own still, and gambling.

Mike felt secure enough in business by 1922 to send Pete to Croatia to bring back their parents, John and Mary; Mike's wife, Masha, and their three children; and Monda Barich, Masha's twenty-year-old sister. Not to be outdone, Paul brought Eva's youngest sister, Marija Barich, to Hibbing in 1923. (She married Marco Dosen, who may or may not have been related to Paul's mother, Mary Dosen Maras. According to Marija's daughter Anna Dosen, Marija and Marco were among the family members who sold moonshine during Prohibition—"My mother was too slick for the feds, but my father was sent to the work farm a few times"—before joining Marija's two brothers in Detroit, where there was more legitimate work.)

Also in 1923, Joseph, now the owner of an auto livery, married Rosie Toddie, who was from Italy. They had no children. Soon after, Pete proposed to Monda Barich. They had a big wedding, raised four boys, and eventually divorced. But for years, business partners Pete and Mike were married to sisters.

The five Maras brothers and their sister, Anna (who had three children with Mike Barich), were married by 1924, and all lived in or near Hibbing, as did their parents and relatives of their spouses. "There were big family gatherings on Sundays, usually at my grandparents' house in Alice," says Peggy Sanborn. "All the brothers and relatives came with their families, and my mother and the other kids played together." It was then that young Rudy developed a love of barbecues that he'd pass along to Roger. He also got his first close look at polio, which had stricken his first cousin Frederick. He didn't know it would affect one of his own sons.

A destination for many kids in the family was Steve's candy store. "Uncle Joe, who called me Irish, would say, 'C'mon, Irish, let's go see Uncle Steve,' " remembers Tilly Sanborn. "And we'd go out to his little candy and pickup store in Leetonia. I loved Steve. He always had a lot of candy and that sure did me good. He and my aunt Katharina were very nice to me. He ran the store and she was a housewife. I'd spend weekends there with the five kids."

Paul and Mike had an increasingly strained relationship, but if there was a harmonious period for the entire Maras family, it was from the early 1920s through 1927. Then in 1928, Joseph, loved by all the brothers, died a few days after turning thirty-five. Tuberculosis was hinted at.

In 1929, the year the Great Depression began, John Maras decided he'd had enough of the New World and returned to Croatia to spend his last years alone. Mary loved America and stayed. "His leaving was a real heartache for the family," remembers their granddaughter Tilly Sanborn.

Steve rode out Prohibition and the Depression by making a modest living selling candy, cigars, odds and ends, and near beer. Mike and Peter made a good living with their various enterprises, although Mike spent some time in jail on a bootlegging charge. But Paul had a reversal of fortune. "My family was secretive and never would talk about it," says Peggy Sanborn, "but Grandpa Paul became an alcoholic and spent money beyond his means and was broke *before* the stock market crashed. I don't know if he asked Mike to help him, although I think he'd set him up in business. But Mike was never good to him."

Paul might have saved himself from ruin if he hadn't sold his shuttle-bus service to "Bus Andy" Anderson and Carl Wickman, then turned down their offer to be a partner. In 1929, the Greyhound Bus Service began operations in Hibbing, Minnesota, and Paul Maras got out of town.

"He ran a small saloon at his resort in Superior, Wisconsin," says Tilly Sanborn. "He couldn't send money home because he was in tough shape for quite a while."

"Eva and the kids were devastated when Grandpa Paul left," Peggy Sanborn says. "My mother, Tilly, has a bitter memory of having no money and being hungry and of having no clothes and not being able to go to school.

They went to Detroit, where all the kids were farmed out to Dosen and Barich relatives there. That lasted a couple of years."

On the day after Christmas in 1929, eighteen-year-old Rudy Maras was arraigned for assault and battery. His arrest probably didn't horrify his father, Steve, because he and all of his brothers, with the possible exception of Joseph, had been arrested at some time on minor charges. Rudy pleaded not guilty, but a jury decided otherwise, and he paid a fine, served time, or did both. This episode solidified his growing reputation as a hot-tempered "duker."

Rudy was a natural-born athlete who excelled at all athletic activities, particularly baseball and ice hockey. Among those he played ball with was Nick Maras (not to be confused with Mike Maras's son "Big Nick"), who, still living in Hibbing, remembers him as "a heck of a player. He played baseball and football in school, and then we played on town baseball teams from when I was about fourteen."

"My dad was a great pitcher, and Rudy, who was a few years older, was a tremendous hitter," says Nick's son, Nick Maras Jr., a former minor league pitcher whose fastball topped out at 103 mph. "They weren't related yet, but were friends with the same last name who played ball and partied together."

Nick Maras's sister Mary was engaged to Rudy's best friend in Leetonia, Steve Starcevic. One of Nick's relatives was James LaFreniere. (Nick and James were about the same age and both of their fathers toiled at the huge Mahoning Mine, which was in their futures as well.) Rudy and James were such good hockey players that they received invitations to try out with NHL teams, which they turned down because the pay was so low. Rudy's greatest attribute was strength, while James relied mostly on speed and agility. Rather than competing for superiority, they admired each other's talents and became teammates on bar teams and ultimately good friends. A few years later, they became brothers-in-law when James married into the family.

At 6' and 195 pounds, Rudy was a solidly built, handsome young man who was considered a catch by the girls in Leetonia and at Hibbing's ice rink. They knew his temper, but the word was he was a nice guy and a fun date. "During the Depression, it was almost impossible to find work," says Bill Starcevic, "but my dad, Steve, said Rudy 'worked' at his father's store because he needed money. Before he went out at night, he'd reach into the cash register."

Rudy dated local girls, but none kept his interest. Then, unexpectedly, someone caught his eye. She was about 5'5" and had a slim figure. She had dark hair and eyes and strong, sharp features. She was so attractive that he couldn't help looking her way when playing sports.

The head-turning teenager told Rudy to call her Connie. Her name was Ann Sturbitz. She attended high school in Coleraine. Her mother was Ana Marich. Following the death of her husband, miner Mihiel Sturbitz, Ana had married another miner, Mike Marich. Connie and her three siblings had kept the name Sturbitz, while the kids born to Mike and Ana assumed their father's name. Rudy Maras must have done a double take when Connie told him that she had a half brother named Rudy Marich. The Marich-Sturbitz family lived in a house in Calumet, a mining town of approximately 1,200 people that was located twenty-five miles west, in Itasca County. Connie probably told Rudy all this the first time they talked, but it's likely it took several dates and a promise of secrecy before she revealed to him what only some of her family members would ever know: Connie had not been born in Itasca County and had not been born a Sturbitz.

Ann Corinne Perkovich was born in Ironton, Minnesota, in Crow Wing County, on December 28, 1913. According to her birth certificate, Connie's parents were thirty-year-old Croatian miner Joseph Perkovich and twenty-four-year-old housewife Annie Perkovich. Ana Alar (no one called her Annie, but she did go by Anne and Anna) came from Croatia to New York on April 1, 1906, departing from Le Havre, France.

On the SS *La Touraine*'s manifest, it was written that Roger's maternal grandmother was a servant from Croatia who was on her way to see her friend Jos. Perkovic in Chicago and possessed $6. She listed her age as eighteen, but when filing her accepted Petition for Citizenship in March 1933, Ana Marich stated that she was born in Yagodne, Yugoslavia, on August 2, 1890. Although that date indicates Ana was twenty-three when Connie was born, it is consistent with the U.S. Census taken three years earlier, which stated she was sixteen when she first married, soon after arriving in America.

It is not known when Ana married Joseph, if the couple tried to make a go of it in Chicago or immediately went to a mining town, or if Ironton was the first place they settled. But according to her birth certificate, Connie was the third child born to Ana and Joseph. Tragically, her older siblings died in infancy, as would a fourth child, a girl born in Ironton in 1915. "I was told one died of measles, another died of mumps, and the other died of something else," said Violet Marich Cortese, Connie's half sister, a few months before her death in 2009. One can imagine the toll the deaths of three children took on the parents and understand why Ana and Connie might have conspired to keep this period a secret. As on the paternal side of Roger's family, stories were left untold.

Ana's fifth child, Mildred, was born on December 19, 1916, 278 miles east, in Greenland, Michigan, in copper country. Was her father Joseph Perkovich? Or after ten strenuous years with Ana, had he mysteriously vanished from her history? Don O'Neil was married for sixty-two years to Jean, as Mildred was called. He says, "Jean never mentioned the name Perkovich. She always said her father was named Sturbitz."

When Ana's sixth child was born on July 16, 1918, he was named Mihiel Sturbitz Jr., confirming she had a new husband. According to at least one document, Sturbitz, too, was six years older than Ana; and though he listed himself as a laborer, he definitely worked in the mines. Mihiel Jr.'s birthplace was Ironwood, Michigan, where vast iron ore deposits had been mined since the railroad came through in the 1880s.

Before long Ana and Connie, who was usually called Anna in early documents, were back in Minnesota, along with Mihiel Sturbitz, Jean, and Mihiel Jr. Mary Louise Sturbitz was delivered on July 1, 1921, in Calumet. She was Mihiel Sturbitz's last child with Ana. He perished in a mining accident, possibly near Calumet but more likely in Ely, in northeastern St. Louis County. Ely was a scenic but "dangerous place to mine," says Bill Starcevic. "When there was a cave-in, they wouldn't even look for the miners."

In Ely, Ana wed Mike Marich on November 23, 1925. Her new husband was a thirty-three-year-old miner from Dubica, Yugoslavia. He had enlisted in the regular army in Youngstown, Ohio, in 1917 and served in Europe. Honorably discharged in 1919, he was granted American citizenship. Connie, who had been toughened by a difficult twelve years in mining country and the death of Mihiel Sturbitz Sr., vigorously protested when her pregnant mother told her she was remarrying. Connie's misery increased with the birth of Rudy Marich on June 17, 1926. "She would never accept my dad as her father or me and Vi as her siblings," says Rudy Marich more than eighty years later.

Violet Mae Marich was born July 19, 1929, back in Calumet, where her father was employed by the Hill Annex Mine. He worked in the relatively safe job of oiler in its washing plant, a separate facility where the machinery was greased. At last Ana had a permanent home, where Roger would spend a lot of time as a youngster.

The Marich house in Calumet wasn't particularly big. There was a kitchen with a huge table, a dining room, and a front room downstairs, and three bedrooms upstairs. There was a glassed-in porch, a two-stall garage, and a big barn. "We had our own cow, chickens, and pigs, so we could be self-supporting," remembers Rudy Marich. "Our kitchen stove used coal and wood, and we had another stove in the living room for heat in the winter. There was a little, grated opening in the ceiling so the heat could rise into the bedrooms. God almighty, the winters were so cold. I'd lie in bed and hear the cracking nails pop out at night. Bang! Bang! Bang!"

Of his parents, Roger's maternal grandparents, Marich recalls, "Mother was pretty and heavyset. Father was slim, handsome, and a bit taller. Both had dark hair and eyes, European high cheekbones, well-defined chins, and their complexion was olive yet distinctly white European. When they posed for pictures, he wore his WWI army uniform and she wore a traditional housedress. Mother was a typical old-fashioned woman who stayed home and took care of the family. She cleaned, sewed, and cooked, using recipes from Croatia."

"My most distinct memory of my mother as a girl was her *potica* and homemade bread," recalled Vi Marich Cortese. "I could smell it walking around the house. She was a pretty, kind person. My dad learned to read and write, but she never did. We always spoke to her in English so she'd pick up the words, but her English was very broken and I think it made her lonely."

According to the 1930 U.S. Census, sixteen-year-old Anna Sturbitz lived with her mother, Ana Marich; stepfather, Mike Marich; thirteen-year-old Mildred Sturbitz; eleven-year-old Mike Sturbitz; eight-year-old Mary Sturbitz; three-year-old Rudolph V. Marich; baby Violet M. Marich; Mike's seventeen-year-old sister-in-law, Anna M. Sertich; and three boarders. Additionally, there were frequent visits from Ana's sisters and their families, who lived in Gilbert. If the Calumet house wasn't already too crowded, Ana was pregnant again.

Connie was eager to get out as soon as the right man came along and she could sweep him off his feet. She swept Rudy Maras off his skates. Quiet himself, he appreciated that she talked enough for the both of them, walked on the wild side, and even had a temper as volatile as his own. They made a dashing couple. By the time Connie turned eighteen in late December of 1931, she had corralled her boyfriend, her escape. That year they stood up for their best friends, Steve and Mary. And when Rudy and Connie married on June 7, 1932, the Starcevics returned the favor. For Rudy and Connie, who had a combined age of thirty-nine, a marriage that began with guarded optimism would in a short time seem to be on the verge of collapse.

CHAPTER TWO

LEAVING MINNESOTA

"Connie had problems with a part of the family," says Tilly Sanborn, Paul Maras's daughter, "but I'm sure she liked us because she visited quite often after we returned from Detroit. She was pleasant to be with and so beautiful. One time Rudy was working the night shift and she didn't want to be alone because she was pregnant. So I stayed with her in a house they rented in Hibbing."

Baby Maras, which was the name on the birth certificate, was born on June 18, 1933. Rudy Jr.'s father was listed as a "laborer for the village," an ambiguous classification that included mining.

"Rudy and my dad, Steve, got their first jobs at Masabi Chief Mine," says Bill Starcevic. "It was hard and dangerous, and they were given 3-p.m.-to-11-p.m. and 11-p.m.-to-7-a.m. shifts. So they quit and got jobs with the Great Northern Railroad doing repairs at the roundhouse in the Kelly Lake location."

Founded by "Empire Builder" James J. Hill, the Great Northern, which connected St. Paul to Seattle, was instrumental in Hibbing's growth as a mining town. Rudy would always work for the railroad.

Another Baby Maras was born at 2 p.m. on September 10, 1934. On Roger Eugene Maris's birth certificate, Rudy wrote that he was a "car repairer, railroad company."

On Rudy Jr.'s birth certificate, the address of his actual birth was 2905 St. Louis Avenue. For Roger it was 2312 Oakdale Avenue. Brenda Macki of Hibbing's Recorder's Office says, "It's my guess that they were both born at home, possibly with midwives, because it lists houses rather than a hospital."

It has been stated that Roger was born in Leetonia, but his birth certificate indicates Hibbing, at his parents' rental.

Rudy eventually passed out photos of his second son buck naked on a bearskin rug. But the merriment surrounding Roger's birth was tempered by the death four days later of Katharina Maras, his grandmother. The obituary in the *Hibbing Daily Tribune* began, "Mrs. Steve Maras, 52, 112 Leetonia location, died this morning at 1:30 a.m. following a lingering illness."

Six months later Steve died of pulmonary tuberculosis, which he had for twelve years. *The Hibbing Daily Tribune* of March 21, 1935, said, "Stephen Maras, 50, a member of the National Croatian Society of America," was survived by his mother, three brothers, and a sister. There was no mention of Rudy's being married, as there was in Katharina's obituary, so Connie was not acknowledged in any way. More disturbing was the mention that fifteen-year-old Sofia, Steve and Katharina's youngest daughter, was "critically ill at St. Mary's hospital in Duluth." She passed away thirteen months later. Tuberculosis was again the prime suspect.

The deaths of his mother, father, and youngest sister in quick succession had to be traumatic for twenty-five-year-old Rudy. However, he wasn't allowed proper time to mourn because he needed to look after three sisters until they married and to support his own family in their first real home.

Rudy and Connie's new house was near the one where he'd grown up, in Leetonia, a location that had made a dramatic transition since the war, when a young, crusading Presbyterian missionary, the Reverend William J. Bell, reported, "Leetonia is bad beyond description. No drainage, no water except . . . in barrels. No ventilation or sanitation. All toilets are outside. . . . Leetonia is a sample of the worst." Fortunately, by the time Rudy Jr. and Roger Maras lived there in the 1930s, conditions had improved.

Roger's childhood chum Bill Starcevic recalls:

Everybody in Leetonia was Croatian, and though everybody but the old-timers spoke English, it was as if you were in the old country. There was a Croatian grocery store, Croatian bars, and a Croatian barbershop. There was a Catholic church. There was a little grade school nearby at the Morton location. My dad and I both went to Morton School. Roger and Buddy went there, too, and were in the same classroom though Buddy was one grade higher. The school had indoor plumbing and nice bathrooms.

The Morton mine was underground till 1950, so we didn't hear any blasting or drilling and the air quality seemed fine. The streets were black-top, and in the summer all us kids got tar all over our feet. People were poor but I'd see some Model T's and Model A's.

Roger lived on First Street. That was the main street with all the bars after Prohibition was lifted. Their house was kind of square and was made of wood and had two or one and a half stories. There was a steep roof so you'd have to walk through the middle or you'd hit your head. I think there were only two bedrooms, both upstairs. Everyone had outhouses. I'm sure they owned the house, though the mining company might have built it.

Roger and Buddy grew up with animals all around them. Everybody had a dog and cat. Everybody had a cow, a pig, and chickens, so there would be a mini-barn on the property. All the yards were fenced in, but everybody's cows roamed freely, so you'd have to find them at night to milk them. Every-one had a big garden to grow food. We'd also kill a pig and a lamb and make sausage and put it away for the winter. We didn't have a refrigerator in those days, so we'd smoke meat. Everybody hunted for food. Deer. Rabbit. We used to can it. If you're hungry, you'll eat the animals you pet.

I liked Roger's mother, Ann. She was really pretty. Rudy was tough and could fight, but he had a gentle side. I didn't realize there was any trouble between them. Roger and I played together all the time. We played hockey in the street, softball, marbles, tag, and Ante-Ante-I-Over. Buddy was there, too. They were quiet, nice boys and always got along. Roger was quite a kid.

Years later Rudy joked that if he knew Rudy Jr. and Roger would turn out to be such good sons, he would have had more children. But the deci-sion not to have more than two kids—although his father had had five and his grandfather six—was not his alone to make. By the midthirties, Rudy and Connie weren't getting along. Their frequent bickering had several valid explanations. One was that they married too young and were discovering they were still strangers.

Another was that Connie was sure that Rudy's family was against her. Also she probably resented that Rudy spent much of his spare time from the railroad not with her but playing baseball and ice hockey. Perhaps Rudy re-sented that Connie was a controlling mother who, according to a neighbor, "wouldn't let her kids out of her sight." More significantly, he didn't like the rumors that Connie was carousing with men while he was working.

Connie often grabbed her boys and retreated to the house in Calumet. Roger and Rudy Jr. were crazy about their relatives and their grandmother's cooking, but they were going from one battle zone to another. Only in this house, their mother didn't go toe-to-toe with their father but with their surviving grandfather, Mike, their young uncle Rudy, and very young aunt Vi. The only Marich who got Connie's seal of approval was Gerald, who was born in 1931, when Ana was forty-one. He was Ana's tenth and final child, the seventh to survive. Uncle Jerry was only two years older than Rudy Jr. and three years older than Roger and was their playmate. Otherwise Connie avoided the Marich kids and spent time only with Jean, Mihiel, and Mary.

"Connie and Jean were very close," says Rudy Marich. "Jean was a lovely, lovely person. She had more class. Connie was intense. She was different from anyone."

Betty Marich, who met her husband, Rudy Marich, in 1976, says, "Jean told me that Connie was a troublemaker and always had to keep things stirred up. If you danced to Connie's tune, she may have graced you by not being mean. And if you didn't, she'd do everything she could do to make your life miserable."

"Father and I tried to be good to her, but she was aloof and always angry," says Rudy Marich. "Maybe she had a hard life, but she made that life for herself."

"Even though I was really young, I knew she didn't like me because she told me so," said Vi matter-of-factly. "She said I wasn't her sister. She said, 'You have a father and I don't.' She hated my dad and they fought all the time. She fought with my mother, too, though they were very close. They fought in Croatian. My mother didn't like that Connie interfered in how we were brought up. Also, Connie wanted my mother to divorce my dad, but she was madly in love with him. Connie just wanted to be an instigator. Roger and Buddy were totally different from her. Roger was more like his dad, who I thought was very kind."

A bone of contention between Connie and her stepfather might have had to do with religion; and in that instance, Ana might have been her ally. While Croats and Serbs spoke the same language (despite having a different alphabet), almost all Croats were Roman Catholics, almost all Serbs were Eastern Orthodox, and religion factored into their division over ethnicity. Ana raised the kids she had before she met Mike Marich as Catholics and probably wanted to do the same with children she had with him. For the most part, he was agreeable, but at times he made things uncomfortable for everyone in the house.

"I was learning the catechism of the Catholic Church," remembered Vi. "When I came home, my father took my books and burned them in the stove."

"I don't recall anything of that nature," says her brother Rudy Marich. "On the occasions Father wanted to attend church, Vi, Gerald, and I would drive with him and Mother to the Serbian Greek Orthodox church in Chisholm, but when he didn't, Mother and the rest of the family attended the Catholic church in Marble. Father hated the Catholic Church and told me never to marry a Catholic because they had no love for the Orthodox pope."

Jane McAlphine Oftelie grew up in her parents' house in Marble, a mile away from the Marich house in Calumet. "I visited Rudy and Mary all the time," she recalls, "because we were closest in age, but I got to know everybody. I thought the whole family was so good-looking and a lot of fun. It could be that Connie had a temper, but they were all at each other's throats quite a bit. There was always a lot of commotion."

As the decade progressed, the family dynamics changed. Jean graduated from high school and took off to begin what would be a successful modeling career under the name Millicent Jean Cartwright. Roger missed her. In the days before he wore a crewcut, he loved when Aunt Jean combed his hair. Roger also missed Mihiel after he married and joined the army. Mary also moved out, but didn't go far. She met Rudy's friend James LaFreniere at a hockey game and was just seventeen when they married on August 24, 1938. The first of their five kids, Jim LaFreniere Jr., was born the following January. By the end of the thirties, only the three Marich kids remained in the Calumet house.

There also were changes on Rudy's side of the family. Paul Maras quit drinking and reunited with Eva and his family in Minnesota. At first he worked at a restaurant-bar at the Howard Hotel in Hibbing, but then he became a barman at a hotel in nearby Buhl. He'd eventually buy out the owner and run it himself.

On December 5, 1933, the Twenty-first Amendment was ratified and Prohibition was over. Mike and Pete kicked pharmacist Homer Webster out of their building but kept his first name for their use, and two weeks later the bar was open for business. Bill Maras says, "Our Homer Bar had its seventy-fifth anniversary in 2008, having never moved from First Avenue."

Mike, who was frustrated in his attempts to get his citizenship until the early forties, resented that Pete got the Homer Bar a liquor license. Even worse for Mike, who never learned to read but considered himself the brains behind the business, was that the license was in Pete's name. Some say that when working side by side through the decades, Mike and Pete never spoke.

Mike's daughter Mary and Nick Stilinovich ran the hotel upstairs, and Nick also put in time as a bartender. They married in 1934 and raised their three children in the hotel. Mary's brother Big Nick also came to work at the Homer Bar, probably reluctantly. "In those days," says his son Michael Maras, "if your father told you to do something, you didn't ask any questions. So my father quit his construction job and gave up his opportunity to try out for the Chicago Bears." The mammoth Big Nick Maras, who stood about 6'3", weighed nearly 375 pounds, and had enormous hands, eventually became the face of the bar and its most dominant personality.

It's unclear whether Paul and Mike had any contact at this time or if they were actively feuding. Nick Maras Jr. says, "Even when I ask my parents about the Maras family feud seventy years later, they hush up. My dad won't say if there was a feud. Some Marases on Mike's side of the family don't think there was one. My dad did tell me that he was in a fight at the Homer Bar between cousins. Maras versus Maras. They threw a bunch of punches and Big Nick got in the middle and stopped it."

Following Steve's death, Rudy probably broke away from his uncles and their extended families because Connie was tired of their disapproval, real or perceived. Her personal feud with the Maras family seems to have been directed at Mike, because his descendants were the first targets of her hostility, but eventually it extended to the whole family.

Members of the Maras family might have sided against Connie for two entirely different reasons. One was that they believed her to be Serbian. "If she was Serbian," says Anna Dosen, the daughter of Eva Maras's sister Marija, "you have to recognize that there has been a tremendous amount of animosity between Serbs and Croats." "Mike Maras was the biggest S.O.B. I ever met," says Nick Maras Sr., "and if he thought Connie was Serbian, that would have been enough for him to want to kick her out of the family."

Individuals on both Rudy's and Connie's sides of the family believe Connie was Serbian. But her biological parents, Ana, who did come from a region with many Serbians, and Joseph Perkovich, were both almost certainly Croatian and Catholic. Her stepfather, Mike Marich, was Serbian and perhaps converted Ana to the Eastern Orthodox religion—she would be buried near the church in Chisholm—and this confused Connie about her own religion and was the probable reason she later chose public schools over parochial schools for her sons.

More likely the reason for the friction was what Connie was doing behind Rudy's back. "There was a bad story about her," says Nick Maras Jr. "My father says she was really into the booze, and she became totally loose. He says, 'I know this was true because I was right there when this was going on.' He told me that they started having trouble and she started drinking and carousing and stuff like that, and it looked like they were going to split up. He can't say if she started it or if Rudy was drinking too much or had gone astray."

"It wasn't Rudy causing problems," says Connie's nephew Jim LaFreniere Jr. "I know some stories and *things* about Connie that I'm not going to tell anybody."

As their squabbling became more heated, Connie no longer seemed to care that her husband knew about her carousing. Rudy worried that the marriage wouldn't survive. He also worried what would happen to their kids. "He tried everything to make her come around," recalls Nick Maras. When nothing worked, he took out his frustrations in his old ways.

"One evening in 1938, my dad, Big Nick, was courting my future mother, Rose Mayerle," says Michael Maras. "He took her for a ride in his fancy car and stopped at the Maple Hill Community Center. And before they got out of the car, my dad realized there was something going on inside. Boom! One guy comes flying out the front door. Boom! Another guy comes out a window. Boom! Another guy comes out a window on the other side. And finally someone charges outside, his fists clenched. It was Rudy Maras!"

In the early forties, work was picking up on the railroad and this gave Rudy an opportunity to change his family's situation. When his foreman was transferred to Grand Forks, North Dakota, he asked Rudy to accompany him with the promise of a better job. Rudy was thrilled, but Connie was the opposite and didn't appreciate those in and out of the family who urged Rudy to accept the promotion on her account.

"He knew that his wife was messing around with someone, and that was the reason they had to leave," says Bill Maras. "According to my dad, Big Nick, Connie was really upset to be going, and that's the reason she later changed her family's name from Maras. She did it just to piss off Rudy and everyone else with that name. If there was any bad blood between our families, it had to do with Connie."

Growing up in the Great Depression in a poor mining town was hard enough, but the constant fighting between a mother he loved and a father he idolized had to have been almost unbearable for Roger. He probably also was aware of his mother's feud with the Marases and friction with the Mariches, though he might not have understood the details. Rudy Jr. had the same experience as Roger, and that made them extremely close. He protected his younger brother from the occasional bully and didn't abandon him to go play with older boys. For that, Roger developed a deep sense of gratitude, admiration, and indebtedness that carried from that day forward.

It is often said that men with a strong worth ethic, integrity, and humility "have never forgotten where they came from." But Roger Maris tried to bury his first seven years. While Roger tried to forget he'd ever lived in Hibbing, or Leetonia, and would forever be secretive about what he did remember, the people there and the experiences he had with them would forever influence his life.

CHAPTER THREE

FAMILY TURMOIL

GRAND FORKS, NORTH DAKOTA, was only one state line and 194 miles from Hibbing, Minnesota, but Roger Maras must have felt as if he had traveled through a time warp to get there. This town was strangely calm and peaceful. The air was fresh; yards weren't overrun by farm animals; many high school graduates didn't immediately try to find work, but instead attended the University of North Dakota; smartly dressed women spent their days shopping; the men on the street weren't grizzled miners with dusty clothes and alcohol on their breath; and Roger and his brother were the toughest kids around.

Located on flat land at the fork of the Red River and Red Lake River, Grand Forks was for decades an agricultural community, but it was making its mark in manufacturing, education, trade, retail, and tourism before being knocked on its heels by the Great Depression. During World War II, the city had an economic revival, due in part to the resurgence of the railroad. At the time the Marases arrived, the population of Grand Forks was a comfortable 20,000, the same as Hibbing in 1915.

The Marases moved into an eight-apartment complex at 624 Fifth Avenue North, across from St. Michael's Catholic Church and its school. It's not known whether the Maras boys attended the church, but they enrolled in a public school.

Don Gooselaw attended St. Michael's, as did Roger's future Yankee teammate Ken Hunt. The son of a barber who rented the apartment next door, Gooselaw was two years older than Roger but only one grade ahead. He was, in fact, in Rudy Jr.'s grade, but he much preferred the younger Maras boy. "Roger and I were friends from the start," says Gooselaw. "We used to eat together all the time, little kids snacking. He never sat down. He always wanted to go outside and play something. Roger was a nice, ordinary kid. But his brother, Buddy, had a very difficult time playing with other kids. His personality wasn't very nice. We got into a fight once and he knocked the crap out of me. I tried to stay away from him."

Where Gooselaw didn't stay away from Rudy Jr. was on the lots, fields, playgrounds, and streets when the boys played stickball, a little baseball, basketball, and their favorite sport, football. "Buddy wasn't friendly, but he was a very good athlete," recalls Gooselaw. "There were telephone wires across the street and we made up this little game where if you got the football over a wire, you got two points. It wasn't so easy because of the distance, but Buddy would drop-kick, punt, and throw it through all the time. He had all the talent in the world."

Roger was comfortable taking a backseat to Rudy Jr. in athletics, as he did in the classroom, where his brother was known as a "brain." Roger realized he was faster, stronger, and more talented than the local kids in every sport from basketball to ice hockey, but Rudy Jr. was older and bigger, so Roger figured there was no comparison between the two of them. That was particularly true in baseball, at which Rudy Jr. excelled and Roger played with decided indifference. Anyway, it wasn't just Rudy Jr. who was a better baseball player, but his father, too, so why would Roger want to set himself up for ridicule?

It was probably good for Roger's ego that his first athletic success came on a team on which he played without Rudy Jr. When Roger was in the sixth grade, Washington Grade School won the town basketball championship, Roger's first sports title. The team had the Lowe twins, the Walsh twins, and the MacDonald brothers, but Roger was on his own with Rudy Jr. in junior high. Roger has a genuinely happy smile in the team picture after the big game. His best friend on the team, Gailen Telander, remembers:

There were probably six grade schools in a tournament, and the championship game was played at the YMCA. Roger was fun to play with because we both passed and moved around the court pretty good. He was a team player, and our coach didn't have to keep him in line one bit.

The sixth grade was in one room and we had about forty kids. He wasn't an honor student, but he was a B guy. He wasn't an outsider; in fact, he was a little more popular than most. I didn't see that he was shy at all, but he wasn't a show-off. Athletically, he was kind of a leader.

We lived two blocks from each other, and every day we played catch or shot baskets or shot a BB gun. We probably even played marbles. There wasn't much I could beat him at, although we were on the track team, and I did beat him in the high jump. He could do the rest.

Our school was on the corner, and across the school yard was the Catholic church and grade school. The snow piled up quite a bit in front of the church, and we'd go over there and see who was king of the mountain. Roger was pretty tough up there and didn't show any mercy to those Catholic kids.

Roger was a little hot-tempered. He was a little bit hyper. He'd have arguments. I don't remember him duking it out with anybody, but when he'd get mad at somebody, he'd push him down and pull his hair or something like that. In the playground, if you happened to kick or run into him, he'd push you down.

Telander is one of the few people who remembers Roger being temperamental, as a child or an adult. Indeed, his lack of a temper, particularly directed at others, was one of his most remarkable traits considering he grew up with three individuals who couldn't control theirs. Roger looked up to a father and a brother who settled many disputes with their fists. That Roger was sweet-tempered was due, perhaps, to a self-protective ability to tune out the tumult around him and not become a participant.

Grand Forks could have been an idyllic place for the Maras boys to grow up. However, nothing had changed in their parents' relationship since Leetonia. "I remember when his mother threw a shoe and broke a lamp on the wall," says Gooselaw, "and when she started doing things like that, Rudy would run away. The old man used to come storming out of the apartment house. My mother told us we had to be in by a certain time on Saturday night. She never drank, but they used to go to a neighborhood bar on Saturday night. It was a ritual. My dad and mom, Rudy and Connie Maras. They would go out and have a few beers, and then they'd come back home, and by that time Rudy and Connie were fighting all the way."

"His father was always working, but I saw his mother a lot," says Telander. "She was dressed up a lot in the apartment—sharply dressed, like a professional woman. She was quite elegant in a way. I also recall that she was a little tough. She'd come out, and, boy, she'd holler at her sons if they were playing too loudly or doing something she didn't like. She was a little stern."

Roger loved quality time with his father, whether playing ball or lazing with him by the muddy Red River or the railroad tracks, in anticipation of the next train passing—it was much more fun being there with a railroad man. With the railway taking on a more prominent role in the war effort, Roger's admiration for his father must have soared.

Roger and his brother accompanied their father when he traveled by rail back to Hibbing to visit the graves of their grandparents in the Old North Cemetery. Oddly, Rudy didn't take the boys to Leetonia to see their friend Bill Starcevic (who never saw Roger again) or his parents, although Rudy and a grown Rudy Jr. would visit Steve and Mary in Kerr from the 1960s to the early 1980s.

Connie brought the boys back to visit family in Calumet and presumably to see her friend Mary Starcevic, with whom she swapped Christmas cards. She badly missed her mother and married sister Mary LaFreniere. She felt alone in Grand Forks and from the beginning insisted that Mary visit her and bring their half brother Jerry for the boys.

Still Connie made no effort to get along with Rudy or Vi, who were now both teenagers. And she expressed no sympathy for Mike Marich, who suffered two work-related injuries. A back strain suffered in October 1944 paled in comparison to the news received a few months earlier: Lieutenant Mihiel Sturbitz had been killed during the Normandy invasion.

A tank officer, Mihiel was felled by a bullet on Omaha Beach. He left behind a wife and child. It was a calamity for the entire family because Mihiel was much loved. "He was a great brother," says Rudy Marich. Jean, who was closest to him, was so upset that it took her sixty years to open the letters he mailed her just before D-Day. Connie, too, never got over the loss. The death of twenty-five-year-old Uncle Mike was the first of a family member that Rudy Jr. and Roger had experienced since they were old enough to understand such things.

Despite turmoil at home, Rudy Maras was doing well as a mechanical supervisor, impressing his bosses with his diligence, popularity with his men, and willingness to get his own hands dirty. It was a significant time for America's railroads, and the managers at Great Northern in Grand Forks felt fortunate to have dependable men such as Rudy on board.

But Rudy wanted another transfer. He still hoped his marriage would survive, but he was growing impatient being a cuckold. What made it worse is that everyone knew about Connie's partying while he stayed home with the boys.

"Connie was running around in Grand Forks with a guy named Gobel," says Don Gooselaw. "She'd go uptown every weekend."

If Connie wasn't going to change her ways, then Rudy was going to change her town. When he was offered a transfer eighty miles to the south, he jumped at the opportunity. Again the Marases packed up and moved.

CHAPTER FOUR

SETTLING IN FARGO

R UDY MARAS HOPED THAT Fargo, North Dakota, presented Connie and him with a brand-new start and real chance to save their marriage. It was a nice, safe, conservative town in which to raise kids, and maybe she'd find contentment just being a mother to their growing boys. As it turned out, Rudy Jr. and Roger were the ones who benefited most from the move to Fargo. They'd spend their formative years there and mature as athletes and individuals, making their difficult home life tolerable.

Postwar Fargo was a small town of less than 30,000 people disguised as a city. Most of the streets were brick, and if you owned a bicycle, you could ride from one end of town to the other. It was a casual community, although the women were nicely dressed and men wore suits to work and hats when they went out. Ice hockey, basketball, and football were popular, but so was baseball and golf despite the early frost. Fierce football rivalries between high schools in Fargo, Moorhead (across the Red River in Minnesota), and other towns in the area aroused keen interest. But also popular were the Fargo-Moorhead Twins of the Class C Northern League. Barnett Field had been built in Fargo on the old fairgrounds in 1936 to house the city's minor league baseball team.

Fargo had weathered the Depression and during the war had a rapid recovery, due in part to the railroad and a national need for agricultural supplies. Much of the economy was connected to agriculture, and farmers came from miles around to buy feed, machinery, and other products sold in town.

Roger's high school friend Dick Savageau remembers the Marases living in two places: on the 1300 block of 5th Avenue and at 731 7th Street North, upstairs in a modest two-story apartment building. Rudy settled in at his new job at the depot, and he and Connie enrolled their sons in another public school, Roosevelt, on Tenth Avenue. That Roger made no lasting friends in Fargo while in his early teens indicates he and Rudy Jr. stuck together. Despite different personalities, they were best friends for life.

In his 1963 novel, *Slugger in Right,* Roger wrote about the fictional Mack brothers, with best friends Billy and the one-year-older Bob the stand-ins for Roger and Rudy Jr., respectively. He said that the Macks were "always together, doing the same things. Yet they were different as day and night." He added, "Billy had a quick temper"; "Bob was calm and deliberate"; "Billy would flare up and say things that he shouldn't"; "Bob always thought out his answers"; "Bob got along with people, could see their side and, as a result, made friends"; and "Billy always thought that people were trying to take advantage of him and, as a result, made enemies."

Significantly, to avoid offending Rudy Jr., Roger made Bob, Rudy Jr.'s counterpart, the more appealing brother and infused Billy, his own counterpart, with not only his character flaws but Rudy Jr.'s as well. In reality, Rudy Jr. was the one with a quick temper and who had trouble making friends; and Roger was calm and deliberate, thought out his answers, saw all sides, and made friends. It's true that Roger, as he wrote about Billy, was prone to saying things he shouldn't, particularly when standing up for himself, but unlike Rudy Jr., he favored diplomacy over violence. Only one statement Roger made about Billy Mack truly described himself. Afflicted by a thin skin and a suspicious nature, Roger, too, "always thought that people were trying to take advantage of him."

The surprise of the novel is that the secretive Maris opened up about himself under the guise of writing about a fictional character. Maris prided himself on honesty, but the book is the only instance in which he was revealing without being pushed and the one time he did any self-analysis. With Jim Ogle at the typewriter, perhaps Roger felt he was protected and could express himself to young readers as he couldn't to an increasingly hostile press during his Yankee years.

Roger's protagonist becomes a baseball fanatic at the age of eleven because of his obsession with Babe Ruth, whose birthday he shares. When Ruth dies in 1948, Billy laments, "The Babe is dead. He'll never see me play in Yankee Stadium. But I'll be there and I'll try to be just like him." It's a bit startling that Maris would write such words in 1963 because, in the previous year's *Roger Maris At Bat*, he wrote, "I have never imagined myself as Babe Ruth."

Billy Mack eagerly joins Bob in Little League. At that age and for a couple of more years, Roger didn't have the same enthusiasm for baseball as Billy. He loved being outdoors and had trouble concentrating on his homework, so if his father or brother suggested a sports break, he'd happily play anything they wanted—except baseball.

According to Harvey Rosenfeld's book *Roger Maris*: *A Title to Fame*, Roger once told a reporter, "It was my brother who forced me to play baseball, and I mean *forced* me. If he went to play, he dragged me along. If he found me sitting around the house, he grabbed me by the ear and pulled me out. If I had been bigger, I might have put up an argument. But I didn't catch up to him until we were in high school, and by that time nobody had to force me to play."

"I was pretty rough on him," admitted Rudy Jr. to Maury Allen in 1985. "If he didn't do what I wanted him to, I'd beat him up."

While the boys scuffled on the ball field, there was an equal amount of conflict inside their house. The problems that had followed Rudy and Connie from Hibbing to Grand Forks had been carried to Fargo, too.

"Connie would get mad at him and jump on a train with Roger and Rudy Jr.," remembers Jane Oftelie. "They'd get off in Grand Rapids and take a bus to Marble, which was as close to Calumet as they could get. Then at two thirty in the morning, sometimes, somebody would wake me up because Connie needed me to drive her and the boys over to her mother's house in Calumet. That happened even during the school year. She'd always calm down and in a couple of days take the kids back to Fargo. I don't know why Connie and Rudy would fight. Maybe she just had a temper. Or maybe she was carrying on a romance and he didn't like it. She was supposed to have had a romance with a ballplayer, but that was years later. I don't know if the boys knew what was going on or were keeping it a secret. In all the years, they never said one word about it."

Connie also brought the boys to her mother's house in the summer for scheduled visits. "She would drop off the two boys at the house in Calumet," says Oftelie, "and their uncle Rudy and I would take care of them." The time Roger spent in Calumet proved fortuitous. It ignited his interest in baseball. Rudy Marich, who at the time was boxing to pay his way through Itasca Junior College, remembers:

> Roger and Rudy Jr. came in the summer to see their grandmother and spent about a month with us. Roger was about thirteen or fourteen and was a fine young man without a mean bone in his body. We had a fellow there named Rudy Drobnick, whose sister was the librarian in town. He was a single guy who was looked at by the Yankees at one time. He was quite a pitcher. His only problem was that he didn't want to work and would rather play baseball all the time. Calumet, which was a small town of 1,200 people, had an old ballpark, nothing fancy. He and Roger would go there during the day and they'd take turns pitching and hitting, and they'd chase the balls. They'd spend at least half a day there *every* day. It was just Roger, not Rudy Jr. After they played ball all day, we'd meet them in the café. Everybody scooted into a booth, and Rudy Drobnick always said, "Roger's going to be in the big leagues!" And the other guys said, "Aw, Rudy, what are you talking about?" And Rudy said, "I know I'm right!"

Roger (who threw right-handed but hit from the left side) must have had ambivalent feelings about being told something positive about his baseball skills that even his talented brother hadn't heard. However, Rudy Drobnick injected him with self-confidence and enthusiasm. Somewhere in the back of his mind, young Roger Maras formulated the crazy idea that if he kept practicing and playing baseball, he really had a shot at the major leagues.

"Their uncle Rudy and I often took the two boys to watch the older kids play baseball at Mallard Park in Marble," recalls Jane Oftelie. "Roger would beg the coach, Windy Anderson, to let them play, too. Windy never lived it down that he wouldn't let them."

When Roger returned to Fargo, he was eager to play ball with his father and brother and to go to the ballpark and watch Fargo-Moorhead. One day in 1949, the Aberdeen Pheasants came to town to play the Twins. The Marases arrived early, and during batting practice a ball was hit against a fence. "A kid jumped over the fence and ran out to pick up a ball," recalls 1958 Cy Young Award winner Bob Turley, who as an eighteen-year-old was in the midst of a 20–3 season for Aberdeen. "When we became teammates in 1960 on the Yankees, Roger told me that he was that boy and that I came over and took the ball away from him. I told him I hated to do it, but we couldn't give away balls back then."

If boys wanted to play organized baseball in Fargo, they waited until summer for American Legion ball, in which both Rudy Jr. and Roger participated. The local schools had no baseball programs, but in the fall the Maras brothers tried out for their school football teams, followed by basketball in winter, and track in the spring. Sports fans in Fargo first realized Rudy Jr. was a special athlete when he starred as a halfback and linebacker as a sophomore on Fargo Central High's football team. Much was expected from him as a junior, and Roger looked forward to joining him as a two-way back on the Midgets as a sophomore. But the new coach sent Rudy Jr. to the bench and Roger to the B team. Roger's later explanation was: "He didn't like us."

Rudy Jr. approached the coach with a demand that Roger would later repeat several times in his professional baseball career: "Either I play ball or I'm going somewhere else." The coach tuned him out, thinking it was an idle threat. What kid in those days would transfer schools just to play football?

The college-bound Rudy Jr. had more to lose than Roger if he didn't get to showcase his football talents in high school, but his shy younger brother was more proactive about switching schools. In *Roger Maris At Bat*, Roger wrote, "I have never been the type of person to let anyone give me the business. I felt that Bud and I were getting the short end of the stick and decided to do something about it."

The Maras brothers wanted to switch to the smaller Catholic school in town, Sacred Heart Academy, and the major reason was Sid Cichy, its innovative coach. Cichy already knew about them from working in Junior Legion baseball. Wanting justice for his sons, Rudy Sr. signed the necessary papers for them to transfer at the end of the semester to the Catholic high school on 13th Avenue and Broadway North, which was run by the Presentation Order of Sisters. How Connie, who wasn't seen at Catholic church with Rudy Sr., felt about her sons switching to parochial school isn't known. But in Fargo, where high school football was a religion, the Maras brothers' transfer to a rival school was akin to a Yankee willingly becoming a Red Sox.

"Bud and I were responsible for splitting the town in half when we switched schools," Roger later contended. "We were surprised to learn that a lot of people resented our shifting schools. . . . We had left the Fargo High basketball and track teams a little shorthanded, and that made some people mad. We didn't let the feelings of the people bother us. Bud and I were only doing what we thought was to our best interests." Roger's sentiments were echoed in *Slugger in Right*, when Billy Mack says, "I have to take care of myself, fight for my rights and never let anyone push me around. It's Bob and me against everybody."

"Sacred Heart Academy was renamed Bishop Shanley High the year Roger and Buddy moved there," recalls 1947 graduate Walt Seeba, who several years later became Roger's brother-in-law. "It had about 250 students, and 80 were young women studying to be nuns. That didn't leave us with a lot of boys to pick for the sports teams. Fargo Central had about 2,500 kids, and none of them were studying to be nuns. But when we got the Maras boys, we had confidence we could beat them."

After the transfer to Shanley in 1950, Roger realized that it was no longer Rudy Jr. and him against the world. The brothers remained close, but Roger broke away and made friends. To become Roger's friend was as easy as climbing a greased pole. It required passing his tests and accepting his personality quirks, including his unwillingness to forgive you if he felt you betrayed his trust even once. In *Roger Maris At Bat*, he explained:

> There is no halfway with me. When I take a liking to someone, then I really like him and stick by him unless one day he proves I was wrong in the first place. Usually when I meet someone for the first time, I'll stay in the back seat on the outside until I make up my mind about him. I am always careful with new acquaintances until I'm sure whom I'm with. . . .
>
> Sometimes it is said that people think I'm tough to get along with just because I say what I think and don't follow the crowd. That's all right with me. If people are going to like me they are going to have to take me as I am. If they don't like me, then there's no way I can change them. In fact, I wouldn't even make an attempt. My friends know me and understand me. The others don't count anyway.

Roger was part of a formidable foursome with his Shanley classmates Dick Savageau, whose uncle ran the floral shop where Roger worked one summer, and Bob Wood, whose father had a beer distributorship, and St.

James Academy student Don Gooselaw, whose family relocated from Grand Forks to Fargo in Roger's senior year.

"We were all different," says Savageau. According to Savageau in Harvey Rosenfeld's biography *Roger Maris*: A Title to Fame*, "Woodsie was ebullient; Goose was amiable, and obliging; and I was thought of as intense and thoughtful. Roger liked to think of himself as an individual who not only could give to his friends but could also learn from them. It would be reasonable to say that Roger's personality was somewhat a composite of his three friends."

There were endless activities for the boys. "We'd play cards or go downtown to the movies," says Savageau. "We played a lot of pickup baseball. If we had time in the evenings and wanted to cool off, we went swimming at a pool downtown. Roger was a very good swimmer. Sometimes in the winter, Roger played basketball in the afternoon and then in the evening we'd go down to the rink and play pickup hockey. Roger was a good skater, too. He was just a natural athlete."

Roger's sports talent ultimately set him apart from his classmates, but Roger never felt like an outsider at Shanley. In *Slugger in Right*, he wrote, "It is only while playing sports that Billy was at ease. Bob was one of the most popular boys in school. Billy, however, had always been shyer and had never attended any of the school's social functions." Again Roger generously made his brother's fictional counterpart the more appealing Mack brother. In the real world, Roger was more at ease when not playing sports, more popular than Rudy Jr., and even attended school functions.

"Buddy was a very good athlete but he was not friendly," recalls Savageau. "He was pretty much an introvert. Roger wasn't an introvert. Buddy and Roger were close because they were the only boys in the family, but they didn't chum around in high school. Buddy stayed to himself. Later he had a girlfriend in Moorhead."

"Buddy wasn't popular," remembers Wayne Blanchard, who knew the Maras boys before they were schoolmates at Shanley because his father, too, worked at the Great Northern Railroad. "He was nice enough, but his problem was that he was more intelligent and grown-up than all of us. He didn't act like a typical fun, hell-raising high school kid; he acted more like an adult."

Roger, on the other hand, could raise a little hell. "We got into trouble the first year there," recalls Bob Wood. "It was cold out, so some of us snuck into the school when it wasn't open and took out the basketballs and shot around. They caught us and made us do some labor around the school." Roger also got into trouble at Shanley's Annual Pancake Dinner. He, Goose-law, and a couple of other pranksters later confessed that they had the bright idea of pouring pancake batter into the nuns' overshoes. The punishment to fit the crime was to clean the gym with scrub brushes.

Roger's pranks at Shanley didn't cause him to fall out of favor with the nuns. They considered him one of the most cheerful, amiable boys in school and admired that he was an athlete who was willing to take typing. "He was not a number one student," says Savageau, "but the nuns liked him and he didn't have to perform. They'd give him good grades because he was Roger and likable. From one nun, he got an automatic A in her class. I don't know if he learned how to type, but he got an A in typing. Sister Bertha loved him."

Roger had a difficult time sitting still in school, so Sister Bertha believed he did so well in her typing class because he could continuously bang away at the keys.

Roger didn't meet his future wife in typing or any class, although she attended Shanley, too. Their fateful first encounter took place in the gym of St. Anthony of Padua Church, at a Friday-night dance. Roger asked a football player named Gene Johnson the name of the pretty girl across the gym with Jeanie Williams. Her name was Pat Carvell, called Patsy by family and friends. When Roger introduced himself, he learned she lived on the opposite side of town from him, on the south side, and was one grade behind him.

When they dated, Roger discovered that Pat was quiet, good-natured, and down-to-earth, as sweet as her smile but with some grit. She was a good student and good Catholic. "Pat went to church all the time but wasn't a fanatic," recalls Wayne Blanchard, her classmate at Shanley High.

Pat came from a large Roman Catholic family. Her maternal grandparents had emigrated from Ireland. Her mother, Grace Victoria McDonnell, was from Whittemore, a little town in north-central Iowa. Grace earned a teaching degree and took a position in Garrison, North Dakota, north of Bismarck. "The four things you needed to know about Grace were that she was Irish, Catholic, from Iowa, and a Democrat," says Walt Seeba.

Al Carvell was, purportedly, descended from French Huguenots who fled to England and then settled in Pennsylvania, which didn't explain why he hailed from Parkston, South Dakota. He became a pharmacist and was working at a shop in Garrison when he met Grace McDonnell. They married just before the outbreak of World War I and had three sons, in 1918, 1921, and 1925, and two of them became pharmacists. There was a gap, then Mary Jo was born in 1931. Their fifth and last child, Patricia Ann, was delivered in June 1935 in Fargo. At the time of his death, Al Carvell had a drugstore in Fargo. He passed away when Pat was nine, and his two daughters continued to live at home with their mother, at 1022 Eighth Avenue South. Mary Jo married Walt Seeba in June of 1951 and lived there while he was in Korea. When Seeba returned, he and Pat's sister raised their kids on the ground floor of the two-story house.

Roger and Rudy Jr. were ineligible to participate in school athletics their first semester at Shanley, so to fill the void they played sandlot baseball during the spring and American Legion ball in the summer. In 1949, Roger had played outfield and pitched for the junior team of the Gilbert C. Grafton American Legion Post. In 1950, when only fifteen, he joined Buddy in the outfield of the post's main squad, coached by Chuck Bentsen.

Larry Sweeney was a pitcher on the team. Nineteen months older than Roger, he remembers him as "a fun guy to be around. He needed a little time when meeting people because he was shy, but after we all got to know each other, he would be like any other kid, playing ball or hanging out at the Dutch Maid eating ice cream. I was a lefty and he batted left-handed, so he liked to see if he could hit my curve. When I first threw it, he'd have one foot in the dugout, but eventually he learned to stand in there."

Roger's swing would someday be admired by no less an authority than Ted Williams. "Roger and I were big Red Sox fans," Sweeney says. "Maybe there were a few Yankee fans on the team, but our idol was Ted Williams."

Roger checked the Boston Red Sox box scores every day to find out how Williams was doing. He was usually doing well. He was the MVP in 1946, when he led Boston to the World Series; then the last man to bat over .400 in a season (.406 in 1941) won batting titles in both 1947 (when he joined Rogers Hornsby as the only players to win the Triple Crown twice) and 1948. Then he copped a second MVP award in 1949 despite the Sox handing the pennant to the Yankees in the final two games of the season. If

Roger read about Williams, he knew of his idol's troubled relationship with the Boston media and fans, which foreshadowed Roger's own problems in New York. He knew that the press in other cities didn't like Williams much better and had spitefully denied him other deserved MVP trophies.

Roger won an MVP award himself after batting .367 in Legion ball. That he beat out Rudy Jr. must have felt awkward, and at no time did he brag about it. He was proud that Fargo won the North Dakota American Legion state championship. However, Fargo was denied the chance to play in the nationals when it lost in the regional playoffs. For the Maras brothers, this was the biggest disappointment of their youths.

Despite Roger's spectacular season, no one expected that he would be a star in the major leagues one day. "Not him any more than the rest of us," Sweeney says.

A professional scout saw it differently. Frank Fahay, who worked in the Cleveland Indians farm system, run by Hank Greenberg, issued a report on the fifteen-year-old after watching him play in the American Legion tournament at Dickinson, North Dakota, in August of 1950. He agreed with the assessment of Rudy Drobnick in Calumet. In Harvey Rosenfeld's *Roger Maris*: *A Title to Fame*, Fahay is quoted: "Roger weighed one-hundred fifty pounds and stood five-eight. My opinion at the time was that he would be a major leaguer if he filled out. . . . He could run and throw and had lots of power."

Although Roger played baseball every summer of his high school years, he worked as well. "I am firmly convinced that my father had the right idea when he insisted that my brother and I get out and work in the summers," Roger later wrote. "It proved to be very valuable to me and, in fact, had a great deal to do with the way I think and the way I act. It was during that period that I learned the hard way the value of a dollar. I learned to appreciate the value of money and what it can do for you."

For a couple of summers, Rudy Sr., who was working as a mechanical supervisor at the depot and in the field, got his sons jobs with the railroad. Roger worked for a time as a mail clerk, but he also did physical section work.

"Roger worked summers hitting rails, and he was a hard worker," Walt Seeba says. "The railroad paid kids a lot better than most summer jobs, but you got messy and suffered in the sun." Roger always was regarded as a wrist hitter, and he claimed his strong wrists were the result of driving spikes into railroad ties while on a gandy gang.

Roger also did odd jobs year-round. "My dad owned a Western Distributor company," says Bob Wood. "Roger and some other friends would come over and unload freight cars full of Pabst Blue Ribbon. We'd load trucks, and once in a while we would get to ride on one. My dad paid us an hourly wage." So a new generation of Marases got into the beer business, at least in a tangential way.

The summer of 1950 ended, school resumed, and Rudy Jr., a senior, and Roger, a junior, were thrilled to not only play on the football team but also start in the same backfield for Sid Cichy's Shanley Deacons. They eagerly donned their red jerseys with white numerals, white pants, and red-and-white helmets. Even the optimistic Cichy didn't anticipate that the Deacons would be transformed from a good team into a powerhouse thanks to the Maras brothers.

The year could not have begun more auspiciously. A crowd of 2,500 turned out to see Shanley play its cross-river rival Moorhead, featuring the long-anticipated debut of the Maras boys. They weren't disappointed. Rudy Jr. had a 30-yard touchdown run called back but on the next play threw a TD pass. Roger ran for two touchdowns and added a third on a 35-yard interception. The Deacons beat the Spuds convincingly, 26–0.

Next came an especially satisfying triumph, before 3,500 fans at Barnett Field. Shanley defeated visiting Fargo Central 13–0 as Buddy threw a 31-yard touchdown pass in the first quarter and scored on a nifty 25-yard run in the fourth period. The victory stamped the Deacons as an Eastern Conference title threat and justified Fargo's decision to replace the coach who hadn't given them playing time.

The following week saw a 7–6 squeaker over St. James Academy of Grand Forks, whose quarterback was Don Gooselaw and star running back was Ken Hunt. St. James took the lead in the first quarter when Hunt intercepted a pass and eventually scored from the 2-yard line. But the point after failed. With a minute left in the first half, Rudy Jr. hit Roger for 21 yards at the 48, and Roger galloped the final 52 yards. "I couldn't catch him," says Gooselaw, shaking his head fifty-eight years later. Quarterback Pat Colliton's kick was the deciding point as the second half was scoreless.

"They were two of the best halfbacks in North Dakota," states Dick Savageau. "Rudy played left halfback and Roger played right halfback. Roger was faster and he was very shifty. I was an end and I always had Roger on my tail because I wasn't fast and he was. We had the combination of Rudy Maras to Roger Maras. Roger and I would go out for a pass and make our cuts, and all the time we knew the pass was going to the guy who would catch it and could run with it."

In the next game, Colliton led the Deacons to a 27–6 shellacking of Devil's Lake. Besides excelling as a ballcarrier and receiver, Roger had an interception and a 60-yard punt return for a touchdown that the *Fargo Forum* described as "a beauty."

By now Cichy saw Rudy Jr. and Roger as the Blanchard-and-Davis of Fargo, North Dakota. Rudy Jr. was already known to be a tremendous football player, but Roger, who had a growth spurt and put on some muscle, had to be a surprise. "He ran out of the single wing and nobody ever stopped him," Cichy told Jerry Izenberg in 1985. "On defense, he would come up from the secondary to cut down the ballcarrier for no gain on one play and intercept a pass twenty-five yards downfield on the next. We'd run him in motion as a blocking back and then bring him back to crack block on the linebacker—it was legal back then—and if you ever saw him hit, you know how the block got its name."

Cichy was impressed by how well the sixteen-year-old Roger already knew the game yet was still eager to learn more, which made him a coach's dream. When the usually quiet boy told him that a practice drill made no sense, Cichy was taken aback but realized Roger was correct. Cichy halted the drill, making it seem like his decision. "Roger hated practice," says Pat Colliton, "but he was always ready to play."

Shanley lost its chance for a perfect season when it suffered a frustrating 19–18 loss to tough Jamestown, led by a gargantuan lineman, Chuck Maxime. The future pro was fierce on defense and, in a key play, rumbled 65 yards with a fumble recovery for a touchdown. Roger scored two touchdowns, one on a pass from Rudy Jr. that covered 49 yards, but they went for naught when the Deacons couldn't score in the final period. A big reason for Jamestown's defensive success was their unusual strategy. "When Roger would come back to the bench, he complained to Coach Cichy that Jamestown was doing something to him during tackles," recalls Savageau. "At halftime, he showed him his testicles, and they were beet red."

The Deacons rebounded from their loss to Jamestown with a 26–6 pounding of unbeaten Wahpeton, featuring future Baltimore Colts kicker Steve Myhra. In Shanley's final home game at Barnett Field, Roger scored all four of his team's touchdowns, including one on a 50-yard pass from Rudy Jr. and another on a 50-yard interception. Two more TD passes from Rudy Jr. to Roger were called back because of penalties. Scoring all the touchdowns probably made Roger uncomfortable in regard to Rudy Jr., who was a senior and supposedly the star of the team.

"People said Buddy was a better athlete than Roger," says Wayne Blanchard. "And I think Roger really believed it. Probably Buddy did, too. But you see, Roger was a better football player. And he might have been a better baseball player, too, although he'd tell everyone he couldn't carry Buddy's glove."

The following week against Park River looked like a repeat of the Wahpeton game. Again Roger was outshining his brother, scoring two early touchdowns. He was heading for the goal line for the third time when he tossed the ball back to Rudy Jr., who scored the touchdown. Rudy Jr. also scored the team's final touchdown on a 45-yard punt return, giving both brothers two touchdowns for the day. "Rudy's scampering was undoubtedly the best of his career," wrote the *Forum*'s Chuck Johnson, "while Roger turned in his usual all-around performance, brilliant in every respect." Shanley won, 33–7.

For years Roger was acclaimed for his unselfishness on the lateral play on which Rudy Jr. scored, and certainly it was deserved. But Roger's two touchdowns had come on a pass from Rudy Jr. and then, significantly, a lateral from him—on a play that covered 70 yards, Rudy Jr. ran 20 yards, then gave the ball to Roger to run the final 50. So when Roger let Rudy score, he was just paying him back in kind. However, he might also have wanted to make sure that Rudy Jr. didn't resent him for stealing the headlines. His older brother never seemed to resent Roger's success, but scoring seven touchdowns to none for Rudy Jr. over two games could have been too much for either of them to handle. Roger didn't want to be the only one represented in their mother's scrapbook.

Shanley concluded its outstanding season with a 34–12 victory over Valley City, as Roger and Rudy Jr. each scored on 26-yard runs and Cichy played everyone on the team. The Deacons' 7-1 record was good enough to win the Eastern Division of the North Dakota East-West Conference. The Deacons were supposed to play Minot, the Western Division champions, in the title game the first week of November, but it was canceled because of a massive snowstorm, and the schools were declared cochampions.

In the United Press coaches' poll, Shanley was voted the best high school football team in the state. Roger was named to the Associated Press East-West High School Football Team as well as All-State. Again Roger received recognition, while Rudy Jr., whose high school football career was over, received none.

If he needed it, Rudy Jr. got some solace by leading a solid Deacons basketball team to two triumphs over Fargo Central. Roger played guard for the Deacons. He was a good shooter, but was more effective on defense, where his speed and aggressiveness worked well in Coach Cichy's full-court press.

At Shanley, Roger never displayed the quick temper he had as a youngster in Grand Forks. But Rudy Jr. never mellowed. Dick Savageau recalls:

> He used to give me a ride home from basketball in the wintertime. One time a car catches us as we enter an intersection. The guy never slows down and runs into the driver's side of Rudy's car and smashes it all in. None of us got hurt, but Rudy gets out and starts raising hell with this guy that hit him. I mean, he's swearing at him like a trooper. I said, "Rudy, Rudy! That's the rabbi!"
>
> One time we were at basketball practice and this kid got into a fight with Rudy. Roger ran downstairs and made a phone call to his dad and said, "Dad, you'd better get out here in a hurry. Rudy's going to beat the hell out of Art." So his dad came out and picked up the two boys after the practice to prevent what could have happened outside. Rudy had a temper, not Roger.

The Deacons had a good basketball season before losing to the taller Grand Forks in the playoffs, despite Rudy Jr.'s 18 points. In the spring the Maras boys joined Cichy's track team, with Roger having more success. It was the last time they participated in an organized sport together and was Rudy Maras Jr.'s final athletic endeavor before graduating from Shanley High in June.

Rudy Jr. accepted a baseball scholarship to Santa Clara College, an all-male Jesuit school in northern California. His plan was to pursue a degree and play baseball in anticipation of signing a professional contract. Roger thought he might follow him to college and they'd play football together, maybe baseball, too. The older brother had first dibs on a life after Fargo, and the younger brother was content to be in his shadow.

Roger played his last year of American Legion ball, without his brother or his friend Larry Sweeney, who were past the maximum age. Under new coach Leo Osman, who played him in right field and had him pitch on occasion, Roger didn't miss a beat, leading the team in almost every offensive category.

"We were walking down the street one day and we were across the street from the Fargo Theatre," recalls Savageau. "A few of the Fargo-Moorhead Twins were giving us grief, so Roger hollers to them across the street, 'You want to see my clippings?' I said, 'Roger!' Because he wasn't someone who bragged. Then he turned to me and said, 'I'm going to play in the majors someday.' I said, 'Yeah, Roger, you're going to play in the majors. So will I. Come on.' "

Roger had secured his driver's license when he turned sixteen and immediately developed a love for being behind the wheel. As an adult, he would often drive long distances and on occasion drive at high speeds. But when he was a high school student, he was content just borrowing his father's 1932 Chevy coupe and riding around with his friends. "Somewhere between our junior and senior years," recalls Savageau, "we tipped it over down in the park that is now called the Roger Maris Memorial Park. It had rained a lot that summer and he was driving and he tried to turn the wheel. It was all mud and we tipped it over on its side. We all got out and tipped it back up. We went to the river and got some water and some rags and tried to clean off all the mud so that his father would never know what we did. He'd have killed Roger."

That summer, newspaper headlines kept Americans posted on the war in Korea and the ongoing UN campaign led by General Douglas MacArthur. There were items on the death of William Randolph Hearst; the jailing of writer Dashiell Hammett for contempt of court for not naming those involved with a Communist-front bail fund; and the excitement over the publication of *Catcher in the Rye* written by J. D. Salinger. There were advertisements for such popular movies as *A Place in the Sun,* with young screen idols Elizabeth Taylor and Montgomery Clift, *David and Bathsheba* with Gregory Peck and Susan Hayward, and *Show Boat* featuring Kathryn Grayson, Ava Gardner, and Howard Keel. TV listings included popular programs starring Arthur Godfrey, Milton Berle, Jack Webb (who wore badge 714 on *Dragnet* in tribute to Babe Ruth's career home-run record), Sid Caesar, Gertrude Berg, Lucille Ball, Red Skelton, Jack Benny, Groucho Marx, and Roy Rogers. And the sports pages were chock-full of events, such as thirty-seven-year-old Jersey Joe Walcott knocking out Ezzard Charles for the heavyweight championship in Pittsburgh; and, in New York, nineteen-year-old phenom Mickey Mantle playing alongside Yankee great Joe DiMaggio, who was about to hang up his spikes because of age (and his difficulty hitting the slider). Roger might have read about all of this in the *Fargo Forum* if he wasn't too busy playing Legion ball.

Unfortunately, a second-half slump dropped Roger's astronomical .480 average to .350—anticipating his brutal second-half slumps in professional baseball. Also, a pitching loss in the final game of the state's double-elimination tourney cost him a second consecutive team MVP award.

He was extremely disappointed to be edged out for the MVP honor by another outfielder and pitcher, Don Gronland. While Roger believed from an early age that work was its own reward, he also felt a person should be properly compensated for the fruits of his labor. He didn't seek acclaim or awards, but he worked hard at sports and wanted proper recognition for his accomplishments. He always had a code of *fairness* that he applied to sports, particularly when he got older and equated playing baseball and business. When he was bypassed for the team MVP, he believed justice didn't prevail and felt hurt, confused, and betrayed.

CHAPTER FIVE

A SCHOOLBOY SENSATION

WITH RUDY JR. AWAY at college, it was harder for Roger to deal with his family life. Although he didn't like talking about the troubles of his parents, it was impossible to keep it from his friends. "Bob Wood's folks had a room with a shower down in the basement of their house," says Dick Savageau, "and at times Roger would get ticked off at his parents and go stay there. I always liked Connie. For whatever reason, she was always so nice to me. Rudy Sr. was a hard-nosed, tough guy. Only a few of us got along with him. He had a temper. I don't remember Connie having one. They were two people that lived together who couldn't stand each other. I remember as a kid growing up, divorce was really something you didn't do, so I went to my mother, who was a very good Catholic, and said, 'Mom, I can't understand this because these people hate each other. Why would they make them stay together?' "

Connie's disapproval of Pat, a good Catholic girl, led to tension and frequent arguments. Connie's dalliances were not a secret in the small town. Roger's friends remained circumspect about her behavior, never bringing it up to him. They accepted his lifelong need for privacy in regard to his family. "Roger was sensitive when one of his friends would talk about it," says Savageau. "He didn't like that. In fact, there was a kid here in town who talked about his mother and Roger wouldn't have anything to do with him."

School, Pat, and football kept Roger occupied in the fall, pushing family turmoil into the background. Roger had a tremendous senior year with the Deacons, but Rudy Jr.'s departure was too much for the team to overcome. The season began with a 33–13 loss to Moorhead. The following week, the

Fargo Midgets crushed Shanley 33–0. Shanley won only three of its eight games.

Roger continued to rack up touchdowns and starred in all three victories. In Shanley's 33–7 win over Oak Grove, he had a 90-yard touchdown run during which, reported the *Forum*, "Shanley's speedy halfback . . . ran through the entire Grover eleven without a hand being laid on him." In a 31–6 defeat of Park River, Roger scored three touchdowns and an extra point.

But the highlight of Roger's season was undoubtedly the game against Devils Lake. Shanley won 32–27, with Roger accounting for all but one of his team's points. Local writer and sports historian Larry Scott says that the familiar story is that Roger scored four touchdowns on kickoff returns, prompting the opposing coach to tell Sid Cichy, "We hated to score because we knew he'd run it back every time." This tale persists because Cichy petitioned to get Roger the national record for most kickoff-return touchdowns in a game.

What Roger actually did was more impressive. He returned the opening kickoff 88 yards, and the kickoff that opened the second half 90 yards. He also had a 45-yard punt return, a 32-yard run from scrimmage, and a 25-yard runback of an interception. So he scored five touchdowns, four on various types of returns, plus an extra point. His five scores totaled 280 yards, or 56 yards a pop. This performance confirmed for many college coaches that Roger was worth recruiting.

"Roger starred in so many games that his name was all over the place," remembers Savageau. "Every Saturday morning, he was what the paper was all about—Maras, Maras, Maras. He was *the* star football player in North Dakota."

"If he liked being a high school star, I wouldn't have known it," comments Wayne Blanchard. "He was never one to brag about what he did."

For the second year in a row Roger was voted All-State. No one had more respect for his gridiron efforts than his coach. In his career at Shanley, Sid Cichy compiled a record of 231-38-3, including fifteen state championships, and a record streak of 59 consecutive wins, earning him induction into the National High School Athletic Coaches Association Hall of Fame. Yet he looked back at the 1951 season with deep regret. "It was one of the two losing seasons I had in thirty years at Shanley," Cichy said, "and it happened with probably the best athlete I had."

With Rudy Jr. gone, Shanley's basketball team also had a downturn. The most depressing losses came at the hands of Fargo Central. Roger moved on seamlessly to track in the spring, expanding his repertoire to the long jump and shot put. The first time he vaulted, he cleared 10 feet. In the season-ending state competition in 1952, Roger finished third in the shot put and second in the 100-yard dash.

When the state sprint champion visited Fargo, Roger challenged him to two 100-yard dashes. The champion accepted, saying, "Loser buys a steak dinner." "It was the best steak I ever had," said Roger years later.

To his mother's chagrin, Roger felt serious enough about Pat to not date other girls his senior year. In between their teenage squabbles and breakups, she wore his football ring. She accepted his invitation to his senior prom. He drove up in his father's beat-up '32 Chevy. He was wearing a suit, a tie, a crewcut, and the familiar half smile that he always had when nervous. In his hand was the first corsage that Pat Carvell ever wore.

Roger and Pat sensed they had a future together, but for now they couldn't commit. She had another year of high school and he expected to leave Fargo in the fall. Maybe he'd join Rudy Jr. at Santa Clara, but football recruiters from big schools were tempting him with offers. Roger and his friend Steve Myhra went on a recruiting trip to the University of Minnesota. He was even more interested in the distant University of Oklahoma, which had an exceptionally strong program under Bud Wilkinson. Though no baseball scouts had made overtures to him, professional baseball wasn't out of the picture.

A dramatic turn of events made Roger's choices about his future even more difficult. In California, Rudy Jr. contracted polio. Though a mild case from which he recovered in time, it ruined his chances of being a professional athlete. He returned to Fargo, and for a time Roger's strong big brother was bedridden.

Rudy Jr.'s illness was life-altering for both brothers. Whatever Roger did in sports from this point on, he would do alone and feel as if he'd left Rudy Jr. behind. Proof of his deep guilt about becoming the one brother healthy enough to pursue an athletic career is found in *Slugger in Right*.

Dreaming of major league careers, Billy Mack and his older brother, Bob, play on an amateur baseball team. Bob, the more advanced player, is a second baseman, Billy is the right fielder. Racing in on a short fly, Billy hurtles into Bob, breaking his leg. "I'm never going to play again," the devastated Billy tells Bob. "I couldn't enjoy myself knowing I was responsible for your not playing." Bob will never play again, and Billy signs a professional baseball contract with enough bonus money to pay for Bob's surgery. His guilt over Bob's injury plagues Billy the entire book because he thinks he should be the one who can't play. Thinking himself less talented than Rudy Jr., Roger probably believed he should have been the one stricken.

Roger still wanted to pursue a sports career, but he didn't feel at ease attempting it without Rudy Jr. or taking on Rudy Jr.'s family burden to be a successful professional athlete. It was a no-win proposition because if Roger somehow became a star, as everyone expected Rudy Jr. to be, he would feel he was having the career meant for Rudy Jr. And no matter how well he did, he would believe that Rudy Jr. would have surpassed him. His father continued to say, unfairly, that Rudy Jr. was a better athlete, and Roger accepted that.

"My father worked in the Grand Recreation on Main, which crossed Broadway," recalls singer Bobby Vee, who grew up in Fargo as Robert Velline. "It was a café with pool tables in back and an extended bar with stools, and they could serve comfort food to about fifty people at a time. Roger Maras's father would have lunch at the counter and talk to my dad, who liked him. I'm certain Rudy Sr. was proud of Roger, but he always talked about what a great talent Rudy Jr. was."

Roger graduated from Bishop Shanley High in June 1952. Thinking that he might accept a full football scholarship to Oklahoma in the fall, he played organized baseball for what he thought could be the last time, in a city league.

"It was amateur baseball," says Savageau, "so he needed a job. Fargo Floral was down on First Avenue, just off Broadway. My uncle Jerry Cossette was the manager, and I started working there in seventh grade. Roger became friends with my uncle and got a job as a delivery boy, driving the Floral car. One day my uncle told me that Roger was having fun teasing the office girls and they couldn't work. He didn't fire him but said, 'Rog, you go over to the Grand Rec, and we'll call you when we need you.'"

Rudy Jr.'s dream of being signed to a baseball contract was on hold while he recuperated from his illness. Meanwhile, he was making all A's at North Dakota Agricultural College, the future North Dakota State University. Roger was leaning toward playing college football and eventually turning pro if he was good enough, but he felt he might still be offered a baseball contract.

Indians scout Frank Fahay had kept an eye on Roger since August 1950 in Legion ball and the city league. He was pleased that Roger had grown a few inches and put on twenty pounds without losing any speed. He believed Roger had all the tools at the plate, on the bases, and in the field—including a strong, accurate arm—and recommended that the Indians give him a try-out. Cy Slapnicka, the scout from Iowa who signed Bob Feller, agreed.

The Chicago Cubs heard the Indians were interested in Roger Maras, so they invited him to an earlier tryout. But when he and Rudy Sr. got to Chicago, they discovered that the team's enthusiasm had waned. They were miffed that Roger was given only a cursory look and the 6', 185-pounder was judged to be "too small" and dismissed.

It was a different story with the Indians. The club's general manager was the onetime great ballplayer Hank Greenberg, and he had genuine interest in left-handed hitters with power. Municipal Stadium was 385 feet in the power alleys, but only 312 feet down the lines, so if Maras learned to pull the ball, he could reach the seats with ease. "I watched him swing and catch some fly balls, and I knew quickly he was a hell of a prospect," Greenberg told Maury Allen in 1985. "I made him an offer, $8,000 or $9,000, the going rate for a kid out of high school."

Greenberg's offer was probably higher, perhaps as much as $15,000, because he was competing with college football for Roger's services. Roger turned down Greenberg and accepted a full scholarship to Oklahoma that included tuition, room and board, a job, and transportation to and from campus.

The popular story is that Roger went to Norman, Oklahoma, in late summer of 1952. He climbed off the bus, saw no one there to meet him, and took the next bus back to Fargo. It wasn't beyond Roger to do exactly this if he felt slighted. However, when he arrived in Norman by bus or train, surely someone greeted him, escorted him around campus, and got him settled, because soon Roger was sitting in a classroom taking an entrance exam.

Roger later said that by mid-exam he'd made up his mind, with some regret, that college life was not for him. So instead of sticking around and eventually playing for an Oklahoma varsity that won 47 consecutive games and a national title, he returned to Fargo after about ten days on campus.

"He never talked about that episode at Oklahoma," says Savageau, who doubts it was the test that did in Roger. "He got homesick. His friends were his security blanket."

Roger called Greenberg to accept his offer, but he no longer had football as a bargaining chip. Greenberg sent Slapnicka to Fargo to make Roger a new offer. Joining him was Jack O'Connor, the general manager of the Fargo-Moorhead Twins, an affiliate of the Indians. Roger was offered a $5,000 signing bonus—still serious money for a small-city teenager in 1952—and an additional $10,000 *if* he reached the majors.

Eighteen-year-old Roger Maras signed the contract, and his professional baseball career began.

CHAPTER SIX

A PRO

DAYTONA BEACH, FLORIDA, WAS the site of Roger Maras's first spring training, in March 1953. Indianville, where Cleveland's eight minor league teams came for spring training, was a twelve-field complex on the future location of the Daytona International Speedway. "It was a navy air base during the war," recalls Mert Prophet, who was the organization's popular minor league trainer. "Everything about it was first-class. The players stayed in a large building with a dining hall. The coaches, club managers, equipment men, and myself stayed across the street where the officers had been. You can't believe how great the food was. The Indians really took care of their players."

Some of the players who were staying in the cramped two-story, U-shaped dormitory saw it differently. "Some old, raunchy guy would walk through the barracks every morning at five thirty firing off blanks with a pistol," recalls Russ Nixon, a catcher from Ohio who first came to Indianville in 1954. "That was our wake-up call. Good Lord, we had players everywhere. You had your little locker, and unless your mother and dad came to help you out, nothing ever got clean. It was a smelly mess, but we got through it."

When he wasn't at the parent club's camp in Tucson, Arizona, Hank Greenberg was in Indianville to monitor activities. He had been the team's scouting director when Bill Veeck ran the club in the late forties. The socially conscious "people's owner" turned it into a contender by matching the Brooklyn Dodgers' penchant for signing black players, including Larry Doby, who broke the American League's color barrier only eleven weeks after Jackie Robinson first played for the Dodgers in 1947. Veeck also signed legendary Negro Leagues pitcher Satchel Paige and Cuban star Minnie Minoso.

When Veeck had financial problems, a syndicate led by Ellis Ryan, who became the owner, and Greenberg, who became the GM, bought out Veeck for $2.5 million and continued his enlightened ways. Rosters throughout the Indians organization were integrated, with blacks, whites, and Latinos playing side by side. This was the first time Roger suited up with ballplayers of color. But to him and the hundreds of players in camp, sock color was more important than skin color.

"The color of your socks told you what class you were in," recalls Dan Osinski, a right-handed pitcher who bunked with Maras. "Players assigned to Indianapolis, the Indians' Triple A team, wore striped socks, Class A Reading Indians players wore green socks. Players at the lower levels wore the least attractive colors—red for Class C, brown for Class D."

As in the other fifteen minor league camps, few players were considered genuine prospects. The majority would be cut, and the function of most survivors was to fill roster spots so that the players with a real shot had teams to play on. Even for the most talented, it was extremely difficult to move up the slippery slope to the major leagues, and many were destined to be career minor leaguers. For those in Cleveland's system it was particularly discouraging to know that the parent club's strong lineup—led by center fielder Doby, first baseman Vic Wertz, third baseman Al Rosen, second baseman Bobby Avila, shortstop George Strickland, and catcher Jim Hegan—and heralded pitching staff—headed by starters Bob Feller, Bob Lemon, Early Wynn, and Mike Garcia—seemed set in stone, and roster openings weren't anticipated for years. It wasn't necessary to put even the best minor leaguers on the fast track.

Two exceptions had been promoted to Reading: Rocky Colavito, a slugging outfielder with a cannon for an arm, and his roommate, Herb Score, a left-handed pitching phenom who had been signed for $60,000 by Cy Slapnicka. Quiet, religious, and polite, both struck up lasting friendships with Roger. That Colavito and Maras hoped to be the Indians' starting right fielder someday never interfered with their relationship.

"The word around Indianville was that Maras was a good prospect," recalls Jerry Mehlisch, a catcher from Iowa who was signed by Slapnicka. "He was fairly good-sized, he was very fast, he had a great arm, he roamed the outfield very well, he had a good stroke, plus he had a good presence. Roger had the whole package."

"You could tell he was going to be a great player," agrees Billy Moran, a shortstop from Georgia who was considered a top prospect despite wearing number 469. "He could do everything, including bust your butt going into second base. He did the rolling block they eventually outlawed. It was like a saw hitting you."

Cleveland's management considered Colavito on a different level from the younger Maras, but other players drew comparisons because they both played right field. "The scouts said Colavito would be a major leaguer, but they weren't sure about Maras," remembers Billy Harrell, an infielder who got only 342 major league at-bats in a career that lasted from 1952 to 1966. "They had the strongest arms in the organization. Roger's was more accurate. They'd run on Rocky, but they wouldn't on Maras. Shoot, Rocky would throw that ball two feet over your head or two feet in front of you. Maras hit the cutoff man. He played the game the right way."

According to some accounts, when Roger agreed to the Indians' contract offer, he stipulated that he play his first year with the Class C Fargo-Moorhead Twins. It's more likely, however, that he decided after negotiations that he wanted to play at home. This became a source of contention between Roger and Cleveland farm director Mike McNally, who wanted the eighteen-year-old to play for the Class D team based in Daytona Beach. Roger said he was too good for Class D. McNally countered by saying first-year players were under too much pressure already, and playing in front of family and friends would make it far worse. Roger disagreed, but he played hard while the tug-of-war continued.

"Coming from the Midwest," says Mehlisch, "Roger was stubborn and hardheaded. But he knew what he wanted and nobody was going to talk him out of it."

Roger dug in his heels, stating firmly, "I'm either going home to play or I'm going home to stay." When a player threatened to quit over any issue, teams always called his bluff, assuming no athlete would turn his back on money to play ball. But the Indians realized that if this obstinate kid from North Dakota said he'd go home and work, that's exactly what he'd do. McNally, perhaps swayed by Roger's exceptional camp, blinked first. Roger donned a pair of red socks.

Maras reported to the Fargo-Moorhead Twins' new manager, Henry John Bonura, a fellow so colorful that he had two nicknames—Zeke and Banana Nose. Born in New Orleans, Bonura became an instant hero in Chicago as a rookie in 1934 by setting a White Sox record with 27 home runs. He'd never hit with such power again, but he batted over .300 in four of seven major league seasons. Bonura was popular because of his affable personality and the way he played first base, which was to give what people called a "Mussolini salute" as balls whizzed past him. He lost favor with management because of his fielding, annual holdouts, and supposed interest in the owner's daughter. He was happy to be traded to Washington because he could sign his name *Senator Henry J. Bonura, Democrat, Louisiana*. By 1940, he was out of the league.

Bonura reestablished himself during the war by organizing baseball operations in Algeria. The "Czar of North African Baseball" failed to make a comeback as a player but in 1953, as an act of goodwill, was given the one-year assignment of taking a team that hadn't won a Northern League title since 1934 and had finished seventh in '52 and making it competitive.

The Fargo-Moorhead Twins' 1953 season began on May 6 with a 12–3 drubbing of Sioux Falls before 10,123 raucous fans at Barnett Field, not only an attendance record for Class C baseball but for a sports event in North Dakota. Despite the threat of snow and *Call Me Madam*, with Ethel Merman, playing at the Fargo Theatre on Broadway, they wanted to see Zeke Bonura's Twins, featuring returning slugger Frank Gravino and hometown boy Roger Maras. Those with night jobs tuned in to Manny Marget's broadcast on KVOX.

Roger got only one of Fargo's 16 hits, but it was the start of a 10-game hitting streak. As Roger's contribution increased, Gravino rocketed pitches into another dimension, and the wins accumulated, fans continued to fill the seats. Families arrived two or three hours ahead of game time with picnic baskets. There were five-hundred-pound drums of salted peanuts, and children could eat as much as they wanted if they helped pack the nuts for the concession stand, which also sold hot dogs, chewing gum, and soft drinks. For fifty cents, kids could purchase season passes and sit in their own sections.

"I sat with the others in the Knothole Gang," recalls Bobby Vee. "I can't begin to say what a big deal it was with the Twins and the crowds they pulled in—10,000 fans in North Dakota!"

"One night, there were just a handful of people there, and we're thinking, 'What's going on?' " says Ray Seif, the pitching ace of the Twins. "Guess who was in town giving a concert? Lawrence Welk!"

"I was ten when Roger played on Fargo," says Vee, "and I knew he could do it all. But my hero was Frank Gravino because I was excited by home runs. I didn't have the nerve to ask for autographs, but I remember those guys coming over and signing things."

Roger's road roommate and mentor, Gravino had an astounding year, belting 52 homers (33 more than the league's runner-up) and driving in 174 runs in the 125-game season. But autograph seekers had a lot of stars to choose from. Twenty-game winners Seif and Don Nance combined to go 40-14. Don Wolf and Bob Borovicka went a combined 23-6. Second baseman Santo Luberto won the batting title with a .361 average and drove in 105 runs. Shortstop Joe Camacho knocked in 90 runs from the leadoff spot and led the league with 139 runs scored. Towering first baseman Ray Mendoza belted 16 homers and had 85 RBIs. Fargo's announcers called many double plays that were turned by Camacho, Luberto, and Mendoza.

At third base on Fargo was John Morris, Roger's first black teammate. "Galion, Ohio, where I came from, didn't have any African-Americans," says Seif, "so John was the first black teammate for me also. Other guys were a little shy of him, but we got along. Whenever somebody charged me on the mound, he'd be the first one to help me."

Maras played mostly in right field and usually batted seventh. In 114 games, he drove in a 80 runs, scored 70, laced 18 doubles and 13 triples, and swiped 14 bases. He batted .325, which would be the highest of his professional career and indicated he could hit for a high average if he hit to all fields. He slammed only 9 homers, but people in Fargo still talk about the one that landed on a porch across the street from the center-field fence. Though a line-drive hitter, he had enough power to partner with Gravino in a home-run-hitting contest against Eau Claire at Barnett Field.

A more significant event at the home park was the Northern League All-Star Game, which pitted the first-place Twins against the top players on Duluth, St. Cloud, Aberdeen, Sioux Falls, Grand Forks, Superior, and Eau

Claire. The bleachers were extended and a new Northern League record of 13,629 fans cheered on the Twins. Roger had 2 doubles and a single as Fargo humbled the All-Stars 8–4.

Roger did well on the road—in Grand Forks, his 2 homers and a single led a 16-hit attack in a 16–2 victory; in Duluth, he hit a ninth-inning, game-winning homer; in St. Cloud, he threw out three runners in a game. But as he anticipated, Roger flourished in his hometown, where his team went 49-14.

"I met Roger's family at the ballpark," remembers Joe Camacho, a future bench coach for Ted Williams. "His mother was a beautiful lady with reddish blond hair. His dad, who was at a lot of games, was a handsome, rugged guy. His brother, Rudy, was a rugged guy, too, and looked like an athlete."

"Our clubhouse was right off right field," says Seif. "The game would end, and by the time rest of the team got in there, Roger would be in his street clothes, leaving. He talked about a girl but I never met her. He probably wanted to get the heck out of the ballpark so he could see her."

That wasn't the case. It's often assumed that since Roger and Pat dated in high school and eventually married that they were together from the night they first met. But that picture-perfect romance didn't happen. "They weren't engaged," explains Savageau. "In fact, during her senior year, Patsy was going out with a kid named Kelly, who was in her class." Perhaps Roger's fine year can be attributed to his focus on baseball.

If he wasn't out with friends, he might have been at St. John's Orphanage playing football with the kids under Sister Bertha's supervision. Unchanged, he was by all standards generous in spirit and kind to a fault. One person he touched was Rob Johnson, who was born with a form of muscular dystrophy. Now the chief audiologist at the Fargo Veterans Hospital, he lived with his parents and cousin across the street from the Marases. He recalls:

Before I went to kindergarten I had a surgery on my legs and they put casts on up to my hips. One of my cousin Diane's responsibilities was to push me around the block in a wheelchair. One time Roger stopped to talk to us and discovered that I loved baseball. Soon he showed up at our house with some balls that had been hit over the fence at the ballpark. Roger asked me if I wanted to play catch. From that day forward, whenever Roger saw me outside, we played catch. Roger gave me a few baseball tickets for the games, and all of us kids became members of the Knothole Gang, attending games for a dime. For years, Roger and his parents brought me baseballs.

Roger also was exploring his entrepreneurial side by pumping gas and changing oil at the small filling station he operated across the river in Moorhead. "Maybe he leased it, but I think he bought it," Dick Savageau says. "At about 7 a.m. it would open up and stay open full-time. When Roger was in town, he'd be over there, kind of running it. When he was out of town during the summer, I ran it for him. Rudy would come over when he was done at the railroad and relieve me. Business was slow and I don't think it was a good deal for him."

"Roger didn't spend time with us in Fargo because he had his own friends," recalls Mehlisch, who caught for Fargo after Bonura requested that he be transferred from Peoria. "But we hung out on the road. One time in Duluth five or six of us went out to eat. We were walking down the street and Roger found a $10 bill. We said, 'Hey, Rog, you can buy us all a beer now.' Roger didn't say anything and we kept walking. There was a homeless guy on the corner and Roger gave him the ten bucks. We yelled, 'Rog!' He just smiled and off we went."

"Roger was a very quiet individual, but he was good to talk to," says Camacho, "and I liked spending time with him. We were both Catholic and always made it a point to find a church service."

"He was quiet and shy and kept to himself most of the time," says Seif. "What I remember most was that Joe Camacho would tell him, 'You've got to eat better,' because every day we ate steaks and open-faced sandwiches and Roger's meals consisted of shakes and burgers. We thought he was stashing away money by eating cheaply."

Roger's teammates ended up visiting Roger in a Grand Forks hospital after a pitch hit him so hard on the head that the ball bounced into the stands. In that pre-batting-helmet era, the only protection players had in their caps were thin strips of plastic inside the rims. "It was scary," says Mehlisch. "I saw young players who lost their confidence because they worried they'd be hit again. I think a defining moment in Roger's career was in his first game back. He hit a home run. He stood right in there and wasn't scared a bit."

Roger got over the beaning and for the rest of his career was able to stand in against pitchers who came inside, including side-arming lefties. However, to protect himself, he moved farther away from the plate. He compensated by striding into the pitch, which allowed him to learn how to pull the ball, even the outside pitch.

The Fargo-Moorhead Twins finished the season 86-39, an extraordinary turnaround from their 44-80 1952 season. In the playoffs, they took both games from St. Cloud, clinching the series with a 4–2 victory in ten innings. Then they won a best-of-five championship series from Duluth, taking the finale 13–5, as Mehlisch went 4 for 5. As a member of the Northern League champions, Roger received a full share of $120.

Gravino was selected the league's MVP, beating out Luberto and Seif. "The fans gave Frank a car at the end of the year," recalls Camacho. "Zeke Bonura was upset because he didn't get one." Gravino would lead Fargo to a second consecutive championship in '54, smashing 56 homers. The 5'9", 185-pound slugger had a two-year total of 108, staking his claim to being the Northern League's best player ever, past or future. But unable to hit well in higher leagues, perhaps because of poor eyesight, he left baseball to work in the construction business in Rochester, New York.

Maras was chosen the Northern League's Rookie of the Year. The only player to have received more votes in league history was Eau Claire's Henry Aaron in 1952. Roger showed what kind of interview he'd be for the duration of his career when all he could tell the *Fargo Forum* was "It's nice to know I won."

Even at that age he wanted to do his job and be left alone. He was proud that he had made the giant step from amateur to professional athlete and continued to win championships for his teams. But there was no gloating to the press or anyone else. That would be left to his parents.

Connie took her boasting back to Hibbing and caused such a stir that it was written about in the *Minneapolis Star* eight years later by a reporter who visited the Homer Tavern. "The man on the next stool," wrote Howard Schaefer, "explained that the rift in the Maras clan stemmed principally from talk among the womenfolk. Some felt they had been 'ritzed' by Mrs. Maras."

Roger's father did his bragging in Fargo, at the railroad and at lunch counters. Those he spoke to realized that whenever he boasted about Roger, he made it a point to add, "But did you know my older son, Rudy Jr., was even better before he got polio?"

His father's words underlined what Roger felt himself—the reason he always felt as uncomfortable being praised as criticized. Rudy Jr.'s misfortune was an explanation for why Roger felt embarrassment throughout his career when discussing his accomplishments.

CHAPTER SEVEN

MAKING A NAME FOR HIMSELF

AFTER HIS FIRST PROFESSIONAL season, Roger decided that it was time to leave Fargo and his family troubles behind. He was delighted that Rudy Jr. had recovered from the polio and was earning a degree in mechanical engineering at NDSU. But Rudy and Connie were becoming more estranged. That in turn made Connie increasingly hostile to other family members, Marases and Mariches.

Tilly Sanborn remembers, "My brother Jack Maras got a job with a company in North Dakota and wanted to visit Rudy, Connie, and their boys in Fargo. He told me he went to their apartment, but Connie wouldn't accept him. He felt terrible because he hadn't done anything."

"Mihiel's widow and daughter made overtures to Connie because they wanted to be part of the family," says Rudy Marich. "They were her sister-in-law and niece, but she pushed them away and we never saw them again."

Connie did welcome her sister Mary to Fargo after her divorce from James LaFreniere. Jim LaFreniere Jr. says, "My mom had a tough time when she lived in Fargo and then Dilworth, Minnesota, right on the border. Roger would visit and fix up her car, put on new tires, do everything to help her out. It was always Roger and his dad who came over. Connie visited once in a great while but never with Roger. My mom had to visit her. Roger was mild-tempered because he hung on to his dad, who was one of the nicest guys I ever met. Rudy Jr. and his mother were very sarcastic, snobbish, and hot-tempered. Connie was pretty bossy, and if she didn't like something, she'd tell you. We had some run-ins."

When another sister moved to Fargo, Connie was less than enthusiastic. Vi Marich was now married to Dominic Cortese, who during the war had been a pilot in North Africa. Soon after, she gave birth to a son, Rick. A daughter, Catherine Anne, was named after her grandmother Ana. In the early fifties, Vi's family moved to Fargo so Dominic could open a pizza parlor. Vi remembered, "One day I stopped by to see Connie with my son, Rick, who was still in a high chair. Rick had one eye that kind of wandered and would need surgery on it. Connie said, 'God is punishing you through your kid. That's why he's cockeyed.' She was very vicious. Roger was there and Connie pointed to a picture of his girlfriend and said, 'That's the biggest tramp in Fargo, North Dakota!' Roger, who was a sweet kid, took off. But first he told her, 'Whether you like her or not, I'm going to marry her!' "

"Roger knew his mother was strange," says his uncle Don O'Neil. "Did he love her? I don't know. I think he tolerated her." For reasons never disclosed, Roger sided with his mother in her feud with the Marases, but he stood up for Pat Carvell.

One time Roger stormed out of the apartment during an argument with his mother and didn't return. Jack Blakely, who worked at the Northwest Beverage distributor, offered Roger an off-season job and accommodations in his basement. Blakely was only four years older than Roger, but in the winter of 1953–54 he already was a successful businessman with a wife, MarLynn, and two young children. While working and playing basketball on a distributor-sponsored team together, he and Roger became close friends.

"Dad said Roger was a good-mannered, soft-spoken kid, but was an absolutely maniacal competitor playing basketball," says Jack's older son, John Blakely.

It was at this time that Roger made one of his greatest catches, and it wasn't on a ball field. Jack and MarLynn's young daughter was eating ice cream in the kitchen. "I remember being in a little chair at a little kids' table," says Pat Blakely. "I was rocking back and forth when the chair fell over backwards through the open cellar door. Roger happened to be coming up the stairs, and his most famous catch should have been me, because he caught me before I flipped and had a serious injury."

The Blakely family relates how Roger once parked his brand-new DeSoto convertible in their driveway. The next morning, the car wasn't there. The police conducted an investigation and found that Connie had the car towed to the front of her apartment building. She pointed out that it wasn't in

Roger's name because he was under twenty-one. Apparently, she wanted him to come home.

"His leaving home had to do with his girl, Patsy," says MarLynn Blakely. "Maybe his mother didn't like her because she was a strong Roman Catholic. Roger was with us on and off over the years, and Patsy sometimes came over and she and Roger babysat our kids."

Pat Carvell and her senior-year boyfriend didn't last after they graduated. Although she and Roger didn't make a commitment to each other, they dated when he returned to Fargo. She was still living at 1022 Eighth Avenue South. Pat and her mother had an apartment upstairs while the Seebas lived on the main floor. "On weekends during the winter, Roger and Pat would come into the living room and we'd watch hockey," Walt Seeba remembers. "He liked hockey because his dad played and taught him. Roger and Pat actually dated for three or four years. But while he was off playing ball, she was dating other guys, and I'm sure he was out dating other gals. Pat was a very attractive, nice young woman, so young men were interested. But Roger never went away entirely."

When Roger reported to Indianville for his second spring training, he again believed he knew best what direction his career should take. He wanted to leave home and be promoted to a higher league. It was a reasonable expectation considering the fine year he'd had in 1953, so he was shocked when he was again assigned to Fargo. The Indians argued he'd get more seasoning under the Twins' new manager, Phil Seghi; Roger said he needed to move upward and improve his game against better talent. Roger stated his position, "Promote me to Class B or I'm gone," and he wouldn't budge. After a couple of days of this stalemate, club officials were steamed. There were accounts of a shouting match and of Roger leaving camp to lie on the "World's Most Famous Beach."

"Roger was bullheaded enough to go home rather than go along with something he didn't agree with," says Jerry Mehlisch, who played again with Fargo. "He didn't like being jerked around. He just wanted to play where he knew he could play."

If Roger hadn't revealed special talent, he would have been shown the door despite the Indians' investment. But Greenberg saw Roger's potential and decided he couldn't let him go. He agreed to Roger's demand and assigned him to Keokuk, Iowa, in Class B, but he did so with the realization that the Kernels' manager, Jo Jo White, could change the line-drive gap hitter into a pull hitter with lift so he could better utilize his power.

Greenberg thought White also had the temperament to make Roger enthusiastic about baseball rather than willing to abandon it when things weren't perfect. In *Slugger in Right*, Pop Colliton, a sympathetic Jo Jo White–like character (named after the Collitons of Fargo), thinks about the troubled Billy Mack: "He has all the makings of a great player, but there's something eating him. Sometimes he acts almost ashamed of being able to play ball." Roger was extremely revealing here in regard to his own guilt about leaving Rudy Jr. behind. What Roger failed to realize, ever, was that baseball was difficult for even the talented, and the odds were that he had already developed into a better player than a healthy Rudy Jr. would ever have been.

By the time camp broke and the Kernels headed for Iowa, Roger knew that the Indians planned to change him into a power-hitting pull hitter. He typically resisted anything that was thrust on him without his participating in the decision, but not this time. The idea intrigued him.

Keokuk was situated in southeastern Iowa, in the heart of the Corn Belt. America's pastime was the biggest sport in the heartland, and the townspeople and fans in the surrounding rural areas loved their Kernels, who had joined the tough Three-I League in 1952. In 1954, the team became a Cleveland Indians affiliate. After fifth- and seventh-place finishes, it was a much improved team under White, and attendance soared.

According to team historian Shane Etter, "Keokuk was excited that baseball was back because it had sort of died out. The fans made Roger Maras and the other young guys feel welcome."

"Keokuk was quite a town," says a sarcastic Joe Camacho. "I still remember the fish flies that kept coming off the Mississippi. In restaurants, we had to knock them off our plates."

"There was a plant that made starch for medical gloves right outside of town," recalls Ray Seif. "It stunk up the whole place when the wind was in the wrong direction, and that included the ballpark. The most exciting thing to do in town was eat watermelon."

This was Roger's first extended period away from his Fargo friends, so he was glad his teammates included ex-Twins Seif and Camacho, and his spring-training roommate Dan Osinski. Osinski recalls:

> We rented rooms in a house owned by an old lady named Madia Harrington. Roger and I shared a big room with two beds. There was no air-conditioning, so we'd be sweating and go out at night and find a place with watermelon to cool us off. Then we went early to the ballpark and I'd throw him extra batting practice. It helped us both. I had a halfway decent year until I came down with something and started losing weight—they didn't know it was mononucleosis yet. Roger really started to blast the ball. I could see he was going to be one heck of a ballplayer and play in the majors. He had the drive.
>
> Roger was a super guy and we got along because we were pretty much the same. We even switched our sports jackets. We'd go out to eat on the road. A $1.25 a day for meal money wasn't much, so a hamburger and a milk shake is what we could afford. We didn't do a whole lot of talking, and we minded our own business. Our biggest conversations were about baseball. I knew he had a girlfriend named Pat, but she never came to stay with him. He didn't talk about his family, but I met his mom, dad, and brother a few times. She was a very, very nice-looking lady. I was told Rudy Jr. was the better athlete of the two.

Taking on the role of supportive paternal figure, Jo Jo White had an immediate effect on the nineteen-year-old Maras. Years later, Roger said, "He was one of the great influences I had in baseball. I can't imagine a young fellow breaking into baseball being in better hands."

"I liked [Roger] right away," White told Leonard Shecter in 1961. "I liked his nerve, the way he'd run into fences for you, the way he slid. He'd rip that bag and the man right along with it. He had what it takes to be a ballplayer—great desire. It stuck out all over him. I knew damn well he could be a big leaguer."

White loved that Roger gave 100 percent, which included stealing bases and breaking up double plays with abandon. Fans in Keokuk still talk about the time Roger, playing center field, ran right through the wooden fence while making a catch. White thought the kid was out for the season, but

Roger was revived and stayed in the game, which he won with a ninth-inning homer

Roger responded to White's guidance and encouragement with an All-Star season—a .315 batting average, 32 home runs (3 behind league leader Ed Barbarito of Quincy), 105 runs, 111 RBIs, and 305 putouts, the most by an outfielder in the Three-I. His 25 stolen bases were 5 more than totaled by the Waterloo White Hawks' Luis Aparicio, a future American League base-stealing king. When the Kernels played in Waterloo, Iowa, Maras beat Aparicio in a 100-yard dash.

Maras acquired a reputation as a tough, hard-nosed player, but White recalled years later, "I never saw Roger look for a fight. If somebody got smart with him, he'd say, 'That's enough. If you keep it up, I won't be responsible for what happens to you.' I never saw anybody accept the challenge. And if somebody started anything with one of our players, Roger would be the first to help out his teammate."

Led by Maras, Osinski, and 20-game-winner and strikeout-champion Stan Pitula, the Kernels finished the season with a record of 78-58. It was 25 wins better than the previous year and put Keokuk only 3½ games behind the Evansville Braves. They lost in the first round of the playoffs to eventual champion Quincy, 3 games to 1, but it was still a successful season that paved the way for a title in 1955, when Russ Nixon hit .385 and Mudcat Grant had 19 victories.

At the end of the season, Roger Maras became Roger Maris. There is the stated reason why Roger changed his name; and there is a reason connected to the mysterious feuding among the Marases.

Everyone in Keokuk knew his name was pronounced like Morris, but public-address announcers and hecklers on the road pronounced his name Mare-ass or a similarly uncomfortable variation. "They used to call him Roger Mary-Ass," remembers Osinski. "He just hated them making fun of him." This was Roger's explanation for his desire to change his name.

Because Rudy, Connie, and Rudy Jr. also changed their names from Maras to Maris, some family members believe the name change was Connie's doing. Her dislike for the Marases was so strong that she saw this as a way for the four members of her family to further distance themselves, payback for the acrimonious Hibbing days. With the name changed to Maris, the

Marases would receive no reflected glory as her son rose up the baseball ranks. That Roger gave his birthplace as Fargo was further indication that he, too, wanted to have a clean break from the Marases of Minnesota.

Not surprisingly, the Marases back in Hibbing were insulted. "They didn't like it *a-tall*," says Jane Oftelie. That was probably the reaction Connie wanted.

CHAPTER EIGHT

DEFIANCE

CLEVELAND'S BRASS WASN'T CONVINCED Roger Maris was headed for major league stardom, but after his excellent season at Keokuk, they decided to let him progress at his own speed despite his age. Now twenty and with a new name, Roger had an air of confidence that fit right in with the organization. The parent club was the reigning American League champion, having won a league-record 111 of 154 games in '54. Although they were swept in the World Series by Willie Mays and the Giants, they took pride that Cleveland beat out the Yankees for the first time since Casey Stengel became their manager in 1949.

The veterans had paved the way—Bobby Avila led the league in average, Larry Doby led the league in homers and RBIs, Al Rosen smashed 24 homers and drove in over 100 runs, and Early Wynn and Bob Lemon each had 23 victories. But young players were also significant contributors, including second-year outfielder Al "Fuzzy" Smith and six rookies—backup receiver Hal Naragon, utility player Rudy Regalado, reserve outfielder Dave Pope, pitcher Dave Hoskins, and particularly righty-lefty relievers Ray Narleski and Don Mossi. It was a good sign to Maris and other farmhands that Al Lopez was willing to use youngsters in the heat of the pennant race. Unfortunately, a new logjam was at the top, which got worse for outfielders with Greenberg's off-season acquisition of his friend, thirty-two-year-old Ralph Kiner, a seven-time National League home-run champion.

The Triple A Indianapolis Indians had won the Junior World Series, and several of their players were ready for the majors, including Herb Score and Rocky Colavito. Score was allowed to advance and move into the Indians rotation, where he was as good as advertised, winning 16 games in 1955, leading the league with a rookie-record 245 strikeouts, and earning the American League Rookie of the Year trophy. But Colavito, who hit 38 homers and drove in 116 runs at Indianapolis in '54, had to spend another year on the AAA team. As if he'd been held back a grade in school, Colavito was now only one year ahead of Maris in the organization.

Roger believed that if he was good enough, a spot would open up for him on the Indians when he was ready. For now, he was on track for a promotion to the Tulsa Oilers, in the Double A Texas League. Tulsa's star was Joe Macko, who hit 28 homers in 1954, only to be assigned to the Oilers again. "I got to know Roger at spring training, and he was a great player and person," remembers Macko. "I was from Ohio, but my folks were from Czechoslovakia, and I spoke Slovak, Polish, and Hungarian. I knew Maris was Croatian, so we'd say 'Good morning' and 'How are you?' in Slovak. He could understand a few words. He was very gracious and forthcoming with me."

Paul "Cooter" Jones, another career minor leaguer, recalls, "I'd broken in with Rocky, and Roger was just like him, a nice loner-type who didn't say much but could really play. Boy, oh boy, if the pitcher made a mistake, *zoomp* it was gone. Roger had that attitude of 'I'm going to make it.' And everyone thought, 'Wow! He's got a shot.' "

"Indianville was like high school, where the older kids don't pay attention to freshmen," says Dick Stigman, a left-handed pitcher at his first spring training in '55. "Roger was higher up than me, but he always greeted me and was nice to me. He was a great, great guy. I was from Minnesota, too, Nimrod, about 100 miles from Hibbing, and idolized him. I'd sit in the stands and watch him. I saw he had special talents."

For someone who usually kept to himself, Maris accumulated a remarkable number of friends each year at Daytona Beach and elsewhere. In a dog-eat-dog setting, those who met Roger were struck by this confident but reticent young man who complimented everyone on good plays and sincerely wanted the best for those competing with him for roster spots. Players who had contact with him, even for the briefest time, were completely taken by him, labeling him not just a "good guy" but a "great guy," and speaking warmly about him for the rest of their lives. Many players over the years professed love for him. He was eerily like Herman Melville's young, innocent sailor Billy Budd, who affected the grizzled sailors on his ship in the same way Roger touched even the most hard nosed ballplayers in the clubhouse.

"I knew Roger at spring trainings all the way through the minor leagues, and everywhere, everyone liked Roger," says Jim "Mudcat" Grant, who would become the American League's first star African-American pitcher. "It didn't matter where you were from or what race you were, you couldn't dislike him. I will say that he was hard to get to know. Sometimes if you asked him a question, he didn't give you an answer until the next day. You never knew with Roger."

One friendship Roger forged in the spring of '55 is noteworthy because it was with someone outside the organization and in the media. Jim Adelson began calling Twins games in 1955, on KXJB-TV, Channel 4, Fargo. He remembers:

Since we were going to televise Fargo-Moorhead games, my boss sent me down to Daytona Beach for spring training to meet the players. I was introduced to Roger, and at dinner he said, "My mother thinks you're cute." "What?" I stammered, then added, "Your mother's pretty cute, too." And we became instant friends. I actually met Roger's mother in a grocery store or some place like that, and somebody introduced her to me as Roger's mother. She was very pretty, with red hair. I thought Roger was a wonderful small-town kid, someone who would go to the ends of the earth for you.

I went to a spring-training game and Roger was playing center field. He said, "Why don't you go up in the press box and give them a little BS." So I went up there and stood right behind Hank Greenberg and Paul Richards, the manager and general manager of the Baltimore Orioles. Two giants of the game. Maris makes a fantastic catch against the wall in right-center field and then makes a perfect peg to second base. He comes up the next inning and lines a double into the gap. And Richards looks at Greenberg and says, "I'll give you a hundred grand for that kid right now." And Greenberg says, "Go to hell." I told Roger later, "You almost went to Baltimore."

Another organization was monitoring Maris in 1955. New York Yankees general manager George Weiss was looking for a left-handed pull hitter to take advantage of the extremely shallow right-field seats at Yankee Stadium, as Charlie "King Kong" Keller and Tommy Henrich had done in the 1940s. Roger was probably on Weiss's radar because Casey Stengel heard good reports on him when he played against Quincy, the Yankees' Three-I affiliate, in 1954.

At the end of spring training, the Cleveland organization decided Roger was ready to move up to Tulsa. He had finally made it back to Oklahoma and planned on staying longer than ten days this time around. "Roger and I and two other players rented a three-bedroom ranch house," says Dan Osinski. "We all had our duties—I cooked, Roger did the cleaning and some cooking, too. When we had night games, we made breakfast and lunch. On Sundays, we'd make a roast. It was a pretty good arrangement."

Eight teams were in the Double A league. "Dallas and Ft. Worth probably drew more than Tulsa, but we drew pretty good," says Macko. "We played right there on 16th Street in Oilers Park. Tulsa was an oil town and it had absolutely great fans. When Roger Maris played there, we were already pretty well established. They put Roger in the lineup at first. He was a good-looking kid with a great swing, but he wasn't connecting. He started hanging his head a little bit."

Maris got along with his teammates, but he had friction with his manager. Lambert "Little Dutch" Meyer, who had played college football, spent time in the Army Air Corps in World War II, and been a journeyman in the majors, was nothing like the patient, supportive Jo Jo White. Meyer worried more about his own job than about how his players progressed, so after Maris struggled early, he played him only sporadically. It didn't help Maris's cause that when Meyer did play him, he hit below .240. And for the first time, his play in the outfield was erratic. "He kept trying to change everything I did," Maris told Leonard Shecter several years later. "According to him, I couldn't do anything right. I was really getting fouled up."

For someone who didn't have the patience to sit in a classroom, sitting on the bench was intolerable. Finally, Maris pulled Meyer aside and said, "I can't help you on the bench, and you can't help me. I'd like to go someplace where I can play regularly." This didn't please Meyer, who expected his judgment to go unchallenged. One night a throw from Maris to third base ended up in the stands, and the error cost the Oilers the game. Meyer had Maris show up at the ballpark early the next day to field balls and throw to third over and over. It was obvious to Roger that this was humiliating punishment, not practice. He would tell Shecter, "I still remember every time I threw to third base that day." In *Slugger in Right*, a spiteful manager makes Billy Mack go through the same drill. After half an hour, Maris caught a ball and instead of throwing it back in, he walked off the field, telling Meyer, "I'm not blowing my arm out for you or anybody else." "If you leave, you're gone," Meyer shouted, but Maris kept on walking.

Maris surely realized he had jeopardized his career with his brazen action, but an apology was out of the question. How would Hank Greenberg react when he heard Roger had gone home to Fargo? Even if Meyer had been in the wrong, this was the third time in three years that Maris had threatened to quit, so Tribe officials wondered if this "troublemaker" was worth it.

They decided he was. Greenberg approved a transfer of Maris from Tulsa to the Reading Indians in the Eastern League, where Jo Jo White was now managing. This was actually a step back for Roger because Reading was in A Ball, but he was relieved to get away from Meyer and back with White. Tulsa, led by Joe Macko, whose 29 home runs wouldn't earn him a promotion, ended up with a winning record, but Dutch Meyer wasn't around to enjoy it. Soon after Roger's departure, he was fired.

A few days after Maris left, it was Osinski's turn to go to Reading. He had a rude welcome. "I got to the hotel room and passed out," he says. "The maids found me the next morning, and Roger took me to the hospital. They said I had mono and kept me for a week. Roger would sneak up the back stairs to my room with watermelon." Once Osinski recovered, he and Maris rented a room together for $5 a week that was conveniently across the street from a golf driving range.

Players preferred playing at home because road trips meant they had to ride the infamous Reading bus. "We had long trips on a bus that had no brakes," says Ray Seif, who was on the shelf with an arm injury that would end his promising career. "We'd go down this big hill and I thought we were all going to die. Zoom, we'd go through red lights and Don Nance, Joe Camacho, and I would be staring at each other terrified."

"It was an old-timey bus with a motor in the back where we carried luggage, and, seriously, it had no brakes," recalls Cooter Jones. "Jo Jo always rode in back because he was afraid to sit in the front."

In Reading, Maris became good friends with Carroll Hardy, who had the distinction of playing baseball in the Indians organization and football for the San Francisco 49ers. "I flew in during the season and met Roger right away," Hardy recalls. "He had the car he'd bought with his signing bonus, so we bummed around together. We were called the Gold Dust Twins because we were both kind of blond and had crewcuts and chiseled features. We ate out all the time, burgers mostly, but we'd get a good meal every once in a while. Roger liked a place in Reading where we could have a beer and listen to some jazz. I was from South Dakota and we were both football players, so we had a lot to talk about. Roger had a football mentality, too—we both played hard."

"Roger never told me he'd played football," says Clell Hobson, a second baseman who was the quarterback who preceded Bart Starr at Alabama (and whose football-star son Clell "Butch" Hobson became a hard-hitting third baseman and manager with the Red Sox). "But we had other things to talk about. I liked that he was just a regular guy. He was real shy when other people would come by, but with me and other fellows, he was fine. He'd kid a lot, but he was very serious about his hitting and fielding."

The move east was a turning point in Maris's career. After hitting only a single homer with Tulsa, he flourished in Reading. In 113 games, he batted .289, with 19 homers, 78 RBIs, 24 stolen bases, and, some swear it's true, 18 successful drag bunts in 19 attempts. There were few errant throws from the outfield; in fact, he had 9 assists. Hitting 19 home runs was no Herculean feat, but Memorial Stadium was a pitcher's park and it indicated that Maris's power was increasing.

One reason Maris was able to come back to form in Reading was his gentle exposure to the press. According to Hobson, "There were only a few reporters who came around after games and asked our reactions. Roger got some valuable experience talking to the press without being hounded at all. He never had any problems."

Reading thrived under its new manager and finished the season in first place. Losing in the first round of the playoffs to Schenectady was disappointing because Jo Jo White's Indians won 13 more games than Pinky May's Indians the previous year, yet that team made it to the finals.

Still, Roger's good numbers with Reading put his career back on track. Now his goal was to have a good year at AAA in 1956 and reach the Indians in 1957, when it looked as if they'd need new blood. The Tribe fell to second place in the American League in 1955 as the Yankees won their sixth pennant in seven years under Casey Stengel. More pennants seemed to be on the horizon with Yogi Berra racking up MVP awards and Mickey Mantle, who hit 37 homers and drove in 99 runs, developing.

Meanwhile, flattering reports about Maris's play at Reading found their way to George Weiss's desk. "Everything we were told convinced us that he was the player we wanted," Weiss said years later.

Unaware of the Yankees' interest, Roger was back in Fargo in the winter and back at the Blakelys. Pat Blakely remembers:

> Roger was living in the basement so Johnny and I were not allowed to go down there and interrupt his privacy. We were little kids, so when Roger was out, we went to the basement and started jumping on his bed. And Roger came home and found us bouncing on his bed. He wasn't very happy and said, "You kids, get out of here." Well, I got him back. We had a cousin who occasionally babysat for us. Her name was Priscilla and I really liked her. One day she was babysitting, and I walked into the kitchen and found her and Roger with locked lips. I didn't know what they doing and I started yelling, "That's my Priscilla, you leave her alone!" Priscilla always told me I was relentless.

If everyone is entitled to one indiscretion with a babysitter, then that was it for Roger. Despite his mother's unwavering disapproval, he decided that the time had come for him to get serious about Pat Carvell. As far as they were concerned, they were on the path to the altar. They only needed to decide if they should delay their nuptials until Roger reached the majors and received the $10,000 bonus on top of a big league salary, or do it earlier, with the confidence that he'd make Cleveland's roster soon after. If Roger and Pat became engaged or set a date for marriage, they kept it to themselves. They looked ahead to what they knew was, in their relationship and in his career, a make-or-break year.

CHAPTER NINE

A TITLE AND A WEDDING RING

IT'S LIKELY THAT RUDY was the only Maris to keep up with the Marases of Minnesota. From his married sisters and Steve Starcevic, he knew that in the fifties the Maras family experienced only trials and tribulations. The decade began with the deaths of Anna Maras's husband, Mike Barich, and ninety-three-year-old Mary Dosen Maras, Rudy's grandmother and Mike, Paul, and Peter's mother. Mike's wife, Mary, formerly Masha Barich, who her devoted grandson Michael says "used to swim in the sea and catch fish with a stick in the old country," became extemely ill with diabetes and had her leg amputated. She passed away in 1957.

Mike and Mary's only son, Big Nick, and his wife, Rose, were cheered by the birth of their third son, Bill, in 1955. But their happiness was shattered when their five-year-old son, Nick, struck his head and died. Paul Maras also was devastated by the loss of his son Jack, at forty-two, in a mining accident. "My dad took it hard," Tilly Sanborn remembers. "He went upstairs and never got well."

"When my grandpa Paul was dying in 1956," says Tilly's daughter Peggy, "he and my grandmother Eva lived upstairs at the Buhl Hotel. Meanwhile Frederick, who used crutches because of his childhood polio, ran the hotel and bar. My uncle Mike came to see Paul. My mother has told me a hundred times that she heard Paul say to Mike in Croatian, 'Please, my brother, give me $10.' She says Mike broke down and sobbed when Paul said that and then left. It was obvious to her that something bad had happened between them that nobody in the family talked about and they would take to their graves. We think that at one time Paul needed money badly and Mike didn't give it to him, not even $10." The brothers never saw each other again because Paul, the first Maras to come to America, died shortly after. Eva passed away a few years later.

Because of his mother, Roger had nothing to do with the Marases, so their difficulties certainly weren't on his mind when he arrived at Cleveland's major league training camp in Tucson for the first time, in 1956. Since 1946, the Indians had trained at Hi Corbett Field and played their exhibition games in the Cactus League against the New York Giants, Chicago Cubs, and Baltimore Orioles.

The Indians had won 18 fewer games in 1955 than the previous year. Greenberg, who in 1956 became the first Jewish player selected to the Hall of Fame, was concerned that despite his farm clubs doing well, only a small number of legitimate prospects were in the organization: pitchers Mudcat Grant, Gary Bell, Bud Daley, Stan Pitula, Dick Tomanek, and Hank Aguirre; catchers Russ Nixon, Dick Brown, and Earl Averill; infielders Gordy Coleman, Joe Altobelli, Billy Harrell, and Rudy Regalado; and outfielders Rocky Colavito, Carroll Hardy, and Roger Maris.

Although the retired Ralph Kiner and traded Larry Doby left behind two open outfield slots, they were going to be filled by rookie Colavito and veteran acquisitions Jim Busby and Gene Woodling, so things weren't necessarily brighter for Maris. Even if another spot opened up the following year, it was expected to go to Hardy. "Roger's advantage over Rocky was speed on the bases and in the outfield, and his advantage over me was power," says Hardy. "He had muscular arms, big wrists, and large, strong hands. He just had to learn to pull more."

The plan was for Maris to spend spring training with the major leaguers, and then be assigned to Indianapolis, the Indians' top farm club in the American Association. Despite receiving conflicting advice from Greenberg, who wanted him to pull, and coach Tris Speaker, who wanted him to hit to all fields, Maris made an impression in the early days of camp. However, he found himself on the bench during exhibition games. Stir-crazy, he didn't hide his dissatisfaction from management, teammates, or the press. He said his bags were packed and he was ready to leave Tucson. "They were looking at Carroll more than at Roger," says Hal Naragon, Jim Hegan's backup. "Maris said, 'Well, if you're not going to give me a chance here, send me to Indianapolis now.'"

On March 15, he got his wish when he and five others were sent from

Tucson to the minor league camp at Daytona Beach. Playing in exhibition games with Indianapolis, he convinced Greenberg and his staff he was ready to make the jump to AAA.

Baseball had been played in Indianapolis, Indiana, since 1887. The Indians made their debut in 1902, making it the second-oldest minor league franchise, after the Rochester Red Wings of the International League. They had been an affiliate of Cleveland's since 1952.

In the team's long history there had never been a manager quite like Kerby Farrell, a onetime first baseman for the Boston Braves and the Chicago White Sox. "Farrell was different," says Mudcat Grant. "One time he took a pitcher out of a game, and before he got back to the dugout, the new pitcher had given up a home run. Kerby turned right around and took that pitcher out. After he gave the ball to the new guy, he ran to the dugout and leaped in before the first pitch."

"Farrell was the goofiest manager I've seen in my life," states Bud Daley, who began the season in Cleveland but was sent down to Indianapolis and went 11-1. "I once saw Kerby dive head first into the dugout and cut his head open. His son was seven or eight and was always there. We used to tie him up and hang him from the rack on the bus. One time a few of us coaxed him into letting the air out of his dad's tires."

"Kerby was really superstitious about a lot of things," says infielder Billy Harrell. "If we won, he'd wear the same suit, the same tie, the same everything, until we lost. After some losses, he'd walk home, refusing to get on the bus. He wouldn't even talk to us."

"Kerby Farrell was different from anybody, but I liked him a lot," says Earl Averill II, the son of the Indians Hall of Famer who put Snohomish, Washington, on the map. "He was adamant that we learn fundamentals, and his record managing in the minors spoke for itself."

Maris initially played every day, but when he got off to a slow start and began putting pressure on himself, his playing time was reduced and he was removed for pinch hitters in key situations. He realized that if he didn't produce, the possibility of a demotion was strong, which would be a big setback to his career and marriage plans. But he felt he couldn't start hitting if he didn't play regularly and without fear of being benched after a bad game.

"They considered sending him down because they felt he was a streak hitter," says Harrell. "He'd get in slumps and it took a while for him to get out of them. The only time I'd see a change in him was when he failed to get a big hit. Then he'd sit off by himself and we wouldn't go near him."

Maris soon made a familiar demand of Farrell: "Play me or farm me out!" Roger was probably a bit embarrassed that he was sounding like a broken record. In *Slugger in Right*, when Maris compares Billy Mack to another character, Maris was obviously comparing Billy to himself and being shockingly self-critical: "There was a great deal of young Mack in the old manager . . . the same quick temper, the same 'me first' philosophy, and the same overeagerness to fight for his imagined rights."

After Roger's ultimatum, Farrell neither banished Maris nor assured him that things would get better. Instead, he and Greenberg tried to find a solution that wouldn't damage Maris's prospects. Farrell offered Maris a deal: he would remain in the lineup for ten consecutive games, even if he went 0 for 40. If he didn't start hitting by that time, he would be demoted. Maris agreed. It turned out to be an excellent bargain for both manager and player. The young ballplayer quickly broke out of his slump and went on to have an extremely productive season. He was the team's right fielder but played center, too, because Hardy was drafted into the army one month into the season.

Maris was a major reason that Indianapolis was able to compete for a division title against the powerful Denver Bears, a Yankee affiliate full of all-stars managed by ex-Yankee backup catcher Ralph Houk. Maris impressed Houk by hitting 2 homers against Denver during a game in April. "I first saw Roger when he was at Indianapolis, and he was a good hitter," remembers Houk. "He was pretty much a pull hitter, already. He was one of the guys we always tried to pitch around. The Yankees asked me about him and I gave them some good reports, saying he could hit and also was an outstanding base runner and outfielder."

The Bears weren't the only team to take notice of Maris. On May 18, he drove in 7 runs with a single, double, and triple in a 24–0 dismantling of lowly Louisville. He also had some of his best games against St. Paul. "I pitched against Maris when I was at St. Paul in 1956," recalls Stan Williams, Roger's future Yankee teammate. "I was a nineteen-year-old pitcher trying to find out where that plate was. Roger was just another trim, wide-eyed kid, but he had the most beautiful short swing I've ever seen. And he could run like hell. He beat me in a ballgame with his speed. It was a 0–0 game with two outs in the ninth and a man on third, and he beat out a push bunt as the run scored. Another time he had an inside-the-park home run. In Indianapolis it was like 483 feet to center field, and he got around the bases before the outfielder even got to the ball."

Other than being treated by Mert Prophet for a bad case of athlete's foot, all went well for Maris. He played every day, hit with consistency, was cheered by fans, was of no interest to the press, and had many good friends on the team, including future Indians teammates Altobelli, Nixon, Averill, Daley, Tomanek, Regalado, and Harrell.

Maris never viewed his teammates through the prism of color and had befriended several black players in the system over the years, including Harrell. Roger had grown up with little, if any, contact with blacks, but being a child of the Depression, he had an understanding and respect for anyone who had struggled to overcome hardships. Harrell remembers:

> When guys came to town after spring training, they got their own places. I was married then and we lived in nice apartments in projects in the black section. Indianapolis wasn't an easy place for blacks and whites to get together at that time. After a game, I'd go home. In all the years I knew Roger, he would tell me "nice play" and all that, but there was no socializing. We were teammates and it was a warm relationship, but we didn't hang out like Roger and Altobelli did. I was good friends with Roger and Joe and we could eat together, but there was no socializing. All socializing was done at the ballpark. When we were inside that ballpark and the clubhouse, it was great. Socially it could have been the same on the outside, but it wasn't set up like that in society at the time.

"Roger really thrived in Indianapolis because everyone liked him so much," says Dick Tomanek. "Still, nobody on the outside got a clear picture of him. I think most people didn't realize how great he was as a player because he was serious, quiet, and not brash at all."

"Roger was an all-around player and great guy," states Regalado, a Californian whose mother named him Rudolph Valentino Regalado after the silent screen's greatest romantic idol. "We roomed together for half a season. He was shy and didn't talk too much, but we hit it off. We had a lot in common. We were both Catholic and went to church on Sundays, plus he had a father and brother named Rudy."

Indeed, when Indianapolis visited Minneapolis and St. Paul, Rudys Sr. and Jr. came with Connie from Fargo and stayed at Roger's hotel. Some players knew Rudy Jr. from practices he attended at Victory Park. After recovering from polio, he played some amateur baseball (and even some football) and still sought the opportunity to play it professionally. Roger arranged a tryout for Rudy Jr. with Indianapolis, as he did with Fargo-Moorhead in 1953, with the same negative result. "He couldn't cut it," remembers Mert Prophet. "He didn't have the same physique as Roger and they weren't similar in abilities."

They may have had similar abilities when they were teenagers, but that was the past, though Roger refused to acknowledge it. He still told everyone that his twenty-three-year-old brother was the best ballplayer in the family and hoped he'd get a chance to prove it. In a quirk of fate, Rudy Jr., once a victim of polio, was drafted into the army, finally putting an end to his baseball aspirations.

Indianapolis edged to within 2 games of first-place Denver in mid-August, then pulled off a sweep of a seven-game series with St. Paul, including three doubleheaders in four days. When the St. Paul massacre was over, Indianapolis led Denver by 1½ games. It was an exciting time for the Indians, but when they checked the sports pages, they discovered that articles about Indianapolis's surge were eclipsed by coverage of Mickey Mantle's pursuit of Babe Ruth's single-season major league home-run record as the Yankees marched toward still another pennant. Mantle would win the Triple Crown in his MVP season, but the pressure wore him down in September, and 52 homers was his limit.

Mantle slowed down, but Roger never let up, getting 4 hits in an August 30 victory that stretched his hitting streak to 16 games and upped Indianapolis's lead over Denver to 3½ games. Indianapolis staked claim to the American Association title on September 5. The Indians finished with a record of 92-62, 5 games ahead of Denver. For all his eccentricity, Farrell looked like a genius.

Despite his bad start, Maris wound up with a .293 batting average, 17 homers, and 75 runs batted in. Indianapolis was the fifth consecutive team that improved from the previous year when Roger joined them.

"Winning a championship in the minor leagues was very important to players in those days," says Russ Nixon, who roomed with Maris for part of the season. "There were many more players in the minors then, so being on a winning club and putting up decent numbers was a way to move up quicker."

The exhausted Indians almost didn't make it out of the first round of the play-offs against Eddie Stanky's dangerous Minneapolis team. In the seventh game, Altobelli hit a decisive seventh-inning homer and John Gray tossed a 5-hitter as the Indians squeaked by the Millers 2–1. Next they went head-to-head with the Denver Bears, with future Yankees Tony Kubek, Bobby Richardson, Marv Throneberry, Ralph Terry, and Johnny Blanchard on their roster. They ran away with Game 1, 13–1, behind strong pitching from Ed Gasque and Daley, a big homer by Nixon, and Maris's 4 RBIs. A 3-run rally in the bottom of the ninth gave Indianapolis a rousing 7–6 victory in Game 2. The Indians took advantage of Terry's wildness and had two 3-run innings to win 6–5 in Game 3. Indianapolis earned the sweep with a 6–1 victory in Game 4, as Maris and Regalado homered and Daley helped his own cause with an RBI single.

Indianapolis moved into the Junior World Series against the Rochester Red Wings, champions of the International League. In Game 1, the Indians went up 3–1 in the top of the ninth on a solo blast by Regalado. However, Rochester loaded the bases with none out against starter John Gray in the bottom half of the inning. The key play of the game and entire series came with one out. Pinch hitter Gary Geiger slashed a single to right that scored the runner from third, but pinch runner Eddie Phillips was gunned down at the plate on a perfect throw by Maris to catcher Allen Jones. Daley came in to record the final out, and the Indians won the thrilling opener.

Roger had more heroics in store for Game 2. On the day Mickey Mantle clubbed his final home run of the season in New York City, Maris had his final home run of the year in Rochester, New York. In fact he had 2 homers and a single to drive in a Junior World Series record of 7 runs in support of Tomanek and Gasque, as the Indians walloped Rochester 12–4 to go up 2 games to none. Indianapolis won Game 3, 3–0, as Stan Pitula, who went 15-4 during the season, threw a 3-hitter, and Game 4, 6–0, behind Daley and in front of 9,000 excited hometown fans.

Everyone celebrated the sweep of the Red Wings for the Junior World Series title, but none more so than Kerby Farrell. It was known that Al Lopez was leaving as manager of the parent club because of problems with Greenberg, and Farrell had his eye on the position. In one story, probably fabricated, Farrell was so thrilled by Maris's great fielding play that saved Game 1 that when Roger came back to the dugout, the tearful manager exclaimed, "Roger, you just got me the Cleveland job!"

A successful season behind him, Roger Maris returned to Fargo with important personal business ahead of him, and a $300 check in his pocket for the Junior Series victory. In *Slugger in Right*, Billy and his fiancée, Dawn, agree not to marry until he makes the majors and gets the $10,000 bonus. But love wins out and they wed before they know if he'll earn a spot on Cleveland's roster. Roger and Pat were of the same frame of mind. They married on October 13, 1956, at St. Anthony's Church in Fargo. Roger had turned twenty-two a month before, Pat was twenty-one. The best man was Don Gooselaw, who ran a beauty salon in Fargo after getting out of the navy. "I borrowed a car because I didn't have one," he remembers. "I went with Mary Kay Swanson—Pat always was trying to set me up with her girlfriends."

"It was a small wedding, with just family, classmates, and friends," says Dick Savageau, who was still waiting to be discharged from the navy. "I don't think there was even a bachelor party." Savageau says it was a happy wedding for the bride and groom, but probably not for Connie, who either had a deep-rooted reason for disapproving of Pat or simply thought no woman was good enough for her son.

"That's what I'd surmise," says Savageau. "But there could have been some things in the family that went on. You know, if Connie says, 'I don't know why Roger would marry Pat,' well, obviously Pat would not be very happy with her! At the wedding, I was talking to Connie and Pat told her, 'You didn't need to say that to Dick.' There was something between them. Pat's very pleasant but she can be tough."

"Nobody in the family treated Connie badly," says her nephew Roger LaFreniere. "She just liked to run the show. When Roger made it into baseball, her head got big and it was like she was the one to talk to about him. Roger's wife didn't care for that."

After the ceremony, with Gooselaw at the wheel, the wedding party drove up the street for the reception at the Silver Star, a dance hall that provided a setup bar, 3.2 beer, plenty of food, and recorded music. Eventually the music died down, the lights dimmed, and everybody went home.

CHAPTER TEN

THE ROOKIE

"I WAS PLAYING WINTER ball in the Dominican Republic and our right fielder got hurt," recalls Rudy Regalado. "So they asked me if I knew anybody in the States that could come down and play. I called Roger and he said, 'Well, I don't know, Pat and I just got married.' I said, 'Perfect. You can come down here for your honeymoon.' And they did it."

At first Roger and Pat's extended honeymoon went smoothly. They stayed in a nice hotel and were treated first class. He played well and his team, Estrellas Orientales, meaning Eastern Stars, won a lot of games.

Maris was disappointed when Regalado was traded to a Puerto Rican team. Then Roger realized that his new name was giving him the same old trouble. "In the Caribbean, they called him *Mary*," says his brother-in-law Walt Seeba. "Somehow the people there got confused by the name Maris and thought he was the Blessed Virgin. Roger also had tense moments with the people paying him over there, because they weren't so dependable."

"That winter I started playing regularly for Aguilas," says Dominican Julian Javier, who was Maris's St. Louis Cardinals teammate in the late sixties. "I saw Roger had talent. I remember most that he was a very good outfielder. But he wasn't in a good organization."

Maris's winter season was cut short when he injured his heel, and, as would happen with the Yankees in 1965, management didn't believe he was hurt. In ESPN's *Roger Maris: Reluctant Hero*, Pat Maris recalled, "They couldn't see it on X-rays or anything, so they couldn't understand why he couldn't play. We decided we'd better get home because he knew it meant his career with Cleveland if it was worse than they thought it was."

Roger and Pat had decided they weren't going to wait for the presentation of the $10,000 bonus check to start a family. Back in Fargo, they announced that Pat was pregnant. Grace Carvell was thrilled that she was going to be a grandmother. It's doubtful that Connie had the same reaction. For a woman who obsessed about looking far younger than her forty-three years, the idea of becoming a grandmother must have been disconcerting.

"She always liked to dress up," recalls Dick Savageau. "She had her hair done all the time and wore a ton of makeup."

"She used to try to look so young," agrees Don Gooselaw. "She'd wear a ponytail and auburn hair. When I had a beauty school downtown, every day at one o'clock in the afternoon, she'd come in and say, 'Oh, Donny, what do you think? You know I had that hair color put in last week and it's not *doing* it.' "

If Connie was unhappy that Roger and Pat were having a baby so soon after their marriage, then the friction in her own marriage probably increased.

"I'm sure there was worry about Rudy and Connie's relationship," says Seeba. "But Roger didn't talk about it. I know everyone didn't like Connie, but I liked her because she did some kind things for us. And I'll say that Rudy was a good man because Connie's mom lived with them in not exactly a huge apartment. He helped look after her. Rudy was very good to his mother-in-law."

Ana Marich lived with Connie and Rudy after she suffered a stroke in Minnesota. She was hospitalized there and Connie visited her. "Connie didn't like the way the hospital was treating her," recalls her brother-in-law Don O'Neil. "She went in and said, 'I want my mother!' She took her home to Fargo and took care of her for two or three years. She really loved her mother. As did Jean, who visited them in Fargo."

Since leaving Fargo after the 1953 season, Roger had received little press and nothing had been critical. So it must have unnerved him when just before his second spring-training camp in Tucson, one Cleveland newspaper took him to task for the previous spring: "A young man described by some as a spoiled brat and by others as a reformed mamma's boy will be the most closely inspected young Indian in Tucson starting Monday. He would be Roger Maris, an outfielder who bats left and throws right, and who impressed very few people favorably out there last year. Maris, who came to camp with the reputation of being a power hitter and a speed boy, did little except run fast. He appeared to sulk and there were some who guessed this was because another rookie, Carroll Hardy, had taken the play away from him."

Although Roger issued annual play-me-or-send-me-elsewhere demands, his squabbles with management had always been kept in-house. But his attitude in his first major league camp had come back to haunt him. Was the story planted by the Cleveland organization to motivate Maris? It's unlikely, because he had a track record of being a winner. He also had a thin skin, and the last thing Cleveland management wanted was for him to receive negative press as he broke into the big leagues. Roger, oddly, didn't fully grasp the concept of someone speaking or writing negatively about another person.

The Indians needed to make major changes after finishing a disappointing 9 games behind the Yankees in 1956. Herb Score, Early Wynn, and Bob Lemon each had 20 victories, and the Indians staff led the American League with 67 complete games, including 17 shutouts; 845 strikeouts, including Score's league-best 263; and 3.32 ERA. But Bob Feller had retired and Wynn, Lemon, and Mike Garcia were aging; and the Indians finished in a tie for last with a .244 team batting average. "In 1956, I thought the club was falling apart even though we finished second," says George Strickland. "Even the pitching was going downhill. Al Lopez knew something when he went to the White Sox."

As a rookie, Rocky Colavito had been a bright spot, despite a brief demotion to San Diego. Coming off a season in which he batted .276 with 21 homers in just 322 at-bats, his bat was needed in the lineup following Al Rosen's retirement. However, there was room for more power hitters, so Maris hoped he was next in line with Hardy stuck in the service (though he came to camp in Tucson while on leave and spent time with Roger at the dog tracks).

Maris saw a familiar face in the manager's office in Tucson, Kerby Farrell, who had Al Lopez's big shoes to fill. Farrell wanted Roger in his lineup. With Colavito in right, Maris focused on center and left fields, knowing that in the cavernous Municipal Stadium he would have to cover much more territory than in most ballparks and make longer throws. Maris also worked on baserunning with Eddie Stanky, the Tribe's new infield coach. Roger was hitting over .300 in exhibition games, but he was not pulling the ball for power. Greenberg sent him to Palm Springs to get special instruction from his disciple Ralph Kiner, now the GM of the Indians' PCL affiliate, the San Diego Padres. Colavito worked with Kiner in 1956, and Greenberg hoped for similar results with Maris. Kiner remembers:

Roger was with me for about ten days of spring training, staying with my players. He was like he was advertised—really quiet and low-key. I liked him. He was a line-drive hitter at the time I got him. Basically Greenberg and I agreed that it was advantageous to pull the ball if you had his power. When I worked with hitters, I tried to get them to move their hip through the strike zone and shift their weight off their back foot onto their front foot. My whole theory was, the sooner you can get on the plane of the ball— and it's coming at you on a downward plane—the better off you are. Because then you don't have to hit it squarely to hit it hard. That was basically Ted Williams's approach. After we had finished, I said to Greenberg, "Maris should be left alone. Don't ruin him."

Having seen them both, I thought Colavito would be the bigger star. But I had no idea Roger would be able to pull a ball down the line as he would do at Yankee Stadium in 1961. He didn't learn that from me.

If Kiner, who idolized Babe Ruth as a kid, knew Roger would make a run at Ruth's single-season home-run record, he might have talked to him about 1949. That year Kiner hit 54 home runs for the Pittsburgh Pirates, the highest total in the majors between 1938, when Greenberg had 58 round-trippers, and 1961. Kiner could have warned him, "I didn't come close to Ruth's record but I was getting hate mail."

Before camp broke, Roger was told he had made the ball club and was issued number 32. It had taken him only four years to receive the $10,000 bonus stipulated in his original contract. He was now a major leaguer, on the same level as his idol Ted Williams, and he couldn't wait for Opening Day.

On April 16, 1957, in Cleveland, Roger Maris made his major league debut as the Indians' starting left fielder against the Chicago White Sox before 31,145 fans. He felt calm after walking to the park with Bob Lemon, who had bought him a beer and reminded him that "he was a good ballplayer or the Indians wouldn't have brought him up." In his effort to beat Pale Hose manager Al Lopez, Kerby Farrell penciled in center fielder Al Smith as his leadoff hitter, third baseman Bobby Avila (Harrell replaced him later in the game), first baseman Vic Wertz (Altobelli replaced him), right fielder Rocky Colavito, Maris (batting fifth as he had done for Farrell at Indianapolis), shortstop Chico Carrasquel, catcher Jim Hegan, second baseman George Strickland, and pitcher Herb Score, the new ace of the Indians.

Score went against veteran Billy Pierce in a matchup of two of the league's best left-handers. In 1955, Pierce posted the only sub-2.00 ERA of the decade (1.97), and in 1956, he won 20 games for the first time. Maris struggled against southpaws, but he went 3 for 5 in his debut against Pierce. However, he wouldn't celebrate because the Indians lost 3–2 in eleven innings, as both pitchers went the distance.

Two days later, in his second game at Briggs Stadium in Detroit, he could fully enjoy the moment after cracking his first major league home run—a grand slam. It was scorched off Jack Crimian in the eleventh inning, leading to an 8–3 victory. Crimian's major league career ended one bad outing later.

As the rookie continued to do well through April, Eugene Fitzgerald in the *Fargo Forum* wrote, "A lot of people are learning where Fargo is."

Pat didn't leave Fargo for Cleveland until a month into the season. She was annoyed to discover that Roger hadn't opened any of the letters she'd written him. He wasn't trying to insult her, but was letting her know that wasn't the way he liked to communicate. "I don't think Roger would write a letter," says Dick Savageau. "If there is one around, they should put it in a museum." Roger and Pat rented a house in Parma, Ohio, less than 15 miles from Municipal Stadium. Colavito was a neighbor, and "he and Roger carpooled to the ballpark, stopping off for mass at St. Francis de Sales Church," remembers Rich Rollins, who was an altar boy there a few years before becoming a major leaguer.

Roger's fast start brought a quick halt to articles that attacked his talent and dedication. In the May 1 issue of the *Sporting News*, the influential Hal Lebovitz of the *Cleveland News* repudiated the critical article that had greeted Maris at spring training, writing, "There has been no trace of moodiness or surliness in Maris this spring. Now 22, he appears to have matured. In truth, we have come to know him as a friendly young man who tells what is in his heart."

Roger probably paid little heed to Lebovitz's contention that he "has the mark of greatness," or that he was "an exciting young player who could approach the stature of Mantle." After being unfavorably compared to his brother his whole life, Maris now probably cringed when he, a mere rookie, was compared to baseball's greatest slugger. However, he didn't mind being compared to other rookies as he continued to bat over .300 into May. Reporters, fans, and teammates alike thought they saw a star in the making. The rookie confided to Carrasquel, "Chico, one of these years I'm going to hit 20 to 25 home runs!"

"Roger was a good-looking player and good people," remembers Cal McLish, a pitcher from Anadarko, Oklahoma, who went 44-23 for Cleveland from 1957 to 1959. "When I first saw him with a bat, I said, 'God damn. This guy's got a little short swing with a pop in it. And he doesn't strike out much. Man, he is going to do some damage.'"

"Roger had as much confidence in his ability as any player I ever saw," Colavito told Maury Allen in 1985. "He may not have been as outspoken about it as I was, but he certainly had it."

While Roger hung out with Colavito, Score, Hardy, Altobelli, and Nixon, he still had the uncanny knack for making new friends despite little knack for conversation.

"Maris was a serious guy who didn't laugh," recalled Gene Woodling in 1993. "But I liked him."

"Roger was just a good old country boy," remembers pitcher Don Mossi. "He was very congenial and without any pretension. He was comfortable hanging around Ray Narleski and me because we were still on the young side and not talkative, so it was an easy fit. In Baltimore, Roger, Rocky, Herb, Ray, and I would go to a fish place and order a big tray of crabs and clean them out—five quiet guys who talked only when it was about baseball and helping our team win."

"It was the funniest thing when we went to New York for the first time," recalls Narleski. "Coming out of the Dakotas, he had never seen anything like it. It was his first time seeing skyscrapers. I can't really say if he liked them or not, but he thought they were quite something."

As Cleveland executives had envisioned, Maris was giving a boost to the offense. Meanwhile, Herb Score was carrying the pitching staff. Unfortunately, one of the most tragic moments in baseball history aborted his trip to Cooperstown.

On May 7, in the top of the first inning, Gil McDougald, the Yankees' second hitter, turned around a Score fastball. In a flash, it shot off the bat and toward Score's face.

"Herbie was throwing almost a hundred miles per hour, and when the ball was hit back at him, it was going almost twice as fast," Narleski says.

"It was a night game," remembered the opposing pitcher, Tom Sturdivant, in 2008, "but we had just changed to daylight savings time and the sun was still in the sky in the first inning. There were slats on top of the Cleveland ballpark, and as Herbie threw the ball, the sun came though the second slat onto his face and he couldn't see the ball coming back at him."

"I thought it knocked his eye out," remembers Preston Ward, who was in the Cleveland dugout.

Maris could hear the sound of bone cracking in center field. "I was sitting in the bullpen and it sounded like a golf ball hitting a tree with no bark on it," McLish says. "It was the damnedest sound. Everybody had a sick feeling."

Al Smith, playing third base, instinctively picked up the ball and threw to first for the out, though the distressed McDougald had raced to the pitcher's mound along with catcher Jim Hegan. "When I got there," recalled Smith in 1993, "blood was pouring out his nose, mouth, and ears. He looked like a boxer had just demolished him. But he never lost consciousness. He kept asking for Mike Garcia, who was his good friend."

In the hospital doctors confirmed that numerous facial bones has been shattered and Score had suffered some blindness in his right eye. He'd be out for the year, and the pitcher who Bob Feller said was going to be better than him would never again be effective.

Score's teammates were devastated by what happened to their friend. And to their season. "It killed our chances," acknowledges McLish.

Farrell must have felt snakebit when two games later his hottest hitter went down with an injury that spoiled his season. In Kansas City, Maris, hitting .315, tried to break up a double play by upending Milt Graff at second base. The rookie second baseman came down with both knees, and Maris wound up with two broken ribs. For the rest of his life he'd be hampered by sore ribs and be unable to lie on his stomach.

Maris was out for a couple of weeks, during which time he sat in the stands in street clothes, not immune from attack by reporters desperate for a story. After allowing that Maris was "a fine young man with a great future," Howard Preston of the *Cleveland News* insisted that he was "sitting too far from the action to learn anything. Here was a chance for him to sit in a seat behind the catcher, to watch what the pitchers threw, to see—close-up—the mannerisms of some of the players he will be playing against for many years. But he was a spectator, that's all, away up in the stands."

When Farrell put Maris back in the lineup, he couldn't find his stroke. The nagging rib injury didn't help matters. Fearing he would be benched, Roger pressed, and his average dropped lower. A sensation early on, he was that bad later. "Rather than [letting me] work myself into shape," said Maris years later, "they just threw me in the lineup, damaging my confidence."

Unfortunately, Roger's slump wasn't an aberration. Sometime in almost every year Maris would stumble through an excruciating dry spell, often after rushing back from an injury. "When Maris had his slumps, a lot of it was psychological," says Ralph Kiner. "The good thing is that he didn't change his swing like some young players do when they aren't going well."

"Roger still made all the plays and was always hustling," remembers Earl Averill, who had also been promoted from Indianapolis. "He was having his ups and downs at the plate, but he was as good an outfielder as you'd want to see." The rookie outfielder had 10 assists for the year despite limited playing time.

Perhaps anxiety about Pat played a part in Roger's poor performance at the plate. Her due date was July 25, yet the couple hoped the baby would arrive before a road trip began on July 22. But Susan Ann was born on July 31, when Cleveland was in Baltimore. "Roger's daughter and mine were born about the same time," recalls Hal Naragon. "We had an open day and somehow it was arranged for us to fly home early."

"The club should have leased a plane for such occasions," Dick Tomanek says. "There was a team party in 1957, and eleven of the wives were pregnant, including Pat."

Maris's hustling and fielding weren't enough reason for Farrell to keep him in the lineup with the offense sputtering. Cleveland's pitching was faltering, too. Warhorses Lemon and Wynn developed bone chips and gout, respectively, and won just 20 games between them, losing 28. In July, rookie right-hander Stan Pitula, a teammate of Roger's at Keokuk, blew out his arm and never pitched another major league game. (His friend Dick Tomanek believes that Pitula's disappointing career, along with a broken marriage and inability to find work, contributed to his suicide in 1965.)

"What happened to Herb Score was the most tragic moment of 1957," says Russ Nixon. "But, hell, everything went wrong. The whole club was falling apart because we had too many older guys. I don't think it was Kerby's fault. He hadn't changed much. He probably got a little more nervous, but he was a little shaky anyway."

"Farrell was a nice man," says Strickland, "but it was just a tough year for him. We'd be having breakfast and he'd hand me a piece of paper and say, 'How does this lineup look for tonight?' I felt flattered to be asked, but I got the feeling that he might have been overmatched a little bit."

"Kerby was very successful in the minor leagues, but maybe he shouldn't have managed in the majors," says Naragon. "He had a difficult time adjusting to the press and players. He held meetings after almost every game. Lopez just let us play."

"Poor Kerby didn't have a chance," remembers Dick Williams, a veteran outfielder/third baseman who was acquired from Baltimore during the season. "He gets his shot in the big leagues and Score gets hit in the eye and the rest of our pitching staff goes down the drain. We didn't have much of a ball club, so there was going to be rebuilding taking place and it would cost Kerby his job."

By August it was apparent that the Indians wouldn't challenge the Yankees for the American League pennant. Again it was an Al Lopez–managed team, the Chicago White Sox, that finished second, 8 games behind New York. Mickey Mantle won his second consecutive MVP after crushing 34 homers and batting a hefty .365. (GM George Weiss offered Mantle a pay cut, explaining that he wasn't as good as in his Triple Crown season.) Another big contributor was outfielder-shortstop Tony Kubek, who won the Rookie of the Year award that earlier in the season seemed to be in Maris's reach.

Despite his brilliant start, Maris batted .235, with 14 homers and 51 RBIs in 116 games. His numbers paled in comparison to those of Colavito, who slugged 25 homers and drove in 84 runs to put a lock on right field. Maris's occasional flashes saddled the rookie with the undesirable label *streak hitter.*

The Indians finished the season 76-77, in sixth place, the first time Roger played on a professional team that did not improve over the prior year. This was Cleveland's worst season since 1946, and someone had to take the blame. On September 27, Greenberg fired Farrell, who never again managed in the majors. He replaced him with former Pirates manager Bobby Bragan. Six weeks later, Greenberg himself departed.

"I was managing in Cuba in winter ball," recalls Bragan, "when Greenberg flew down there to hire me to manage Cleveland. Shortly after that, they fired him as general manager. I might have been one of the reasons!"

Some accounts stated Greenberg was fired by Indians owners William R. Daley and Ignatius A. O'Shaughnessy. These local businessmen had purchased Cleveland for $3.96 million in February of 1956, then watched as the team went downward in the standings and in attendance. They thought Greenberg was doing little to stop the slide. Other accounts said Greenberg quit in frustration because he was unable to get league approval for his financially strapped franchise to relocate in Minneapolis. His replacement at general manager was Frank Lane, who had been GM of the St. Louis Cardinals. Roger had tangled with Dutch Meyer at Tulsa in 1955, but Frank Lane would become the only person in baseball Maris said he actually *hated*.

CHAPTER ELEVEN

TRADED

FRANK LANE ARRIVED IN Cleveland after a spotty, frenetic record in Chicago and St. Louis. In his seven years as the general manager of the White Sox, he orchestrated 241 transactions, earning the nicknames Trader, Wheeler Dealer, and Frantic Frank. Lane, in effect, ultimately sent himself to the St. Louis Cardinals. In two years as GM, he infuriated the fans by sending the beloved Red Schoendienst to the Giants and Enos Slaughter to the Yankees. Owner Gussie Busch blocked his attempt to trade Stan Musial, probably saving him from being tarred and feathered. This unpopular executive with extraordinary hubris then found safe haven in Cleveland, where he proceeded to eviscerate the team Hank Greenberg had assembled over the years.

Roger Maris was one of the few Indians Lane was excited about when he took the GM job. It took only a few phone conversations for him to change his mind. Maris was furious that Lane told the press that he hit poorly in the second part of the season not because he came back too soon from his injury but because pitchers figured him out. Lane later told *Baseball Quarterly* that he sent Maris a 1958 contract with a $1,500 raise, which the outfielder sent back unsigned and ripped in half. So Lane called Maris to tell him he would be sending him an identical contract and felt confident it wouldn't be "accidentally" torn again.

Since Maris had missed 46 games, Lane wanted him to find his groove by playing winter ball on the Tigres del Licey team in the Dominican Republic. Roger said no. He had disliked playing winter ball the previous year, wanted to spend time at home with his wife and new baby, and had already accepted a job working for a radio station in Fargo. Lane was appalled to have been rebuffed by a twenty-three-year-old coming off a mediocre rookie season. "That did it," he told *Baseball Quarterly*. "I made up my mind that this guy was going to be too difficult to handle to make it worth my while."

Roger remained in Fargo and worked at KVOX, providing tremendous PR to one of the three local radio stations. Officially, his title was account executive and his job was to sell advertising, but what he really did was five-minute sports reports a couple of times a day. "I think he read from the AP wire," remembers broadcaster/deejay Rod Lucier. "I'm sure he didn't make much money, but he did it because he loved Fargo. Sometimes between his spots, we'd sneak off for burgers and bowling at Northport Lanes on North Broadway. There was no star aura to him and he had no problem when people asked for autographs."

Meanwhile, Lane was thinking about how he could unload his impertinent player. He knew that the Yankees were even more interested in acquiring Maris with Greenberg gone. But he wouldn't return their calls. The jealous executive so disliked the arrogant Yankees that he vowed never to trade with them again. He figured that if Maris got off to a good start, another team would make him a solid offer.

That spring, Maris reported to Tucson, surprised that Trader Lane hadn't dealt him over the winter. But he knew better than to buy a house in Cleveland. During the off-season Roger had again stayed away from the Marases of Hibbing, Minnesota, but in spring training one came to him. Nick Maras Jr., the son of Rudy's close friend, was now a top pitching prospect in the Pittsburgh Pirates chain. He recalls:

The first time I met Roger was when we were introduced by Branch Rickey Jr., who was the head of the Pirates at that time. I'll never forget him saying, "I heard about you. Your father and my father worked together." And I said, "Well, Roger, I sure know about you." It was a brief conversation. Roger seemed shy, but he was nice to ask me a question or two instead of the other way around. It was obvious that he didn't want to open up about anything personal. I think he was only talking to me because I wasn't one of the Marases he had trouble with and we were *distant* cousins. Of course, I didn't bring up his name change. We exchanged a few more words and then he said, "Good luck, have a great season." I said, "Thank you," and that was it until the midsixties, when I called his hotel in Anaheim and he invited me to breakfast with several of his Yankee teammates.

"At spring training it was obvious that Roger was the best athlete on the team," says Billy Moran, who split time at second and short in his '58 rookie season. "I didn't understand why Cleveland didn't want to keep him. Of course with Lane, all the players were thinking they might be traded at any moment. That continued throughout the season."

The Indians players worried with good reason. On February 18, Lane dealt Jim Hegan and Hank Aguirre to Detroit for Hal Woodeshick and J. W. Porter. On April 1, he swapped Bud Daley, Dick Williams, and Gene Woodling to the Orioles for former Indian Larry Doby and pitcher Don Ferrarese.

Bobby Bragan, the new Indians manager, had never met Lane before. He recalls, "In Arizona, I got to know Frank pretty good because he sat next to me during the exhibition games. He was aggressive, he was impatient, he interfered, he took credit for what anyone else did, and he was negative about everything. He was difficult to work for. I never felt real secure managing under him."

Finding himself being platooned once the season began, Maris, now wearing number 5, assumed Bragan was in cahoots with Lane. Bragan denies this: "Lane never talked to me about Maris and I didn't know they had problems."

"Roger was mad at Bragan because he kept him off the field," says Mudcat Grant, who went 10-11 as a rookie in 1958. "If you're thinking about benching Roger Maris, you're crazy."

"I saw him as a fourth outfielder behind Minoso, Colavito, and Gary Geiger," explains Bragan. "But I liked Roger and we got along fine. I didn't think he disliked me. A couple of balls went over the fence he had a chance to catch, and the coaches and I thought he was fence shy and needed practice running back to the fence to catch a ball. Every day we spent a lot of time hitting fly balls over his head in right field. He was cooperative and didn't complain."

Maris's fear of going back on long flies and hitting the fence after what had happened to him in Keokuk was the opposite of Billy Mack's fear of coming in on short flies and colliding with the second baseman in *Slugger in*

Right. Maris didn't protest Bragan's drill because, unlike Dutch Meyer's throwing drill, its purpose was to teach him something, not punish him. In fact, when he overcame his fear of fences, he was able to play shallower than other right fielders.

Carroll Hardy completed his military service but was still hampered by a shoulder injury he received playing army ball. He, too, became a platoon player and pinch hitter. Ironically, his first major league home run, on May 17, came when he pinch-hit for Maris in the 11th inning of a 4–4 game against Chicago. With two Indians on base, Al Lopez brought in left-handed Billy Pierce to face the left-handed Maris, and Bragan lifted Maris for Hardy. Neither manager realized that Maris had had a lot of success against Pierce. It was a moot point because Hardy took Pierce over the fence to win the game.

"Roger was happy for me," Hardy recalls. "We pulled for each other all the time, two guys from North and South Dakota." Hardy's run of bad luck hadn't run its course. The next day he was stricken with appendicitis and had to have surgery. "That ruined my season because when I got back, I didn't play much." Lane later sent him to Boston.

With Hardy out of commission and Altobelli back in the minors, Roger hung out with other teammates, including Don Ferrarese, a 5'9" lefty. Ferrarese recalls, "I went out drinking with him and his good buddy Russ Nixon on the road. Beer was Roger's favorite. Russ would tease the shit out of him and they'd both laugh. He was a friendly, modest guy who barely talked and didn't like fanfare or bullshit. He was very serious in uniform. He did everything well, without any flair. Even the way he ran wasn't flashy, with his head down."

In June, Maris's average had dropped to .225 despite batting mostly against right-handed pitchers. He had only 9 homers. His once-bright future with Cleveland was dimming fast. He went 1 for 8 as Bell and Grant pitched the Indians to a doubleheader sweep over Washington, as they improved to 29-30, 8½ games behind New York. His career with the organization that had signed him in 1952 was over. (Cleveland would finish at 77-76, a reverse of 1957, 14½ games behind the Yankees.)

The ax fell on the June 15 trading deadline, three days after Lane had sent Chico Carrasquel to Kansas City to vacate the shortstop position. Roger Maris, Dick Tomanek, and Preston Ward were dealt to Kansas City in exchange for All-Star first baseman Vic Power and outfielder-shortstop Woodie Held, who would replace Carrasquel. A's owner Arnold Johnson had inquired about Colavito, but Lane explained that trading away his matinee idol would result in a big fan backlash—an argument he'd forget when he traded him to Detroit just before Opening Day 1960. Johnson took Maris instead, agreeing to the condition that he'd have to wait until 1959 to trade him to the Yankees.

"I didn't think I'd be traded," says Ward. "I'd gotten off to a great start, batting .338, which was third in the league. I loved being in Cleveland, but that madman had to make trades."

"We were flying back from Washington to Cleveland, and Bragan told us about the trade while we were up in the air," remembers Tomanek. "My wife heard it on the radio before we knew about it. Roger seemed surprised, too."

"Roger was shocked when he got traded," recalls Ray Narleski. "He came over to my house in tears. I said, 'Roger, don't feel bad. You are going to Kansas City but will end up with the Yankees.' I don't know if he liked that idea."

"I wasn't surprised Maris was traded considering who the general manager was," says Bragan. "If Lane had traded Minoso or Colavito, I would have been surprised. It was his decision, but I agreed with the trade because I got Vic Power, who was probably the best defensive first baseman who ever played."

"That was a bad deal for us," insists Grant, who became close friends with Power, "because Roger was better than both players we got for him. The guy was a star!"

"Roger had reason to hate Frank Lane," remembers Earl Averill. "He was a tyrant. In the hotel, you could hear him through his door, screaming about trading players."

Joe Altobelli recollects, "Within a three-year period, Frank Lane traded everyone who was on the forty-man roster when we had spring training in 1958. Hal Naragon and Rocky Colavito were the last two guys he traded who were on that original forty-man roster. He traded everybody. Including me!"

Apparently, Lane didn't have much patience with managers either. After only 67 games, the shortest stint for an Indians manager ever, Bragan was fired. Cleveland had just lost 2–1 on a ninth-inning home run by Ted Williams off Cal McLish. Lane told Bragan, "I don't know how we're going to get along without you, but starting tomorrow we're going to try." Bragan's replacement was Joe Gordon, whom Lane would tire of and trade for Tigers manager Jimmy Dykes in 1960.

Bragan was one of only eight people to show up at Frank Lane's funeral in 1981, and he was one of four representing the commissioner's office. Bragan says, "He must have traded his friends away, too."

CHAPTER TWELVE

AT HOME IN KANSAS CITY

T HE KANSAS CITY ATHLETICS were in their fourth year of existence when Roger Maris became part of their history. Arnold Johnson, a Chicago businessman, purchased the storied Philadelphia Athletics franchise from Connie Mack's family and moved his new team to Kansas City for the 1955 season. Kansas City fans were excited to have a major league team and said fond farewells to the AAA Blues, who departed for Denver, and the Negro Leagues' Monarchs, who became a full-time barnstorming team.

The original Kansas City A's generated a lot of optimism but had finished sixth, eighth, and seventh in their first three years. Manager Lou Boudreau was replaced by his coach Harry Craft. With attendance waning, Johnson might have moved his team to Los Angeles if the Brooklyn Dodgers didn't beat him to it for the 1958 season. By the time they acquired Maris, the A's were regarded as an also-ran and, worse, a virtual farm team of the Yankees.

Merle Harmon, who was the Kansas City A's announcer at the time, recalled in 2008:

> Ernie Mehl was the big, tough, loud, cigar-chomping sports editor of the *Kansas City Star*. He was the ringleader, along with Kansas City sportswriter Parke Carroll, in getting Arnold Johnson to buy the A's and move them to Kansas City. Mehl was a good friend of Del Webb, who along with Dan Topping owned the Yankees. Webb made his money as a construction magnate and real estate developer, and when Johnson needed the 19,000-seat Blues Stadium transformed into the double-decked Municipal Stadium in just ninety days, who do you think the contract went to? The Del Webb

Construction Company. So Johnson was beholden to Webb, and Carroll, the new A's GM, would do *anything* for his good friend Yankees GM George Weiss.

Another reason Johnson was indebted to Del Webb was that he held a second mortgage on Municipal Stadium totaling $2.9 million. That certainly was a factor when Johnson and Carroll agreed to lopsided trades in which key A's players became property of the Yankees for little in return. Whenever the Yankees were a player short in their run for the pennant, Weiss simply dipped into the A's talent pool. But he had to be patient with Maris because, as Carroll explained to him, Johnson had promised Frank Lane that he wouldn't deal him to the Yankees that year.

Surely Maris heard rumors that he'd wind up a Yankee, but he was dubious about the Yankees really coveting a .235 benchwarmer who rarely saw eye-to-eye with management. In *Slugger in Right*, a Yankee scout rejects signing Billy Mack, saying, "You're a good looking ballplayer. You can hit, run and throw, but you're not the Yankee type. You have a quick temper, sulk when things don't go your way and act as if you think everyone is against you." That is how Maris assumed the Yankees viewed him. So rather than worrying about moving again, Roger wanted to play his heart out for the team that wanted him and prove that the team that discarded him made a big mistake.

When Maris arrived in Kansas City, A's manager Harry Craft was curious about the player who got under Frank Lane's skin. So he turned to his veteran outfielder Bob Cerv. Cerv remembers, "Harry said, 'I'm going to room you with Maris, the new guy, and I want you to find out about him. I hear he's a red-ass or something.' In those days if someone put a label on you, it was hard to get rid of. So we went on the road and Rog got suspicious and asked, 'Why am I rooming with you?' And I said, 'Roger, I'll tell you the truth. The skipper said I've got to find out what the hell makes you tick.' He thought it over and said, 'I like guys who tell me the truth.' And we were good friends after that. We'd eventually be godfathers to each other's kids."

Years later, Craft told Maury Allen, "I called him into my office and . . . told him I didn't care what happened in Cleveland . . . because none of that mattered in Kansas City. I just wanted him to hustle for me, play hard, and if he did that, he would never have any trouble. And that's what he did. I got to really like Roger."

Maris's first game with his new team, which was playing .500 ball and was in second place, was against the Baltimore Orioles. The first three players in Baltimore's lineup had been traded from Cleveland by Frank Lane: left fielder Dick Williams, center fielder Jim Busby, and right fielder Gene Woodling. The lineup for the Athletics had Chico Carrasquel at shortstop, Bill Tuttle in center, newcomer Preston Ward at third, Bob Cerv in left, number 35 Roger Maris in right, Hector Lopez at second, former Indian Harry "Suitcase" Simpson at first, Harry Chiti behind the plate, and forty-one-year-old knuckleballer Murry Dickson on the mound. Making an appearance as a pinch hitter would be Whitey Herzog, the future manager who would become one of Maris's best friends. In the bullpen was Bud Daley, who was traded to the A's soon after Lane traded him to the Orioles.

Maris singled to right in his first at-bat as an Athletic, driving in Ward for the second run of the first inning. But eighteen-year-old O's rookie Milt Pappas settled down to strike out the side and kill the rally. He'd give up only two more hits in his seven innings of work as Baltimore came from behind to win 5–3. Maris flew out twice to Busby in center and lined out to Williams in right to finish 1 for 4 before 10,843 fans.

Later that night, Maris met two of those fans, Jim Cosentino and his younger brother Jerry, future supermarket magnates. Jim became Roger's best friend in Kansas City. He passed away in 1971, but Jerry Cosentino remembers:

Our grocery store was on Blue Ridge Parkway and was maybe forty feet wide and sixty feet deep. It was the two of us who ran it, and it was a struggle. When Roger played his first game for the Athletics, Jim and I were at the stadium. It was an evening game and afterward we went back to the store. Roger came in and my brother recognized him because he had that distinct look. They started chatting and struck up a friendship. They had a lot in common. Jim had been a third baseman in the Cardinals organization, including with the Duluth Dukes a few years before Roger played in the Northern League. Jim played semipro ball for the Barrett Meat Company after he gave up pro ball to get married. When we met Roger, it was on his terms, so it wasn't hard getting to know him.

Kansas City also lost its next game to the Orioles. But the A's then won 6 straight against Boston and Washington. Then in a three-game series that attracted a season's-best 93,000 fans to Municipal Stadium, the Yankees beat them twice, but the A's crushed them in the third game, 12–6. Maris got 4 hits, including a round-tripper off Art Ditmar, drove in 2 runs, and scored 3 times. "I was disappointed I wasn't playing as much," recalls Bob Martyn, who lost his right-field job to Maris, "because I was leading the league in triples. But I saw that Roger hit a fair number of home runs and played good defense. We'd talk in the outfield prior to games, but I never complained to him about my situation after the trade."

Roger's manager and new teammates saw that he played hard every game, particularly against Cleveland. In the 1994 book *We Played the Game*, Vic Power, the key player the Indians acquired in the Maris trade, spoke of an incident that nearly led to blows:

> I was playing second for the Indians and Maris slid very hard with his spikes high and caught me in the ribs. I warned him that the next time he slid like that I was going to give him an eye for an eye. I had seen how Jackie Robinson would jump over a sliding runner and land on top of him with his spikes, and that's what I planned for Maris. And the next time he slid hard into the base, I jumped into the air. But he slid past the base and I realized that I was about to come down directly on his face. It would have looked like an accident if I came straight down, but I quickly split my legs and landed with my spikes on both sides of his face. I didn't hurt him, but I did teach him a lesson.

Power, a dark-skinned Puerto Rican, wondered if Maris's run-in with him was racially motivated. Maris was known for getting along with players of color, so it's more likely that he wanted some form of payback on Frank Lane's team. And who better to go after than the player for whom he was traded? Perhaps Roger's most satisfying game all year came against the Indians, when he broke up starter Hal Woodeshick's no-hitter in the seventh inning and won the game with a 2-run homer in the tenth inning off Mudcat Grant.

Maris enjoyed playing for Harry Craft, a genial man from Mississippi. "One thing I like about him," Roger said, "is that if you do something wrong, he'll call you aside later on and explain how the play should have been made. You don't learn anything from a manager that just chews you out." Craft had been Mickey Mantle's first manager, on Independence in the Kansas-Oklahoma-Missouri League in 1949, and then, in 1950, on Joplin in the Western Association, when Mantle played shortstop and drove in 136 runs in 137 games to earn a promotion to the Yankees. Years later, Mantle said, "I was lucky to have Harry as my skipper my first two years. He started me out right."

The A's faithful didn't expect much in value when there were trades or call-ups from the minors. So they cheered their new player as he stretched singles into doubles, beat out bunts, busted his tail on the basepaths and in the outfield, and invariably threw to the right base or hit the cutoff man. It wasn't every day that a comet landed in town.

"Maris was popular with the fans because he hustled so much," says Ray Herbert, who was part of a solid rotation with Dickson (until he was traded to the Yankees), Ned Garver, Ralph Terry, and Bob Grim. "He played hard all the time out there. He was a good teammate and he loved baseball, and that's what the fans saw."

Ernie Mehl of the *Kansas City Star* wondered, "Have the Athletics found in Roger Maris the outstanding performer they have been searching for ever since the franchise moved here?"

Merle Harmon recounted in 2008 that Craft had spoken confidentially about Maris to his close friend Tom Greenwade, the Yankee scout who had signed Mickey Mantle. "Craft told Greenwade," said Harmon, " 'I have a player who can be the next Mickey Mantle. He will be a great hitter. He's already a great outfielder.' "

Craft was also impressed that Maris was willing to sacrifice his body and his statistics to help his team win. And he didn't accept defeat easily. Harmon saw Maris's dedication:

As Kansas City dropped in the standings, it was clear it was a bad ball club. But most of the players were still happy-go-lucky because they didn't expect much in the first place. After a loss in Baltimore, I was sitting on the bus going back to the hotel when a bunch of the guys got on. They were all carefree, telling each other, "Where do you want to go tonight? Let's hit the streets!" Roger came aboard in a bad mood and stomped down the aisle.

One guy said, "Nice game, Rog!" because Roger had hit a home run. He turned on him and said, "What do you mean, nice game?" And the guy says, "Well, at least *you* had a good night. You don't have to be upset about it." And Roger said, "I don't give a *such and such* what kind of a night I had. We lost." I tell you, that bus was silent all the way back to the hotel. He didn't talk a lot, but he had leadership qualities in him. He was a winner.

Jim Cosentino, his wife, Frances, and his brother Jerry were among many individuals who welcomed Roger and Pat to Kansas City. Susan was less than a year old, and Pat was pregnant again, so Roger was relieved that the quick relocation was made easier by the kindness of strangers who became close friends. Jim Cosentino even got Roger a weekend job with the Armour Meat Company, signing autographs.

"If there was an evening game on the weekend, he'd go into a store from maybe one to two in the afternoon," recalls Jerry Cosentino. "When there was a day game, he'd go after it was over. They paid him $75 for only two days a week, so that helped him out. It wasn't so hard to do and it paid good money, but it was a chore for Roger because he didn't like that kind of publicity or attention. He did it because he was making only around $8,000 playing baseball."

Like most ballplayers in the fifties, Roger was glad to find part-time work to supplement his salary, but he would have preferred something outside of baseball. "He would play ball but then not want to talk or boast about what he did at the ballpark," says Cosentino. "A lot of people considered Roger surly or aloof, but he was just quiet. He liked to laugh and have a good time, but otherwise he was pretty sedate and private."

"Roger Maris was a different breed of cat," says Bill Grigsby, who was Merle Harmon's partner in the A's radio booth. "He was a first-class person and his wife was a sweetheart. If I'd been in a barroom fight, I would have wanted Roger with me because he didn't back off from anybody. And yet he was shy. I tried to make it easier for him by introducing him to my friends."

Although he had become wary of the media in Cleveland, Maris was comfortable enough to appear several times on Harmon's pregame show. "All Roger wanted was to be treated fairly," remembered Harmon a few months before his death in 2009. "During the broadcast of the game, I'd tell the listeners what Roger said on the pregame show. I knew that I had better repeat *exactly* what he told me because if I tried to embellish it in any way and he heard about it, he wouldn't have been happy. He trusted me, and we became good friends."

If you wanted to be Roger's friend, you had to earn and keep his trust. "Roger and I got along very well," recalls Ralph Terry, a cerebral right-hander from Big Cabin, Oklahoma, "but the big difference between us was I could laugh off things and Roger couldn't. If he trusted you and you crossed him, you wouldn't get a second chance."

Harry Craft had set a goal of 70 victories for the A's in 1958, and the club gave him 3 more wins than that and an impressive 14 more than in 1957. But that still wasn't good enough to escape another seventh-place finish. "We had a chance to wind up in the first division," says Ned Garver, a veteran right-hander who got 20 of the last-place St. Louis Browns' 59 wins in 1951. "But Parke Carroll let the Yankees take Murry Dickson from us to help them win the pennant, and we didn't get a thing for him. That was a dirty-handed trick."

Roger and his teammates had the ignoble experience of watching the Yankees clinch the pennant on their field. He had no idea he'd take part in many such moments with the Yankees. He also had no inkling that what took place on the Yankees' train trip to Detroit would have a profound impact on him. During the wild pennant celebration, inebriated reliever Ryne Duren and Ralph Houk had a brief scuffle, with the Yankee coach accidentally cutting Duren over his eye with his World Series ring.

Leonard Shecter of the *New York Post* would have ignored what transpired, as did the other writers on the train, but his editor was angry that he'd just been scooped by Til Ferdenzi of the *New York Journal-American* on a story about the Yankees front office hiring detectives to trail its players. Desperate, Shecter told his editor, Paul Sann, by phone about the minor incident. Sann, in turn, wrote it up under Shecter's byline as a knock-down, drag-out fight.

Until then, the understanding was that what reporters saw on trains, "family stuff," was kept quiet. As Duren puts it, "A trust was betrayed and players weren't so open with reporters after that." The nonexistent fight became a huge story, and the editors of the other New York dailies were furious with their reporters for letting Shecter get the exclusive. They wanted more stories like his. This event is often cited as the one that most transformed sports journalism, allowing sensationalism to do battle with etiquette. Though the stage was set, change didn't really occur until more reporters like Shecter were willing to go beneath the surface for stories. That would happen in 1961.

The A's unlikely star in 1958 was Cerv, who came into his own after years of collecting splinters on the Yankees' bench. During the season, the seemingly indestructible thirty-two-year-old Nebraskan suffered a broken jaw, a broken hand, two broken toes, and various knee and ankle injuries. Yet he batted .305 with 38 home runs and 104 RBIs and was voted the American League's left fielder in the All-Star Game, ahead of batting champion Ted Williams. Cerv's support in the lineup came almost only from Lopez, who had 17 homers and 73 RBIs, and Maris when he was hot.

Maris's 19 home runs and 53 RBIs in 99 games with Kansas City gave him a respectable two-team total of 28 homers and 80 RBIs in 150 games. Although his stats didn't compare to Rocky Colavito's 41 homers and 113 RBIs in his breakthrough season with Cleveland, they were second to Cerv's on the A's.

"He was one of those guys whose eyes lit up when there were men on base," Cerv told Maury Allen years later. "He was about as tough a hitter as there was with a man on third and less than two outs, or a man on second in a close game. . . . Roger could have batted .300 easy if there was a man on second every time he came up all season."

Batting only .240 in an injury-free year was embarrassing to Maris, but he finished seventh in the American League in home runs, tenth in total bases, fifth in at-bats, and seventh in runs scored. He had left his mark. If he did better than he hoped, there's no way of knowing because he never boasted about his accomplishments to anyone other than the person negotiating his contract.

He certainly wasn't going to brag when Rudy Jr. was visiting. "I got to know Roger's brother quite well because he visited Roger quite often," says Jerry Cosentino. "He seemed haunted by what might have been if he hadn't gotten sick. Roger always said, 'He was a much better player than I was.' "

"I met Roger's parents when they came down from Fargo," said Merle Harmon. "His dad looked like a movie star with wavy, silver-gray hair. His mother was very beautiful. They were super people who were easier to hold a conversation with than Roger when you first met him. They always told me that Rudy Jr. was a better ballplayer than Roger before he got polio. I wasn't sure that was true."

Typically, Maris felt he was an outsider whenever he moved to a new place to play ball, but it was different in Kansas City, a city with 450,000 people that felt like a small town. Roger and Pat had found a home away from Fargo—which they still visited regularly—a Middle American community with friendly, straight-shooting "common" folks, fine schools and churches, and the best barbecue Roger ever tasted. There were lovely fountains, wide boulevards, and diverse music, including jazz, which Maris enjoyed. Roger was grateful for the quiet and privacy afforded him by Raytown, the suburb that he and many other ballplayers settled in with their families.

"Roger and Pat had a beautiful home in Raytown," remembers Maureen Tomanek. "Dick and I moved there, too, a couple of miles away. I was friends with Pat, who was very nice and more social than Roger. We talked about our children, and we'd go shopping and occasionally sit in the stands together. The four of us socialized, sometimes with Bob Cerv and his wife, who lived there, too. We had cookouts and picnics and would go out once in a while, which was difficult because Roger was uncomfortable when people recognized him. But usually when the guys were home, they wanted to spend time with their own wives and kids."

At the age of twenty-four, Roger's goal in life was simple. He wanted to play baseball as long as he could make a decent living and provide for his family. Then he intended to work at something else with Rudy Jr. Maybe they'd run a car dealership, or a beer distributorship as did his teammate Joe De Maestri with his father in California. Beer had been part of Roger's world since his early youth in Minnesota. Baseball was fun, but Roger saw it as his temporary profession until he found a lifelong career, such as his father had with the Great Northern Railroad. For now he was content plying his trade in a hassle-free community where he could raise a gaggle of children.

When he wasn't at the ballfield, he wanted to leave the game behind and spend time with family and friends. He wanted to relax, not talk about baseball. That's why he was glad that the press in Kansas City pretty much left him alone once the game was over. He couldn't imagine playing in a town where it was any different.

CHAPTER THIRTEEN

THE ALL-STAR

E VERY WINTER IN BASEBALL'S pre-agent days, players checked their
mailbox for their annual contract with their general manager's salary
offer. Then they returned the contract, signed or not signed. Roger had
hated going through negotiations with Frank Lane, so after his second year,
he bucked protocol. According to George Selkirk, the A's director of player
personnel, Maris entered his office one day in February and wrote a figure
on a piece of paper. He told Selkirk, the right fielder who'd replaced Babe
Ruth when his Yankee career ended, not to call him until the Athletics agreed
to pay him that salary.

"When I phoned him later to see if we could work out a salary that was
mutually agreeable," Selkirk told a reporter a few years later, "Maris told me
I had nerve to call him before I was ready to pay his price." Parke Carroll
took over the negotiations with Maris.

Merle Harmon remembered:

I saw Roger one day and he said, "I'm going over to fight with Parke Carroll
over my contract." I was doing a local show on radio and TV in the off-
season and I said, "Hey, do me a favor. I want an exclusive. Call me from the
ballpark and tell me what happened at the meeting." And he said, "Well, I
can tell you what's going to happen right now. He's going to put the contract
in front of me, and I'm going to put it back on the desk and say good-bye."
I didn't think Roger would call me later, but he did and he was in an upbeat
mood. I said, "Well, how did it go?" He said, "Boy, Parke put that contract
in front of me and I couldn't believe it. I had to grab a pen and sign it before
he changed his mind." Obviously Roger got a pretty good raise.

Maris accepted $16,000, doubling his 1958 salary. He called it "the best contract I ever signed."

Roger and Pat made a point to return to Fargo during the off-season to visit family and friends, but they were in Kansas City in February 1959 while Roger negotiated his contract and they adjusted to life with their second child. Roger Maris Jr. had been born in November, one of the few times Roger was home when Pat gave birth.

On February 3, news from Fargo-Moorhead made headlines even in Kansas City. A plane en route to Moorhead carrying famed pop-music stars Buddy Holly, Ritchie Valens, and J. P. Richardson, the "Big Bopper," had gone down in a blizzard near Clear Lake, Iowa, killing all three before they could headline "The Winter Dance Party." The concert had been booked in Moorhead by deejay and promoter Rod Lucier, Maris's friend from KVOX, for the grand sum of $750. The music world was in shock, and the people of Fargo-Moorhead were traumatized. (The show went on with Bobby Vee stepping in.)

Roger's mother received bad news of a personal kind that month. Her mother, Ana, had passed away in Minnesota. She was sixty-nine and had been in the United States for fifty-three years. "Connie looked after her in Fargo until it became too difficult," says Don O'Neil. "And then she was placed in a nursing home in Duluth. It was there that she passed away."

"She fell and broke her hip and over a period of time passed away," recalls Rudy Marich. "Connie came to her funeral at the Greek Orthodox church in Chisholm. At the time, Jean and Jerry were living in California, Mary was living near Fargo, and I was teaching physical education in Colorado. Vi and Dominic eventually moved to Colorado, too. After the funeral, I was driving my father back to the Veterans Hospital in Fargo. He said, 'You kids are all well taken care of and I don't have to worry about you, so it's time for me to go, too.' I said, 'Dad, don't talk like that.' Sure enough, he passed away three months after we buried Mother."

"Connie didn't come to my father's funeral and I wasn't surprised," said Vi Marich Cortese. "She hated my dad. So did Gerald, who changed his name to March. It didn't have to do with his being gay because my dad didn't push him away, but I don't know the reason. My dad tried to talk to him at my mother's funeral, but Gerald wouldn't acknowledge him. That was the last time they saw each other. Connie had nothing more to do with

Rudy or me, but Jean kept in touch with everybody." As with the Maras family, the Marich family had conflicts that were never resolved and secrets that were never revealed.

Roger was in a good frame of mind when he went to spring training in Florida. He was happily married with two kids, with another already on the way, and settled in Kansas City. If Maris was reluctant to wind up in New York, he started out the 1959 exhibition season doing the wrong thing. Against the Yankees at their facility in St. Petersburg, he crushed a tape-measure homer that was witnessed by an impressionable boy, Ralph Wimbish Jr., a future *New York Post* sports editor whose eminent father led the fight for desegregation of the Grapefruit League facilities. It was the first time the youngster saw anyone hit a ball that "landed outside the stadium, bounced across First Street, and jumped into the lobby of a hotel."

The A's played their first ten games of the season against the White Sox and the Indians. Roger was brimming with confidence and did as well against tough left-handers as right-handers. "I was a lefty with a good curveball, but he didn't bail at all," recalls Don Ferrarese, Roger's teammate on Cleveland. "Roger hit a home run off me the second series we played them when I jammed him with an inside fastball. He pulled that thing and POW! GONE! He was something special by that time."

The A's started slowly before having a little hot streak to end April with a 9-7 record. Maris, wearing number 3—the same number as Babe Ruth—was batting cleanup and hitting .328. And he didn't let up. On May 14, he hit his 8th round-tripper against tough Baltimore left-hander Billy O'Dell and upped his average to .343. At Yankee Stadium on May 17, he drilled his 9th homer off Don Larsen. In support of Ray Herbert, his 10th homer was a 3-run blast off Boston's Bill Monbouquette at Fenway Park on May 20, lifting his RBI total to 26. With Cerv struggling with injuries, Maris was carrying the offense and making headlines.

Then it ended. On May 21, Maris was rushed from his home to the hospital for a 2 a.m. emergency appendectomy. The surgery was successful, and while he convalesced, he received stacks of cards and telegrams from well-wishers, proof of how much he was appreciated in Kansas City. One card came from out of town. "I had my appendectomy the year before," says Carroll Hardy. "Roger and Pat visited me when I was recuperating, so I sent him a card. I wrote, 'You'll be all right. Just give yourself a little time.'"

"Roger had his appendix operation and I was out with a sore shoulder," recalls Dick Tomanek. "So when the team was out of town and we weren't bass fishing, we worked out at the ballpark. I take some credit for Roger hitting left-handers so good. He stood far away from the plate but could still pull the ball. He had a little bit of a closed stance. He had quick hands and wrists and power to the opposite field also. Against me, he practiced taking left-handers the other way."

Before the season, Harry Craft said, "For the first time we're in a position where we don't have to make trades." However, with Maris on the sidelines and the team falling below .500, the A's agreed to another deal with the Yankees. If Maris hadn't landed in the hospital, he would likely have been the centerpiece of the transaction, but the struggling Yankees needed offense immediately and asked for the healthy Hector Lopez instead. The A's also gave up their ace-in-the-making, Ralph Terry. Lopez and Terry would play important roles for the Yankees for several years. In return the A's received two past-their-prime pitchers, Johnny Kucks and Tom Sturdivant, and backup shortstop Jerry Lumpe. After going 2-6, Sturdivant would be traded at the end of the year; Kucks would pitch pretty well in '59, but after a 4-10 record in 1960, his career ended. Surprisingly, Lumpe was the prize of the deal for the A's. He was converted to second base and became an All-Star.

"I didn't think of Roger as a star yet," says Lumpe. "But I saw he had a lot of ability. I didn't really know he was slumping in the second half of the season because I was learning a new position and trying not to get killed turning the double play."

Eager to help the Athletics, who had fallen 5 games under .500, Maris returned to the lineup in one month, in time for a four-game series against the visiting New York Yankees. Roger picked up where he'd left off. He had 2 doubles with 2 runs and an RBI in the first game. Mantle had 2 homers and 6 RBIs for the Bronx Bombers. For the four games, Maris went 7 for 17 to raise his average to .331, with 3 runs and 4 RBIs, but the A's dropped three of the games and fell farther back in the standings.

Maris must have been running on pure adrenaline because after the Yankee series he went into a tailspin. He had obviously returned before he was fully recovered. A week later, when the A's record stood at 32-40, Maris's average had dropped to .298.

"Any slump is a matter of timing," Maris said. "Anytime I've been out,

I've found it takes quite a while to adjust my timing after I get back in. It's how fast you can get back your timing that determines whether you're back on the beam or in a slump. The longer it takes you to get it back, the more likely you are to press, and once you start pressing, you're in trouble."

This time Maris got out of trouble with a 15-game hit streak that raised his average to .332 on July 7. He hit only 2 homers during this stretch, confirming that when he didn't go for homers, he could hit for a high average. Maris's hot bat ignited the entire team. They won three in a row before being shut out by Washington in the game Maris's streak ended. Then the A's embarked on an 11-game winning streak that improved the team's record to 50-49. The entire city was excited.

"In my five years in Kansas City," says Joe De Maestri, "the biggest thing that happened is that we won 11 games in a row. Parke Carroll wanted to give everybody a watch, but that never came about."

"That streak was the biggest thrill for everybody," agrees Bud Daley, who went 16-13 for the A's in 1959. "*Sports Illustrated* wrote a story about me. I was called 'the Pork Chop All-Star.' There were some festivities with hundreds of fans, and the mayor gave me a live pig."

Bill Grigsby recalls:

We came to town after a road trip and Harry Craft collapsed and they rushed him to a clinic. There were rumors he had a breakdown, but the truth was he was drinking too much. The team looked better to him when he was drinking. So with Harry in a clinic, Bob Swift, the third-base coach, took over as a manager. And we started winning every day. The town was going crazy, and you would have thought we'd won the World Series. So Harry became a hostage in the clinic because if he got out and the A's lost, the people would kill him. We got a laundry truck and put him in the back and sneaked him out of the clinic and took him to the Phillips Hotel. He was on about the 10th floor and they didn't have central air-conditioning then so the windows were open. And there was a guy on the corner selling papers and yelling, "Read all about it, Harry Craft fired as A's manager!" Harry paid somebody to get the paper, but there wasn't anything in it about any firing. The newsboy had found out that Harry was up in that room and was putting the needle to him. Harry gets out and we're in third place and there's no way Harry's not going to come back as manager. Well, the Yankees came to town and then we went on a road trip. We lost 13 in a row. And Harry's days were numbered.

By going 0 for 9 in the final series before the All-Star break, Roger's average had decreased from a league-leading .344 to a still outstanding .331 when he played in his first All-Star Game, on August 3, in Los Angeles. It was the second All-Star Game of the year. (From 1959 to 1962, a second game was added to benefit the players' pension fund.) Maris went 0 for 2 with a strikeout. It was still a thrill, particularly playing with Ted Williams. Dressing near him in the locker room, Roger was too shy to say anything.

Maris hit well into August, and if he had continued to do so for only seven more weeks, he could have ended the season batting around .335, with 25 homers and 100 RBIs. Such stats would have changed his legacy, denying future critics the opportunity to say he never batted .300 or had an outstanding season before 1960. But Maris couldn't hang on. He stopped hitting entirely, erasing the memory of four outstanding months. When he faded, the A's did, too, losing 22 of 29 games.

"We all stunk," recalls Joe Morgan, a future major league manager who arrived in a trade with Milwaukee only to have Harry Craft ask him what position he played. "When you're losing all the time, it's no fun. The A's fans were very quiet and left the game early. We were told they lived a long way from the ballpark so they needed to leave about the seventh inning."

Maris couldn't understand how his swing would make him at times one of the most feared hitters in baseball and at other times fail him against even the least effective pitchers. As he said, "When I'm not hitting, even my wife can get me out."

"When Roger was going well and had his sweet stroke," says Bill Grigsby, "a big group in town bought him a pair of matched shotguns because he loved to hunt. They were going to give it to him in a big ceremony. Well, Roger went something like 6 for 106 and they didn't give him the guns because they were afraid he'd shoot himself. I think they got him a ticket out of town instead."

He was in the midst of his dreadful slump on August 21 when friends and neighbors from Fargo traveled to Kansas City to honor him between games of a doubleheader. In the first game, he struck out in the ninth with two outs and the bases loaded. "I wanted to climb into a hole and pull it in after me," he told reporters.

Among those who attended "Roger Maris Day" at Municipal Stadium were Pat, Rudy and Connie, Rudy Jr., and Roger's high school coach Sid Cichy. Fargo residents had chipped in to buy the Marises a piano and a plaque signifying he was the city's only major leaguer. His A's teammates had passed the hat, and catcher Frank House gave him the proceeds to purchase singing lessons because his vocalizing in the shower was maddening to them.

Maris never got back on track. He wound up batting .273, which was a huge improvement on his .240 in 1958 but was extremely disappointing considering he was leading the league at one time. Because he missed a month after the appendectomy, he finished with only 16 home runs and 72 RBIs, down in both categories.

The Athletics had only 66 victories in 1959 and finished a distant seventh. Cerv led the team with just 20 home runs and 85 RBIs, as he battled knee problems. Center fielder Bill Tuttle batted .300 to lead the team.

After the disappointing season, the Athletics fired Harry Craft, who would next coach and manage in the National League. At the winter meetings in Miami Beach he told Casey Stengel, "If you have a chance here to trade for Roger Maris, don't hesitate. He's ready to be a star."

Maris was on the trading block, along with everyone else on the A's. Finally he was there for the taking, the player the Yankees needed in order to rebound from a poor season in which they finished third, behind Chicago and Cleveland. Incredibly, Weiss hesitated and almost lost him.

During the winter meetings, Joe L. Brown, the GM of the Pittsburgh Pirates, was searching for a left-handed power-hitting outfielder. So he approached Parke Carroll, who was looking for a shortstop with Joe De Maestri ready to retire, and expressed interest in Maris. He offered Dick Groat in return. The general managers agreed to the swap. "I heard it was cut-and-dried," says Groat. "Then Kansas City asked Brown and our manager Danny Murtaugh to step out of the room for a few moments. And when they got out in the hallway, Danny said, 'I don't want to trade Groat.' And they called it off. Thank God! Had I gone to Kansas City, I'd have been buried for my career. And Roger went to New York instead, and ironically, we were the MVPs the next year. It sure worked out for both of us."

With the Pirates out of the picture, Carroll turned to the Yankees. It would seem that George Weiss would have been salivating at the prospect of Maris, with his short stroke, pulling balls into the right-field seats, which were only 296 feet away down the foul line and had only a four-foot-high railing. Yankee outfielder Norm Siebern was a fine left-handed hitter, but not the pull hitter Weiss and Stengel desired. So why was there hesitancy in taking Maris?

Weiss always wanted a roster with twenty-five "Yankee types." He wondered what an outspoken malcontent would do to team chemistry. He hadn't appreciated Maris's reaction in the spring when he was asked about the prospect of being dealt to the Yankees. Maris told a reporter, "I wouldn't want to join the Yankees because I don't believe I'd be happy. . . . They get on their ballplayers a lot and try to make them do things just the way they want it. I don't go for that sort of thing. When someone starts getting all over me, I just get mad." Maris was the one player in the majors who didn't dream of wearing pinstripes.

Weiss also was concerned that Maris was the quintessential streak hitter, when consistency was what the Yankees were after. The upside was that Maris was already an outstanding fielder and at the age of twenty-five still had time to develop as a hitter. Mantle had only 75 RBIs in 1959, so it was imperative to bring in someone who could share the load, and Maris seemed like the best bet on the market. Stengel would soon turn seventy, so a decision had to be made now.

Weiss struck a deal with the Athletics on December 11. The Yankees received Maris, first baseman Kent Hadley, and De Maestri, who put off retirement because he finally had a chance to win a championship. Weiss gave up Don Larsen, the perfect-game pitcher in the 1956 World Series, Siebern, Marv Throneberry, who swung like his idol Mickey Mantle only when he missed the ball, and aging right fielder Hank Bauer, a vital cog in the Yankees' pennant seasons.

It was one of the last trades Arnold Johnson approved. The following March he left Connie Mack Stadium in West Palm Beach after an exhibition game and, while driving, died from a cerebral hemorrhage. He was fifty-three.

Maris was in a supermarket in Independence, Missouri, when a delivery-man told him that he had been traded to the Yankees. He scoffed because he was used to trade scuttlebutt. Later in the day, however, Pat called him to confirm the deal. She heard the news on the radio.

"I was shocked when he was traded to the Yankees," remembered Merle Harmon. "Dumbfounded. You can't trade a player like that. What we needed was a hero in Kansas City and he was the guy. If he had his druthers, he would have been happy in Kansas City even at a modest salary."

That Maris had escaped a seventh-place club and could start fresh elsewhere in 1960 should have been outstanding news for any young ballplayer. That he was going to the New York Yankees, sports' greatest franchise, was a huge bonus. But when Maris was asked about the trade, he said bluntly, "It doesn't thrill me, and it sure fouls things up. I just built a home and expected to spend a lot of time with my family. Now they've traded me about as far away as they could."

To another reporter he said, "Kansas City is my home now. I've got nothing against the Yankees, but I'm sorry to leave here. And I'll expect more money."

Maris's words didn't endear him to the members of the New York press. And when they were printed in their papers, the Yankee organization and its devout fans considered him an ingrate. How could anyone not want to come to New York City and be a New York Yankee?

CHAPTER FOURTEEN

THE NEW YANKEE

Y EARS AFTER IIE RETIRED as a ballplayer, Roger Maris admitted that he was less nervous about coming to New York City than fitting into a Yankee team of big-name stars wearing World Series rings. Although Norm Siebern was the key player the Yankees traded to the A's for him, Maris was apprehensive that his new teammates might resent his taking the right-field spot that had been the province of the popular team leader Hank Bauer. But his anxiety was unnecessary. While the New York Yankees organization had a corporate image, its players were strikingly sentimental and genial and immediately saw anybody who donned the pinstripes as family.

"When I came over with Roger and put on the uniform for the first time," remembers Joe De Maestri, "I looked around and Yogi Berra, Gil McDougald, Mickey Mantle, Whitey Ford, and Bill Skowron were dressing around me. They welcomed me and told me words I'll never forget: 'Joe, when you walk out on that field, you are screwing around with our money.' In those days on the Yankees, if you were dissatisfied with your contract, they'd tell you, 'Don't worry, you're going to pick up a World Series check in October.' "

The Yankee players knew they'd miss Bauer on a personal level, but they were excited by the prospect of a budding star helping them get the Series money that slipped through the huge holes in their bats in 1959. Especially with Berra on the downside of his career, Mantle needed a power-hitting cohort, and the moribund, third-place team needed an injection of youthful energy.

The day of the trade, the Yankees' third-string catcher, Johnny Blanchard, switched on his television at his home in Minnesota and found out that his former AAA opponent was going to be his teammate. "I turned to my wife," recalled Blanchard forty-eight years later, "and said, 'I'm getting a new car.' Nancy said, 'Are you kidding? We can't afford it.' I said, 'We can now. We got just what we needed and we're going to the World Series in October.' I knew what Roger could do. I had a battle with the wife, but in January I bought a brand-new Pontiac Ventura for about four grand. I paid for it in October."

"I thought Maris was the one guy we needed," said Whitey Ford, the ace of the pitching staff. "He was a complete player who could field, throw, and run."

"He played hard and played hurt and was one on the fastest guys in baseball," recalls Ralph Terry, his former Athletics teammate, who fulfilled his promise on his second tour in the Bronx. "Roger was a great player and I was glad he was coming to New York."

Unfortunately, the individual who negotiated Maris's first Yankee contract paid no heed to unsolicited testimonials. Sixty-five-year-old George Weiss, the Yankees' farm director from 1932 until he replaced Larry MacPhail as general manager in October 1947, was arguably the most successful executive in major league history. The Yankees had already collected 18 pennants and 15 Series titles during his tenure. The humorless, antisocial Yale graduate, whom Blanchard called Hog Jaws, didn't win any popularity contests with the players, who wanted him to spend less money on building the farm system and more on them. Even Mantle's salary was kept in check by periodic pay cuts or minimum raises, and Ford, Berra, and Skowron never received salaries commensurate to their star status.

"George Weiss was a cheap, aloof buffoon who we all hated for exploiting us," states Ryne Duren, the Yankees' relief ace, who'd received a contract on Christmas Eve with a 25 percent cut despite his 1.88 ERA.

"George Weiss wasn't very pleasant," states Arlene Howard, the widow of Elston Howard, the only black Weiss brought up. "But since there were no agents then, inexperienced ballplayers went alone to talk about salaries to the owners and general managers."

Maris expected more money to come play for the Yankees because he had to spend most of the year more than a thousand miles from his family. He requested $20,000 for 1960, a surprisingly modest $4,000 jump in salary. Weiss made a firm offer of $18,000, telling him, "I don't care what you did for Cleveland or Kansas City. It's what you do for the Yankees that counts."

Disappointed that he got the same raise he would have received with the less affluent A's, Maris told Weiss, "You'll pay plenty next year after I help you win a pennant." He was stating a fact, not making a threat.

Upon arriving at his first Yankee spring training, at Miller Huggins Field in St. Petersburg, Maris was greeted by members of the New York metropolitan-area press corps, who had a lot more interest in him in pinstripes than when he'd been a visiting player. "The beat writers realized from the start that this was a different sort of guy," remembered Jim Ogle, a scribe for the *Newark Star-Ledger*. They could tell he had no clue that for them to write a story, he would have to supply the quotes.

Some reporters revisited his comments about not wanting to leave Kansas City. Instead of backing off, Maris stated the truth: "I don't much like big cities." When asked how many homers he expected to hit in 1960, he gave another short reply: "20 to 25." Considering that Maris's highest home-run total to date was 28, his answer made sense. Still, it disappointed the reporters because his modesty and veracity were getting in the way of a good story, a common occurrence during Roger's years in New York.

When reporters watched Maris play in Grapefruit League games, they wondered if his cautious prediction had been too *high*. Roger got the playing time he always coveted in the spring, thirty games, but he hit only one ball over the fence. He didn't worry because he hit a solid .315 and his bat was quick enough to impress the press, his manager, and his teammates.

What did concern Maris was that while he was given the number 9 worn by Bauer, the previous right fielder, Stengel stationed him in left throughout spring training and kept praising him. Maris didn't make waves, but it was no secret that he didn't want to play the sun field at Yankee Stadium, which had been the ruin of Siebern and other left fielders since Gene Woodling in the early fifties. His uncharacteristic silence was due to his respect for Casey Stengel, whose teams had been accruing World Series checks since Roger was in high school. Because of what Weiss was paying him, money was an issue for the young husband and father.

Charles Dillon Stengel, who looked old when he was forty, was already sixty-nine when he became Roger Maris's manager. However, since he was baseball's most successful and prominent manager as television came into America's homes, baseball fans didn't think he looked silly in a baseball uniform but exactly how they pictured a great manager. He came across as the father figure young Yankees listened to and veteran stars needed to keep them in line. And he was the "Old Professor," who could impart his baseball wisdom on his twenty-five pupils. In truth, he had mixed results both disciplining veterans, since he drank late into the night himself, as well as teaching youngsters as he grew older and more impatient.

Stengel had spent twelve years in the majors playing for a handful of teams, during which time he clubbed exactly 60 home runs in the regular season, a total that Babe Ruth equaled in 1927 in 3,748 fewer at-bats. When his playing career ended, he was the manager of the talent-deprived Brooklyn Dodgers and Boston Bees and Braves between 1934 and 1943 without ever finishing higher than fifth place. He saved his reputation in the minors, guiding the Milwaukee Brewers to the AAA title and the Oakland Oaks to the Pacific Coast League crown.

Stengel and George Weiss had known each other in the Eastern League in the 1920s, and when Weiss was promoted to Yankees GM, he hired him to replace Bucky Harris as manager for the 1949 season. Dan Topping and Del Webb, who'd hired Stengel to manage Kansas City in 1945, approved of Weiss's choice.

This time Stengel had great players and led the Yankees to five consecutive world championships. After the Indians captured the American League flag in 1954, the Yankees won pennants in the next four years, and world championships in 1956 and 1958. The Yankees of 1959 had only 79 victories and finished third—which resulted only in pitching coach Jim Turner's being replaced by onetime Yankee junkball pitcher Ed Lopat—but Stengel's nine pennants in eleven years were still more than the Yankees' most heralded managers, Miller Huggins and Joe McCarthy, ever won.

Because of Stengel's unprecedented success, players were reluctant to complain about how he used them. So strong were his teams that some potential stars wasted away on the bench, others in the minors. "I'm not sure Casey ever knew who I was," claimed Blanchard. "I think he thought my name was Hey You." Other managers lauded Stengel for devising a formula that utilized an entire roster and still resulted in winning titles, but it's likely that his strongest motive was to help George Weiss win pennants while keeping salaries down. Because he platooned many of his players according to whether the opposing pitchers were right- or left-handed, since 1950 no hitters other than Mantle, just twice, and Berra (the most feared clutch hitter in baseball), four times, had driven in 100 runs. And because pitchers who might have started every fourth game elsewhere were held back until they could face an opponent they did well against, only two pitchers since 1952 had won 20 games—Bob Grim (20-6 as a rookie in 1954) and Bob Turley (21-8 in his 1958 Cy Young season). Without bigger numbers, no one could demand large salary increases. So the hungry ballplayers were intent on reaching the World Series to collect the money that should have been in their contracts.

Stengel controlled the media that flocked around him as much as he did his players. He told coach Ralph Houk his simple philosophy: "Never admit to the press that you're wrong." Especially when the cameras rolled or reporters tossed him softball questions, he delivered long-winded, stream-of-consciousness mini-speeches that amused one and all until they tried to put together a coherent piece later. He invented "Stengelese," the speed-talking language of someone who should be administered a Breathalyzer, and delighted in double-talking inquisitive people into confusion.

Until Maris came into his life, Stengel confounded players, not the other way around. But no player had been as unresponsive as Maris. Stengel carped to a reporter, "I ask Roger a question and I'll stand there and wait for an answer and he never gives it to me." Stengel couldn't communicate with Maris, but he loved how the new Yankee stood at the plate and unleashed a quick bat, channeling all his power into a short blur of a swing. He believed Maris would be a tremendous addition to a lineup that was in need of a left-handed pull hitter with power. With a sudden scarcity of topflight left-handed pitchers in the league, Stengel was excited that he'd have four excellent left-handed hitters in his batting order—Maris, the switch-hitting Mantle, Berra, and Kubek. He particularly liked the prospect of running out this formidable group at Yankee Stadium, with its short porch in right and the foul pole just 296 feet from home plate.

The Yankees finished the exhibition season with only 11 wins in 32 games, but when camp closed, Stengel was optimistic. He had heard whispers that Webb and Topping were thinking about replacing him when he turned seventy—and that they'd even made overtures to his friend Al Lopez of the White Sox, who rejected them—but he assumed that couldn't happen if the Bronx Bombers won their twenty-fifth pennant.

CHAPTER FIFTEEN

AN INSTANT STAR

THE SEASON OPENED FOR the Yankees in Boston on a chilly April 19, in front of 35,162 rabid fans at Fenway Park. There were two things on Stengel's lineup card that puzzled Maris. First, Stengel placed him at the top of the batting order. Even though Maris displayed little home-run power in the spring, it's unlikely Stengel thought of him as replacement for Bauer as an effective leadoff man. The move was only temporary. The sly manager just wanted his eager new player to break in as a leadoff hitter so he would be patient and not overswing. Equally peculiar was that after raving about Maris's play in left field the entire exhibition schedule, Stengel moved him back to his preferred position, right field. Surely he hadn't forgotten Mickey Mantle playing right field and wearing number 6 (an inverted 9) against Boston in his debut with the Yankees in 1951. And his career had turned out just fine.

Against right-handed Tom Brewer, Maris was followed in the batting order by second baseman Bobby Richardson, third baseman Gil McDougald, left fielder Hector Lopez, center fielder Mickey Mantle, first baseman Bill Skowron, catcher Elston Howard, shortstop Tony Kubek, and right-hander Jim Coates. "Whitey was left-handed so Stengel never pitched him in Fenway," remembers Bob Turley.

Playing in front of his hero Ted Williams, Maris had one of the greatest debuts in Yankees history, going 4 for 5 with 2 home runs and 4 RBIs. His second round-tripper, a 2-run shot in the fifth inning off Ted Bowsfield, was the game-breaker in an 8–4 victory, and he felt embarrassed when his teammates congratulated him in the dugout with such fervor.

Maris went 1 for 4 in the second game against a Sox team that had little chance of contending, knocking in the only run in a 7–1 loss. After that, Stengel moved him into the cleanup spot, where he'd remain for much of the season, usually following Mantle. Maris, in his third game, went 2 for 4 in a victory over Boston to up his average to .538, with 2 homers and 5 RBIs for his first series as a New York Yankee. The season was young but Roger already recognized two major benefits to playing for the Yankees rather than the A's: even when he was hot, pitchers didn't pitch around him; and every game had pennant implications so he would get many more meaningful at-bats, which was when he was at his best.

The most repeated Roger Maris fish-out-of-water story has to do with his arrival in New York City. It begins with Bob Cerv phoning his friend Julie Isaacson in Brooklyn and asking him to greet Maris's plane and help him get settled. Did that happen? "Hell, no," says Cerv, though he knew Julie well, having been introduced to him by his Yankee roommate Irv Noren in the early fifties. "Big Julie," who stood 6'3" and tipped the scales at well over 200 pounds, pitched in the Brooklyn Dodgers organization in the 1940s but was now the well-connected president of the International Doll, Toy & Novelty Workers Union; a fight manager (he'd guide Ernie Terrell to a heavyweight championship in 1965); a racing fan; and someone who enjoyed doing favors for athletes. This Runyon-like character had ties to the underworld, but since he wasn't involved with gambling, the Yankees couldn't shoo him away.

At the airport gate, Big Julie spotted a young man with a crewcut wearing a polo shirt, corduroy jeans, and white buckskin shoes. According to the 1987 book *Sixty-One* by Tony Kubek and Terry Pluto, as they exchanged a strong handshake, Isaacson told Roger, "Yankee ballplayers don't dress like that. These Pat Boone shoes, they've got to go. I don't think the Yankees are going to like this."

Maris gave him a hard stare and said, "The hell with them. If they don't like the way I look, they can send me back to Kansas City."

Isaacson checked Maris in at the Manhattan Hotel on West 43rd Street near Times Square. Then he went with Roger to a nearby Thom McAn shoestore, where the new Yankee purchased two more pairs of white bucks. The next day, Opening Day at Yankee Stadium, Isaacson picked up Maris to go to the ballpark and saw that he was wearing the same outfit with the addition of a Sears Roebuck seersucker jacket. "Red-ass" Roger had arrived in

New York, and his don't-mess-with-me philosophy had come with him. Soon Maris got endorsements from clothing companies that would supply him with expensive shirts and suits that he'd wear to banquets and award ceremonies, and he'd learn to be comfortable in such attire. But his defiant attitude never changed.

Maris was not new to Yankee Stadium—in fact, George Vecsey of the *New York Times* remembers fans chanting "Cha-Cha" to the visiting out-fielder "because of how he moved his feet in anticipation of defensive plays." However, Friday afternoon, April 22, was the first time he played Babe Ruth's position in pinstripes. Maris went hitless against Baltimore's supreme knuckleballer Hoyt Wilhelm. But the Yankees sent the 36,386 fans home happy with a 5–0 victory behind the pitching of Whitey Ford and Ralph Terry and home runs by Mickey Mantle and Hector Lopez. The Yankees defeated the Orioles again on Saturday, 3–2, with Maris delivering a first-inning single that drove in the their first run. He was banged up on a play at third and was replaced later in the game by outfielder Ken Hunt, his friend since they were kids in Grand Forks. He missed the rest of the homestand.

In the clubhouse, Roger lockered between Johnny Blanchard and Elston Howard and across the room from Mickey Mantle, Yogi Berra, and Bill Skowron. He was befuddled that reporters covering the Yankees gathered around him rather than proven players. Their biggest surprise was his physicality. Arthur Daley of the *Times* observed, "There is nothing small about Maris. He's a 197-pound six-footer who doesn't look it. His build is compact and symmetrical. In street clothes or baseball uniform he seems ordinary in size—or less. But when he's sitting in front of his locker in the Yankee Stadium clubhouse, a truer appreciation of his physique instantly hits the eye. His upper arms and shoulders are heavily muscled. In the vernacular of the trade, 'he strips big.' "

"Roger was in great physical shape," remembers Maury Allen, who was with *Sports Illustrated* before moving to the *New York Post*. "He had a thick back, like Sandy Koufax's, and his shoulders were big. Mantle had thin legs, Roger's were thick and muscular. I understood why people said he could have been a world-class football player. He was big, and when he hit you, he hurt you."

Maris quickly became friends with veteran clubhouse man Pete Sheehy, who found the uniforms that fit his football-player build. Sheehy came to regard Maris as his favorite Yankee. Agreeing with that assessment was Bronx-born teenager Fred Bengis, who was a Yankee batboy from 1960 to 1962. He recalls, "Roger and Bobby Richardson were the two nicest players I ever met. I'd sit in front of Roger's locker in the mornings and give him a piece of devil's food cake, and we'd talk about baseball and everything else for the half hour he dressed for batting practice. He was just a super guy, a bright guy, and a great teammate who cheered the other players and always gave 100 percent because he wouldn't risk letting them down. Once he put his uniform on, everything was baseball."

Roger missed three games but closed out the month just as he began it, with a 4-RBI game on Jim Coates's behalf. His 3-run first-inning homer off the Orioles' Milt Pappas propelled the team to 16–0 victory and into first place, ½ game ahead of the idle Tigers and defending champion White Sox. After 14 games, Roger's average was a robust .476, to go along with 4 homers and 16 runs batted in, one behind team leader Bill Skowron in both departments. "For the first few games I'd hear guys yelling for Bauer," Maris told a reporter, "but not much anymore."

The Yankees got Maris because of Yankee Stadium, and a decades-long misconception was that he suddenly became such a good hitter because he was dropped into a ballpark with dimensions that gave pull hitters an unfair advantage. What Maris was proving in early 1960 was that he was dangerous in *all* ballparks. He had developed into an excellent hitter *before* he came to New York, but his lengthy stat-eating slumps had obscured that. He was even better in 1960 because of a natural progression rather than a change of venue.

"I saw improvement since his rookie year," states Billy Pierce, then an All-Star left-hander for the White Sox who had trouble with Maris. "He no longer went after bad outside pitches, and he now could handle pitches on the inner part of the plate exceedingly well. The reason he could hit left-handers is that he never bailed out. He didn't have any fear."

A's lefty Bud Daley faced his former teammate in early May: "I said, 'I'm going to knock him right on his butt.' And I knocked him down good. And the very next pitch, he hit a line shot right through the middle and knocked me down good. I looked over and we grinned at each other." Roger was a pull hitter, but as Stengel advised, he sometimes went up the middle against tough left-handers.

"Give Roger credit for being a great pull hitter," says Jim Landis, an exceptional center fielder for the AL champion White Sox. "It takes talent to be that. He stood away from the plate but strode into the ball, so he could pull anyone."

Maris was treated well by his teammates in spring training, but not until the regular season was under way and he was producing did he feel comfortable with the players who hadn't been his teammates in Kansas City. "Roger was a bit shy when he joined us," recalls Berra, "but then he fit right in. Everyone liked Roger."

"He had the reputation for being surly and problematic, but the press made it up," says Duren. "He needed a comfort zone and we gave it to him. Around strangers he was quiet, but he felt comfortable around us. There were no cliques. If Roger didn't want to drink, he could go out with Tony Kubek, Bobby Richardson, and Bobby Shantz. If he did, he could go out with Mantle and Ford."

According to Ford, he, Mantle, and Hunt gave Maris a Yankees' baptism-by-firewater after the team returned from Baltimore. They took Roger to Toots Shor's, the famous restaurant at 51 West 51st where athletes and other celebrities gathered each night. "We wanted to break Roger in," Ford told Maury Allen in 1985. They drank double scotches, and Maris "kept up for a while, but he wasn't like me and Mickey. He slowed down around midnight." When the bar closed at 3 a.m., the gang moved over to Shor's Park Avenue apartment, and the drinking resumed. At 8 a.m., the group piled into a cab for a scheduled workout at Yankee Stadium.

Roger was more likely to pal around with Hunt, Duren, and Clete Boyer than high-salaried players such as Mantle and Ford. Besides, he knew they were too wild for him. Roger occasionally drank something stronger than beer, but he wasn't among the "seventy percent of us who abused alcohol," states Duren. And he was not a carouser. Most nights in New York, Maris stayed in his hotel room or had a quiet dinner with Julie Isaacson, often at Lindy's or Isaacson's house with his family. Outside of teammates, Big Julie became Maris's closest friend in New York, although Maris was a Catholic from North Dakota, Isaacson was a Jew from Brooklyn, and Maris preferred anonymity, while Isaacson enjoyed being the center of attention.

Maris had superb starts in both 1957 and 1959, but nobody paid much attention. But now that he was on the most famous team in sports, he was "the next big thing." Articles were written about the Yankees' new sensation everywhere the team traveled, and since the Yankees boosted national TV ratings, he was frequently seen playing ball on television from coast to coast, including in small towns such as Fargo, North Dakota. "Roger became the town's lifeline to the big time," recalls Fargo native Bobby Vee, who by 1960 was churning out gold records. "When he became a Yankee, some of that dust landed on us and we were rocking in Fargo!"

"Every Saturday I'd go up to Connie and Rudy Sr.'s apartment to watch baseball," recalls Don Gooselaw. "They were just starting it with Pee Wee Reese and Dizzy Dean, and she'd make spaghetti or chili for the old man and show me the scrapbook she started when Roger and Buddy were in high school."

In late May, the Yankees had a Saturday-afternoon game on NBC against the White Sox in Chicago. Roger's brother-in-law Walt Seeba recalls:

Mary Jo and I were in Raytown visiting Pat and their kids, expecting Roger to come in that night before the Yankees began a series against the A's on Sunday. I had the television on but the weather was bad and they said it was unlikely the game would be played. So I turned it off. That night Pat, Mary Jo, and I picked up Roger at the airport. Then we got coffee in downtown Kansas City. While we were talking, some guy came up and said, "Hi, Roger! Great game today!" And I asked Roger, "What great game? You guys didn't play." "Oh, we played," he said. "We got started an hour and a half late." Then the guy mentioned that Roger hit a couple of home runs. Roger had come off the plane straight-faced. He wasn't even going to bring that up. Talk about humility.

In *Slugger in Right*, Maris's stand-in Billy Mack laments, "Dawn, for the moment, was running second to baseball. Unfortunately, that was to be the story of her life." Maris's priority in life was always Pat and their kids, but the peripatetic nature of his business meant that other than when the Yankees played in Kansas City, Pat didn't see much of her husband during the season. "When I get wistful about anything," wrote Pat Maris in a 1962 *Look* magazine article titled "My Husband," "it's that our children don't have their dad around more."

"Perhaps I'll bring them east next year," the lonely Yankee told Walter

Bingham of *Sports Illustrated.* "Unless my wife is pregnant again next year, which she probably will be."

Maris was pleased when the Yankees, in need of a strong right-handed hitter to come off the bench, acquired Bob Cerv from the A's on May 19. Now he had someone to commiserate with about missing family back in Raytown. "We both missed our families in Kansas City," recalls Cerv. "When one of our wives was pregnant like Pat was, we'd get nervous, especially when it got close to the due date."

The two initially lived together in a roomy apartment at the Manhattan Hotel that didn't have much appeal for the older Cerv. "It was like a dorm situation," he recalls. "We had frigging cots for sleeping and there were guys everywhere. I wasn't sure who lived there and who was just visiting."

Eli Grba pitched for the Yankees in 1959 but was sent down on Opening Day. When the witty, bespectacled pitching prospect was recalled from Richmond, he was invited to move in with Maris and Cerv. He remembers:

Cerv was like Roger's surrogate mother. They always compared notes on how many kids they were going to have. Cerv had about ten. We'd play a lot of cards, pinochle or maybe hearts. Cerv used to agitate the shit out of Roger, but Roger didn't care. I liked my broads and liquor, so I went out by myself and tried to hustle rather than hang around with my married roommates. I found out New York was a lonely town, but when I was with Maris and Cerv, it was beautiful.

Both of them were frugal and went where they could get a meal for nothing. Sometimes, we'd go after a day game to Danny's Hideaway and get free steaks if we'd sign autographs. Every day we'd go for breakfast to the Stage Deli and pee our pants laughing at Jack E. Leonard, the insult comic, who had an apartment upstairs. He was a great guy and nuts! Roger had a little devil behind that smile and a good sense of humor and took all his zingers. Every morning the four of us would sit together and they'd give us a free breakfast.

Maris's favorite breakfast was eggs with baloney, which made him an easy target for Leonard, "the Mouse That Roared." Maris was a bit more sophisticated at dinner now that he had a big leaguer's salary. Steaks had replaced hamburgers, and when he was in Boston or Baltimore, he devoured seafood.

"Roger could really eat," marveled Moose Skowron, who got his nickname not because he looked like the animal or Archie Andrews's friend but because his grandfather thought he resembled Benito Mussolini. "We both wore crewcuts and were bashful guys, so we'd go out together and eat. It was nothing for him to put away the bushel of crabs they'd bring us in the clubhouse in Baltimore. And then we'd go out and have a big steak."

Maris's average dipped to .322 by the end of May, but his 11 homers and 30 RBIs led the league. Mantle had skidded to .244, so the players and fans were grateful that Roger was hitting. They also appreciated that he wasn't a one-dimensional player, but someone who could play defense and run the bases. "Before he was traded to the Yankees, he was the guy who made me change the way I turned the double play," said Richardson, who finally got to play every day at second base. "When he was on first, he'd knock me into left field. He'd do a come-up slide and there was no way to avoid him."

"If I came up with a runner on third and Roger was on first," said Skowron, "I knew I'd get an RBI if I just hit the ball on the ground. No way there would be a double play. Roger always took the fielder out at second base and the run scored."

"The press hadn't written how good he was," claims Duren. "Roger Maris was the best all-around player I ever played with, even better than Mantle. I'm not saying he was a greater talent, but he was more consistent and probably as good as any player I ever saw because he did everything right."

"We were sad when Hank Bauer was traded," recalls Bob Turley, "but, oh, God, we were happy to get someone with Roger's talent. He was a great outfielder who played in close and went back on a ball better than anyone I ever saw. He had a great arm and he was almost as quick as Mickey going to first and could run the bases faster than anyone. He could do it all, not just hit."

Probably the most appreciative of Maris's all-around play was his manager. "From the beginning," remembers George Vecsey, "Stengel raved about all the things that Maris could do instinctively, like make the correct throws, and how good he was on the hit-and-run, whether he was the runner or the hitter. Casey loved how Maris never made a mistake."

According to Maury Allen, "Casey liked Roger so much because he had a great sense of the game. Maybe it was reflex, maybe genetics, maybe instinct, but Roger had it. Mickey didn't. Mickey had tremendous physical gifts, but all he thought about was looking for a ball to drive five hundred feet. He had little sense of the game."

In the early part of 1960, Mickey's physical gifts abandoned him. Not completely recovered from various injuries, including a bad shoulder and knee, he was scoring runs but his average and power numbers were low. Even with Maris hitting, the Yankees were as many as 6 games out of first in early June. This was during a brief period in which Ralph Houk took the managerial reins while Stengel was recuperating in the hospital from a virus and, it was whispered, chest pains.

After Maris and Mantle each took Boston's Tom Brewer deep on June 5 to help improve the Yankees' record to 21-20, Maris's average stood at .333 with 14 homers and 36 RBIs, while Mantle was batting .237, nearly 100 points less, with only 8 homers and 17 RBIs. With Berra the only other Yankee hitting above .300, Maris was clearly the reason the club remained in contention.

If there was a time for Mantle to have resented Maris's presence on his team, this was it. If it had been in his nature, he could have poisoned the water by turning his teammates against the new man. But by the 1960 season he was secure in his position on the team and never felt jealous of anyone who wore the same uniform.

"There was only one Mickey Mantle," says Terry. "He was just in another league from anybody else. And he was the greatest guy that ever lived. He didn't act like a big star, and the young guys felt comfortable coming up to him. He was all for Roger."

"Mickey was great to Roger and me," says De Maestri. "He never acted like a star—he was more like a class clown."

Above all else, Mantle wanted the Yankees to win and was thankful to Roger for hitting for two while he wasn't producing. He'd never had a teammate so capable of hitting home runs and regarded Roger as a partner rather than a rival. There were clear reasons why he felt a strong kinship to the newcomer, though their paths to the Yankees were very different. Mantle and Maris, three years apart in age, were both born in mid-American mining towns, in Mantle's case Spavinaw, Oklahoma, and raised in similar surroundings during the Depression. Both had hardworking fathers with whom they closely identified, Rudy Sr. and Mutt Mantle, a miner who died at only thirty-nine of the same hereditary disease, Hodgkin's lymphoma, Mantle expected would kill him before he reached forty. Both were natural athletes with strength and speed, who were celebrated in their hometowns. Both got homesick and had to be talked out of quitting early in their careers. Both idolized Ted Williams and were influenced early on by Harry Craft. Both met their wives, Merlyn and Pat, while teenagers and started big families when young.

Both were country boys who were unprepared for the fast pace and bright lights of New York City. Stengel's nickname for Mantle was Ignatz, as in a bumpkin or rube. Mantle could relate to Roger's not being a fashion plate when he joined the Yankees. When Mantle arrived, he carried a straw suitcase and two pairs of slacks, a cheap blue sports jacket, and argyle socks. "Hank Bauer was told to care for him," recalled Blanchard in 2008, "and Mick told me, 'Jeez, he threw my new argyle socks away. I almost died.' "

In Mantle's early years with the Yankees, wrote Dick Schaap, "his conversation consisted almost entirely of 'Yes' and 'No,' and a string of curse words reserved for use upon himself whenever he struck out. It wasn't that he had difficulty communicating. He simply didn't communicate."

Mantle recalled the cold reception given him by Joe DiMaggio, who resented the youngster taking his place on center stage. In a 1960 issue of *Sports Illustrated*, Tom Meany wrote, "Mantle used to actually squirm when photographers asked him to pose with Joe DiMaggio, feeling as if it was a pushy, cocky act on his part." Mantle didn't worry about Maris replacing him and welcomed him to the team. Maris never forgot that graciousness.

Mantle related to Maris's humility. His own came from feeling he was never as good as he was supposed to be. When Stengel first saw Mantle, he went overboard in assessing his talents, saying, "I never saw a player who had greater promise" and "with his combination of speed and power he should win the Triple Crown every year." Mantle felt that he disappointed Stengel and the fans, who booed him for striking out and never being mistake-free like DiMaggio. For years at the plate, his crutch was Bob Turley's tipping pitches to him with unfailing accuracy, by whistling. He homered and received cheers, he whiffed and it was jeers.

Mantle admired Maris for never being visibly upset when he struck out. Mantle treated every failure at the plate as Armageddon. "When Mantle struck out," said his former teammate Tom Sturdivant in 2008, "his neck became red and he'd kick over the watercooler and throw some bats, and I wouldn't have fought him with a shotgun."

"Roger recognized that you couldn't hit a homer every time up, but Mickey didn't," says Maury Allen. "Mickey was a classic bipolar, if you get into psychiatry. He had the very high highs and the very low lows. Roger's highs and lows were pretty close. He never expressed depression at going badly, whereas with Mickey it was obvious."

Finally, Mantle related to Maris playing despite physical ailments. Mantle did that his entire career. His legs had been in pain since he was a youth because he suffered from a bone disease, osteomyelitis. Then, in the '51 World Series, he caught his foot in a drain and wrecked his knee. By 1960, both knees were in terrible shape and needed to be wrapped. Sometimes he could barely stand, yet he played with intensity every day and appreciated Maris for doing the same.

Maris and Mantle were different in as many ways as they were similar, but rather than clashing, they complemented each other. When they hit at the same time, they were baseball's most dynamic twosome. That's what happened when Mantle finally caught fire in June, about the time Stengel returned to the dugout with the vow not to drink for the rest of the year. The Yankees steamrolled to seven straight victories over the White Sox, Indians, and A's as Mantle (who missed two games with a slight injury) went 7 for 16 with 4 homers and 8 RBIs and Maris went 9 for 28 with 4 homers and 8 RBIs. The Yankees were back in second place, only ½ game back, and seemed primed to make their move.

Stengel had for the most part settled on a rotation of Whitey Ford, Art Ditmar, Bob Turley, the emerging Ralph Terry, and Jim Coates, who was 7-0. Youngsters Eli Grba, John Gabler, and Bill Short got spot starts in Sunday doubleheaders. Most of the starters also took turns in the bullpen to support Duren, Shantz, Duke Maas, and Johnny James. Stengel tweaked his lineup by alternating Kubek and Richardson in the leadoff spot and inserting former Athletic Clete Boyer at third in place of McDougald. With Boyer, one of thirteen siblings of St. Louis's star third baseman Ken Boyer, the Yankees had more pop and exceptional infield defense.

Baltimore manager Paul Richards hadn't forgotten his failed attempt to obtain Maris in 1956 from Hank Greenberg. He stated, "Without Maris, the Yankees would be just where they were last year." That would have been ideal for him because his Orioles sat perilously atop the American League standings. His "Kiddie Korps" of starters all under twenty-three years old—Milt Pappas, Steve Barber, rookie Chuck Estrada, and Jack Fisher—were all having such terrific seasons that Wilhelm was now a reliever. They were led by power-hitting shortstop Ron Hansen, who would be the American League Rookie of the Year; twenty-three-year-old Brooks Robinson, a wizard at third; and pull-hitting first baseman Jim Gentile, who was realizing his potential after being buried in the Dodgers organization for eight years because of Gil Hodges. The question was whether this untested squad could hold up against veteran teams down the stretch.

The Yankees put on the pressure by winning thirteen out of fourteen games and moving into first place on June 22. Maris was now batting .340 with 20 homers and 52 RBIs, Berra and Skowron were over .300, and Mantle was up to .281 with 16 homers and 34 RBIs. Although the Yankees didn't increase their lead, they finished the month with a 21-10 record to stand at 40-25. For June, Maris had 14 homers, Mantle 12. Writers began making Ruth-Gehrig comparisons and referred to them as the "buzz-saw team." One striking article title was "Double M for Murder." Mel Allen, the Voice of the Yankees, called them "the gold dust twins" and "the magic marvels."

Roger had adjusted well to his team but was still having trouble feeling at home in New York. Bob Cerv felt the same so they asked Julie Isaacson to find them an apartment in Queens. "It was in a building out by the airport," recalls Cerv, "and we split the rent. We also lived there in 1961 and 1962."

At the All-Star break, the Yankees were 45-35 and up by 2½ games on Cleveland, 3 on Chicago, and 4 on the slipping Orioles. They would have been farther ahead but stumbled into the break, losing their last three games. Coates even suffered a defeat on July 9 to Boston, after going 9-0 to begin 1960 and winning his last five decisions in 1959. The slender Virginian, whose nickname was the Mummy because he slept with his eyes open—Edna Stengel once told her husband on the bus, "Dear, I think one of your players is dead"—was heading to the All-Star Game.

Maris was the top vote-getter on the American League's team, which was chosen by players, managers, and coaches. He was pleased with the locations of the All-Star Games. The first was played on July 11 at Municipal Stadium in Kansas City in front of his family, friends, devoted fans, and the red-faced A's front office, which had foolishly traded him. The National League prevailed 5–3. The second game, two days later, was in Yankee Stadium, and manager Al Lopez batted him third in front of Mantle, Skowron, and Berra. The American League lost again, 6–0, as Vern Law bested Whitey Ford, and Willie Mays homered in his return to New York. Maris went hitless in the losses, but perhaps his biggest regret was that Ted Williams, who had a pinch single, didn't play the outfield with him and Mantle in his final All-Star appearance.

Afterward it was back to the daily grind of trying to win a pennant. The Yankees began unimpressively, losing three of four to the Tigers, who were led by Rocky Colavito and Al Kaline. In the second game of a doubleheader at Briggs Stadium, the Yankees were trailing 2–1 in the top of the eighth inning when Bill Skowron hit a liner into the right-field seats that first-base umpire Joe Paparella called fair for a homer. In the bottom of the inning the right-field fans went berserk, hurling debris onto the field, most toward Maris. He was almost struck in the head by the jagged wooden arm of a seat, an incident often wrongly placed in 1961.

"Why did they throw that stuff at me?" asked the furious Maris after the game. "They were angry at Paparella. Why didn't they throw the stuff at him? . . . idiots . . . morons. Why should I take my life in my hands because an umpire's decision gets the fans all steamed up?" Maris's comments were in the next day's newspapers. His relationship with the Detroit fans never recovered in his Yankee years.

The White Sox arrived at Yankee Stadium and won three straight over Turley, Ford, and Coates to take over first place. Chicago won the first game of the Sunday twinbill, 6–2, before 60,002 spectators, Yankee Stadium's largest crowd of the season. The Yankees needed to win the second game to stop the bleeding.

Stengel started Eli Grba against Herb Score, who had been traded to the Sox by Indians GM Frank Lane at the beginning of the season—immediately after Colavito was dealt to Detroit. Roger's friend hadn't regained his form since being struck in the eye against the Yankees in 1957. In the second inning, the Yankees were down by a run with Chicago's Al Smith on first base when Gene Freese drilled a liner to deep right-center. Maris galloped over and, with his back to the plate, reached high and gloved the ball, almost crashing into the auxiliary scoreboard and the railing of the Yankee bullpen.

Thanks to Maris, a rally never materialized. Grba settled down and pitched a complete game, while Score faltered. The Yankees prevailed 8–2. Maris made several astonishing catches during the season, including one in Cleveland when he leaped into the six-foot Cyclone fence to rob Tito Francona of a grand slam. "That was the greatest catch I ever saw," states Ryne Duren forty-eight years later. But none was more important than the one he made on Freese because the Yankees left town trailing the Pale Hose by only 1 game rather than 3.

"There is always a game you could look back on, maybe even one play, and say to yourself, 'This is the one,' " Ford said. "We could have been out of it if Roger hadn't caught the ball Freese hit."

Ditmar shut out the A's in the final game of July, as the Yankees ended the month 52-39, 1½ games behind Chicago.

The day before, Stengel turned seventy. He was in the second year of a two-year contract. Though it had not been enforced in his case, Webb and Topping had previously announced that sixty-five was retirement age in the organization. Stengel feared that if the Yankees did not replace the White Sox as league champions, the owners would implement their age policy. Stengel hoped that an outcry by fans and the members of the press would keep them from doing anything so drastic.

But it could have been a false hope because the press was not as kind to Stengel as in the past. "There were two kinds of reporters then," says Maury Allen. "I was one of those who loved Casey and was fascinated by his humor and baseball knowledge. But there were others who thought he was an old fool and had enough of him."

Stengel was losing some of his players, too. "The single most significant change in the Yankees that year was in Stengel himself," wrote Mickey Mantle in *All My Octobers*. "I think age and the pressure—not just to win, but to finish first every year—were catching up to him. He had gotten more cantankerous. He was drinking more. . . . But the big change was in how he dealt with the younger players."

"Casey could demoralize a young player," Richardson remembered. "Quite often he would pinch-hit for you in the first inning. Those things would make you mad." The young second baseman hadn't forgotten how Stengel once evaluated him to reporters: "He doesn't drink, he doesn't smoke, he doesn't stay out late at night, but he still can't hit."

Maris might have heard the rumors about Stengel fighting for his job and wondered if he was a jinx for managers. None he'd played for in his seven years of professional baseball had returned to the team the next year. If Stengel was to be let go, then in Maris's four years in the majors, all four of his Opening Day managers were unemployed by Christmas.

CHAPTER SIXTEEN

A PENNANT

ROGER MARIS WAS THE biggest story in baseball. It wasn't only the sports magazines that were covering him. *Time* did a piece on the new Yankee slugger. Even the high-brow *New Yorker* printed a long profile of Maris, its first baseball article in six years. The writer described him as being "roughly as garrulous as Calvin Coolidge." While "chewing industriously on a wad of tobacco," Roger talked about signing with the Indians, riding the buses in the minor leagues, and having his '59 season marred by the appendectomy. He spoke innocuously about his family, how "the crowds have been great to me here in New York," and spending his off-seasons hunting and bowling, though the last winter he worked two months as a salesman for Armour & Co.

When asked about his chances of breaking Babe Ruth's single-season home-run record, he said modestly, "Nobody's ever going to break that record. Not me or anybody else." He was at his most boastful when he said, "I must admit I'm going pretty good this year." The reporter did him one better, stating, "The difference between this year and last year [on the Yankees], everyone seems to agree, is an outfielder named Roger Maris." Maris paid the article his highest compliment: "It didn't get too many things wrong."

As much as he hated attention, Maris told the *New Yorker* that he was pleased to get his first endorsements through Frank Scott, a onetime Yankees traveling secretary who in the fifties became baseball's first agent. While Scott wasn't permitted to negotiate salaries, he got his Yankee clients—and eventually almost all major leaguers—fair compensation for endorsements and appearances (including on pre- and postgame shows). Scott discovered that Maris was as much in demand as Mantle and Berra, who promoted the

chocolate-flavored soft drink Yoo-Hoo. Scott landed Roger his first television commercial, for Camels, which he smoked incessantly. (According to
Bob Wood, "Roger smoked only a little in high school," but eventually
"chain-smoked unfiltered cigarettes.") Soon Scott was making deals for
shaving-cream and razor-blade commercials as well. "They pay a lot of
money and it takes no time at all," said Maris, beaming.

The *New Yorker* article hit the newsstands when Roger was mired in his
worst slump of the year, resulting in his average dropping below .300 for the
first time. "Roger had a better swing than Mantle," says Turley, "so it was
surprising he'd have such bad slumps. It would look like he never played
baseball before, and then suddenly he'd break out of it."

Maris broke out of his hitting funk in Kansas City. Spending time with
his very pregnant wife and two kids, eating home cooking, and sleeping in
his own bed did wonders. In the first game of the series, he hit a 2-run
homer, and in the second game he went 3 for 4 with his 34th and 35th
homers and a season-high 6 RBIs. After the first week of August 1960,
Maris, who is still often called a "one-year wonder," was ahead of Babe Ruth's
1927 home-run pace.

Whenever Maris was asked if he had a shot at hitting 61 homers, he
could rehearse what he'd say early in 1961: "I'm not interested in breaking
Babe Ruth's record. I'm only interested in having a good year for myself and
seeing the Yankees win the pennant." He wasn't pressured into giving a different answer. Maris always regarded 1960 as his favorite year in New York
because he had a civil relationship with the press. Leonard Shecter's story
about the Houk-Duren train scuffle in 1958 had changed the rules for
sportswriters, but even the most powerful still followed the example of
Grantland Rice and built up celebrities. Not until 1961 would a gang of irreverent reporters take over the scene and not mind knocking star players off
their pedestals.

Maris's replies were not always interesting and were spoken in a dry
monotone, but after years of receiving stock answers from Yankee players,
the press was impressed by his candor. "Maris may not be one of the most
articulate of modern ballplayers," wrote Tom Meany in *Sport* magazine about
"The Man Who Shook Up the Yankees," but "he . . . doesn't play games
with interviewers, not because frankness is his long suit, but because he can't
be bothered being evasive."

"As a young reporter," recalls George Vecsey, "I was warned that Mantle could bite your head off if it was the wrong question or wrong time of day or he was hung over. I love Yogi now, but his typical reply to our questions then was 'How do you expect me to know?' Now here came Maris, who was more even-tempered than Mantle and talkative than Berra. He was salty, sarcastic, sardonic, and self-deprecating. He hadn't yet divided the world into the people who were for and against him and didn't give you smart-ass remarks. He was just being himself."

"Mantle would look through you with a steely glare as his way of trying not to deal with questions," recalls Stan Isaacs, who was with *Newsday*. "But I liked Maris. He was outspoken in a grumpy way, like a guy in the army who complained and said things you wished you could say."

Maris was willing to talk about baseball, but not family. Indeed, he was taken aback when anyone expected him to reveal anything personal. Sherry Hunt, who married Ken Hunt after his playing career, explains, "People in North Dakota tend to their own business, and what happens in the family stays in the family. Roger was very private, and it would have been devastating to him if there had been unflattering things written about his parents and family in newspapers across the country."

Stengel enjoyed jousting with reporters, so at times he stepped into their paths before they could reach Maris's and Mantle's lockers. He may have been trying to protect them, or he may have wanted the attention for himself. In either case, his verbal pyrotechnics took pressure off Maris, although for the most part Roger didn't feel the need to avoid the press in 1960.

In the Kansas City series, Maris's average shot back over .300, and though a weeklong homer drought followed, his timing was back. That he had stayed hot for so long was really impressive considering he didn't get much sleep on long train trips. Most nights he sat up talking baseball with team statistician Pete Kalison, another Pullman insomniac. Apparently Maris could perform well without rest, but an injury was a different matter. Against Washington on August 12, he tried to break up a double play by bowling over second baseman Billy Gardner. As had happened on a similar play in 1957, he wound up on the disabled list with badly bruised ribs. Maris had only a remote shot at catching Ruth, who hit 17 homers in September, but if the injury bug didn't bite him again, resulting in missed games and a subsequent slump, he was on track for 50 homers, 125 RBIs, and a .300 average.

Particularly galling about Maris's being hurt while hustling was that Mantle hit the grounder and didn't run hard, allowing the double play to happen anyway. Mantle waited near first for someone to bring him his mitt; instead the outraged Stengel sent out Cerv to replace him. The boobirds were back at Yankee Stadium as the home team lost the game in fifteen innings and dropped to third behind Chicago and Baltimore. A guilt-ridden Mantle hit a pair of 2-run homers in the next game to supply Ditmar with exactly enough support for a 4–3 win against Baltimore. After the second homer, Mantle tipped his cap to the cheering fans. The determined Mantle went on a hitting spree, leading his team to 13 wins in 17 games and back into first place. Fans with short memories began to think of him rather than Maris as the team's top MVP candidate.

The Yankees went 22-11 in August, despite Maris going down and Ford battling the tendonitis that limited him to only 12 victories in 1960. The pitching staff improved substantially with the call-up of right-handed starter Bill Stafford and Weiss's acquisition of the Reds' veteran lefty reliever Luis Arroyo, who had reinvented himself as a screwball pitcher. Stafford won 3 of 4 decisions and posted a 2.25 ERA in eleven appearances. Arroyo, a stocky Puerto Rican whom Stengel called Yo-Yo, replaced the struggling Duren as the closer and won 5 of 6 decisions while saving 7 games. "Who'd ever think a guy like that would be lying around dead somewhere?" Stengel wondered aloud.

Baltimore also won 22 games in August so the Yankees' lead remained at just 1 game. The White Sox, now 4 games back, wouldn't be a factor. Shockingly, the "Baby Birds" swept the visiting Yankees in a three-game series, 5–0, 2–0, and 6–2, behind Pappas, Fisher, and Estrada, to move into first place in early September. None of the Yankees were hitting, and that wouldn't really change. When they won, it was because they got clutch hits, mostly by Mantle, and outstanding pitching.

Now the father of three—Pat had given birth to their second son, Kevin—Roger returned to the lineup on August 31. He'd spent 17 games on the shelf, and his timing was off and his power nonexistent. His frustration built as his average fell well below .300 and he hit only 4 homers for the rest of the season. Mantle replaced him in the cleanup spot.

In September, Mantle didn't get many hits, but most came at crucial moments, especially his 10 home runs. In Detroit, he hit a ball that cleared the right-field roof and wound up in a lumberyard. The *Guinness Book of Sports Records* credited him with a record 643-foot shot, far longer than his more famous 565-foot blast out of Washington's Griffith Stadium in 1953.

Despite playing only .500 ball in early September, the Yankees moved back into a first-place tie with the Orioles. A fight to the finish was anticipated, but the Yankees smelled the money and left Baltimore in the dust by sweeping a four-game series at Yankee Stadium. In the decisive finale, Terry's 2–0 shutout put the Yankees up by 4 games. "That virtually ended our 1960 hopes," says Brooks Robinson.

As Stengel used numerous lineups and juggled pitchers, the Yankees won their final 15 games, including 3 in extra innings. On October 1, they defeated Boston, 3–1. Exactly one year before their historic confrontation, Sox reliever Tracy Stallard fanned Maris the first time they ever faced each other.

Having clinched the pennant on September 25, the Yankees wound up with 97 victories, 8 more than Baltimore. Stengel equaled John McGraw's record of managing 10 pennant-winning teams. The club broke its own American League record with 193 home runs, 79 of them by Mantle and Maris. Mantle hit his 39th and 40th homers on September 28 off Washington's Chuck Stobbs, the victim of his storied 565-foot blast, to pass Maris and snatch his third and final home-run crown.

On that same day at Fenway Park, their idol, Ted Williams, clouted his 521st homer onto the roof of Boston's bullpen in the final at-bat of his illustrious career. It was hit into the teeth of a strong wind off the Orioles' Jack Fisher. Replaced by Carroll Hardy, Williams left the outfield for the last time, refusing to acknowledge the cheering fans he'd battled with for years with a smile, tipped cap, or curtain call. "Ted had the courage of his convictions right to the end of his playing days," Maris told the *Christian Science Monitor*'s Ed Rumill in 1968. "I admire that."

Setting the stage for 1961, the Yankee fans and reporters had taken sides during the late-season race between Maris and Mantle. After years of being booed, Mantle was cheered, and the outsider heard the catcalls. Maris was confused and uncomfortable being treated like the enemy in his home park while engaging in a healthy competition. Disappointed to have lost the home-run title so late in the season, he aspired to engage in another duel in 1961. Years later Maris confided to his Cardinals teammate Mike Shannon, "I figured I was going to hit more homers than Mickey. It was nothing against Mickey. It was the damn writers and the fans booing. I just got sick of it, and I wanted to shut everyone up."

CHAPTER SEVENTEEN

THE MVP

IT WAS HARD TO dampen Roger's spirits as he played in his first World Series, but his parents managed it. They attended the games with Rudy Jr., Connie looking elegant in a fur coat, and the gents looking refined in suits and ties. Photos were taken of them talking over a railing to Roger, who was in uniform. This was probably the last time the family posed together. Roger was told the big news: on July 27, Connie had filed for divorce from Rudy after twenty-eight years of marriage. Their divorce would be finalized on October 24, 1960, with the stipulation that Rudy pay Connie $115 a month (and keep her on the railroad's health plan and as the beneficiary on three $1,000 insurance policies). Roger, a devoted son who still obeyed when Rudy told him to get a haircut, kept quiet about his reaction to his parents' separation.

The 1960 Series was a rematch of the 1927 Series when the Murderers' Row Yankees swept the Pirates, two years after they had been world champions. Pittsburgh hadn't played for the title since then. Most pundits believed the '60 Yankees could sweep, too, but New York's dominance was highly exaggerated.

Surely the Yankees had a stronger offense, but the Pirates did have National League batting champion Dick Groat, soon to be selected the league's MVP; Bill Mazeroski, the majors' best defensive second baseman; and awesome right fielder Roberto Clemente, who was coming into his own. Plus they had strong pitching, led by Vern "Deacon" Law, a lock to capture the Cy Young Award after winning 20 games; and Bob Friend, who had 18 victories. They also had a unique closer, Elroy Face, a forkball artist who had gone an incredible 18-1 in relief in 1959 and won 10 games and saved 24 others in 1960.

"To me the Yankees were just like any other hitters," says Face. "I'd pitched against Stan Musial, Willie Mays, and Hank Aaron. I wasn't intimidated."

Pirates manager Danny Murtaugh told his team that they'd win the close games, as they'd done all season, and if the Yankees' bats exploded, they'd take their lumps and move on to the next game. The Pirates got to see the Yankees' power in the first inning of Game 1, courtesy of Maris, batting third. The press had questioned in bold headlines whether Roger could handle the pressure of playing in a World Series. His answer was a homer off Vern Law in his first Series at-bat. Law recalls:

> That winter Ted Williams asked me, "How did you want to pitch to Roger?" I said, "Inside." And he said, "What? You're crazy, man!" And I said, "Ted, I mean six inches inside *off* the plate." That way if he did hit the ball, he'd pull it foul. So the first time I faced him, I threw a hard slider belt high on his hands, about six inches inside, but he checked his swing because he had a good sense of the strike zone. I realized that if I continued to throw off the plate, I'd walk him with Mantle on deck. So I put it on the corner. At Forbes Field, we had a brick wall and then a screen, and he hit it over that screen. So I got acquainted with Roger Maris real quick. He was an excellent hitter.

It was easy for Law to shrug off Maris's homer because the Pirates stormed back in the bottom of the first to score 3 runs off Art Ditmar. The "Deacon" combined with Face for a 6–4 home-field victory.

Law and Face again pitched the Pirates to victory in Game 4, 3–2, over Ralph Terry at Yankee Stadium. It was Harvey Haddix and Face who stymied the Yankees in Game 5, 5–2, with Ditmar taking a second hard loss. In the other games, the Yankees' bats did explode. Mantle homered twice in Game 2 in a 16–3 victory behind Turley. "Mantle was one of the greatest players who ever lived," says Dick Groat, "and we were awed by his gigantic homers and said, 'Hey, did you see that!' Then we looked forward to the next game."

Mantle homered again in Game 3, when Ford shut out the Pirates on 4 hits, 10–0, at Yankee Stadium. But surprisingly, Richardson did the most damage, with a grand slam off Tom Cheney and a single-game World Series–record 6 RBIs (a feat matched in Game 6 of the 2009 World Series by Hideki Matsui of the Yankees). In the Yankees' next win, in Game 6, Richardson tripled twice and drove in 3 more runs to establish a Series record with 12 RBIs, proof that he was as good an all-around second baseman as there was in baseball. The Yankees knocked out 17 hits while Ford threw a 7-hitter for his second shutout, 12–0, this time in Pittsburgh.

Through 6 games, the World Series had followed Murtaugh's script. "The three games they won, they kicked our asses," remembers Groat, "but every game we had a chance to win, we won. In Game 7, we matched their power."

The final game in Pittsburgh was, arguably, the most exciting World Series game ever played. Maris was one of the few participants who was a non-factor, going 0 for 5, with an error and a big foul-out in the ninth inning. Even with a second homer off Haddix in Game 5, he played an insignificant role in the entire Series, batting .267 with just the 2 RBIs. Even though much was on his mind, he must have been dissatisfied with his disappearing act.

In the wild seventh game, the underdog Pirates broke out to a 4–0 lead against Bob Turley and Bill Stafford, but Law couldn't hold it, and the Yankees roared back to take a 7–4 lead into the bottom of the 8th inning. Their big blow was a 3-run, go-ahead homer by Berra off Face in the 6th. "It was a fastball down and in that I wanted back," remembers Face. "It wasn't where I wanted to throw it, but Berra hit everything."

The Yankees seemed to have things under control in the 8th inning with Coates on the mound, but a double-play ball caromed off a pebble and struck Kubek in the throat, sending him to the hospital with a damaged windpipe. Fate had played its part, and the Pirates took advantage. Hal Smith staked his place in baseball history by slugging a stunning 2-out 3-run pinch homer off Coates as the Bucs rallied for 5 runs and a 9–7 lead. The Yankees came back gallantly to tie the game in the top of the ninth, thanks to some brilliant baserunning by Mantle.

That set the stage for the bottom of the ninth, when the first batter, Bill Mazeroski, faced Ralph Terry. Terry recalls, "I pitched a whole game in the bullpen. I got warmed up five times. It was a little bitty bullpen with a steep slope, and everything I threw was high. In Forbes Field, the real mound didn't have a slope like that. Did they make the mound in the bullpen slope intentionally to throw us off? That's a good question. It would have been okay if I'd warmed up only once, but I got adjusted to the slope. So I threw two pitches to Mazeroski and my ball wouldn't go down. The second pitch was kind of a half-assed cutter-slider, but it was the only thing I had working."

"I was putting on my helmet and getting my bat out of the rack," recalls Groat. "When Maz hit it, we all yelled, 'Get off the wall! Get off the wall!' "

"I didn't think it was a home run," remembers Yogi Berra, who was playing in left field, "or I wouldn't have run back toward the wall."

Berra watched the ball sail over the wall, and Mazeroski became the first hitter to end a World Series with a home run.

A few moments later, the Yankees were in their clubhouse shaking their heads in disbelief. Maris slammed his locker shut and exclaimed, "I've never seen such a lucky team in all my life!" Mantle, who had batted .400 with 3 homers and 11 RBIs, openly cried. His Yankees outscored the Pirates 55–27, but they got the rings and $3,200 more than the Yankees' $5,214 loser's share.

"They just thought that automatically they were going to be the winners," says Face, "but we had the desire to go out there and beat them."

In 1960, many events in America signaled the country was moving forward. The United States launched the first weather satellite. The Food and Drug Administration approved the sale of birth-control pills. The U.S. Supreme Court ruled that anyone who was arrested had the right to an attorney. The first fifty-star flag was unfurled in Philadelphia. Senator John F. Kennedy of Massachusetts and Vice President Richard Nixon staged the first three televised presidential debates. Major League Baseball agreed to expand the American League to ten teams in 1961 and increase its schedule from 154 games to 162 games, with the National League to follow suit in 1962. And on October 18, the Yankees replaced manager Casey Stengel because, the owners explained, he was seventy. "I was surprised," says Berra. Others saw it coming.

Before the press at the Savoy Hilton in New York, an irked Stengel, who thought a tenth pennant in twelve years would be enough to save his job, said, "I'll never make the mistake of being seventy again." He didn't confirm the owners' contention that he had retired rather than being forced out. Instead he had a drink at the bar.

The sportswriters who were fond of Stengel and many of his players believed that the reason he wasn't offered a new contract wasn't his age but that he blew the World Series to Pittsburgh by making numerous blunders. The one most often cited was not starting Ford in Game 1, and thus the era's best big-game pitcher wouldn't get three starts, including in Game 7. Surely Stengel compounded his mistake by not taking out Ford early in his blow-out victories, so he would be rested enough to relieve in Game 7.

Topping and Webb wanted Stengel gone because of both his age and his World Series mistakes, but the biggest reason was that they wanted to promote Ralph Houk to manager rather than lose him to another organization. Kansas City was definitely interested in Houk to replace Bob Elliott, and the two new expansion teams also were looking for managers. The Yankees offered Houk a one-year $35,000 contract, $65,000 less than they were paying Stengel. "I would have signed anything they asked me to sign," Houk stated in *Season of Glory*, written with Robert W. Creamer. "I would have done it for nothing. . . . The highest salary I'd had with the Yankees before was $10,000."

So it was that seventy-year-old Casey Stengel was replaced by forty-one-year-old Ralph Houk, just as seventy-year-old President Dwight Eisenhower made way for forty-three-year-old John Kennedy. The new manager, like the president-elect, was handsome, charismatic, and a World War II hero who preferred looking toward a hopeful future than reveling in the glories of the past.

Ten days after Houk's press conference, Webb and Topping fired George Weiss, the 1960 American League Executive of the Year, and replaced him with Weiss's assistant Roy Hamey. At his own press conference, Weiss handed out a one-sentence statement confirming his retirement. Then he said softly, "I want to thank you fellows. It's certainly been swell. See you around." That was it. He couldn't continue because he broke down in tears.

But Weiss would have the last laugh. The organization agreed to keep him on as a paid consultant under the condition that he not become general manager for another team. Weiss surprised Webb and Topping by signing on with the expansion New York Mets, who had shrewdly hired Casey Stengel to be their first manager for 1962. Although Weiss's official title was team president, he'd function as a general manager.

"I think most of the players thought Casey was going to be gone," recalls Turley, the Yankees' player rep and the only player who really knew and liked Weiss. "The big surprise for me was that they let Weiss go when it had been him who created the great Yankee dynasty. It was only a matter of a few years before the team declined."

Another election took place the day after Kennedy nipped Nixon by 100,000 votes. In Raytown, twenty-six-year-old Roger Maris picked up the ringing phone and was surprised to hear that the Baseball Writers' Association of America had selected him the American League's Most Valuable Player. Was this the biggest day of his life? "All I know," he replied, "is that I'm happier now than I would have been if anybody else got it." He said bluntly, "I'm the same player I was with the Athletics in 1959, but it always helps to play for a pennant winner." Then he acknowledged, "That trade was the turning point in my career, and without it I would never have received the Most Valuable Player award." The press must have wondered who wrote this guy's material.

Maris prevailed by only a slight margin, 225–222–211, over Mickey Mantle and Brooks Robinson, who would have won if only the top three places on the ten-place ballots were counted. Mantle actually got the most first-place votes, 10, to 8 for Maris, 3 for Robinson, 2 for Minnie Minoso, and 1 for Ron Hansen.

As would be the case from 1960 to 1964, Maris's and Mantle's statistics were similar. Maris batted a career-high .283, with a league-leading .581 slugging percentage, 98 runs, 39 homers, and a league-leading 112 RBIs. Mantle batted .275 (his lowest average since his '51 rookie season), with a .558 slugging percentage, a league-leading 119 runs, a league-leading 40 homers, and 94 RBIs. Mantle was unquestionably the most valuable Yankee in the two months after Maris's injury, but MVP voters noted that if Maris hadn't been the team MVP from April to early August, Mantle's heroics would have occurred when the pennant was out of reach. Mantle himself said that Maris deserved to win much more decisively. And he meant it.

Maris had ignited an offense that was dormant before his arrival. "Roger was a hell of a team player," said Blanchard in 2008. "We couldn't have done what we did without him. He was the key. When we threw him in the lineup, good Lord! Roger Maris in 1960 was the best baseball player I ever saw."

The eight voters may have gotten it right, but Maris's winning the league's top prize further antagonized the many New Yorkers who had been rooting for Mantle in the home-run and MVP races. They had figured Mantle's winning the first race guaranteed he'd win the second and were peeved. In 1961, they would make it clearer whose side they were on.

CHAPTER EIGHTEEN

THE M&M BOYS

THE OFF-SEASON FOR BASEBALL'S newest star was hectic. Roger probably intended to spend most of the winter relaxing at home with Pat and the kids, but after he was named the American League's MVP, his time was no longer his own. He found himself back on the East Coast juggling banquets, award ceremonies, and personal appearances on behalf of companies whose products he was endorsing, including Spalding Sporting Goods. Maris was excited to pick up extra money and get credit for what he'd achieved, but he was a dreadful public speaker and hoped never to do the banquet circuit again.

As in most off-seasons, Roger found time for a brief respite in Fargo, visiting family and close friends. "Roger was a little upset because when he came back here, people were treating him like a big hero because he was the MVP in 1960," says Wayne Blanchard. "When his friends treated him like a celebrity, he read them the riot act."

"I said to him, 'You're on the stage now and I don't want to get in on your show,'" recalls Dick Savageau. "And he said, 'You know, that's what ticks me off with you guys. You're my friends and you're the ones I want to be with. I don't want to be with those other people."

Roger and Pat, who was pregnant again, intended to take a brief family vacation in St. Petersburg prior to spring training. But their plans went awry. "It was about ten p.m. when we heard a rap on the door," recalled Johnny Blanchard in 2008. "Nancy and I were staying on Treasure Island, and a visitor that late was highly unusual. I opened the door and Roger was standing there with a baby in his arms. He said, 'Hey, Blanch, can you and your wife keep the baby for a few days? Patty's in the car bleeding.' He handed the baby to Nancy and they took off for St. Anthony's Hospital."

In the "My Husband" article in the April 24, 1962, issue of *Look*, Pat Maris told interviewer Deirdre Budge (the wife of tennis legend Don Budge) that their car had broken down in rural Georgia. "I was pregnant," she said, "and being towed twenty-five miles over bumpy roads caused me to wind up in the hospital when we arrived in St. Petersburg. Having lost one baby, we were both anxious not to let anything happen to this one if we could prevent it. When he was worrying about me in the hospital, I was worrying about leaving him with the job of looking after our youngsters by himself. . . . Like most men, Roger isn't too handy at changing diapers and making formula, but he 'kept house' beautifully for Sue and little Rog."

Roger enjoyed his babysitting chore because it gave him the rare opportunity to be with his kids constantly in Florida. But when spring training itself began, he asked his mother to come help care for the children.

Maris looked forward to his second year with the Yankees, although he wasn't thrilled that he'd be playing eight more games in 1961 due to the addition of two teams, the Los Angeles Angels and—with the original franchise becoming the Minnesota Twins—the new Washington Senators. He believed baseball should have reduced rather than expanded the number of games played in order to keep a balanced schedule. At least his salary was much larger than in 1960, and he could now offer his family security, which he insisted was the reason he played baseball for a living. Years later, as his love of the game waned, he'd say cynically, "If I could make more money down in the zinc mines, I'd be mining zinc."

Maris hadn't the satisfaction of going to George Weiss and demanding fair compensation for his great year, but Weiss's successor, Roy Hamey, made him the third-highest-paid player on the Yankees, behind only Mantle and Berra. Hamey didn't give him the $40,000 he asked for, but his salary more than doubled. Mantle received a meager $10,000 salary bump despite his finishing second in the MVP race.

If not for Pat's problems, Roger might have reported to spring training with focus and enthusiasm. But he was there in body only and had an awful exhibition season. "Maris couldn't hit a balloon in spring training," Ralph Houk wrote in his 1962 book *Ballplayers Are Human, Too*. That didn't make things easy for the new manager, especially since only Mickey Mantle and rookie right-hander Rollie Sheldon, who came out of Class D, fared much better. The Yankees lost 8 of their first 9 games and two-thirds of their games overall. New York had lost seven players in the expansion draft, including Roger's good friends Bob Cerv, Eli Grba, and Ken Hunt, who all went to the Angels, but Houk was patient because the core of the team was intact.

Before it was clear that Casey Stengel was being pushed out, thirty-five veteran reporters signed a petition urging him not to retire. So they weren't inclined to give his neophyte successor much rope. Arthur Daley of the *Times* and Joe King of the *World-Telegram & Sun* were among the influential reporters who ripped Houk as the losses mounted. The younger reporters, who were trying to establish their own identities, didn't necessarily take a pro-Stengel stance, but they were in an attack mode as well. What Houk endured while his team lost games of no consequence made it obvious that the tenor of sports reporting had changed and that 1961 would be exactly the wrong year for anyone to get on the wrong side of the media.

Fortunately, Houk had the ability to parry the blows of even the most powerful reporters. As an Army Ranger who rose to the rank of major during World War II, he had fought at the Battle of the Bulge, survived a sniper's bullet that passed through his helmet while it was on his head, and received the Purple Heart, Silver Star, and Bronze Star. He wasn't afraid of reporters with pencils and typewriters. When he was hired, he stated that he'd be "a player's manager," and he proved himself to his team when he accepted all the blame for his team's spring struggles.

Pat left the hospital under strict instructions not to do anything for at least three weeks. According to *Roger Maris At Bat*, Maris sent his pregnant wife and their three kids to New York, and when camp broke, he joined them in a hotel. Maris always stated he didn't want his family to live in the big city, yet they looked for a place near Yankee Stadium so they'd be together during the season. After three days of the five of them in one room, Roger and Pat decided that she and the children should return to Raytown. Pat would have a difficult pregnancy, but doctors assured them that she and the baby would be fine. Roger could finally concentrate on baseball.

It had been a lost spring training for Maris, and when the season commenced, he had no timing and was unable to get any loft, the two skills he thought were essential to his hitting well. Maris spoke incessantly about the need to hit the bottom one-eighth inch of a ball to hit home runs, and he wasn't doing that. In the first 10 games of a soggy April that resulted in several rainouts and a seven-inning tie with the Orioles, Maris hit an anemic .161, with no extra-base hits and a lone RBI on a sacrifice fly. Batting third, fifth, sixth, and seventh, he finished the month at .204 with only 4 RBIs, 2 on sacrifice flies. His only homer came off Detroit's Paul Foytack on April 26, in the eleventh game of the season.

In the same game as Maris's 1st homer, Mantle smashed his 6th and 7th homers as the Yankees won, 13–11. Already people were talking about Mantle chasing Ruth's home-run record as he had in 1956. The struggling Maris was left out of the discussion because it didn't seem possible that he'd hit 60 more homers in the final 152 games.

Through April, Mantle batted at a .327 clip with 17 RBIs. In the winter Houk had gone to his center fielder and told him that he expected him to be the leader of the team. Tony Kubek believed Mantle was more vocal and assertive in '61, but the majority of teammates didn't know Houk had appointed him unofficial captain. According to Blanchard, "Mickey turned down Houk. There was no difference in him that year. I loved Mickey, but he didn't mature till the day that he died."

Perhaps Mantle hadn't matured—"None of us had grown up," insists Ryne Duren—but in truth his teammates had long considered their idol their leader. How could they not when they'd watch him wrap his painful legs in bandages before every game and then go all out on the diamond, where he was the most feared hitter in the American League. "To fully appreciate Mickey," said Kubek, "you would have had to see him after a ball game with his legs taped from his thighs to the ankles. He wore these awkward rubber wraps, not the sophisticated braces of today. I'd look at the scars on his knees and wonder how he even stood up, much less played."

"He is the only baseball player I know," said Clete Boyer, "who is a bigger hero to his teammates than he is to the fans."

The other player Houk approached prior to the season was Ford, who was expected to be the anchor of the rotation with Terry, Ditmar, Turley, and on occasion Coates and Stafford. Houk hired Johnny Sain, the greatest pitching coach in history, to replace Ed Lopat. Sain believed pitchers benefited from throwing as much as possible, so he and Houk decided Ford should pitch every fourth day, rather than every fifth or sixth game, as Stengel had used him. If he tired late in games, Luis Arroyo would be ready in the bullpen. Ford loved the idea of getting more starts because he got bored waiting for his turn and saw this as a chance to finally win 20 games. He also allowed Sain to change his style. Instead of throwing mostly fastballs and curves, he'd now throw mostly sinkers and sliders (or "slurves"). He was beaten at Yankee Stadium on Opening Day, 6–0, by Minnesota's Pedro Ramos, but then was virtually invincible. Veteran hitters never adapted to the transformed Ford in 1961, and younger players were overmatched.

Maris's average remained low into early May, but he managed 2 more homers. The first came off Ramos in the Yankees' first series ever in Bloomington, Minnesota. Three days later, at 28,000-seat Wrigley Field in Los Angeles, he went deep off a high, outside pitch by his ex-roommate Eli Grba in a loss to Gene Autry's expansion Angels. Coming one day after Alan Shepard became America's first man in space, it was Maris's 100th career home run and carried over the left-center-field fence. His one homer the opposite way in 1961 was a reminder that Maris was a pull hitter by design, not because that was all he could be.

Again Maris's 35-inch, 33-ounce, tapered, thin-handled bat went ice-cold. On May 16, a full month into the season, he was batting .208 with 3 homers and 11 RBIs. He worried that he was playing himself off the team. "The Yankees don't hold on to outfielders who hit .200," he said. Mantle was batting .309, with 10 homers and 26 RBIs. After breaking up a no-hit bid by Washington's Hal Woodeshick with a sixth-inning homer on the sixteenth, Mantle was five games ahead of Ruth's 1927 pace.

Maris trailed Mantle by 7 home runs and it looked as if another home-run race with his teammate wouldn't materialize, but, as Robert W. Creamer wrote, "like a long-dormant volcano he was beginning to rumble." In actuality, he was about to erupt. In his next 134 games, he smashed 58 home runs and drove in 131 runs.

In early May, the Yankees reacquired Bob Cerv along with reliever Tex Clevenger from the Angels for Ryne Duren—whose ugly late-night drinking episodes were no longer tolerated now that he wasn't pitching as well—Lee Thomas, and Johnny James. Having the supportive Cerv around helped Maris. So did a meeting with Dan Topping, who instructed him to keep pulling the ball with power and pay no attention to his batting average. But

Maris got back on track mostly because his timing returned. He'd spent March in a fog while worrying about his wife, so in effect the first thirty days of the season served as his real spring training.

On May 17, in the Yankees' 29th game including the tie, Maris clouted his 4th homer on a fastball thrown by Washington's Pete Burnside. It was his first homer at Yankee Stadium in '61 and his first of 12 off left-handers. In the 30th game he crushed his 5th homer off the Indians' Jim Perry. It was his first of 7 first-inning home runs in 1961, 10 less than Babe Ruth hit in 1927. His 6th homer came in the Yankees' 31st game off onetime teammate Gary Bell. The following day, Maris drilled his 7th off Baltimore's Chuck Estrada. "Roger had such a quick bat that Milt Pappas, Steve Barber, and I never threw anything from the middle in that he could pull," says Estrada. "He told me I was the only pitcher he couldn't pull, because he couldn't get around on my outside fastball, but he still got me that one time."

With 4 homers in 4 games, Maris was out of his slump and there was suddenly a home-run race, but the Yankees lost 10 of 14 games to fall 5½ games behind Detroit. Houk was booed by fans and criticized in the New York papers. The Tigers were proving to be a formidable contender, with a potent lineup featuring Al Kaline, Rocky Colavito, and Norm Cash, and a strong staff headed by veterans Frank Lary, Jim Bunning, Don Mossi, and Paul Foytack. "It was the first good team I'd been on," says Kaline, whose twenty-two years with Detroit began in 1953.

Although Roger's hitting had picked up since meeting with Topping, he fulfilled his promise to him to have his eyes examined. That night before taking the field against Baltimore, he administered eyedrops the optometrist had given him. He had an allergic reaction and in the bottom of the first had to be removed for the only time all season for a pinch hitter. "Houk Sees Red," read the headlines the next day. "We finally get Roger hitting," grumbled Houk, "and he shows up blind." "I was a little scared," wrote Maris in his book. "I knew that Houk was angry at me, but I was just following orders. . . . That was the last time I tried that."

The Yankees fell to a season-high 6 games back, but then won 2 games from Boston. In the first game, on the 24th, Maris hit his 8th homer off 6'8" NBA forward Gene Conley, the majors' tallest player. The Yankees next played a Sunday doubleheader against the White Sox. In the second game, Maris hit homer number 9 off his former Indians friend Cal McLish. "I tried to throw him a cross-seam fastball on the outside part of plate," recalls McLish, "figuring if he did hit it, it would be on the ground. But I got it up a little bit and he hit it to deep right-center field." The Yankees moved to 4½ games back, and Maris was pleased that his homers were now coming in victories.

The Yankees went to Boston for a four-game series, and the M&M Boys, as they now were being called (causing a big boost in sales of the candy), went wild. In the first game, Ford lost a 2–1 duel to Ike Delock, his last defeat until August 15, with Mantle's 11th homer accounting for the only Yankee run. On a memorable Memorial Day, Mantle and Maris each homered off both Gene Conley—the first of many pitchers to give up multiple homers to Maris in 1961—and reliever Mike Fornieles as New York crushed the Red Sox, 12–3. For the first time, Maris and Mantle hit back-to-back home runs. Moose Skowron also knocked two balls over the fence, making this the second time in American League history that three teammates homered twice. The next day, Maris and Mantle each homered off future Cardinals pitching coach Billy Muffett.

Through May, Mantle had 14 home runs and was exactly on pace with Ruth's record. Maris had 12 homers when he'd had only 3 two weeks before. He also picked up 19 RBIs in the twelve games in which he came to the plate, lifting his total to 30. He no longer worried that the Yankees might trade him.

The Yankees' record stood at 23-17, 3½ games back. Richardson (batting eighth) and Lopez were the only two players not hitting. Lopez's continued struggles prompted Houk to give Berra a lot of time in left field, and he responded by playing solid defense and having his eleventh and final 20-homer season. Catching duties were handled by Elston Howard, who hit .348 for the season, and Blanchard, who got playing time from Houk and cracked 21 homers in 243 at-bats. At the corners were Skowron, who hit a career-high 28 homers in '61, and Boyer, who his teammates swore was as good as Brooks Robinson at third base. Richardson eventually came around and was moved to the top of the order, and he and Kubek became invaluable table-setters for Maris and Mantle, as well as giving the team exceptional up-the-middle defense.

In May, only the pitching received mixed reviews. Ford, who was about to embark on a 14-game winning streak, and Terry were thriving under

Houk and Sain. As a twosome, they were on their way to an eye-popping 41-7 record and were the reason the Yankees' 4-game losing streak from May 16 to May 20 was their longest of the year. But Ditmar and Turley struggled mightily, and after six weeks Houk replaced them in the rotation with Stafford and Sheldon, who claimed to be twenty-three but was really twenty-six. Houk's tough decision paid big dividends, as they went 25-15 between them and Stafford finished second in the league in ERA. Ditmar was traded to the A's for Bud Daley, while Turley spent the rest of the year as a spot starter and long man in the pen. When Houk needed a fifth starter, he usually called on Coates or Daley. The sunny-faced Daley, a lefty with a slightly withered right arm, who had been Maris's teammate in Cleveland and Kansas City, turned in several clutch performances in the tight pennant race.

Remarkably, the supremely confident Ford went 8-0 in June. Maris homered in five of his wins, Mantle in the other three. Arroyo, the other chief member of his support team, picked up 5 saves. "Sometimes around the seventh inning I would get tired, especially pitching every fourth day," Ford recalled in the documentary *Pinstripe Power*. "I'd be in the dressing room first and I'd have two beers right by Luis's locker opened and ready."

As good as Ford and Arroyo were on the mound in June, Maris matched them at the plate. After hitting 9 homers in the last two weeks of May, he slugged 15 more between June 2 and June 22. Pat Maris was feeling well enough to join Roger in the Windy City for a weekend series, June 2, 3, and 4. Maris homered in all three games to the chagrin of Cal McLish, Bob Shaw, and Russ Kemmerer. Maris said, "That was the best series I ever had in Chicago." If Roger had been able to spend more time with Pat during 1961, it's likely he would have better handled the intense pressure that lay ahead.

CHAPTER NINETEEN

CHALLENGING RUTH

HAVING WON 2 OF 3 games in Chicago, the Yankees came home to host the Twins. They swept a doubleheader, in which Maris was homerless, then won two single games in which Maris hit his 16th homer off Ed Palmquist (the least known of his homer victims) and his 17th off Pedro Ramos, to put him 2 up on Mantle.

Maris's 18th homer came three games later off Ray Herbert, in a 5–3 victory over the visiting A's. "I tried to sneak a ball past him on the inside corner," Herbert remembered forty-seven years later. "I realized then that I couldn't throw hard enough and my ball didn't move enough for me to do that against him anymore." Mantle also hit his 16th against Herbert and then crushed his 17th the next day against the A's reliever Bill Kunkel.

About this time, the two stars noticed that an unusually large number of writers gathered around their lockers after every game. It was too early in the season for them to be questioned about breaking Ruth's record because they lagged behind his 1927 pace, but not about their personal home-run battle that seemed like an extension of their race in 1960. Both insisted that all they cared about was winning games.

"The very true fact," recalls Ralph Houk, "is that they were just trying to win the pennant, but the writers would come in and all they wanted to talk about was home runs."

Maris tried to be polite to the press, but his lack of interest when talking about himself and home runs came across as arrogance. He was prone to speaking out of the right side of his mouth, and the reporters thought he was sneering at them. When Roger was angry, annoyed, or upset, renowned sportswriter Roger Kahn observed, his "mouth changes into a grim slash in a hard face." His piercing green eyes made him seem even more menacing.

Adding to his aggravation was that the press was calling him a "whiner." Maris was a hard-nosed ballplayer who never asked out of the lineup even when hurt, but part of his daily ritual when getting in and out of his uniform was to grouse à la Roberto Clemente about bruises, a stiff neck, sore muscles, tired feet, a tense back, and all the other reasons he wasn't hitting as well as he hoped. His teammates got a kick out of his shtick, and when appointing a mock presidential cabinet of his teammates, Whitey Ford, "the Chairman of the Board," designated Maris his "Secretary of Grievances." But some new reporters on the scene wrote seriously about his moaning and groaning. He came across as a high-salaried athlete who wasn't appreciative of anything, including the great year he was having.

Maris felt it was becoming increasingly difficult to open up to reporters because a high percentage wanted him to slip up so they could write about it. Feeling guarded, Maris became increasingly stone-faced as the season wore on, which subjected him to even more ridicule. The media—particularly television reporters—expected the man chasing Babe Ruth to also be dynamic, garrulous, and bigger-than-life, but Maris wasn't even good copy.

The streaking Yankees had won 8 of their last 9 games, and the next day, they swept a doubleheader from the visiting Angels. In the first game Maris made one of the greatest catches of his career, robbing his chum Ken Hunt of a home run that would have tied the game in the seventh inning. The Yankee right fielder jumped as high as he could and stretched his arm and glove into the stratosphere to snare the ball. He fell into the lap of a lady in the front row, but no cameras clicked. In the ninth inning, he reached over the bullpen fence to take another home run away, this time from Ted Kluszewski. Maris again showed that even when he wasn't hitting homers, his fielding was worth the price of admission.

In game two, Maris hit number 19 on a bad "newfound curve" thrown by Eli Grba, his second homer against his old apartment-mate. "Despite what Roger wrote, I always had a curve," says Grba, who won 11 games with the Angels in 1961. "But that was a hanger. That year, anything going into him on the inner half of the plate, he killed." Number 20 for Maris came later in the game against Johnny James, "on a sinker that stayed up," the ex-Yankee remembered long after his retirement. Maris detested doubleheaders and had a self-fulfilling prophecy that he'd play poorly in them. However, he'd remember the twin killing of the Angels on June 11 as "one of the greatest doubleheaders of my life."

The Yankees headed for Cleveland tied for second place with the Tigers and trailing the surprising Indians by a game. The Yanks and Tribe split the first two games with Maris homering in each against the same pitchers he went deep against on May 19 and 20. His 21st came off Jim Perry on June 13, the thirteenth anniversary of the dying Babe Ruth's final appearance at Yankee Stadium; and his 22nd came off Gary Bell. "Batting left-handed, Maris and Mantle were lowball hitters, and I was a high-fastball pitcher," says Bell. "I'd try to go up the ladder on them and hoped they'd chase the high pitch, which Mantle did more often. I struck them both out a few times, but every once in a while, they'd make it disappear into the crowd."

A natural lowball hitter, Maris uppercut the ball, but as pitchers began to work him upstairs, he learned to hit down on the ball so that he wouldn't pop up. "In '61," Maris told Bob Broeg of the *St. Louis Post-Dispatch* years later, "I couldn't believe how consistently the opposing pitchers kept the ball up, when it seemed obvious, at least to me, that I'd learned to hit that pitch as well."

With 10 home runs already in June, Maris set his sights on the single-month home-run record set by the Tigers' Rudy York. In August of 1937, York smacked 18 home runs, one more than Ruth had hit in September of 1927, and Maris thought that record was reachable. But the next day, it was Mantle who hit his 19th off Mudcat Grant, as the Yankees notched their 16th victory in 20 games.

With a record of 37-21, the Yankees were a few percentage points ahead of both the Indians and the Tigers as they began a three-game weekend series in Detroit that would attract 147,000 fans. In the Friday game, the Yankees made 5 errors, including one by Maris, as the Tigers won 4–2. Houk took his aggravation out on an umpire and got tossed from the game. On Saturday, Maris ripped a curve thrown by Don Mossi into the upper deck for his 23rd homer. It was his first homer against the former Indians reliever, who won 17 games in '59 and 15 games in '61 starting for the Tigers. "Roger was getting tougher to pitch to all the time," recalls Mossi. "He had better control of his bat, a better idea of the strike zone, everything just improved for him." Mantle hit his 20th off Paul Foytack in relief, but the Tigers won the slugfest, 12–10, to drop the Yankees 2 games back.

Ford went 12-0 in games after Yankee losses during 1961, and in the must-win finale, he and Arroyo whitewashed the Tigers, 9–0, leaving the Yankees only 1 game out instead of 3. Maris slugged his 24th homer off Jerry Casale. This homer put him on pace with Babe Ruth after 62 games, which was startling considering Maris's beginning to the season. Until now he had thought only of trying to beat Mantle in the homer race, but inadvertently he was challenging baseball's most sacrosanct record.

The Yankees traveled to Kansas City to begin a four-game series. Essentially, Maris spent time at home with his pregnant wife and three kids, then went to the ballpark and slammed home runs. Number 25 came against rookie left-hander Jim Archer to move Roger seven games ahead of Ruth. It came in the ninth inning and put the Yankees ahead 3–2, but it didn't spoil the managerial debut of Hank Bauer. The A's pulled out an improbable 4–3 victory in the bottom of the ninth on an inside-the-park homer to deep center by Norm Siebern off Sheldon, followed by a homer over the right-field fence by pinch hitter Wes Covington off Arroyo.

Maris did help ruin player-manager Bauer's second game with a first-inning homer that propelled the Yankees to a 6–2 victory. His 26th homer came off veteran left-hander Joe Nuxhall. "I was sitting on top of the world," wrote Maris. "I felt I was in the sort of streak that all home-run hitters dream of. I was getting good loft to the ball with enough power to scale the walls. Not even left-handers were stopping me, and that made it extra special in my mind." At this time, Maris felt true appreciation for Bauer's coach Jo Jo White, who at Keokuk in 1954 changed Roger from being a spray hitter. "If he hadn't turned me to pulling," said Maris, "then certainly I wouldn't be hitting so many homers."

In the third game of the series, Maris contributed a couple of hits, but Mantle did all the serious damage. He hit his 21st and 22nd home runs and drove in all the Yankee runs in a 5–3 victory. In the finale on Thursday, June 22, however, Maris had a 3-run blast off rookie Norm Bass in an 8–3 win behind Ford and Arroyo. Maris had 3 more hits in the game, including a pair of doubles, to raise his average to .258, 50 points higher than it was on May 16, the day before he broke out of his slump.

Maris was now 5 homers ahead of Mantle and 12 games ahead of Ruth's pace. He had homered in 5 of his last 6 games and 15 times in 24 games in June. An even bigger accomplishment was that from May 17, when he hit his 4th home run, through June 22, when he hit his 27th, Maris had smacked 24 homers—and driven in 48 runs—in 38 games. In *Season of Glory*, Robert W. Creamer wrote that what Roger did in the five-week span "deserves to be ranked with DiMaggio's 56-game hitting streak as an example of sustained, unrelenting achievement." It was one of the great overlooked feats in baseball history.

Maris didn't want the press to call attention to what he was doing and bug him for interviews. Yet the rub was that he wanted acknowledgment, if not accolades, from these same people. He certainly didn't want anyone comparing him to Babe Ruth. It was hard enough being compared to Mantle, whom he considered the best player in the game. As when he'd been compared to his brother, Maris conceded that Mantle was superior to him, although only batting average set them apart statistically.

The Yankees' next stop was Minnesota for a three-game series with the Twins. In early May, the crowds at three Yankees-Twins games were modest: 16,669, 18,158, and 18,179. Now with Maris and Mantle providing fireworks in almost every game in June, 30,940, 35,199, and 35,152 fans charged through the turnstiles. They were disappointed that Maris and Mantle hit no "big tonks," as Roger called home runs, and their Twins managed only one victory.

By now the pressure was building on Maris. He had come to understand why that word began with the letters p r-e-s-s and was getting the reputation for being a tough interview. But when Jerry Ruff, a columnist for the *Fargo Forum* he'd never met, came to the park, Roger, after posing with American Legion ballplayers from Fargo, invited Ruff into the dugout. Ruff wrote, "They say Maris was tough on newspaper guys. Maybe he was sometimes. Except if you were from Fargo."

The Yankees took the final two games from the Twins and flew into L.A. "There was a lot more press than usual following Roger everywhere he went," recalls Billy Moran, who had become a star second baseman for the Angels.

Mantle homered twice in the three-game series, off Ken McBride and Ryne Duren, but Maris again couldn't connect in the homer-friendly park. His chance to catch Rudy York vanished, and he blamed his homer drought on the added pressure he put on himself while pursuing the record. The Yankees finished June back in New York, with Ford defeating Washington, 5–1, as Mantle hit an inside-the-park homer off former White Sox pitcher Dick Donovan. Ford joked, "I'll have a great year if Arroyo's arm holds out." It would. The dependable lefty was baseball's best closer in 1961, with 15 victories, a major-league-record 29 saves, a 2.19 ERA in a league-leading 65 appearances, and 87 strikeouts in 119 innings.

Arroyo averaged nearly two innings an outing, but he still needed a set-up man at times. That role was admirably filled by Coates (whose 11–5 season gave him a three-year record of 30-9) and recent call-up Hal Reniff. Reniff was "one of the few baseball players I ever met that hated playing," recalls Maury Allen. "He hated the game and going to the ballpark, but he loved the competition and the money. Maris also was in it for the money, but he loved baseball—it was New York that he hated." Reniff befriended Maris, who loved his biting sense of humor, and played poker with him, Lopez, and Clete Boyer.

Although Maris didn't homer in the final seven games of June, he concluded a sensational month with a total of 27 homers and 65 RBIs, just ahead of Mantle's 25 homers and 64 RBIs. After 73 games in 1927, Ruth had, fittingly, 26 homers.

Mantle passed Ruth and caught Maris in his first two at-bats the next game, against Washington. He rocketed a solo homer over the 457-foot sign in left-center and 3-run shot off switch-hitting left-hander Carl "Stubby" Mathias, a rookie who was making one of only three major league starts. A tie-breaking homer in the top of the ninth by Dale Long, who had been drafted from the Yankees by the Senators, threatened to negate all Mantle's heroics, but Maris's competitive juices were flowing and he pulled Dave Sisler down the line for a 2-run homer. His 28th home run put him ahead of Mantle and won the game to keep the Yankees 2 games behind Detroit.

The next day, the Yankees moved to a game behind the Tigers by trouncing the Senators, 13–4. In game 75, Maris hit his 29th off Pete Burnside and his 30th off Johnny Klippstein, and Mantle hit his 28th off Klippstein. It took Ruth 70 games to hit his 28th homer, 83 games to hit his 30th.

"It was so much fun watching those two guys," recalls Bud Daley. "Every time they came up, I thought they were going to homer. The difference was that as soon as the ball left Mickey's bat you'd say, 'Oh, it's gone.' With Roger you'd say, 'It's going to go . . . it's going to go . . . ' But it made no difference because his balls went out, too."

The back-and-forth home-run race didn't divide the M&M Boys, but united them through mutual respect for their talents and, as Hemingway so famously put it, "grace under pressure." They were like the homesteader and the outsider who bond while taking turns attacking a huge tree trunk with axes in the classic passage in Jack Schaefer's *Shane*. Only they understood what the other was going through, and there was no need to express it verbally to each other and no way to articulate it to anyone else. The uniqueness and magnitude of a shared experience separated them from everyone else in the universe, as it did in the same decade to the four Beatles and the Mercury and Apollo astronauts who ventured into space and eventually landed on the moon. This isolation pushed Maris and Mantle together, but if anything inextricably linked them, it was their front-row view of the aggressive, ungovernable new media in action.

CHAPTER TWENTY

THE ASTERISK

"HERE'S THE WAY IT worked," recalls George Vecsey. "Reporters would come in when the clubhouse opened and talk to players while they were undressing. Nobody was self-conscious about that part of it because there weren't women reporters in those days. They'd be sitting there in their jocks and having a beer or whatever, and eventually they'd say, 'All right. Enough of this.' " *Except* if it was Roger Maris.

Maris was still a relative newcomer in the player-reporter game, which Mantle had mastered. Maris didn't understand the concept of exchanging good quotes for favorable stories. Mantle routinely raced past reporters, as well as autograph seekers, but if he'd had a really good game, he'd hold court, regaling the press with hilarious stories, few of which were printable, and discussing his latest moonshot. "Mantle," remembers Maury Allen, "had the attitude 'I want the broads to know I hit a home run, and all you guys gather around and I'll bullshit you for half an hour.' Roger was extremely modest and looked at baseball as 'This is my job, and though I just hit a home run to win a game, I don't have to tell anybody about it.' "

Mantle, as Houk's leader, was more accessible to the press in 1961, but he still didn't bother to give real responses to questions that required serious thought. Maris felt obligated to answer *every* baseball question to the best of his ability, even if that meant he couldn't leave the ballpark for an extra two or three hours. He was usually disappointed to read the next day that he had been unresponsive or had acted surly toward the reporters, who scoffed when he insisted that he cared more about winning than hitting hanging sliders over the fence.

By July, the home-run race was a national story. Being relentlessly hounded by a growing number of reporters was difficult enough for Maris, but worse was that many reporters were obviously rooting against him. "Is the ball a lot livelier this year, Rog?" "Rog, how much does it help you batting in front of Mantle?" "Rog, is the pitching a lot worse because of expansion?" "Do you think you've just been lucky, Rog?" "Rog, with that low a batting average, do you think you can call yourself a good hitter?"

The last two questions struck a nerve. "There had been a whisper here and there that I was lucky," he recalled in *Roger Maris At Bat*. "People were asking how I could hit home runs and only be hitting around .250. It was getting under my skin. I didn't like it, not a little bit." If the reporters got a rise out of him by inferring he wasn't much of a hitter, so much the better because in their articles they could refer to him as "red-necked Roger" or "The Last Angry Man," borrowing the title from a popular 1959 movie. Dealing with the media was wearing down Maris, and it became increasingly worse as even more reporters showed up at the ballpark and the team's hotels.

The reporters who were the most trusted by Yankee players were part of the establishment, including Dan Daniel of the *World-Telegram*; John Drebinger, Arthur Daley, and Louis Effrat of the *Times*; Red Smith and Harold Rosenthal of the *Herald Tribune*; Milt Richman of UPI; Leonard Koppett and Milt Gross of the *New York Post*; Ben Epstein and Ken Smith of the *Daily Mirror*; and Til Ferdenzi of the *Journal-American*. These were the guys who didn't "rip" players or resort to gossip to sell newspapers.

The reporter Maris trusted most was Jim Ogle of the *Newark Star-Ledger*, who was so loyal to the Yankees management that he was unpopular with the younger New York scribes. But Maris would also confide in fifty-year-old Jimmy Cannon, the revered columnist for the *Journal-American* and the King Features Syndicate who was known for his superlative boxing coverage. "Cannon was an older guy," says George Vecsey. "I loved his stuff and he had an acerbic wit and knew his shit, so I enjoyed his company, too. He had actress girlfriends, which impressed the hell out of me."

In addition to Ogle and Cannon, there were other veteran reporters who Maris had enjoyed chatting with and even needling since coming to New York. However, in 1961 that became problematic. "I gradually found it necessary to stop kidding around," Maris wrote in *Roger Maris At Bat*. "I never knew when something I would say as a gag would get into the papers as if I meant it. . . . It was the beginning of my going on the defensive when the writers were around me. For some strange reason anything I said now was news."

The young man from Fargo still couldn't fathom why anyone had more than a passing interest in what he had to say or why his private life was of more interest to young reporters than what pitch he'd hit on his last home run. He was such a bad interview because he grew up being secretive about his family and, even more so than other Midwesterners, thinking questions of any type were rude and an invasion of privacy. He believed that most reporters made their living by wasting his time.

He was certain that many young reporters were trying to make their reputations by ruining his. Maris's misfortune was to become the biggest sensation in sports at exactly the time a new wave of irreverent sportswriters took over the asylum.

"Nineteen sixty and '61 was a transition time for the newspaper business in New York," recalled *Newsday*'s Steve Jacobson, in a 1998 ESPN *SportsCentury* profile on Maris. "Some of the older, established writers essentially worshiped at the shrine of the Yankees. And the younger writers . . . were identified as 'Chipmunks' [and] we looked for other kinds of stuff. The box score was not what we were looking for. We wanted some kind of insight into who people were and why they did what they did."

Among the Chipmunks were Stan Isaacs, Steve Jacobson, and George Vecsey of *Newsday*, Phil Pepe of the *World-Telegram*, and Maury Allen and Leonard Shecter, who had been around longer, at the *Post*. "A bunch of us were talking during a game," recalls Allen, "and Jimmy Cannon, an old-fashioned reporter who didn't like chatter in the press box, started stammering, 'You-you-you're a bunch of fucking Chipmunks.' He used that expression *chipmunks* because Phil Pepe happened to have big teeth. It became sort of a status term for us. We had the idea of writing about players as human beings who had wives and families and hobbies, and we really cared about the guys' personalities, thoughts, attitudes about different things, relationships with other players. We got quite a lot of fan mail because people liked what we did."

Isaacs contends the first Chipmunks were actually him, Shecter, and Larry Merchant of the *Philadelphia Daily News* and were called the Rat Pack before they took a liking to Cannon's moniker for them. "We were irrever-ent," Isaacs says, "but prided ourselves on honest, solid journalism."

"We were going to the ballpark, not church," said Merchant. This was his way of explaining why reporters no longer treated even baseball's biggest stars with reverence. Fearful of reprisal in the reporters' columns, some ball-players fawned over them and gave interviews on demand. Though coopera-tive, Maris saw no reason to charm the media.

"Maris might have lumped us all together," says George Vecsey, "and said, 'They're all a bunch of assholes,' but we were reasonably sympathetic. The reality is that most of the players talked to us easily before and after games."

The players may have talked to those they knew best, but they no longer confided in them over drinks at the hotel bar. "Guys were pissed off after a loss and would be cussing and saying certain things," recalls Bob Cerv, "and there it was in the paper the next day." Only sex remained a taboo subject.

The Chipmunks were an aggressive lot who, their detractors felt, too often went over the line or below the belt and also, as individuals or as a pack, skewered a player just to demonstrate their power. "Writers tend to be selfish and ego-driven," says Allen almost fifty years later, "and if a guy is not a good interview, we tend to write about the negative parts of his career and use adjectives like *surly* or *sour.* I wrote negatively about Maris for one reason—he didn't help my career. But should I have punished him because he didn't tell me funny stories about his childhood? I look back and I say, 'I'm embarrassed. I was not fair to him. I hurt him. I think a lot of us feel that way.' "

The saving grace for the Chipmunks was that the individual writers had striking talent and, at least in their own minds, a nobility of purpose. Un-fortunately, the same couldn't be said of their legion of imitators around the country who couldn't distinguish between cynicism and cruelty, or between profiles written after an interview and gossip written when there was no in-terview. "Roger told me that he would get angry with reporters who would get drunk and chase women at night and then be indisposed," remembers Bob Wood, one of Maris's closest Fargo friends. "Because they were doing their carousing, they'd have no time to do the interview. So they'd make it up."

"If there was irresponsible conjecture, it was mostly done by older reporters," says George Vecsey. "We Chipmunks did our research, whereas the older guys were too fucking lazy to go down and talk to somebody. If they had one quote or just a glimmer of an idea, they'd make up a story."

Maris was spending so much time dealing with the press at the stadium that he wanted to assure himself of privacy once he left. But reporters were calling his room and hanging out in the hotel lobby, and autograph seekers were chasing him into restrooms and churches and interrupting his meals in restaurants, which was one of his pet peeves. So again Maris and Cerv asked Julie Isaacson to get them an apartment in Queens. "He found us a nice apartment," recalls Cerv. "One day Mickey came up to us. The reporters and fans were hounding him to death at his hotel, so he said, 'How would you like a roommate?' It took me a few days to think about it. I told him, 'We've got rules, you know.' He went along with them."

The first-place Tigers landed in New York to play the Yankees in a big doubleheader on Tuesday, July 4. The next time the two contenders were scheduled to play wasn't until September 1, so 74,246 excited fans were on hand, the biggest crowd of the year. In the first game, Whitey Ford improved his record to 15-2, striking out 11 and giving up only 5 hits in a 6–2 victory over Don Mossi as the Yankees moved into a tie at the top of the standings. In the second game, Frank Lary shut out the Yankees until Maris tied the game with a 2-run homer, his 31st, over the glove of a leaping Al Kaline. "I tried to pitch both Maris and Mantle low and outside so they'd hit 400-foot outs to center field," remembers Lary, "but sometimes I'd have to throw them inside sliders." Lary drove in the winning run with two outs in the 10th inning off Stafford with a bunt single. The Tigers moved back into sole possession of first place.

The fading Indians arrived in New York for a two-game series after 5–0 and 5–1 losses in Baltimore. After being shut out, 6–0, on a 4-hitter by Sheldon, and 4–0, on a 2-hitter by Stafford, they fled home. Maris hit his 32nd homer in the first game off the Indians' relief ace, Frank Funk. That gave him 75 RBIs, 4 more than Mantle. (Some statisticians believe Maris was erroneously credited with an RBI in the third inning when Kubek, who had reached third on Maris's single, raced home on a bad throw.) By going 4 for 7 in the two games, Maris lifted his average to .280. "I was prouder of my climbing batting average than anything else at this point. . . . When my batting average moved up . . . I think my disposition improved, too. No one likes to be called a lucky hitter."

The first game of a Sunday doubleheader against Boston was the Yankees' 81st game that counted in the standings, and the midway point of the season. Sheldon threw his second consecutive shutout, this time on a 5-hitter. Maris provided the final insurance run in the 3–0 victory with his 33rd home run in the seventh inning, on a slider by Boston ace Bill Monbouquette, that wrapped around the foul pole. He remembers, "I preferred facing Mantle to Maris because he was easier to strike out. Maris didn't have much power the other way, but in Yankee Stadium, whoa!"

Roger headed into the All-Star break twelve games ahead of Ruth's pace, with Mantle 4 homers behind him and one game behind Ruth's pace. The Tigers clung to a ½-game lead over New York.

Nineteen sixty-one's first All-Star Game was played in San Francisco at the Giants' new boondoggle, Candlestick Park, where swirling, bone-chilling winds found a home in the summer. When local reporters asked him about the ballpark, Maris said he'd ask to be traded rather than play there. The story of the game was the gales that caused 7 errors. Most memorably, Giants reliever Stu Miller was charged with a balk when a gust of wind caused him to sway in midpitch. The Yankees had four players in the starting lineup, Maris, Mantle, Kubek, and Ford, and Howard and Berra as alternates. Paul Richards finally got to manage Maris and played him all nine innings. Maris had one of the American League's 4 hits, but Miller, who possessed an extraordinary changeup, struck him out in the top of the 10th with a runner on third and his team ahead only 4–3. The National League came back to win, 5–4, when Willie Mays, playing in front of his home fans, doubled in the tying run, then scored on a single by Roberto Clemente.

Maris and Mantle came back strong after the break. In a 6–2 victory over the White Sox, facing future Hall of Famer Early Wynn, they hit back-to-back homers for the second time in the season to move the Yankees into a tie for first place. Yogi Berra thinks this may have been the first time he said, "It's déjà vu all over again." Mantle's 30th homer was the 350th of his career; Maris's 34th homer gave him 16 round-trippers from June 10 to July 13, to go with 37 runs batted and a .377 average. He was now hitting .288, and .300 seemed in reach despite his pulling everything.

Maris worried about having another of his second-half slumps, but figured he could avoid one if he stayed healthy and disappoint all the people who wanted him to fail. That included Frank Lane. When asked about the home-run race, Lane, now with Kansas City, was not charitable: "Apparently, they'll both break the record, unless Maris falls flat on his face in the last six weeks of the season. That's been his pattern. He did it with me [on Cleveland], with the A's, and the Yankees last year."

Juan Pizarro shut down the Yankees the next day, 6–1, but Mantle smacked his 31st homer. In the finale, the Yankees came from 6 runs back to win, 9–8, in ten innings. After the game Maris was annoyed that the press surrounded him rather than Tony Kubek, who had the winning hit. But Maris did deserve attention because he ended a Sox rally by nailing speedy Luis Aparicio trying to score on Jim Landis's short fly, doubled to tie the game in the ninth inning, tripled, and slugged his 35th homer off Ray Herbert, who now had given up a longball this season to Roger as an A and a White Sox. "I told Al Lopez I'd done well throwing Roger sinkerballs down and away, because that's real hard to pull," says Herbert. "But Lopez insisted I come inside. When I came into the dugout, I said, 'See!'"

Baltimore was New York's next stop. Despite his reputation, Maris enjoyed a good prank now and again. But he preferred not being the recipient, as he was at Bob Turley's home in Maryland. Turley recalls:

> Roger, Elston, Mickey, Whitey, and a lot of other Yankees were there, and we cooked steaks around the pool. We knew that Roger was a swimmer in high school up in Fargo. After a few drinks, Mickey said to Roger, "All I hear about is how good a swimmer you are. I can beat you any day of the week." He said he was a champion in Oklahoma when the truth was he couldn't swim at all. But he and Whitey had a plan. One guy hollered, "Go!" And they both jumped in the water. Maris started swimming and didn't see that Whitey had the skimmer hanging over the side of the pool. Mickey grabbed it and Whitey dragged him all the way down to the other end. When Roger got down there, he said to Mickey, "How did you get here?" Mickey said, "I told you I could swim."

Mantle won the swimming race at Turley's house and the first baseball game at Memorial Stadium, beating Steve Barber, 2–1, with his 32nd homer in the fourth and RBI double in the ninth. Mantle hit his 33rd homer off

Milt Pappas in the first game of Monday's scheduled day-night double-header, as Ford coasted to a 5–0 victory. Maris took a collar, striking out and fouling out twice. "If Maris was in one of his streaks, it didn't matter where you threw it, he was going to hit it," says Pappas. "Outside, inside, up, or down, it was just 'Katy, bar the door!' That was true for almost all of 1961. But when he wasn't in a streak, you could get him out anywhere you threw the ball."

In the nightcap, Maris homered in the first inning and Mantle homered in the fourth inning. Unfortunately, the skies opened up and the game was canceled before it became official, thereby nullifying both home runs. Maris's almost-homer on July 17 was one he needed in his attempt to catch Babe Ruth in 154 games. The reason anyone thought it necessary to hit 60 homers in the same number of games the Yankees played in 1927, rather than in 162 games, was that the baseball commissioner, on that very day when the M&M Boys had homers wiped from the books, stated that's what it would take for it to count as a genuine record.

If Maris had challenged Babe Ruth's single-season home-run record in 1960, 1962, or any other year but 1961, it wouldn't have been the same. That year marked a new era in America. There was a new president (Kennedy). There was a new manager of the Yankees (Houk). There were new baseball teams (the Los Angeles Angels, Washington Senators, and Minnesota Twins). There was a new schedule (162 games). There was a new age of television (impacting news, sports, politics, and entertainment). There were new heroes (astronauts). There were new villains (Adolf Eichmann, Fidel Castro). There was a new frontier (space). There was a new destination (the moon). There were new trouble spots (Berlin, Cuba, the Congo). There was a new and ambitious program for the idealistic (the Peace Corps). There was new fashion (anything worn by the first lady, Jacqueline Kennedy). There was a new dance craze (the Twist). There was a new folksinger taking New York City by storm (Bob Dylan). There was even a new boyfriend for Barbie (Ken). Indeed, the only person stuck in the past was Ford Frick.

Frick was a sportswriter before he served as president of the National League from 1934 until he became baseball's third commissioner, in 1951, following Judge Kenesaw Mountain Landis and Happy Chandler. He had been Babe Ruth's friend and ghostwriter earlier in his career—"I really liked the Ruth book they did together," remembered Ernie Harwell, the longtime broadcaster of the Detroit Tigers, in 2009. Frick was even at Ruth's deathbed in 1948. He considered himself the guardian of Ruth's cherished record, but when he hastily agreed to expansion to stop the formation of the rival Continental League, he set the wheels in motion for the record to be threatened. Frick could have instituted a schedule of 144 games or, better, 153 games, to protect Ruth, but instead he sanctioned a balanced 162-game schedule as a means to generate more revenue. He told Arthur Daley of the *New York Times* in the fall of 1960 that he didn't expect Ruth's record or other records to fall with the addition of only eight games.

When Frick realized he had been shortsighted, he needed to figure out how to derail the M&M Boys before it was too late. So on July 17, he asked a group of veteran sportswriters for ideas to prevent Ruth's record from being surpassed by a player who played more games. The influential Dick Young of the *Daily News* suggested that an asterisk be placed on a home-run record that was set in more than 154 games. Frick liked this idea. He didn't remind anyone in the room that Ruth wasn't given an asterisk in the record books in 1919 when he slammed 29 homers in a 154-game season to surpass the record 27 homers the Cubs' Ned Williamson hit in 1884 in a 112-game season. Frick formally announced that if Ruth's record was broken *after* 154 games, "a distinctive mark" would be placed in the record book next to the number of homers. In that way everyone would know that 60 homers remained the true record. Although Frick refrained from using the word *asterisk*, it became part of baseball's lexicon.

"Frick caused such a big problem," said Harwell, "because he changed the rules in the middle of the season. Considering he had a background in publicity before he became the president of the National League, it was a grievous error. It took some of the bloom off what Mantle and Maris were doing."

"What Frick did was take the joy out of the race," agrees Maury Allen. "Up to that time, it was a fun competition, but he stepped into the middle of it and made it ugly. Mickey went along with it much easier than Roger, who took it very, very hard and personally. He felt, 'They are making a ruling to hurt *me*. Babe Ruth is the Yankees and Mickey Mantle is the Yankees and I'm an outsider.' I think he looked at that ruling as a Frick-Yankee ruling. It was as if the Yankees told Frick to protect the Babe's image that they still were selling every day."

A week later, Walter Bingham of *Sports Illustrated* became one of the most prominent journalists to take a stand against Frick's pronouncement. "It was a foolish, pathetic little statement," he wrote, "foolish because it makes so little sense, pathetic because it will be ignored." It wasn't ignored. A poll of New York sportswriters voted to support Frick's ruling by a 2–1 margin. These same sportswriters couldn't understand why Maris wasn't eager to open up to them the rest of the season.

The commissioner's statement was tantamount to baseball itself rejecting pretenders to the throne, primarily Maris, who was two ahead of Mantle in the race. It caused deep divisions in the baseball community in the middle of the 1961 season and to this day. Those who backed Frick included baseball purists who believed eight additional games really did give current players an unfair advantage, as well as die-hard fans and writers who couldn't handle anyone but Ruth being the home-run king. Generations of fans grew up believing Ruth's 60 homers wasn't a benchmark but a record set in stone. To them, Babe Ruth and his seasonal and career home-run records were baseball, and if the foundation crumbled, the game itself would be diminished.

Those who opposed Frick, including the American League president, Joe Cronin, and many young fans who wanted a new home-run champion, believed a season was a season, and that if a player broke a record, it didn't matter how many games it took. Most people who favored Maris thought anyone who could withstand the pressure of being under the microscope in New York and still challenge Ruth earned their support. However, in the city where it was happening, at Yankee Stadium, and on WPIX, Channel 11, courtesy of broadcasters Mel Allen, Phil Rizzuto, and Red Barber, the great majority of fans and sportswriters concluded that if the record was going to be broken, then it should be done by a lifelong Yankee, not a two-year Yankee.

Also, they wanted it done by a true, career-long home-run hitter, someone who sent balls to the summit of Mount Olympus. Mickey Mantle might not have been the god Ruth was, but at least he was a Titan. Roger Maris, being a mere mortal, was unacceptable.

CHAPTER TWENTY-ONE

THE UNRELENTING PRESS

S UDDENLY MARIS FOUND HIMSELF in a bad slump with no injury for an excuse. After going hitless in a three-game series against Washington, he was 0 for 19 and his average was down to .272. He blamed himself, not Frick for burdening him and Mantle with a new sense of urgency in the home-run race. But the ruling was on his mind because reporters had changed their maddening question from "Are you going to break Ruth's record?" to "Are you going to break Ruth's record in 154 games?"

It was a loaded question. Not wanting to come across as being bigger than their sport, both Maris and Mantle told the press that they went along with the majority of ballplayers (including Whitey Ford, Jim Gentile, Stan Musial, and Norm Cash) who, when polled, agreed with Frick's ruling. Overly diplomatic, Mantle even said, "If I should break [Ruth's record] in the 155th game, I wouldn't want the record."

Maris was more honest: "I think the commissioner shouldn't have made any 154-game ruling when he did. But if Mick breaks it, I hope he does it in 154 games. The same goes for me."

Mantle stayed white-hot. He passed Maris with his 36th homer, off Washington's Dick Donovan, to give him 5 homers in 4 games and 7 homers in 7 games, not including the homer in the rainout. The Yankees, however, lost a doubleheader to the seventh-place Senators and fell into a tie for first place.

The losing pitcher in the second game was a recent call-up from Class A Binghamton. Al Downing, the Yankees' first black pitcher, remembers, "I hadn't been to spring training, so I hadn't seen Roger play in person. I'm a kid sitting on the bench watching him and thinking, 'Man, this guy really knows how to play baseball,' even when he wasn't hitting. If he were playing today, he would be on highlight films every night. Seriously. He was that good an outfielder, thrower, base runner, and everything else. I liked that he never got upset and was supportive of all us young players. He'd never demean us if we didn't do well. He would joke and say, 'Go home, eat dinner, and I'll see you tomorrow.' "

The Yankees concluded their long road trip with a three-game series in Boston. Maris couldn't shake his slump, yet still hit his 36th homer, in the first inning of the first game, against Bill Monbouquette. Mantle followed with his 37th homer to regain the lead. "I can't ever forget that they hit back-to-back home runs on fastballs over the bullpen and over different exit signs," recalls Monbouquette. The biggest hit of the game was delivered by pinch hitter Johnny Blanchard, a grand slam off Mike Fornieles with two outs in the ninth inning to give the Yankees a stunning 11–8 victory. "This was one of those games that makes you proud to be a Yankee," wrote Maris in his book. Blanchard hit another ninth-inning pinch homer the following game as the Yankees rallied for 3 runs and won, 11–9. Maris went 0 for 6.

When Maris and Mantle returned to New York, they read in the local papers that they had been feuding and it was just a matter of time before these bitter enemies would stage a duel at sunrise. "Apparently, the people who wrote the gossip columns," said Maris, "never read the sports pages." Unfortunately, the reporters who contributed to the sports pages believed the gossip columns because word of the nonexistent Maris-Mantle feud spread like wildfire and further polarized the fans. Most assumed Maris was at fault.

All the Yankee players knew the story was ludicrous because their right fielder and center fielder were blissfully living together in Queens with their backup left fielder. "I'd laugh because I'd read they were feuding," recalls Cerv, "and meanwhile we're all getting along fine. They were just starting to get lousy, gossipy sportswriters then, and I was thinking, 'How can these guys make up that garbage?' "

Their living situation was ideal because their neighbors left them alone and didn't reveal their whereabouts to the media. Their phone number was unlisted. Mantle and Cerv had twin beds in the bedroom, and Roger slept on a green studio couch in the large living room. They paid $251 a month in rent. They killed time by watching television—*The Andy Griffith Show* was a favorite—playing gin rummy and hearts for no money, and having marathon putting contests on their carpet with pennies on the line. According to Maris, they often listened to music, sometimes Maris's LPs—he mysteriously enjoyed Dixieland, swing, jazz, and dinner music—but usually Mantle's country records. Julie Isaacson told Tony Kubek for *Sixty-One* that when he visited the apartment, he'd put on his Hebrew albums: "Mickey and Roger would humor me for a while before they would change the record. But one day, Roger really surprised me. I took him to a friend's son's bar mitzvah, and Roger stood up and sang 'Hava Nagila.' He had learned the whole thing from listening to my record when I wasn't around. It really meant a lot to me. . . . He didn't do it as a joke, but as something to please a friend."

The three roommates drank beer in moderation and ate cold cuts, pizza, and, if someone had the energy to shop and cook, steak or something fried. Roger's kidney stew, his specialty, followed by raisin pie, wasn't in demand. In the mornings after a night game, they'd have breakfast and watch game shows. Cerv made eggs for himself and Mantle, but the finicky Roger insisted on making his own, "on the well-done side," the way only his wife and mother had perfected.

"The only thing we argued about was over who did the dishes," said Mantle years later. "And if Roger told him to, Cerv would do them."

A few hours before a game, the threesome climbed into Roger's new Oldsmobile convertible and headed toward the Bronx, discussing the pitcher they'd face. "They'd kid each other," reminisces Cerv. "One would say he was going to homer that day, and the other would say he'd hit two."

Before the game, Roger often sat at the huge oak table that had been in the middle of the clubhouse since the days of the Murderers' Row. Most players, but not Mantle, spent a half hour each day at the table signing autographs. "[Roger] had this game, it was a box about a foot wide and three inches deep," wrote Kubek in *Sixty-One*. "Inside there were two small wooden platforms with forty holes. The idea was to maneuver a little steel ball from one hole, through the maze, and one level to another. Roger was fascinated by it and would play the game for hours. He had a routine in which he could smoke his Camels, drink coffee, and play the game all at the same time." Other Yankees played the labyrinth game, but no one was in Maris's class.

A commemorative plate features the Maras brothers bowling team at the Ryan Hotel, 1912–14. From left: top row, Joseph, Peter; bottom row, Roger's paternal grandfather Steve, Mike, Paul.

Rudy Sr. and Connie Maras attend the wedding of Connie's sister Mary Sturbitz and James LaFreniere (*center*) in 1938.

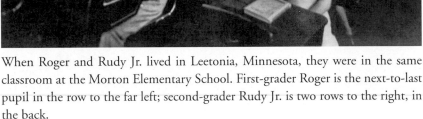

When Roger and Rudy Jr. lived in Leetonia, Minnesota, they were in the same classroom at the Morton Elementary School. First-grader Roger is the next-to-last pupil in the row to the far left; second-grader Rudy Jr. is two rows to the right, in the back.

Roger (*kneeling, center*) and Rudy Jr. (behind Roger's right shoulder) starred on the Fargo team that won the North Dakota American Legion state championship in the summer of 1950. Roger was voted team MVP.

Roger was an all-state football player for two years at Bishop Shanley High School. In 1950, when he and Rudy Jr. played together in the backfield, the Deacons were voted the best high school team in North Dakota.

Roger was eighteen when he broke into professional baseball in 1953 with the Class C Fargo-Moorhead Twins, which won the Northern League championship. In the team photo, he is in the middle of the front row, with John Morris to his right and Joe Camacho to his left. Frank Gravino is on the far left of the middle row. Jerry Mehlisch is the second from the left in the top row, Ray Seif is three players to his left, and manager Zeke Bonura is to the far right. *(Courtesy John Jensen and Jerry Mehlisch)*

Maris broke into the majors with the Cleveland Indians in 1957.

On the basepaths, Roger specialized in breaking up double-plays with hard slides into second, as he does here while playing for the Kansas City Athletics in 1959. On a ball hit by Bob Cerv, he upends Boston second baseman Pete Runnels.

With the addition of Roger Maris, the Yankees had a new Murderers' Row from 1960 to 1962 that included (*from left*) Yogi Berra, Mickey Mantle, and Bill "Moose" Skowron. *(National Baseball Hall of Fame Library, Cooperstown, NY)*

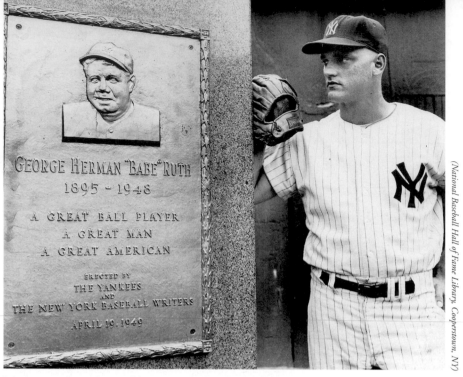

(National Baseball Hall of Fame Library, Cooperstown, NY)

Maris poses by Babe Ruth's monument in center field at Yankee Stadium, looking respectful, daunted, and almost apologetic for challenging the baseball god's single-season home-run record.

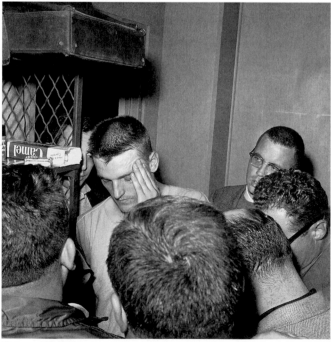

Late in the 1961 season, when it appeared that Roger had a real chance to break Babe Ruth's record, the pressure from the press became relentless. There was no escape, especially not in the locker room after games.

(Bettmann/CORBIS)

ABOVE: The shot that both won and broke hearts: Roger Maris connects on a Tracy Stallard fastball on October 1, 1961, at Yankee Stadium, and becomes the first player to hit 61 home runs in a single season. *(National Baseball Hall of Fame Library, Cooperstown, NY)*

BELOW: Sacramento restaurant owner Sam Gordon eyes the ball that Roger Maris hit for his 61st homer. Sal Durante, the man who caught it, and his new bride, Rosemarie, look on.

In 1962, President John F. Kennedy welcomes the thrilled Roger to the White House in honor of his home-run record, and the two autograph a baseball for charity. After he retired from baseball, Maris proudly displayed this photo in his office.

(National Baseball Hall of Fame Library, Cooperstown, NY)

Maris's exceptional defense was overlooked by fans and reporters, but not by opposing hitters. He often went into the stands to take away home runs, as on this play on May 7, 1962, on a ball hit by the Senators' Ken Retzer. *(National Baseball Hall of Fame Library, Cooperstown, NY)*

In 1965, Roger and Pat Maris make one of their frequent off-season visits to the famed Catskills resort Grossinger's. They were close to the owners and continued to holiday there after Roger's retirement. Roger and Pat were married twenty-nine years and had six children.

(National Baseball Hall of Fame Library, Cooperstown, NY)

ABOVE: Prior to the 1966 season, Maris and Ralph Houk assure the press that Roger's hand is in perfect shape following surgery. It isn't the case.

RIGHT: Andy Strasberg, Roger Maris's biggest fan, visits his idol at Yankee Stadium in 1966, Roger's last season in New York.

(Photo by Arnie Cardillo. Courtesy Andy Strasberg)

From left: World Series MVP Bob Gibson, a delighted Roger Maris, and Lou Brock celebrate a world championship for the St. Louis Cardinals in 1967.

(National Baseball Hall of Fame Library, Cooperstown, NY)

The prodigal player returns: On April 13, 1978, Roger comes back to Yankee Stadium for the first time in twelve years. The reunited M&M Boys receive a rousing ovation from the Opening Day crowd.

Some of the participants in the 1984 Cracker Jack Old Timers Classic were (*from left*) Whitey Ford, Warren Spahn, umpire Tom Gorman, Ed Lopat, Roger Maris, Jerry Coleman, and (*crouching*) Johnny Bench. *(Courtesy Dick Cecil)*

From left: Mickey Mantle, Roger Maris, Ken Hunt, Moose Skowron, Whitey Ford, and Rudy Maris Sr. help kick off the inaugural Roger Maris Celebrity Benefit Golf Tournament in Fargo, North Dakota. It would be held every June, beginning in 1984.

Roger and Arlene Howard, the widow of his good friend Elston Howard, are at Yankee Stadium on July 22, 1984, when the club retires the teammates' numbers. Because of illness, Roger will make only one more appearance at Yankee Stadium before his death in December 1985.

Roger Maris's grave at Holy Cross Cemetery in north Fargo, North Dakota. He is remembered by family, friends, and fans by the words inscribed on the gray, granite tombstone: "AGAINST ALL ODDS."

The famous photo of Roger Maris's picture-perfect swing as he becomes, on October 1, 1961, major league baseball's single-season home-run champion, breaking Babe Ruth's 34-year-old record. *(National Baseball Hall of Fame Library, Cooperstown, NY)*

After an exhibition game between the Yankees and the Giants—at which 47,000 fans revived the 1950s argument about who was the better center fielder, Willie Mays, who drove in 2 runs, or Mickey Mantle, who homered—the regular season resumed on July 25. Maris wasn't looking forward to his least-favorite event—a twi-night doubleheader. He was ready for the worst, but instead had his biggest day of the season.

In the first game against visiting Chicago, Maris hit a 2-run homer off Frank Baumann to tie Mantle for the league lead with 37 homers, Mantle followed with his 38th homer off Baumann to go one up again, and Maris again tied him with his 38th homer off former Yankee Don Larsen. Ford's record improved to 18-2 with a 5–1 victory. Stafford then tossed a 6-hit gem, as the Yankees routed Chicago, 12–0. Boyer had 2 homers and 4 RBIs, but Maris kept his pal from being interviewed by blasting number 39 off starter Russ Kemmerer and number 40 off reliever Warren Hacker with Richardson and Kubek on base to give him 8 RBIs for the two games. It was the only 4-homer day of Maris's career.

After 96 games, including the tie, Maris was now twenty-four games ahead of Ruth's pace, a season high. Dick Young, the creator of the asterisk, wrote, "Roger Maris is running away from Babe Ruth like a scared kid in a graveyard." In his last sixty-eight games, he'd hit 37 home runs. Sixty-seven games were left in the season. It was easy to do the math.

All Maris wanted to talk about was how the Yankees had moved ½ game ahead of Detroit. The press backed off criticizing Houk, who obviously had everything under control.

Mantle hit his 39th homer, his final longball in July, in the next game, against Ray Herbert. But the hero of the 5–2 victory over Chicago was Blanchard. He hadn't batted since hitting 2 pinch homers in successive games the previous week. His first two times up he took Herbert over the fence to tie the major league record with 4 consecutive home runs. In his next at-bat he came within a whisker of being the only player ever to homer in five straight at-bats, but right fielder Floyd Robinson caught the ball in front of the fence. "I was still happy," said Blanchard with a wink in 2008.

The Yankees finished the sweep of Chicago the next day as Sheldon bested Billy Pierce, 4–3. Maris was having his usual success against Pierce, with an RBI double and a single in two at-bats, when he pulled a hamstring.

Because he had the thick, muscular legs of a football player, he was susceptible to this injury for the rest of his career. With his leg heavily wrapped, he played the next day as the Yankees' 4-game winning streak ended against Baltimore. But because a drizzle made the field slippery, he was kept out of the lineup when Ford notched his 19th victory on Old-Timers' Day. Baltimore made it three out of four against the front-runners with a doubleheader sweep on Sunday, as Barber and Pappas held the Yankees to a single run. As a pinch hitter, Maris made the final out in the first game, grounding to first. This was typical of his recent outs of late, as he was having trouble lifting the ball.

Maris had a single in three at-bats in the second-game loss, but was lifted for a pinch runner. He made the trip to Boston to participate in the All-Star Game, on July 31, but his bad leg limited him to pinch-hitting. Rain halted the game after nine innings with the score 1–1, the first tie in All-Star Game history.

With Frank Crosetti as the temporary manager in place of the suspended Ralph Houk, the Yankees resumed play on August 2, ahead of Detroit by 1½ games after having won 20 of 29 games in July. Also picking up where it left off was what Maris called "the ding-dong chase" with Mantle. Although stuck on 40 homers, Maris was 1 homer ahead of Mantle and still eighteen games ahead of Ruth.

The reporters came out en masse, particularly in New York, which added to the pressure Maris felt trying to break out of a homerless streak. He didn't come through the first day back, in a doubleheader sweep against visiting Kansas City. But in the first game he scored the winning run in the bottom of the ninth inning by knocking the ball out of catcher Joe Pignatano's mitt with a hard slide. In the second game, he had an RBI double to left field in the first inning off ex-Yankee Art Ditmar, preceding Mantle's 40th home run to tie him for the league lead. Ditmar plunked Maris his next time up, forcing him to exit the game on two gimpy legs.

Maris had 2 hits in the final game of the series to raise his average to .284, but not until the next day against Minnesota did he hit his first homer since July 25. His 41st homer came on August 4, the day America's 44th president, Barack Obama, was born in Hawaii. The 3-run wallop in the first inning gave him 101 RBIs for the season and was extremely satisfying because it came off his nemesis Camilo Pascual after five years of futility. Still,

Maris tried to direct reporters to Blanchard, who won the game with a 3-run homer with two outs in the 10th inning.

Maris didn't homer again for a week. This longball drought, from July 26 through August 10, was even worse than the first month of the season. Significantly, his power outage lasted the length of the homestand. Not only were reporters trying to make him feel unworthy of breaking Ruth's record, but the fans were also getting into the act. The hate mail piled up. The anti-Maris element also reared its head at Yankee Stadium.

Yankee fans had booed Mantle for ten years for not being the all-around player DiMaggio was, for striking out too much, and even for being a draft dodger—they didn't believe the fastest man in baseball got a medical deferment during the Korean War. Now they embraced him as the quintessential baseball hero. They wrote Houk and told him to forget about the best lineup for a pennant run and switch Mantle to third so Maris could no longer benefit from his bat behind him. None mentioned that when Babe Ruth hit his 60 homers, he batted third in front of Lou Gehrig, who hit .373 with 47 home runs (as well as 52 doubles and 18 triples) and 175 runs batted in.

According to Merlyn Mantle in *A Hero All His Life: A Memoir by the Mantle Family*, it became clear "that Mickey was the people's choice. In a way it was weird. They sometimes booed Maris for hitting a home run. . . . Mick actually tried to help him with the press and the public. Boy, talk about a role reversal. It took his duel with Maris to get the fans to appreciate what he had done, and their ovations seemed to say, 'We should have told you sooner, but it's not too late. We love you, Mick.' "

Maris was baffled about home fans turning against him when he and Mantle were teammates. Why did it matter to them who hit the homers as long as the Yankees won? He had worried about fitting in with the Yankees when he'd joined the team in 1960, but that year he felt everyone accepted him. Now the fans and the New York press reminded him of his outsider status, and it was disheartening.

"What happened in the history of the Yankees," says Maury Allen, "was it went from Babe Ruth to Lou Gehrig to Joe DiMaggio to Mickey Mantle. But it never went from Mantle to Roger Maris. Roger knew intuitively that he was never going to be accepted as one of the historic Yankees figures." Unfortunately, as long as Maris was in a slump, he was an easy target, blood in the water.

Mantle seized the opportunity to take over the home-run lead. In a doubleheader sweep of Minnesota on August 6, he smashed 2 home runs off Pedro Ramos and another off Al Schroll. His 43 homers put him 2 ahead of Maris and nineteen games ahead of Ruth's pace, and it seemed clear that if anyone was to set a new record, Mantle was the man. Maris went 2 for 12 in the two games. The Yankees won the opener in fifteen innings, after Blanchard tied it in the tenth with another clutch homer. Houk believed what all Yankees believed: "Blanchard was amazing."

The Yankees took four close, low-scoring games against the visiting Angels, without either Maris or Mantle connecting. Maris's most discussed at-bat was a squeeze bunt in the first game. In the final game of the series, Ford and Arroyo stifled the Angels, 3–1. For the first time in his tremendous Hall of Fame career, Ford won his 20th game. Even the reporters came to his locker. "It was the damnedest thing," said Ford. "I'd been with the Yankees for ten years, and for ten years I'd been hoping to win twenty games. Now I win twenty-five, and all anybody asked me about was home runs." He still had to share headlines with the hitless M&M Boys.

The next day, the Yankees, boasting a 75-37 record and a 3-game lead, hit the road to play their final series ever in Washington's Griffith Stadium. The slumping Maris was extremely anxious. Wally Moses, the first-base coach and batting instructor, spent four hours talking to him in the men's room on the train. "Wally's mantra was, 'Keep your head behind the ball and drive it,' " says Jim Kaat, then a young left-hander on Minnesota. "If Roger was opening his shoulder and pulling *off* the ball, Wally told him to keep his front side closed as long as he could while striding *into* the ball."

Moses's advice helped Maris return from the brink. In the four-game weekend series that the Yankees split with the Senators, he homered in all four games. His 42nd, coming eight games after his 41st, was on a fastball off Pete Burnside, his third longball of the season off the left-hander. It was one of his few Mantlesque drives of the season, going halfway up the light tower in back of the right-field fence. Mantle also took Burnside deep to maintain his 2-homer lead. The next day, however, Maris produced the Yankees' lone run off Dick Donovan with his 43rd homer.

In the first game of a Sunday doubleheader on August 13, Maris's 44th homer and Mantle's 45th accounted for the Yankees' only runs in a loss to Bennie Daniels. In the nightcap, Marty Kutyna was the victim of Maris's

45th homer, a drive that cleared the thirty-one-foot fence. Coot Veal, the Senators' shortstop in 1961, remembers, "I was hurt and in the bullpen in center field and watched Maris and Mantle hit all of those home runs. Both of them hit balls high off the wall in right-center field that bounced into the bullpen. I've still got those two balls. I didn't think they'd have value at the time."

Even teammates were awed. "You're sitting there watching two guys having just a fantastic year, and it was game after game," says infielder Joe De Maestri. "Every time they came up, we would stand up in the dugout to see who was going to hit the next one."

Frank Scott received some press when he predicted that Roger could pick up $250,000 off the ball field if he broke Ruth's record. That would include television appearances, such as the one Scott had booked for the M&M Boys on an upcoming *Perry Como Show*, and endorsements, such as the $45,000-a-year, three-year deal he had in the works for the Mantle-Maris Wear line of clothes with the Uni-Wear Company. In every city, reporters asked Roger if he was anticipating a large salary increase and more lucrative endorsement deals following the season. Maris explained that while he was pleased to have more security for his family, money in itself was of little interest to him.

The truth was that both Roger, who held many jobs as a youngster, and Pat, who sold nylons at JCPenney during vacations from school, were children of the Depression who even then worried about earning and saving money, spent it wisely and thriftily, and never lived high off the hog. Even as he moved into a higher tax bracket, Roger played card games and other games for pennies or fun, and if he lost a few dollars at the racetrack, that was too much. After an afternoon of watching the ponies run, Julie Isaacson remembered, "Roger was down six bucks and he said to me, 'To hell with this. I'm not coming out here to throw my money away.'" The frugal ballplayer who once ate hamburgers and drank milk shakes every meal still existed.

Maris and Mantle returned to New York for a brief series with the White Sox. After 117 games, they were tied with 45 homers, fifteen games ahead of Ruth. In his book, Maris wrote, "The pressure was beginning to hit both Mickey and me. It became difficult for either of us to deny that the record was on our minds. . . . The fans talked about it, the papers were full of it. Now we not only had the New York writers who travel with the club, but magazine writers began to come around while the out-of-town writers were constant visitors. From here on it became quite a struggle."

"You had eleven dailies in New York in those days," Downing recalls, "and all the time you had twenty to thirty writers lurking in the middle of the clubhouse waiting for either Roger or Mickey to come through the door. They'd go right after them before they even got their clothes off."

"Nobody can measure the pressure that was on those two guys," says Maury Allen. "For Mantle, it was a little bit easier as a result of 1956. But what made it so hard for Maris was that he was not only fighting the memory of a dead hero, but also—and this was even more important to me—trying to beat out a current hero. The whole Yankee fandom, the whole Yankee organization, the whole country, wanted Mickey Mantle to break Babe Ruth's record and said, 'Who the hell is this guy Roger Maris standing in his way?' That was an enormous burden for him."

Maris never came close to reaching the level of acceptance enjoyed by Mantle, especially while headlines blared that the rivalry between them was spinning out of control. This fiction sold papers. They tried to take the allegations in stride and get a few laughs out of them. Mantle told the story about Maris returning to their apartment with coffee and the morning newspapers and saying, "Wake up, Mick, we're fighting again!" During warm-ups, when Mantle spotted a reporter standing near Maris, he trotted past them and called, "Maris, I hate your guts!" The next morning they'd check the papers to see if the reporter fell for it.

Bob Cerv was the ideal housemate for Maris and Mantle because of his attitude toward their home-run race: "It was exciting but I didn't really care who broke the record. What everyone cared about was making money by getting to the World Series."

"I think there were more than twenty players on that team that wanted Mantle to break the record," says Maury Allen. "He happened to be a lovable guy. Mickey bought them dinner, bought them drinks, gave them the goodies. That was part of it. They also wanted to experience the reflected glory Mantle brought to the team. They enjoyed being a part of Mickey Mantle's Yankees."

"I know all of the fellows at that time," said Bobby Richardson in the video *Pinstripe Power*, "and this is certainly not a put-down of Roger, but they were pulling for Mickey to win the home-run championship. Maybe because they were trying to break Babe Ruth's home-run record and he was a great Yankee and they thought that Mickey should be the appropriate one to do that."

Being a sensitive person, Maris must have been hurt that his teammates chose sides, but he knew they weren't rooting against him and were genuinely delighted when he homered. He was also buoyed by the knowledge that Mantle himself was rooting for Roger to continue what he was doing. A truly extraordinary aspect of the home-run race of 1961 was that both men were unselfish enough to want the competition to stay alive to the last day rather than for one to run away with the crown. Such was their awe and respect for each other. They inspired each other to stay focused and undeterred in their mission.

Almost 50,000 fans were at Yankee Stadium on August 15 to watch Maris and Mantle and see if Ford could win his 15th straight decision for a Yankee record. The White Sox scored 2 runs in the second inning, and that was enough for Juan Pizarro, who gave up only 4 hits. Two were by Maris, his 46th homer on a fastball in the fourth inning and a double in the eighth, after he hit one of many long flies in '61 that went just right of the foul pole. Chicago's 2–1 victory ended Ford's winning streak. Maris's homer streak was now five games long. He remained ahead of Mantle for the rest of the season.

Maris's "cousin" Billy Pierce took the mound for the Sox the next day, August 16. On the thirteenth anniversary of Babe Ruth's death, Roger drilled a pair of 2-run home runs into the upper deck, one on a fastball and one on a curve. Maris said that he was studying lefties more than right-handers at that time, but it also helped that he guessed what Pierce was throwing. "Regardless of the weather, Billy wore a long-sleeved sweatshirt," recalls Turley. "I told Roger that when he was going to throw a curveball, his hand went further up in his glove and you couldn't see his bare skin by the palm of his hand. When he was going to throw a fastball, he didn't go up as far and you could see the bare skin."

With his 47th and 48th home runs in the Yankees' victory, Maris, who tied his career high with 112 RBIs, moved 3 homers ahead of Mantle. He was informed that he had tied a major league record by belting 7 homers in 6 consecutive games and broken the American League record of 6 homers in 6 consecutive games held by Lou Gehrig, Ken Williams, and Roy Sievers.

In passing Gehrig, he set his first home-run record on "Babe Ruth Day." Mrs. Claire Ruth was present for the festivities to commemorate her husband's death and had the misfortune of seeing one of the Yankees she hoped wouldn't break his record inch closer. Maris was sympathetic toward her, but it didn't help his image when the press reported that he was trying to break an elderly widow's heart.

Maris continued to accommodate reporters, even after he had miserable games and really wanted to be left alone. The unwarranted attention embarrassed him in front of his teammates, but fortunately they were amused rather than resentful. Maris wanted privacy but the Yankee organization didn't provide it.

"Maybe Casey would have taken pressure from the press off Maris better than Houk," says Berra, "because he always handled the press real good and loved talking to them." Houk wanted no part of the wolf pack. So, although Maris didn't think it was part of his job description, he obligingly subjected himself to being grilled by the press, posing for photographs—Mantle joked they did so many back-to-back photos that they felt like Siamese twins— and, shy as Roger was, being interviewed while television cameras rolled.

Maris even helped Leonard Shecter with a quickie book he was writing for only a $1,000 advance called *Roger Maris—Home Run Hero*. In his 1969 book *The Jocks*, Shecter remembered:

> I accepted on the basis that a little money is better than none and that I liked Roger Maris. . . . So I spent about 40 separate hours with him over the next several months. He was friendly and amenable, talked with great freedom, revealed himself a lot more than he probably intended. But once it became apparent that he might break Babe Ruth's record of 60 home runs, he was besieged, bedeviled, bugged, blinded by flash bulbs and put upon in a manner only television reporters—and the American *paparazzi*—could conceive. I thought that by and large he responded rather well.

The Yankees departed on a four-city trip starting in Cleveland. Roger was reminded that East Coast reporters didn't have a monopoly on stupid questions. "Rog, do you consider yourself as good as Babe Ruth?" "Rog, did you get a good swing on that home run?" "Rog, does it help that Mantle bats behind you?" "Rog, are you going to homer today?" Maris's Fargo friend Dick Savageau says, "Roger was the kind of guy who would tell reporters, 'You want to know if I'm going to hit a home run today? Well, if I knew, I'd tell you.' And they didn't like that. But he was telling the truth. He didn't know. It was kind of a Midwestern thing, where Roger would say, 'Don't you understand what I just said?' "

"If he'd go 0 for 4, we'd try and get an answer as to why he did," recalls George Vecsey. "He was polite, but the third time somebody said, 'Yeah, but it didn't look like the pitcher was throwing that hard,' he might curse and say, 'Then *you* try to hit him.' "

Maris also was aggravated because every time he admitted he had a chance to beat Ruth's record, he was put on the defensive, as if he'd offended a deity. "I don't want to be Babe Ruth," Maris insisted. "He was a great ball-player. I'm not trying to replace him. The record is there and damn right I want to break it, but that isn't replacing Babe Ruth." Another time he stated, "Maybe I'm not a great man, but I damn well want to break the record."

Maris also hated being asked if he, Mantle, and other sluggers in the American League were hitting so many homers because of expansion. The implication was he was homering off Triple A–caliber pitchers, when in fact he hit almost all of his home runs off veterans, and even the rookies were real prospects. He pointed out that the eight-team National League was homering at a near-record pace as well. In response, the reporters asked him if all the homers in both leagues were the result of the ball being juiced, Maris said no, that hitters had changed and now left the dugout swinging from their heels.

"The press wouldn't leave Roger alone, even in the bathroom," says Tex Clevenger. "One day after he had a good game, he knew that they were going to jump on his ass so he went into a restroom and locked himself in one of the stalls and sat down on top of the toilet. Those sons of bitches came in and broke the door off its hinges so they could talk to him."

"Everything regarding Maris and Mantle and the reporters was so wide-open and disorganized," recalls Maury Allen. "Nothing was scheduled, everything was out of control. I myself knocked on his door in hotels. It would be ten o'clock at night and I'd need a quote so I'd go down the hall to his room. I'm sure other reporters did it, too. Even when he didn't homer, there'd be twenty reporters around him after a game. I didn't want the same quotes that everyone else got, so I tried to speak to him before a game, at his locker, or even on the bench until it was time to play."

Fans, too, knocked on Roger's and Mickey's doors late in the night. And they camped out in the lobby, hoping for autographs or just to touch the stars. The duo was forced to sneak out service entrances. Even that was difficult because often a young kid did sentry duty on their floor, and when they emerged from their rooms, he sent word to the autograph seekers that the M&M Boys were on the move. It got so bad that they often stayed put and ordered room service. Cerv, Maris's road roommate, monitored all calls and served as his bodyguard when they left the hotel for the team bus.

Dick Tomanek tried to give him some relief from the chaos. He recalls, "I had quit by then because I had a sore shoulder and was living about twenty miles from Cleveland. I went to the game and picked him up afterward and brought him to my house for dinner, old roommates getting together. We didn't tell anybody that he was coming, but our kids knew. So we had a traffic jam of kids on bicycles around the house, peeking in. I guess he was getting used to that kind of thing."

Maris and Mantle didn't homer in the first two games against Cleveland, but both got to Jim Perry in the first game of a Sunday doubleheader before 56,000 fans. Maris's 49th home run came in the Yankees' 124th game, putting him eleven games ahead of Ruth. It was his only hit in 18 at-bats, including his 0 for 2 in the second game, as his average fell below .280. Worrying about Pat's impending delivery likely played a part in his mini-slump. Mantle's 46th homer, in a 6-RBI day, was his first in a week and kept him alive in the pursuit of Ruth.

The Yankees, with twice as many wins as losses, moved on to Los Angeles. Maris's improbable year continued when on an off-day he, Mantle, and Berra went to Hollywood to make a cameo appearance in the romantic comedy *That Touch of Mink*. The three stars, who might have been working on the railroad, in the mines, and at the brickyard if they hadn't excelled at baseball, found themselves in a movie with box-office megastars Cary Grant and Doris Day.

Back at the hotel, Maris was thrilled to find a message informing him of the birth of his fourth child and third son. After a rough pregnancy, Pat gave birth a month earlier than expected, which surely helped Roger relax and focus on baseball during a pivotal period. In fact, he celebrated in his next game with a 2-run blast off Ken McBride to dead center field. Maris became the 9th player in history to hit 50 home runs in a season, the last being Mantle in 1956, and the first to do it before September, which was a major achievement. Like his 4-homer day on July 25 that gave him 40 homers, his 50th-homer day, in the Yankees' 125th game including the tie that wasn't counted in the standings, served notice that his pursuit of Ruth was for real. If he hit 11 home runs in his next 30 games he'd meet Frick's criteria for a new home-run champion.

Because Maris hit a monumental home run, the press didn't let up on him for the rest of the series, while Mantle, 4 homers behind, was no longer in such demand. "I could tell the pressure was building, so I didn't try to approach him even though we were friends," says his former Indians teammate catcher Earl Averill, who called for the pitch that resulted in Maris's 50th homer but later hit a game-winning homer off Luis Arroyo. "I couldn't believe all the attention he was getting. Man, the press was following him every inch of the way from the dugout to the cage, listening to every word he said. There was usually a certain air of nonchalance to Roger, but that wasn't there. He wasn't his easygoing self. Instead he was kind of rigid. I can't imagine what he was going through."

Neither could Roger's friend Ken Hunt, who had become a star outfielder for the Angels after the expansion draft. "In 1961, it seemed to Ken that each time they met, Roger was increasingly bitter toward the press," says Sherry Hunt. "He thought it would have been different if Roger had family support close by."

In the second game of the series, the Yankees and Angels were tied 6–6 after nine innings. Maris, who had gone 0 for 2 with 3 walks, came to the plate in the top of the tenth with two outs and Richardson on first. He tripled over Hunt's head to score Richardson, then came home himself on a wild pitch, as the Yankees won 8–6. Naturally, Maris was excited about his role in a big victory that upped his team's lead to 3 games, but he was disappointed as well when Hunt told him that his ball had struck the wall only two inches from the top. With the number of games to play dwindling, almost-homers were opportunities lost.

Maris's long 51st homer came off the A's Jerry Walker, in Kansas City. As proof he was slumping, it was his only hit in a three-game sweep. Roger usually thrived in Kansas City because he was able to relax with his family. This time, however, Pat and the baby remained in the hospital while her mother looked after Susan, Roger Jr., and Kevin. Roger was ecstatic to spend time with the kids, but they were all under siege in their home because a local newspaper printed their address when the baby was born. Fans came from a hundred miles away to see if they could catch a glimpse of Kansas City's biggest hero. They were cruising up and down the street, pulling into the driveway, peeking into his windows, and ringing the doorbell in hopes of an autograph. Maris phoned the paper to voice his outrage.

On Monday, an off-day, the tourists were gone, and Pat and the baby, named Randy, finally checked out of the hospital. Roger was pleased to spend at least one day with his entire family because it was his final trip home during the season. "During that long summer," stated Pat Maris in the *Look* article, "I followed the progress of Roger and his team like any avid fan, but it wasn't until late August . . . that I had my first glimpse of him. . . . Although I was naturally wrapped up in my happiness, I couldn't help noticing the strain and tenseness that Rog's face showed during that brief visit. It was so different from his usual easygoing expression."

The Yankees' final destination on their road trip was Minnesota. Maris went 1 for 10 against Camilo Pascual, Jim Kaat, and Jack Kralick, as the Yankees won only the middle game. Mantle reentered the race with Maris with his 47th homer off Kaat and 48th off Kralick in the Yankees' 133nd official game. He had passed Lou Gehrig's 47 home runs in 1927 and joked to the press, "I caught my man. Now Roger has to catch his." Apparently he believed that only Maris had a realistic chance to beat Ruth. While both men were ahead of Ruth's pace, they realized that Ruth began his amazing stretch run to 60 homers in his 132nd, 133rd, and 134th games, played on September 6 and 7, 1927, by slamming 5 homers to up his total to 49. After that, Ruth hit 11 homers in 20 games, a torrid pace that neither Mantle nor the struggling, worn-out Maris expected to equal. So it was essential to stay ahead of Ruth.

To avoid the fans in Minnesota, Roger spent most of his free time cooped up in his room with Cerv watching television, but he ventured outside to see his parents and brother. Rudy Jr. had worked with Allis-Chalmers, the Milwaukee-based corporation that sold bright orange tractors and other farm and industrial equipment, but he was now located in Cincinnati and saw Roger whenever he could. Among the many Fargo acquaintances who saw Roger play in Minneapolis was the town's popular mayor, Herschel Laskowitz, who reminded Roger that everyone in Fargo was rooting for him and passed out business cards boasting he was from "the hometown of Roger Maris." Also in attendance were the Blakelys, who had moved to Coon Rapids, Minnesota. During the game, Jack Blakely unfurled a large banner that read FARGO WELCOMES YOU, giving Roger a much-needed laugh.

Roger was always happy to see people from Fargo. Visitors from Hibbing were another matter. Michael Maras remembers when his father, Big Nick, took a few of the Homer Tavern's best customers to see Roger chase Ruth:

> They went to a gate at the baseball field, and out came the players. My dad met Whitey Ford, Mickey Mantle, and Yogi Berra. And then here came Roger. And my dad said to him, 'I'm your cousin Nick from Hibbing, Minnesota.' And my dad told me that Roger snubbed him and walked right past him. When Roger was on the bus, he pushed his face against the glass and gave my father the finger. He didn't know my father, so it had to do with his mother and our side of the family. She had to be the reason, because soon after she called the tavern and said, "Big Nick, leave us alone. We don't want to have anything to do with you." My father passed away in 2002 when he was ninety-three years old, and he lamented about his meeting with Roger until the day he died. He'd say, "Michael, I don't know what happened," and would just shake his head.

Although shy, Roger was known for being cordial with strangers, even aggressive autograph seekers, so his rudeness toward Big Nick and the Hibbing contingent could be dismissed as a bad moment caused by the tremendous pressure he was under. However, it wasn't the only time that he stepped out of character and slighted Marases. Whatever his mother had told him about her relationship to Rudy Sr.'s side of the family had put him firmly on her side, a willing participant in the long-standing feud. That never changed.

New York went 22-9 in August, for its third consecutive month with at least 20 victories. But Detroit had matched them and was still only 1½ games behind, with a three-game showdown at Yankee Stadium coming up. For the Yankees and Maris and Mantle, with 51 and 48 homers, September promised to be a do-or-die month.

CHAPTER TWENTY-TWO

DOWN THE STRETCH

Through the decades, the New York Yankees had dominated in September. Numerous contenders had believed they were the Yankees' equals until the month of reckoning, then found out the shocking truth. Still, the Detroit Tigers were a confident team when they arrived in New York for a three-game series that was anticipated by fans and reporters with the same zeal as a heavyweight championship bout. The Tigers, winners of 11 of their previous 14 games, were intent on sweeping so they could leave town with a 1½-game lead.

A major reason they believed they were title bound was their starting pitching. Frank Lary had 19 victories, future Hall of Famer Jim Bunning had 15, and Don Mossi, the opening-game starter, was 14-3. Detroit didn't have as strong a lineup as the Yankees from top to bottom, but the middle of the order was exceptional. First baseman Norm Cash, who batted fifth, was having what would in most years be a Triple Crown, MVP season, with 32 homers, 111 RBIs, and a league-leading .365 average thus far. Rocky Colavito, who batted fourth, had 39 homers and 122 RBIs, 2 ahead of Maris and 2 behind league-leader Jim Gentile. The team's longtime star, Al Kaline, was on his way to a .324 season, with 116 runs and a league-leading 41 doubles. The model of consistency and excellence, Kaline had for years been compared to Mantle as the league's best all-around player. Now he also was compared to Maris, because they both played an excellent right field and had terrific arms, and both were so shy and modest that they were accused of being aloof.

The first game was played on Friday night. Despite the oppressive heat, Yankee Stadium was packed with 65,566 fans and a few policemen who were there because Luis Arroyo had received a death threat from someone with anti–Puerto Rican sentiments. Two potent offenses proved ineffectual against Mossi and 22-game-winner Whitey Ford, as well as Bud Daley, who replaced Ford after he strained a hip muscle in the fourth inning. With the nail-biter scoreless in the top of the eighth, Daley walked veteran center fielder Billy Bruton. Kaline then slashed the ball into the left-field corner. Berra dug it out and fired to second to catch Kaline trying to stretch a single into a double. "Yogi has never let me forget that play," says Kaline. After an intentional walk to Colavito, Cash, who'd win 1961's batting title with a .361 average, popped to the catcher to end the threat.

The Yankees failed to score in the bottom of the eighth, and Houk brought in Arroyo, his third left-hander, to start the ninth. He told his nervous pitcher, "You better get them out or *I'll* kill you." Arroyo did, despite feeling he had a huge bull's-eye on the back of his jersey.

Mossi had given up only 5 hits through eight innings and got two quick outs as the hitless Maris—"I was in a terrible slump," he wrote, "one of the worst of my career"—flied out and the hitless Mantle, who was bothered by a pulled muscle in his arm, struck out for the third time. But this Yankee lineup was much more than two men. In a flash, Howard singled to center, Berra singled to right, and Skowron singled to left. Howard crossed home plate, and the Yankees had pulled out a 1–0 victory over the shocked Tigers, who dropped to 2½ games back.

Among the 50,261 fans at Saturday's game was Jerry Mehlisch, Maris's teammate on the Fargo-Moorhead Twins in 1953. Before the game, they spoke briefly in the dugout. Mehlisch remembers, "He looked tired and stressed. It was really sad when you think about all the pressure he was under from all directions. We didn't really talk much about that, but he did say that he was hoping to get out of Yankee Stadium down the line because 'the fans are really vultures. The more you do, the more they want.' Just before I left I said, 'Rog, I wish you a lot of luck with the record.' He looked at me and said, 'You know, Jerry, what will be will be. If it comes, it comes. I'll give it all I've got.' "

In the blistering ninety-six-degree heat, Ralph Terry, with an 11-2 record, matched up against "Yankee Killer" Lary, who was primed for his 20th victory. After being shut out the previous night, the Tigers scored 2 runs in the first on a Kaline single and Colavito's 40th home run. But that was it for their scoring. The Yankees came up with a run in the second when Mantle walked and Skowron doubled, then tied the game in the fourth when Maris doubled, advanced to third on an error, and scored on a squeeze bunt by Mantle. After hitting two balls to deep center, in the sixth inning Maris pulled a 3-2 slider by Lary, and number 52 landed beyond the right-field fence to give the Yankees a 3–2 lead. He had equaled Mantle's home run total from 1956, and the M&M Boys were now the first teammates since Ruth and Gehrig to smash 100 home runs in a season.

Maris came up next in the eighth inning after the Yankees scored 2 runs and had a man on first. Detroit manager Bob Scheffing brought in left-handed Hank Aguirre, then watched Roger pull another ball into the right-field stands. Number 53 was the most home runs hit by a Yankee since Babe Ruth smashed 54 in 1928. "Maris has a way of rising to every occasion, doesn't he?" asked Ralph Houk rhetorically. Jerry Mehlisch came to the right game. The Yankees' 7–2 victory put them 3½ games ahead of Detroit.

Roger was now eight games ahead of Ruth's pace, and the writers and photographers didn't leave him alone. Former batboy Fred Bengis remembers:

There was a reporter for the *Daily Mirror*, Ken Smith, who was at all the games with his photographer. He was a really short man, maybe five feet tall. He came up to me in the dugout and said I was getting in the way of the pictures they were taking of Roger crossing home plate. So he asked me to stand back toward the dugout so he could get his shots. That game I stayed back after Roger homered, and in the locker room later he asked me why I wasn't up at home plate like always. I told him what Ken Smith said. The next day Roger went up to him and said, "Listen, Freddy's part of the team and he's been coming up to the plate and shaking my hand every game this season, and that's where he's going to be coming, and don't ever tell him anything like you said again." And the guy just backed off.

Hoping to see the Yankees hammer a nail in Detroit's coffin, more than 55,000 fans showed up for the finale. A record 171,503 fans had come for the three-game series to determine the American League's best team. It was another broiling afternoon, with Stafford going against Bunning. Cash reached the seats in the first to give the Tigers a quick lead. In the bottom of the inning, Bunning disposed of Richardson and Kubek, then faced Maris. "That year, in fact during Maris's peak years," remembers Bunning, a future U.S. senator from Kentucky, "I had to make very good pitches to him because he was a clutch hitter and hit mistakes really well." Bunning held Maris to a single, but Mantle, who was day-to-day because of his painful forearm, followed with his 49th homer. Leading off in the bottom of the ninth inning, Mantle tied the game by launching his 50th homer into the right-field bleachers off Gerry Staley. Mantle joined Babe Ruth, Jimmie Foxx, and Ralph Kiner as the only players with more than one 50-homer season. And for the first time in history, two teammates had reached 50 homers. Maris was proud of this record.

Later in the inning, with two outs, Howard lashed a 3-run homer to left field. With the crushing 8–5 triumph, the Yankees swept the series and ended Detroit's World Series dream. The stunned Tigers lost a doubleheader the next day to Baltimore and eventually lost 9 straight games. As the Tigers folded, the Yankees won 13 consecutive games, building their lead to an insurmountable 11½ games.

The ailing Mantle sat out the Yankees' doubleheader sweep of the Senators on Labor Day. Maris went 0 for 4 in both games, as Blanchard and Boyer provided the big hits. Naturally, Maris was anxious because he was slumping at the worst possible time, and he wasn't in the mood to stand in the outfield and hear foul-mouthed Yankee fans insult him and his family. When approached by reporters after the game, he lit into the fans, without distinguishing between those who had been riding him and the others in the stands: "They are a lousy bunch of front-runners, that's what they are. Hit a home run and they love you, but make an out and they start booing. Give me the fans in Kansas City every time." He went on to warn the bad fans not to come around asking for autographs because he'd "walk through fifteen million of them and never look at one of them. I have as much love for them as they've got for me."

Maris was contrite when he read his quotes in the paper the next day. But the die had been cast, and the number of fans jeering him increased tenfold in Tuesday's victory. Mantle crushed his 51st homer against overmatched rookie Joe McClain, but Maris was unable to come up with a big hit to shut them up.

The next day, however, his one hit was his 54th homer, tying the record set by Babe Ruth in 1920, the first of four times he smashed over 50 homers that decade. It was yet another homer Maris hit in 1961 in support of Ford, who dominated the Senators, 8–0, for his 23rd victory. The victim was ex-Pirate Tom Cheney, who would set a major league record in 1962 by striking out 21 Orioles in 16 innings. "I didn't want to walk him," remembered Cheney in the 1994 book *We Played the Game*, "[but] if he got a ball from the center of the plate in, he didn't miss it. He hit my pitch." The Yankees had 5 homers in the game, as Blanchard homered twice, and Skowron and his seldom-used backup, Bob Hale, each homered once. Mantle fell 3 homers behind Maris, as well as 1 home run off Ruth's pace through 140 games, including the tie.

Maris, back up to seven games ahead of Ruth, was a bit happier when speaking to the press than in previous days, but he felt "embarrassed"—a word he used repeatedly to describe himself in 1961—that reporters clustered around him rather than Blanchard or Hale, who hit his only homer of the year. And he had no patience when he was presented a list of eighteen questions sent by a Japanese journal. After he answered a handful he quit and then found out that the next question was about how well he was handling the earlier questions.

Neither Maris nor Mantle admitted to the press that they thought the pennant race was over because they didn't want to talk only about their home-run race. But that's what they were asked about anyway. Tom Tresh, a young shortstop who was brought up on September 1, saw how Maris and Mantle were being suffocated by the constant demands of the media. "They couldn't have a normal day when they could just relax," recalled Tresh in 2008. "As soon as they arrived at the stadium, they started answering questions. The reporters kept talking to them in the clubhouse and even when they went out for fielding practice. The hardest part was after the game, when the writers wouldn't let them dress and go home."

In the documentary *Pinstripe Power*, Richardson recalled, "We had a walkway from the dugout into the clubhouse, and there would always be five or six reporters there and all they would say was, 'Roger, I need to talk to you. Roger, I need to talk to you.'"

"Roger wouldn't get a chance to change out of his clothes," remembers Joe De Maestri. "He'd be stuck inside his locker with twenty guys around him throwing questions at him. He tried to answer every single one seriously, and Mantle was laughing like hell, saying, 'That's it, Roger, you tell him.' Some of us would chuckle about it, but it turned out it was killing the guy."

Blanchard "felt sorry for Roger. I lockered next to him, and after a game I'd take my clothes and dress in Lopez's or Elston's locker. It was so crowded that some reporters came around and asked him questions from my locker. Roger sat inside the wire pen, and it was like confessional. There were always about twenty to thirty reporters around him, all asking the same questions. He couldn't say they were stupid questions because he would have been cru-cified. Maybe he came up with only one-line answers when the guys wanted long dissertations, but he didn't say anything derogatory. He always handled himself like a real professional."

"The press was unbearable," recalls Fred Bengis. "It was difficult for me to bring the bat bag into the locker room after a game because it was so crowded. The press hounded him everywhere he went and even cornered him to ask their ridiculous questions. Sometimes I could see him shake!"

On the air, Yankee broadcaster Mel Allen wondered aloud if someday someone would write about the pressure Maris was enduring down the stretch. In a rare in-studio interview, Roger told Allen that having to talk to all the reporters and pose for photographers before and after every game was the only thing that was difficult. "As far as playing the game, there is no pressure," he said. "Playing is the easiest part of it."

At times Roger looked terrified when surrounded by reporters. His eyes were those of a hunted animal. "It was as if I were in a trap and couldn't find an escape," Roger wrote in his book. "It was really beginning to get to me now. I was even afraid to go out for a haircut."

Somehow, amid the turmoil, Roger did sneak off to the barbershop be-cause he felt he was beginning to "look like a shaggy dog." The barber an-gered him by saying whoever gave him his last crewcut in Kansas City had done a hatchet job. He showed Roger his reflection in the mirror so that he could see several uneven spots on the back of his head. He trimmed Roger's hair short to cover them up, but as Roger's hair grew back in the next few days, the same spots showed up. He was losing his hair. He believed he had a scalp disease and postponed going to a doctor.

"At first it was pretty comical that Roger had to deal with the press be-cause he hated publicity," recalls De Maestri, "but then we could see a change in his face and eyes. It was like he'd been beaten. Then it was amazing to see his hair fall out."

"It was only when Roger started losing his hair that we understood what kind of pressure he was under," said Boyer.

"Nobody can measure the pressure that was on Maris," states Maury Allen. "It was the most any athlete endured in my fifty-five years in sports."

At times when Maris struggled at the plate, it took only one home run to get him back into a groove. The Cheney homer apparently did the trick because he homered again in the next game, on a fastball thrown by Cleveland's Dick Stigman, in a 7–3 Yankee victory. "I wanted to get ahead of him so I could get him out with curveballs," recalls Stigman. "He didn't like left-handers throwing curves. But if you don't have good control of your curveball, you're going to throw fastballs if you're behind." Maris's landmark 55th homer was the most by a major leaguer since Hank Greenberg's 58 homers in 1938. He was touched when he read in the paper what Mantle said about him, "He's a cinch. . . . And he deserves it. I'm rooting for him. Let's everybody root for him. I want to see him do it and I'm sure he will."

Roger was receiving up to three thousand messages a day. Letters, telegrams, and phone calls. The entire country was caught up in the homer race. It was being covered on the front pages of newspapers and featured in most magazines. Charts comparing Maris's and Mantle's homer paces to Ruth's in 1927 appeared daily. Back in Fargo, sportscaster Bill Weaver and the proud Rudy Maris Sr. spent evenings watching the Western Union ticker in the newsroom as it gave details of every Yankee game. Weaver remembered, "It would tick, tick, tick. It would go *hr*—home run—*ny*—New York. Then *m*, then *a* . . . Mantle or Maris? Which is it?"

After denying it for months, Maris finally admitted to himself, "I have a burning desire to break the record." Surely he wanted to hit 61 home runs because there was no bigger achievement for a baseball player. But he wanted to do it just as much to silence his critics, all those people who insisted he was a lousy hitter and had no business challenging Ruth. He took it personally when Hall of Famer Rogers Hornsby, who batted .424 in 1924, said that Maris's low average should disqualify him from being a true record holder.

One simpleton reporter from Texas got under Maris's skin by asking,

"What would you rather do, hit sixty-one home runs or bat .300?" Of course, Maris said that he'd rather hit more home runs than anyone else in history than be one of countless players to have hit .300. "What would you do?" Maris asked the reporter. "Bat .300," he said. "To each his own," said Maris, shaking his head. Mantle had the perfect answer in 1956 when a reporter asked him if he'd rather bat .400 or hit 61 home runs: "I'd rather hit .400 because if I did that, I'd be sure to hit sixty-one home runs."

Needing another 2-homer day to jump back in the race, Mantle had to settle for 1 homer in the next game, off Gary Bell, as the blazing Yankees scorched the Indians 9–1. His 52nd homer gave him and Maris a combined total of 107 home runs, tying the teammate record of Ruth and Gehrig that was set in 1927, when no club but the Yankees totaled more than 56 homers.

The long-standing two-player record was broken the next game, on Saturday, September 9, when Maris smashed his 56th home run off Mudcat Grant, equaling Hack Wilson's National League record set in 1930. "For the first time," says Grant, "I saw Roger other than as the all-around hitter he always had been. Now he was trying to beat you with the home run. I said, 'What the hell? What's Roger doing? Where did this guy come from?' "

Maris and Mantle reached 108 home runs in 142 games, excluding the tie, a dozen games before the 154-game deadline. Ford Frick said nothing. It was a great afternoon for the team as well, as it rallied for 4 runs in the bottom of the ninth inning for an 8–7 victory on "Whitey Ford Day." The big hit was a bases-clearing double by Blanchard.

Maris needed 5 more home runs to claim the record. It looked good on paper that he was 3 homers and six games ahead of Ruth with the 154th game (155th, including the tie) in Baltimore a week and a half away. But Maris had no cushion because from Ruth's 147th game until his 154th game in 1927, the sultan swatted 7 balls over the fence. Roger knew he had to add to his total before he reached 147 games so he wouldn't have to match Ruth's incredible pace from then on. So it was extraordinarily frustrating for him that when the Yankees swept a wild doubleheader from the Indians on Sunday, September 10, Roger's 27th birthday, he managed only a single in each game—despite priests in Fargo and Kansas City including him in their sermons.

"Time grows short when you reach September," wrote Joe Trimble in the *Daily News*. "Well, it's choking M&M in what is beginning to look like a fruitless pursuit of Babe Ruth's ghost."

Maris's first single against Cleveland drove in 2 runs as the Yankees batted around in a 6-run second inning, but the big hits in the first game were a 2-run homer by Blanchard and Bob Cerv's RBI single in the bottom of the eighth for a 7–6 victory. The memorable game featured Jim Coates drilling archrival Vic Power after he hit a 3-run homer against him; and the Indians' high-strung Jimmy Piersall decking one fan who ran toward him in center field and kicking another in the pants and—after order was restored— robbing Blanchard of another homer. Although the Yankees coasted to a 9–3 victory in the second game, the fans booed much of the time after a bad call by an umpire. They did cheer Mantle's 53rd homer off Jim Perry. No one expected that his 54th was almost two weeks away.

The Yankees began their final road trip in Chicago. They won their 13th consecutive game, 4–3, for their 100th win against only 45 losses. But it was another homerless game for Maris and Mantle. A steady rain caused the game to be called after six innings, and Maris told skeptical reporters that he didn't mind being denied more at-bats because the Yankees had won. Maris walked, singled, and scored twice in the game, but all the press was interested in was his being called out on strikes by home-plate umpire Hank Soar his second time up. Maris made a few innocuous statements about Soar missing the calls, but in the papers, Maris came across as a crybaby who was blaming umpires for his own failures. Also in print, Soar took Maris to task. Maris and Soar met privately and both denied saying the negative remarks attributed to them.

All month long, Maris felt that he was being misquoted or misinterpreted in the papers. "I'm not trying to knock anybody," wrote Maris in his book, "but when you're trying to answer one question, someone else butts in with another thing, and another guy comes in on half of what you said, and they misinterpret."

Maris grew up believing that a person was only as good as his word, so when a reporter deliberately twisted his words, it was tantamount to a betrayal of trust. He neither understood nor tolerated it.

When the press ran out of baseball questions, they'd get more personal, and Roger invariably cringed. One time he almost went after a reporter for

Time. Roger Kahn, who followed Maris for *Sports Illustrated*, reported this exchange:

> TIME WRITER: Do you play around on the road?
> MARIS: I'm a married man.
> TIME WRITER: I'm a married man myself, but I play around on the road.
> MARIS: That's your business.

Roger usually avoided answering questions about his wife, but he did say that when he spoke to her on the phone, she never mentioned home runs. Pat didn't want to add to her husband's stress, so she made him think she was too busy with the kids to pay much attention to baseball. But the truth was much different.

"When he was chasing the home-run record, it was a real mess for his wife," recalls Jerry Cosentino. "She had to put up with people in church, at the grocery, and at the mall across the street from her house. People kept asking, 'How's Roger doing?' And she'd have to say, 'He's doing the best that he can.' She had to take care of all their kids and at the same time endure the same things he did. She had it pretty hard."

On September 14, the Yankees' winning streak came to a rough ending when they lost a doubleheader to the White Sox, behind Herbert and Pizarro. Maris collected 3 singles in 8 at-bats and his 132nd RBI, but had trouble driving the ball. Suffering from a bad head cold, Mantle went 0 for 7. Mantle still needed 7 homers to tie Ruth, so he had no chance to reach 60 homers by Frick's deadline. Although he told reporters he was out of the race, he still realized that if he shook off his cold, he had an outside shot to match the record in 162 games. Maris, who insisted Mantle was still in it, still hoped to break the record by the twentieth, but he was now just 1 homer and one game ahead of Ruth's pace.

Detroit was 10½ games behind New York and hopelessly out of contention, but 42,000 fans attended a Friday doubleheader that kicked off a four-game series. Whitey Ford captured his 24th victory as the Yankees pounded the Tigers, 11–1. Berra became the fifth Yankee to hit 20 home runs, Howard became the sixth the following day, and Skowron's 25th was the Yankees' 222nd of the season to break the major league record set by the Cincinnati

Reds in 1956. Maris and Mantle didn't homer in the first game or the night-cap, which was won by Detroit 4–2.

One didn't know why his hair kept falling out in patches; the other didn't know why his cold wouldn't go away. Both were having trouble putting good wood on the ball. After 149 games in the standings. Maris and Ruth were now deadlocked at 56 homers. Mantle was 3 homers behind and fading.

That day, Maris read in the papers that he had been seen with movie actress Ava Gardner. She had dined at the New York restaurant where Maris and Cerv celebrated Roger's birthday, and their saying hello was enough for the press to start a rumor. He'd already been linked to other celebrities, including actress Janet Leigh, to whom he supposedly dedicated a home run. Another time some excitable reporters caught him having lunch with a good-looking woman and asked him who his date was. Maris, who had been baiting them, said, "Hey, guys, meet my mother," and their faces drooped. Every time there was gossip about a new paramour, Roger had to call Pat to prepare her for an avalanche of mail about her wayward husband.

So Maris wasn't in the mood to chat with reporters that morning, and he really didn't want to talk after going homerless in his second consecutive doubleheader and spending hours in right field being taunted by crude fans. Instead he holed up with his brother in the trainer's room, off-limits to the press. "I hadn't seen Bud in quite a while," wrote Maris. "It was just about this time that we were discussing a plan to have him become my business manager and financial adviser. We had things to talk about."

The reporters, who needed quotes for their daily Maris story—Shecter claimed he wrote about Maris thirty consecutive days—didn't want the brothers to talk on their time and staged a near mutiny. They demanded that Houk order Maris to talk to them. "It was pretty much a ritual," said Phil Pepe in the ESPN *SportsCentury* profile, "[that] when the game was over, you'd go to Mantle's locker and then you'd go to Maris's locker and get their thoughts on how they performed that day. It was our responsibility to talk to Roger, and [we] had to do it every day whether he hit a home run or struck out three times."

Houk felt that Roger deserved one day off from being grilled, especially when he went 1 for 9 that afternoon. He yelled back at the reporters. Reflecting on his outburst forty-seven years later, Houk says with a rueful chuckle, "I tried to protect him by letting him hide in the trainer's room, but that caused an even bigger uproar. There was no escape for Roger."

It was the most protective of Roger that Houk was all year. Would Stengel have stepped between him and the reporters when it got to be too much? Reporters of the day and his teammates are split on this. They do agree that the Yankees organization should have taken better care of Maris. Years later Maris said he was "left out to dry, by myself, and being a young kid it was very difficult." After he'd retired, the popular Yankee publicist Bob Fishel admitted with deep regret, "What I should have done was hold a daily fifteen-minute press conference in each city we went to. That way, Roger could have met his obligations and had the rest of the day to himself. But I didn't think of it."

Maris finally emerged from the trainer's room and was surrounded by disgruntled reporters. He was not contrite, but rather, according to Robert W. Creamer, "caustic and sarcastic" and refused to answer any questions, saying spitefully that if they wanted him to concede he wasn't going to break the record, then he conceded. He had warned Rudy Jr. not to let anyone interview him because the reporter might throw him a leading question and then make a big deal of his answer. In Maris's book, he said tellingly, "As I saw him standing there, looking at the whole thing, I wondered what was really in his mind. Actually, except for a tough break, it could have well been Bud in the middle of this rather than me." At the height of his accomplishment and fame, Roger still felt that he was living the career meant for Rudy Jr. before he got polio.

Maris was never given a free pass when he lost his cool around reporters, even when they were obviously pushing him over the edge. So the headline of Louis Effrat's unsympathetic article in *New York Times* read, "Maris Sulks in Trainer's Room as Futile Night Changes Mood."

"An unfortunate image," said Detroit icon Hank Greenberg, rallying to the defense of the player he signed to a professional contract in 1952. "I know him, he's just a boy. They get him talking, and he says things you don't say to reporters. The year I hit fifty-eight, drunks called me 'Jew bastard' and 'kike,' and I'd come in and sound off . . . then the next day . . . I'd know I'd been wrong. But the reporters protected me then. Why aren't the writers protecting Maris now?"

Roger Kahn, who quoted Greenberg in his *SI* article, explained, "Even if they chose to, reporters could not 'protect' Maris because Maris is being covered more intensely than any figure in sports history. Not Ruth or Dempsey or Tilden or Jones was ever subjected to such interviewing and shadowing for so sustained a period. No one can protect Maris; he must protect himself. But to do this he would have to duck questions and tell half-truths, and both are contrary to his nature."

It also was contrary to Maris's nature to concede that he was out of the home-run chase, especially when he didn't believe it. His most neglected achievement in 1961 was that he was able to homer late in the season although he couldn't hit a lick. He did this through sheer determination. Looking back at the season, Maris said, "I knew the chase after the home-run record had fouled up my swing." He didn't get his swing back and repeatedly struck out, popped to the shortstop, and fouled out to the catcher—"When I'm going bad, it's like I'm hitting in a silo," he told Shecter—and grounded into double plays. Yet he willed himself to homer just enough times.

Jerry Mehlisch believes Roger's background was the reason he was able to persevere despite enormous pressures and obstacles: "Roger and I had similar work ethics because of where we grew up. We were taught that you work until the job is done. When things got tough, we got tough. You don't have any excuses. That gives you the ability to concentrate. Roger had the will to do what needed to be done, but he wouldn't have been able to do it if he couldn't concentrate and put all the bad stuff out of mind. He was mentally prepared for the task."

Maris seemed to be dead in the water in Detroit, after a week without a homer. Then he crushed his 57th, his lone hit in a 10–4 loss to the Tigers. His 3rd homer of the year off Frank Lary came on an outside fastball and struck the facade in right-center field. "It wasn't a hard-hit ball," recalls Lary, who went 23-9 in 1961. "But it was high and that upper deck hung ten feet out over the field, and his ball caught the front of it. I won the game so it didn't matter to me. I heard Babe Ruth, Babe Ruth, all my life and wanted to see somebody from my time hold the record. I was pulling for Maris."

Al Kaline retrieved the home-run ball when it ricocheted back onto the field and threw it toward the Yankee dugout. "I didn't really get to know

Roger until the 1970s," says Kaline, "but I figured that ball had historic importance and wanted him to have it."

Roger was in a better mood when he faced the press, but he got himself into more trouble when Detroit writer Watson Spoelstra asked him if Kaline had made a gracious gesture. Maris agreed it was but said innocent words he later regretted: "Anybody would have done it."

Frank Lary says, "He was right that anyone would have done it," but at the time Roger's words were taken as a knock on the Tigers' most popular player.

"As I was witnessing it," recalled Stan Isaacs, "I said to myself, 'Roger, say that was a nice thing to do.' But that was Roger. He came across as an ungracious lout."

The Detroit papers detailed Maris's "slight" of Kaline, who today says, "I don't even remember it." The next day, in the final meeting between the Yankees and the Tigers, the 44,219 fans at the corner of Michigan and Turnbull booed Maris's every move.

Maris had moved a game ahead of Ruth's pace, but he needed to homer this day, too, because Ruth had hit his 57th homer, a grand slam, in the 151st game that counted in the 1927 standings and the 152nd game including the tie. In his first three times up against Jim Bunning, Maris walked, struck out, and walked again. Ever since 1961, Maris's detractors have pointed out that he received no intentional walks all year, as if that stat confirms he wasn't a dangerous hitter. The negative implication was that on every 2–0 and 3–1 count, the pitcher gave him a fastball down the middle rather than walk him with Mantle batting behind him. But even Mantle, who tied for the team lead, received intentional walks only once every seventeen games. Maris received 94 walks in 1961, 32 fewer than Mantle, but 29 more than Boyer, who batted in front of the pitcher, and 59 more than anyone else. Moreover, he was hit by the pitch a career-high 7 times, which was 7 times more than Mantle. In truth, pitchers were extremely careful facing Maris. When they came inside, they stayed off the plate. They gave him a high number of what baseball people call "unintentional intentional walks," including in September, when Maris complained that few pitchers offered him anything decent to hit as he neared Ruth.

The Tigers took an early lead against Stafford, but Boyer's 2-run homer put the Yankees on top, 3–2, in the fourth inning. With two outs in the top of the seventh, Kubek singled and Maris followed with a triple to increase the lead to 4–2. But the Tigers tied the score and the game went into extra innings. Luis Arroyo settled in for the Yankees, doing battle with the Tigers' standout reliever, Terry Fox, whose ERA would be a minuscule 1.41 for the year. In the top of the twelfth, Kubek singled with two outs, bringing up Maris, who had flown out against Fox in the tenth. Fox remembers:

> Tony Kubek wrote a book about the season, and supposedly Maris stepped out of the box and watched a flock of geese fly over. I don't remember that happening. Then he said Roger hit my first pitch out of the park, and that wasn't so. I think it was on a 2-1 count.
>
> Roger was geared to hit the inside pitch. I tried throwing him an inside pitch earlier in the year in Detroit, and he almost took off Cash's glove with a liner down the first-base line. So now my thinking was that I couldn't surprise him with an inside pitch and sure couldn't throw it by him, so I had to go away, which I usually did against left-handed hitters. The pitch that he hit was a curve on the outside part of the plate. It was probably a ball. He was channeled to pull the ball, and he had the stroke most hitters want. He pulled it to right-center field, to the upper-deck facing.

Maris's 58th home run in the twelfth inning of the Yankees' 6–4 victory was one of his most dramatic of the season. He had tied Jimmie Foxx (who clouted 58 homers in 1932) and Hank Greenberg for the most home runs ever hit by a ballplayer not named Babe Ruth. He kept one game ahead of Ruth's 1927 pace and still had three games to play under Frick's guidelines. Moreover, and this was vital to Maris, it had shut up the Tigers fans, and "it had come in the clutch, thus annoying the people who claimed I wasn't a clutch hitter."

CHAPTER TWENTY-THREE

BABE RUTH'S GHOST

O NE OF ROGER MARIS'S many unusual exchanges with reporters in 1961 went this way:

REPORTER: Who's your favorite male singer?
MARIS: Frank Sinatra.
REPORTER: Who's your favorite female singer?
MARIS: I don't have a favorite female singer.
REPORTER: Would it be all right if I wrote Doris Day?

Another went like this:

REPORTER: What's a .260 hitter like you doing hitting all those home runs?
MARIS: What are you—a writer or a fucking idiot?

And another went like this:

REPORTER: Why are you hitting all these home runs?
MARIS: How should I know? Why is the Pope Catholic?

It's little wonder that by mid-September Maris felt that he was "a freak in a sideshow" and "was ready to crack up." "Half-goofy" was how his concerned father described him to the *Fargo Forum*. This was Maris's first year without injury, but he was losing his hair and losing his mind. Drinking water was like swallowing ice cubes, and his digestive tract wasn't working so well, either. He told Jerry Izenberg of the *Newark Star-Ledger*, "I am never really going to be as healthy as I was before this whole damn thing started." Repeatedly, he said that he wished the season were over, and more than once he seriously thought he had to quit or go off the deep end.

Mantle, the only person who truly understood what Roger was going through, told him there was a light at the end of the tunnel and to hang in a little longer. "After a while, he came to me and said, 'I can't take it anymore, Mick.' And I had to tell him, 'You'll have to take it, you'll just have to.'" When Maris was set on sitting out a game of the doubleheader prior to the 154th game (not including the tie), Mantle and Cerv told him he couldn't do it. Besides, an off-day preceded the twinbill and he could rest then.

"When Roger came to Baltimore," says Dick Williams, "he was met at the train station by Whitey Herzog, who was then playing for the Orioles. They were close friends in Kansas City and hunting buddies. Whitey rescued him by keeping him at his house where no one could get at him during the day."

Maris and Herzog sneaked past fans, reporters, and photographers to twice visit a sick boy in Johns Hopkins Hospital. Four-year-old Frank Sliwka was the son of a former Senators farmhand. "The kid is so sick," Maris confided to a friend, "it shakes me up." The press was kept in the dark because Maris never wanted publicity when he visited hospitals during his career. In fact, he didn't show for a scheduled interview with the *New York Post*'s Milt Gross so that he could see the boy, who passed away two days later. Roger refused to give Gross an explanation, freeing him to write a nasty article.

Ironically, Mantle, who gave Maris a pep talk so he'd play, felt too ill to take the field in either game against Baltimore on September 19. In his only appearance in the series, he struck out as a pinch hitter for the final out of the first game. The Orioles scored the game's lone run against Ford in the bottom of the first inning. A tough Steve Barber limited the Yankees to 4 singles, none by Maris.

In the second game, against right-hander "Skinny" Brown, Houk moved Maris to center field and inserted Berra in left and Blanchard in right. The Yankees clinched a tie for the pennant by winning, 3–1, as Daley threw a 5-hitter and the offense contributed 12 hits, including a 2-run homer by Skowron. Maris, pressing, got only an infield single. In his last at-bat he faced Hoyt Wilhelm. "Hoyt has the greatest knuckle ball in the business," wrote Maris in his book. "You have to be lucky to even hit the ball, to say nothing of hitting a homer. I didn't hit it. I struck out."

After the doubleheader, Maris trailed Ruth by 2 home runs. In Ruth's 152nd game, not including the tie, he hit his 58th and 59th homers, the second being another grand slam. In the 153rd game that counted in the standings, Ruth slammed his famous 60th homer off Washington's Tom Zachary. Ruth did not homer in his team's finale, the 154th game to count in the standings and the '27 Yankees' 155th official game. After 153 games that counted in the '61 standings, Maris had 58 homers. According to Frick, he had only one more game left to tie or pass Ruth. Though Maris actually had nine games left, he hoped to end all arguments by tying the record the next day in Baltimore, Ruth's birthplace. That the Yankees needed one victory to clinch the pennant was extra incentive.

Milt Pappas was slated to be the Orioles' starting pitcher. "The night before the game," Pappas remembers, "Mickey and Roger were coming down the hallway behind the clubhouse and I ran into them. I told Roger, 'It's really horseshit what Frick is doing with the asterisk. So I'm going to throw you nothing but fastballs tomorrow night, and if you see me shaking my head, I'm shaking off either a slider or the changeup.' He looked at me quizzically and said, 'Jesus, are you serious?' And I said, 'Very much so. I want to see you break the record.' Mickey said, "Hey, what about me?' I said, 'You're on your own, big boy.' "

Some have disputed Pappas's story, but he has stuck by it. "Knowing Milt," says Dick Williams, "I'd say it's true. But knowing what's coming can screw up hitters, which is why most don't want to know."

Roger spent the next afternoon relaxing at Herzog's house. After an early meal, his former A's teammate drove him to the ballpark and wished him luck. A slight drizzle and reports of near-hurricane winds in the area meant the game might be canceled. Maris sat in the clubhouse chain-smoking, reading newspapers, and accepting the good wishes of his teammates. With Mantle out of the race, every Yankee was wholeheartedly rooting for Maris. "Our allegiance switched over," said Richardson in 2005, "and we really wanted to see Roger break the record." Mantle, still too ill to play, was leading the cheers.

Rollie Sheldon remembers, "The reporters kept asking, 'Are you going to do it tonight, Rog?' So he left the clubhouse and I followed him outside, and suddenly we were there by ourselves amidst some construction work at the stadium. He was smoking a cigarette and I talked to him a little bit about how he was going to have a good night. It was the one tender moment I had with him."

Maris returned to the clubhouse. "Everybody was on tiptoes," recalled Jim Ogle in the ESPN *SportsCentury* Maris profile. "Nobody went near Roger. He just sat there. Nobody seemed to want to talk. It was an eerie, unnatural situation."

Batting practice was canceled, but not the game. This was appreciated by the 21,032 fans in the stands and a huge audience for a special national, prime-time television broadcast. Hank Greenberg was the television analyst for the historic game. Pat Maris planned to watch a closed-circuit broadcast set up for her by KMBC-TV in Kansas City, and Claire Ruth was going to watch in New York City.

Behind the scenes, Maris lost it. He went to Houk and, almost in tears, pleaded with him for the night off. Houk felt compassion but reminded him that the people in the stands and baseball fans all over the country expected him to play. Houk finally told him, "You start the game, and after an inning or two, I'll take you out." Roger agreed only because Houk promised a quick hook. But each time he ran from right field into the dugout, Houk looked in the opposite direction. Maris said nothing, Houk said nothing. Maris went all nine innings in what he called "the toughest game I ever played."

In the first inning, Maris got hold of a Pappas fastball, and for a moment everyone *thought* it was gone. The line drive faded in the wind and was caught in front of the fence by right fielder Earl Robinson.

In the third inning, Maris really got hold of a Pappas fastball and everyone *knew* it was gone, a 400-foot drive to deep right field. Yankee broadcaster Mel Allen made his signature call: "There's one! It is going, it is going, it is gone! Number fifty-nine!" History had been made. Maris had broken the tie with Hank Greenberg (who was in the booth) and Jimmie Foxx (from whom he'd receive a congratulatory telegram), and equaled Babe Ruth's record-breaking total from 1921, the second most homers ever hit in a season. It was his 31st homer outside Yankee Stadium in 1961.

Maris, Joe Trimble wrote in the *Daily News*, "saw it crash against a concrete step adjacent to an unoccupied box seat. As it hit, Maris happily flung his bat away and began to jog around the bases."

Maris was greeted at home plate by Berra, the on-deck hitter. He was receiving congratulations in the dugout when Berra also homered. Blanchard then doubled and scored on a single by Howard. Maris was pleased that he and the three catchers, two of whom flanked Maris in the outfield that day, had put the Yankees up 4–0, but the rally resulted in Pappas's early departure. "I wanted to win the ballgame," says Pappas, "but I was glad Maris hit the home run, and if I stayed in, he might have set the record that night."

It's possible that between innings Roger met Bob Reitz, who caught the home-run ball, and when Reitz asked $2,500 for it, Roger said, "Good luck to you," and walked away. But according to Bob Hale, "Roger made an appointment to see these people the next day to talk about the ball. He was going to offer them an all-expenses-paid trip to the World Series. But when he arrived, a bunch of TV trucks were there and he turned back. Roger really wanted the ball, though, so he spoke to the guy who had it on the phone. I guess he wanted a lot of money, so Roger said, 'Forget it.' "

In the fourth inning, Maris faced tough veteran reliever Dick Hall, a 6'6" former outfielder. Maris hit a fly to deep right field that had a chance. It curved foul. The wind had strengthened and was now blowing in and toward the first-base line, making it difficult to pull a ball and keep it fair. Maris became one of Hall's 7 strikeout victims that night.

In the seventh inning, with the score 4–2, Maris faced Hall again. He hit another long fly down the right-field line. Everyone held their breath. It had the distance, but again the wind pushed it foul. Then with two strikes, Maris unloaded and hit a long drive to right-center field. It was the hardest-hit ball of the night. In July, the rain in Baltimore had washed out a home run that would have given him 60 already, and now the wind protected native-son Ruth. Robinson made the catch about ten feet from the wall. "I thought Ruth was up there and knocked it down," said Blanchard.

In the ninth inning, Maris came to bat for the final time. The manager brought in Hoyt Wilhelm, who had given up only 5 home runs in 112 innings. He was, as Roger stated in *Life*'s September 29th issue, "the last guy in the world I wanted to see." A story persists that Orioles manager Paul Richards told Wilhelm he'd fine him if he threw Maris anything but knuckleballs, but it's a fabrication. By this time Richards was an executive with the 1962 National League expansion-team Houston Colt .45s and had been replaced as Orioles manager by his coach Lum Harris.

"I felt awful when Luman Harris brought in Wilhelm," Herzog told Kubek for his book *Sixty-One.* "It just wasn't fair. The game was pretty much over. There was just no reason to use Hoyt, other than to make it tough on Roger personally. . . . They just didn't want Roger to break the record in Ruth's hometown."

Nobody had to order Wilhelm to throw knuckleballs because that's what he threw. An uncertain Maris barely fouled off the first pitch, taking a half stroke. On the second pitch, the ball struck the bat rather than vice versa, and it dribbled weakly to Wilhelm. Running to first, where Wilhelm tagged him out, Maris looked deflated, as if the air of enthusiasm had been sucked from his body. "In his heart he had failed," said Maury Allen in ESPN's *Roger Maris: Reluctant Hero.* Maris tossed his helmet to the ground.

Blanchard brought him his glove at first base and told him that he was proud of him. "He smiled at me, but I know that he was ticked off," Blanchard recalled in 2008.

Ralph Terry went the distance, yielding only 4 hits in the 4–2 victory, and the Yankees clinched the pennant that had been theirs since early September. When the team left the field after the two-hour game, the Orioles fans gave an ovation. It was obviously meant for Roger, the outsider on the Yankees, and not the hated champions, who had won their 11th pennant in 13 years. Maris hit only a solo home run in 5 at-bats in his 154th game, but his performance would be remembered as one of the gutsiest in baseball history.

Bob Maisel reported in the *Baltimore Sun,* "Roger Maris gave it such a stern battle that he seemed to have most of the 21,032 Memorial Stadium fans on his side at the end. One man seemed to express the feelings of the crowd when, while leaving the stadium, he said, 'I came in here hoping the guy would never hit another home run, and I left pulling for him to tie Ruth. I never would have believed it possible, but he gave it such a try that he converted me.' "

However, some journalists couldn't be swayed. Fred Lieb, the veteran Associated Press and *Sporting News* sportswriter, who originated the term *The House That Ruth Built,* wrote, "Perhaps it may sound corny, but my biggest sports thrill of 1961 was seeing Roger Maris hit a weak squib to Hoyt Wilhelm. It wasn't that this writer had anything against Maris, but as one of the Old Guard who had been close to Ruth and who has sent word of the 60th homer over the AP wires, one can't be blamed for having nostalgic memories and rooting for the good old Babe."

"Roger Maris's failure to break Babe Ruth's record of 60 home runs over a 154-game stretch evokes no great regrets here," wrote Oliver Kuechle of the *Milwaukee Journal.* "Not that records are not to be broken or that Maris did not make a gallant, exciting try for it, but that when the record is broken, as some day it must be, it should be by somebody of greater baseball stature and of greater color and public appeal. There just isn't anything deeply heroic about the man, and the American public loves its heroes, particularly a record breaker of something as Babe's mark, to be of the heroic mold."

Roger Maris appeared on the scene at an exciting time when America wanted heroes, be they dynamic presidents, brave astronauts, or record-breaking home-run hitters. He was a hero for the taking, and those few who took him to their hearts picked the right man, as his teammates could have guaranteed. But most of the baseball world, from fans to sportswriters, rejected him. Instead of being lionized, the shy, kind, and talented Roger Maris was taking his place as the most unpopular and vilified athlete in America.

"He did heroic things, there's no question about that," said Robert Creamer in *Roger Maris: Reluctant Hero.* "But it's the perception of heroism on the part of the press and the people [that] amplifies one man to heroic status while another one is dismissed. Maris didn't have that quality that let the public adulate him."

Some sportswriters who had been following Maris around the country packed their bags once the 154th game was played, with Maris 1 homer short. Roger Kahn turned in his Maris profile to *Sports Illustrated* (for which a complimentary Maris later told him, "Of all the horseshit that got written, yours was the best"). Leonard Shecter finished his book. Even the *Life* magazine article that Maris supposedly wrote about the 154th game had as its subtitle "The nerve-wracking last chance to beat the Babe's record." Maris concluded that article with a sentence that began with words registering finality: "I made a pretty good run at Ruth's record . . ." And similarly, during the celebration in the clubhouse following the pennant clincher, a smiling Maris told reporters, "I tried. I'm lucky I hit as many as I did. And now I'm completely relieved." So was it really all over with eight games still on the schedule?

If Maris truly believed that the pressure was off and he could relax for the rest of the season, it was self-deception. He never really bought into Frick's contention that Ruth's record must be broken in 154 games. His mind was still on catching Ruth—because it still had meaning. As for there being no pressure on him anymore, he'd soon find out that the opposite was true. "It was worse than ever," he'd say days later.

On "Oriole Appreciation Night," Maris was the only everyday starter in the lineup besides Richardson, who didn't play all nine innings. Maris's head probably wasn't in the game as he went 0 for 4 against Jack Fisher, who 3-hit the faux Yankees 5–3. But Maris had a cheerful moment when he was informed at home plate prior to the game that he'd been selected the "Sultan of Swat" by the Maryland Professional Baseball Players Association for the second consecutive year. He proudly accepted the honor and promised to attend a ceremony in January at which he'd be given a $2,000 jeweled crown.

When the Yankees arrived in Boston, Maris was surprised that his anxiety had escalated and interest in his pursuit of Babe Ruth had not diminished. Clearly some reporters were even more negative toward what Maris was trying to accomplish. They viewed the proposed asterisk as the sign of an opportunist and cheat. "Before the game we'd go behind the screen so we couldn't be seen talking," recalls Carroll Hardy, who played center field for Boston. "Roger told me, 'My hair keeps falling out. I can't take this pressure.' "

Although he still felt sickly, Mantle returned to the Yankees' lineup on Saturday, September 23. His first time up, he smashed a long 3-run homer off Don Schwall, the American League's Rookie of the Year in 1961. Mantle's 54th homer was his first since September 10 and the last of his sensational season.

In the Yankees' 8–3 victory, Cerv hit his major-league-record 12th career pinch homer. Whitey Ford earned his 25th and final win in the best year of his Hall of Fame career. For the 15th time, Luis Arroyo saved a Ford victory. Maris had an RBI single in three official at-bats and walked twice. He also walked his first time up against Bill Monbouquette in Sunday's 3–1 loss to Boston, and again stroked a single in three official at-bats. With only five games left, he was getting frustrated. He felt he had no recourse but to chase balls off the plate because the pitchers preferred walking him to giving up his 60th homer.

The Yankees returned to New York. Maris and Mantle heard and read the gossip about how their feud had caused them to move out of their Queens apartment. In truth, they'd checked into a hotel because their wives were coming to the city to spend the last days of the season with them.

On the off-day before Merlyn Mantle's arrival by train from Dallas, Mickey took the recommendation of Yankee broadcaster Mel Allen and saw Dr. Max Jacobson, an East Side doctor, to make sure his bad cold wasn't really the flu. "Dr. Feelgood" had treated such celebrities as Tennessee Williams, Truman Capote, and Elizabeth Taylor, so Mantle hoped he could cure what was ailing him. In *The Mick*, Mantle recalled:

> Dr. Max. He greets me at the door wearing a white smock with bloodstains all over it. . . . He stuck the needle up too high. It felt as though he'd stuck a red hot poker into me. . . . The next morning I wake up in my hotel room and realize I'm sweating, sick, burning up with fever. . . . I can't make it to the toilet, let alone to Penn Station. . . . A couple of hours later my fever is worse. I'm really dizzy and there's Merlyn at the foot of my bed. "What happened to you?" "Nothing much. I just got sucked dry by a vampire." I finally had to call Ralph Houk and tell him I couldn't play ball that night. It nearly broke my heart. . . . I ended up in Lenox Hill Hospital, where they lanced the wound, first cutting a three-inch star over the hip bone, then letting it drain. It left a hole so big that you could put a golf ball in it.

Dr. Jacobson sent a bill. Mantle never paid it. He checked out of the hospital and started the next game. He walked in the first inning and was taken out for a pinch runner. He returned to Lenox Hill for the rest of the season. Cerv also was a patient at Lenox Hill. In the final game in Boston, Cerv, who played his entire career with no ACL, blew out his knee and needed surgery. He and Mantle had to watch Maris's pursuit of Ruth on television in the hospital. Roger was a frequent visitor.

Roger's reunion with Pat wasn't as dramatic as that of Mickey and Merlyn, but it also involved a doctor. In her article "My Husband," for *Look*, Pat Maris recalled:

When I spoke to him, I knew the words weren't registering. I was afraid he'd crack in two. I'd never seen him so tense. But I still knew he was glad I was there. . . . In the first few seconds after we'd kissed hello in New York, I took a quick, nervous look at his scalp. The papers had been playing up the fact that his hair was falling out from the nervous strain. I expected to see him practically bald. He caught me looking and we both chuckled, because his head did look as if a bad barber had slipped with his clippers. I told him he looked like a molting bird. Then we went off to see a doctor.

Back in the clubhouse, Blanchard took another look at Roger's head and "I accused him of having ringworm. Roger told me, 'Blanch, the doctor gave me pills for my nerves and says the hair will grow back.' 'It ain't growing back,' I said. 'You'd better get yourself a crewcut wig.' He laughed."

The Yankees' 159th official game, including the tie, was against the Orioles on Tuesday night, September 26. Right-hander Jack Fisher followed up his 3-hitter against New York the previous Thursday with an 8-hit complete game. Fisher had given up Ted Williams's career-ending homer the previous year, and on this day he again found a moment of infamy.

On a 2–2 pitch in the third inning, Roger Maris pulled Fisher's high curve down the right-field foul line. "I threw it," said Fisher, "and the minute I did, I said to myself that does it. That's 60."

Yankee broadcaster Mel Allen said excitedly, "There it is. If it stays fair . . ." It stayed fair by about five feet. It hit the facade of the upper deck, a blow that was worthy of Babe Ruth, and bounced back onto the field. Earl Robinson threw it in. Maris floated on air as he circled the bases, his mind blank. When he saw all the fans and his teammates standing and cheering, he knew for certain that he'd just hit his 60th home run and tied, finally, the monumental record of Babe Ruth.

A thrilled and incredulous Mel Allen told his viewers, "A standing ovation for Roger Maris, who got number 60. They are calling him out of the dugout! This is most unusual! They are asking him to come out of the dugout. Now this is something. They are standing and they are asking Roger to come out." It would be a long time before curtain calls were in vogue in baseball. The smiling but dazed Maris complied with the crowd's wishes, awkwardly waving his hat before quickly disappearing into the dugout.

After the Yankees' 3–2 victory, Maris spent a long time with a horde of reporters. The main point he made was: "This is easily the greatest thrill of my life." Maris also stood in front of Stadium cameras with Claire Ruth. She took his hand and congratulated him on behalf of her husband. Roger kissed her cheek and said sincerely, "I'm glad I didn't break the record in 154 games. This record is enough for me."

Sportswriters around the country were already busy writing articles that belittled his accomplishment, reminding everyone that it had taken Maris an additional five games to match Ruth and conjecturing that if Ruth had played in a 162-game season, he might have hit 65 home runs.

In 1990, Tom Grimes published the seriocomic novel *A Stone of the Heart*, about a brilliant boy who in 1961 escapes the misery of a dysfunctional family by rooting for Roger Maris as he chases Babe Ruth's record. Fourteen-year-old Michael, who has a mute brother named Rudy, protests "that Maris's record was already tainted by the one hundred and sixty-two game season. . . . The fact that Maris had hit sixty home runs in six hundred eighty-four at bats, Ruth in six-hundred eighty-seven, was hardly mentioned. To question the unassailability of Ruth's record, to tamper with the established order, was somehow almost subversive."

Actually, Grimes totaled *plate appearances* rather than at-bats to come up with 684 for Maris and 687 for Ruth when they hit their 60th homers. Maris had 579 at-bats, 91 walks, 7 sacrifice flies, and had been hit by pitches 7 times. Ruth had 537 at-bats, 136 walks, and 14 sacrifice hits at the time of his 60th, before going 0 for 3 with a walk in his final game in 1927. Maris reached 60 home runs in 3 fewer *plate appearances*. At the time, Ruth's devotees and Maris's critics ignored the plate-appearance comparison that favored Maris and kept pointing to the less significant games-played comparison. Over the next half century that didn't change.

The Yankee organization was guilty of a grave offense against Roger Maris in addition to not protecting him from reporters. After 154 games, they did not publicize that he was still pursuing the home-run record, as they might have done if it had been Mickey Mantle closing in on Ruth. By ignoring Maris in the final week of the 1961 season, the Yankees in essence told their fans that Frick was correct in ruling that home runs hit after the 154th game didn't really count.

"Look how mindless the decision was from a marketing standpoint," points out Marty Appel, Bob Fishel's successor as the Yankees' publicity director. "They played to empty seats those last eight games. There was little excitement because they'd 'legislated' against it."

Because the Yankee organization didn't go to bat for Maris, none of the last five games of the season attracted even 25,000 fans. And the crowds would have been even smaller if Sam Gordon, a jovial, publicity-driven Sacramento restaurateur, hadn't made an offer of $5,000 for Maris's 61st home-run ball.

For the Wednesday, September 27, game, the finale against Baltimore, only 7,594 fans showed up, and they might not have been there if they'd got word that Maris wasn't going to play. Roger finally convinced Houk to give him a game off. He spent some of the day in the clubhouse reading congratulatory letters and telegrams, which presumably outnumbered the hate mail and death threats. Then, at the suggestion of Dan Topping, he left the park and spent time with Pat in the city. He said it was his most relaxing day of the year. Meanwhile, the Yankees lost a meaningless game, 3–2, which made the Orioles the only team to so much as break even with the Yankees in their season series. "We came to the ballpark and Roger Maris's name wasn't in the lineup, if you could believe it," recalled Phil Pepe in ESPN *SportsCentury*, "when he had a chance to break the record."

Bobby Richardson recalled, "I remember wondering at the time, 'How can you do this?' because we were all pulling for him so much to break the record."

"Maybe he was right to take the day off," said Steve Jacobson, "but I thought he was foolish." Years later Maris agreed with him.

Roger's nerves were still at war when he returned to the lineup on Friday, September 29, as the Red Sox came to town for the season's final three games. He was greeted by reporters who expressed outrage that he had taken a game off. Maris had no sympathy for those who criticized him for missing a game after criticizing him all along for trying to break Ruth's record by playing more games than he did.

Of the 21,485 fans at Yankee Stadium, many were jammed into the stands in right field, hoping to catch a $5,000 ball. But with three games left to pass Ruth, Roger didn't connect on Friday night. Boston's starting pitcher, Bill Monbouquette, remembers, "I was rooting for Roger on a personal level, but who wants a record broken against you, especially that one? I'm glad he didn't hit his 61st off me. The next day he said, 'You were tough. You didn't give me anything to hit last night.' I agreed with him. I was going for my 15th win against Ford and I got beat 2–1. Roger wasn't mad at me, but why would he care that I was going for a big win? He was thinking, 'Give me something good to hit!' "

Maris didn't get any hits off Monbouquette, but after he walked for the second time in the ninth inning, he had the satisfaction of scoring the winning run on Blanchard's single. It was the twelfth time that Blanchard won or tied a game with a late-inning hit. Ford threw six innings of shutout ball in his last start before opening in the World Series, but Sheldon got the win in relief.

On Saturday, September 30, only 19,061 fans saw the Yankees play on "Youth Day" at Yankee Stadium. In the Yankees' penultimate game, Maris went 1 for 3 with a walk and single. The Yankees won 3–1 as Terry finished his season at 16-3. The Yankees went 21-8 in September, the fourth consecutive month they had won at least 20 games. Only one game was scheduled for October.

CHAPTER TWENTY-FOUR

MAKING HISTORY

Each day that Maris did not homer down the stretch, a typical headline was "Maris Fails Again." Rather than allowing Maris pleasure in his accomplishment, a high percentage of reporters chose to make him squirm. Sometime during the 1961 season, a rampant negativity virus had infected the press. Quite clearly, the Roger Maris/Babe Ruth story was a turning point in the history of American sports journalism because for the first time failure was an even more important theme than success.

Although Maris wanted to leave the park early after games and have quiet time with Pat, he dutifully continued to make himself available to the press until the final question was asked and answered. A few years later Dick Young wrote in the *Daily News*:

> Down the stretch of 1961 . . . Maris would walk to his locker after each game, take off his spikes and shout out, "Let me have a beer, Pete!" Then Maris would sit on the short stool inside his locker, move it against one wall, tilt back and put his stockinged feet against the other wall. Pete Sheehy would stick a cold bottle of beer in Maris's hand. Roger would take a refreshing slug, look up at the newsmen gathered around and say, "OK, fellows, shoot." Roger Maris, under all that unprecedented pressure, was not the surly, short-answered, unsociable cur he has been made out to be. Quite the contrary. He handled it the way he handled so many things, like a man.

"Even at the end," wrote Leonard Shecter in *The Jocks*, "when he was losing what little cool he had he never became the monster he could have. . . . I said that he was a young man behaving well under the most difficult circumstances. I felt sorry for him and somehow close to him."

"I don't think there's ever been an athlete," said Tony Kubek in *Pinstripe Power*, "who had as much pressure over the length of time Roger did and handled it better."

Maris had only one more game to silence the critical media and reward his unwavering fans. When he arrived at Yankee Stadium on October 1, he was relieved that his agonizing, months-long back-and-forth with reporters would end in only a few hours. Still he wondered about their first question to him after the game. Would it be, how upset are you that you didn't break the Babe's record? Or would it be, how did it feel to hit the home run that broke Babe Ruth's record?

All his teammates wished him luck. For days they had been on an emotional roller coaster with Maris. "You kept waiting for him to break the record," recalled Tom Tresh in 2008. "All of a sudden it's the last day and his last chance. It was nerve-racking."

Maris was anxious but felt less pressure than before the 154th game. He just hoped that a Boston pitcher finally threw him strikes. He didn't know much about Tracy Stallard, Boston's rookie right-hander, other than he was a big guy, 6'5", who threw hard and was uncomfortably wild. His record was 2-6 and he had a high ERA, but the twenty-four-year-old Virginian usually got in trouble by walking hitters rather than giving up hits. Maris couldn't remember getting a hit off Stallard. Mantle had homered off him in July, but he wasn't at Yankee Stadium to give Roger advice on how to approach him.

Mantle and Cerv were in the hospital in front of televisions. "I couldn't believe how few people were in the stands," says Cerv. "There should have been a full house."

Two of the 23,381 people in attendance were nineteen-year-old Sal Durante and his seventeen-year-old girlfriend, Rosemarie Calabrese. She had been to only one game in her life, and since destiny was at work, it had been on September 26 when Maris hit his 60th home run, not far from where they were sitting. "The first game I'd ever been to was very exciting," she remembers, "so I wanted to go again the last day of the season. I forced Sal into going rather than watching it on television. I even paid for the tickets."

Sal Durante recalls:

It always has been written that I was a truck driver, but I actually made deliveries in a car for Stuarts Auto Parts. I took home $60 a week. I didn't have any money that day, and the stadium was a long way from Coney Island, so I wouldn't have gone if Rosemarie didn't insist and buy the tickets. I was a Mickey Mantle fan, but when he dropped out, I rooted for Roger to break the record. My cousin John and another girl went with us. I had read about the $5,000 Sam Gordon was offering for the 61st homer, but didn't think of that. I hoped to catch a ball in batting practice, so that's why we sat in the right-field stands.

Game number 162 in the standings and 163 officially, including the tie on April 22, took place on Sunday afternoon, October 1. With the two teams totaling only 9 hits, 2 walks, and 1 run, its 1:57 duration made it the Yankees' quickest game of the year. "We all had our bags packed and the players wanted to get the hell out of there and were swinging at everything," recalls former umpire Bill Kinnamon. "I could have called a pitch over a player's head a strike and he wouldn't have said anything. The one thing that made this different from other getaway games is that Roger Maris was going for the home-run record. Alex Salerno was scheduled to be the home-plate umpire, but he was young and up only a couple of weeks, so the supervisor for the umpires, Cal Hubbard, came in and moved me from first base to home plate, where I'd been when Maris hit his 60th homer."

The season's final game began with Bill Stafford striking out the side in the top of the first. In the bottom of the first, Stallard gave up a one-out single to Tony Kubek. Maris came to the plate for the first time, causing a stirring in the packed right-field stands and the Yankee bullpen. "Every pitcher on our staff, from Whitey Ford on down, had their gloves on, hoping to get $5,000 if they caught the ball," remembers Bud Daley. Maris shocked everyone by going with an outside pitch and driving it to deep left field. It would have been a strange quirk of fate if the game's top pull hitter broke the record with a drive into the nearly empty seats in left. But Carl Yastrzemski made the catch with room to spare. Roger realized that if he had pulled it, it would have been his 61st home run.

Stafford and Stallard both had good stuff and pitched shutout ball for three innings. Maris came to bat again with two outs in the fourth inning. Again the fans in right field got ready. Maris had vowed to leave the dugout swinging all game, but his bat didn't leave his shoulder as Stallard threw two balls, one high and away and the other inside and low and almost in the dirt. Stallard heard the fans boo him. Maybe he got a little mad and decided to prove to them that he wasn't trying to walk Maris and prove to Maris that he could get him out. He made his 2–0 delivery to his catcher, Russ Nixon, at 1:46 p.m. It never reached the mitt.

"Tracy was a fastball pitcher and not anything else, so that's what I called for," remembers Nixon. "And Roger was a fastball hitter. And we got one inside. Tracy didn't have enough speed or good enough location for Roger that day."

"I didn't want to walk him," Stallard later said about the low point in what may have been the best game he ever pitched, "so I came in with a fastball and that was it. . . . I'm not going to lose any sleep over it."

"It was a good fastball, but maybe he had got it too good," Maris clumsily wrote in his book about the '61 season. "I was ready and connected."

"He hit it right on the nose," Kinnamon remembers.

"Hell, I knew it was a homer right away," says Nixon. "I had the best seat in the house."

"As soon as I hit it, I knew it was number sixty-one," wrote Maris.

In the stands were Jim O'Toole and Joey Jay of the Cincinnati Reds, who were scheduled to pitch the first two games of the World Series against the Yankees. "We went there to scout the Yankees, not to see Maris break the record," says O'Toole. "I couldn't believe that I saw that happen. We sat directly behind home plate, and in the *Sporting News* there would be a picture of us and our wives watching the ball as it went toward the seats in right field."

While Red Barber's call on television was low key, Phil Rizzuto said excitedly on the radio, "Hit deep to right! This could be it!"

"I thought I would catch it," said right fielder Lu Clinton, who moved back to the fence. Then he looked up.

"Way back there!" Rizzuto exclaimed. "It's out of there! Holy cow! He did it! Number 61 for Roger Maris!" He later claimed that he shouted so loudly that he had a headache for ten days.

"When I saw that ball go into the stands, I couldn't move," said Pat Maris. "I guess I was the only one not standing and clapping. I think I was crying, perhaps saying a little prayer. I had prayed to St. Jude that morning, asking him to help Roger reach his goal, if he thought he deserved it. I felt that was my answer."

Finishing his classic home-run call, Rizzuto said, "Look at them fight for that ball out there . . ."

In Jon M. Young's fictional short story "Roger Maris Died Yesterday," which was published in 2004, the delusional narrator reflects back in 1985, to when he and his father attended the final game of the 1961 season at Yankee Stadium. In his flight of fancy, his father retrieved Maris's record-breaking home-run ball from a mob of fans rolling on the concrete and gently handed it to his young son. In reality, the person who cleanly caught the historic ball that sailed over Clinton's head was sitting in the lower right-field deck, in Box 163 D, Section 33, about 360 feet from home plate, ten rows back from the field. Sal Durante remembers, "I watched Tracy Stallard go into the windup and the release of the ball and Roger swinging. I don't think I heard the crack of the bat. But I watched the whole flight of the ball. As soon as he hit it, I felt it was going over my head. I played baseball so I had good judgment and climbed up on my seat. I was falling backwards and a woman grabbed my feet—she later wrote me and asked if she could buy my shoes. I caught the ball in the palm of my hand. It didn't hurt at all. It was perfect."

As a pertubed Stallard stood on the mound, looking down and holding his glove against his hip, Maris jogged around the bases as calmly as he had after his previous 60 home runs. His keeping his emotions in check was reminiscent of Baltimore Colts quarterback Johnny Unitas, who also wore a crewcut, when he turned and walked off the field rather than celebrate Alan Ameche's sudden-death touchdown run against the New York Giants in the 1958 NFL title game at Yankee Stadium.

"Roger Maris was a gentleman," says Frank Malzone, who was playing third base for Boston. "He wasn't jumping up in the air, he was just taking his regular stride, and when he got next to me, I said, 'Nice going, Roger.' And he gave me that nice smile. I was secretly rooting for him and I thought it was so nice he acknowledged me."

"Nobody in our dugout clapped," reports Bill Monbouquette, "but we were saying to each other, 'Jeez, he just broke Babe Ruth's record.'"

A message flashed on the stadium scoreboard: MARIS 61 HOMERS BREAK RUTH'S 1927 RECORD FOR A SEASON. By the time Roger came down the third-base line, everyone was standing, even O'Toole and Jay.

When Maris reached home, he briefly clasped hands with Berra, due up next, and batboy Frank Prudenti. "I made sure he touched the plate," recalls Kinnamon.

Roger tried to descend into the dugout, but several jubilant teammates pushed him up the stairs to take a curtain call. Maris followed their orders to tip his cap, which his idol Ted Williams refused to do after his 521st home run.

"Even as I was standing on the steps," wrote Maris, "something inside was telling me that now I had hit more home runs than anyone in history ever hit in a single season. I felt very proud, but also humble."

Maris walked the length of the dugout, accepting handshakes and pats on the back. When he found a teary Fred Bengis, he put his hands on the batboy's shoulders and said, "We did it, Freddy. We did it."

Sal Durante recalls:

The police picked me up and carried me through the bullpen and then took me underneath somewhere and I met Roger. And I offered him the baseball. Sam Gordon didn't even cross my mind. Roger said something like, "You keep the ball, kid. Sell it and make yourself some money." I told the guards, "You'd better get my girlfriend." And that's what they did. They took us to the Yankee restaurant and gave us some pie. Then we went up to the executive office and spoke to some gentleman who said, "We would like you to keep the ball at the stadium because, God forbid, somebody will mug you." And I said, "Well, how am I going to know it's the same baseball when I pick it up later this month to take to the man in California? How about if I put my initials on it?" So that's why that ball in the Hall of Fame today has my initials on it.

Maris couldn't get over the generosity of Durante, who was willing to give him the ball although it was worth nearly two years' salary to him. It was as if Roger's faith in humanity had been restored. He'd tell reporters, "Now what do you think of this kid? He's got bills . . . and he wants to give me the ball. That goes to show you that there are still some good people in the world." Maris even talked to Russ Nixon about Durante when he came to the plate to face Stallard in the sixth inning and on a 3-2 pitch struck out for only the 67th time in 697 plate appearances; and when he faced Chet

Nichols in the eighth inning and popped up in his 590th and final at-bat, and the Yankees' final at-bat, of the incredible 1961 season. His 698 appearances in 1961 were 7 more than Ruth had in 1927—but he had one more home run.

Maris's final out was caught by rookie Chuck Schilling, who also set a record that game, for fewest errors in a season by a second baseman, with only 8. In his case, the 8 extra games made setting the record more difficult. No one mentioned an asterisk.

Luis Arroyo set down Boston in the top of the ninth and with his record 29th save preserved Stafford's 14th victory. For the only time in his career, Maris had homered to win a 1–0 game. It was the Yankees' 240th homer of the season, a new team mark that would stand until 1996. Maris and Mantle had combined for a new teammate record of 115 home runs, 8 more than Ruth and Gehrig. Also, the longball gave Maris 142 RBIs and the American League title by one over Jim Gentile, and 132 runs to tie him with Mantle for the league lead. The Yankees concluded the year with 109 victories, 8 more than Detroit, and only 1 less than the 1927 Yankees. Their 65 wins at home, while losing only 16 times, was a major league record.

"Everybody in the clubhouse was ecstatic after the game," remembered Blanchard, "and when Roger came in, everybody was all over him. Believe me, he was happy, but he kept everything inside and wasn't laughing and throwing up his arms. He wasn't that type. He just went over to his locker and sat there and said thank you to whoever congratulated him."

When Sal Durante was escorted into the clubhouse, Maris seemed to enjoy posing with him, holding up the baseball and a jersey with a big 61 on its back. Members of the media crowded around Maris's cubicle. "It's great, great, great," he told them, answering several questions at once. "Yes, it was the biggest home run I ever hit," he confirmed, which was somewhat akin to Casey Stengel telling a reporter after Don Larsen's perfect game in the 1956 World Series that it was the best game he ever pitched. "I thought nothing could match the thrill I got when I hit my 60th, but this beats everything," said Maris in Joe Reichler's column for the Associated Press. "Whether I beat Ruth's record or not is for others to say, but it gives me a wonderful feeling to know that I'm the only man in history to hit 61 home runs. Nobody can take that away from me."

When the last reporter put away his notepad, Maris left Yankee Stadium with Pat and Big Julie and Selma Isaacson. Their destination was the Spindletop on 47th Street in Manhattan. A Catholic church across the street was conducting a Sunday-evening mass, so Roger and Pat went inside while the Isaacsons waited at the restaurant. But after five minutes they reappeared, explaining that they had to leave when the priest recognized Roger and began talking about the homer. The two couples were joined by Milt Gross, who got the dinner invitation to make up for the missed interview with Roger in Baltimore. There was no champagne for the new home-run king. Instead, Maris had two glasses of wine to accompany a meal of shrimp cocktail, salad, steak, baked potato, cheesecake, and coffee. He had three cigarettes, admitting, "I haven't unwound yet." Still, the dinner was relaxed, even though a teenager approached Roger to sign and date her menu.

After the celebratory dinner, Roger fulfilled a promise to visit Mantle and Cerv at Lenox Hill Hospital. As Maris entered, Mantle grinned and shouted, "I hate your guts!" The three men spent time laughing until a nurse shooed out the visitor. Possibly Mantle told Maris what he'd tell everyone for the rest of his life about Roger's new record: "That was the greatest feat in sports ever."

Roger didn't write much about his parents in his book about 1961 and didn't mention their divorce. He said they were in Fargo at the time of his 61st homer: "I heard from my mother and father, and, quite naturally, they were very happy about it all. They had written me often during the season, and their letters helped me a lot."

That was it for his parents. He quickly moved on to a telegram he received from President John F. Kennedy, which said, "The American people will always admire a man who overcomes great pressure to achieve an outstanding goal." Kennedy didn't realize that Maris was the exception to the rule.

CHAPTER TWENTY-FIVE

WORLD CHAMPIONS

THE MAN WHO WOULD BE HOME-RUN KING was physically exhausted and emotionally spent heading into the World Series against the Cincinnati Reds. Also, despite hitting his 61st homer, his stroke hadn't come back. With Mantle hampered by his leg infection, it was worrisome. But Maris decided to relax rather than work out on Monday. He lazed around the clubhouse, reading his mail and even chatting with some reporters who needed material for their World Series coverage. He kept in touch with Pat, who had agreed to be on *To Tell the Truth* that night. Four panelists on the popular CBS quiz show would try to figure out that she was the wife of Roger Maris.

To many the Series seemed almost anticlimactic after the thrilling 1961 season. But Maris and the other Yankees didn't want to taste defeat again after the 1960 disappointment, particularly when they desired the victors' share of the purse. They also needed to win to validate the '61 Yankees as the greatest team of the era and earn comparison with the 1927 team that went 110-44. The players also badly wanted a title for Ralph Houk to prove the Yankees were smart to hire him to replace Casey Stengel. That was pretty much the theme of the first in a series of ghostwritten Series articles by the M&M Boys that was syndicated nationally by King Features. Ironically, Maris was now a sportswriter.

The Reds, managed by Fred Hutchinson, were led by Frank Robinson, who would be voted the National League's MVP after batting .323 with 37 home runs and 124 runs batted in, and Vada Pinson, who hit .343 and covered a lot of territory in center field. They had three excellent starters, Joey Jay, who tied Warren Spahn for the National League lead with 21 victories;

lefty Jim O'Toole, who had 19 wins; and 16-game winner Bob Purkey, an All-Star. Also they had one of baseball's top relievers, Jim Brosnan, an icono-clast who was writing a follow-up to his bestselling baseball journal, *The Long Season*. It was a very good Reds team, but they were going against a Yankee machine.

The Yankees' twenty-sixth World Series opened at Yankee Stadium, and Houk started Whitey Ford, who had gone 25-4 during the season. He stopped the Reds cold, 2–0, giving up only a bloop single to shortstop Eddie Kasko in the first and a solid single by veteran outfielder Wally Post to lead off the fifth. In pitching his third consecutive Series shutout, Ford struck out 6 and induced numerous ground-ball outs. Clete Boyer dove to his left and to his right, showing the country what the Yankees already knew about their third baseman. "Boyer made plays I hadn't seen all year," losing pitcher Jim O'Toole recalls.

O'Toole gave up only 6 hits before being replaced by Brosnan in the eighth inning. Three were harmless singles by Richardson, but 2 were solo homers by Howard and Skowron. "I lost," says O'Toole, "but pitching against my idol and the Yankees was the highlight of my career." Maris, play-ing center field, went 0 for 4. "It was a challenge to pitch to him after the season he had," says O'Toole. "I just kept the ball away and had good luck."

Joey Jay, the first Little Leaguer to play in the majors, also held Maris hit-less in Game 2. Mixing up his pitches and locations, he held the other Yan-kees in check, too, except for Berra, who briefly tied the game with a 2-run homer in the fourth. Jay threw a 4-hitter to get the victory, 6–2, beating Ralph Terry. "I've been one of the guiltiest guys on the club as far as swing-ing at bad pitches was concerned," wrote Maris in his newspaper column.

Game 3, played at Crosley Field, was the pivotal game of the Series, so Mantle made an effort to play. He got no hits, but his teammates were in-spired by his presence. Unfortunately, that didn't translate into breaking through against Purkey. The Yankees trailed 2–1 with two outs in the eighth when Blanchard hit a pinch-hit home run to tie the game. In the top of the ninth, Maris, who was 0 for 10 in the Series, faced Purkey. Since early Sep-tember, Maris had hit homers at clutch moments despite being in a slump; and now, after not hitting a ball out of the park in three days of batting prac-tice, he knocked Purkey's first pitch over the chicken-wire fence fronting the bleachers, 360 feet from home plate. "I got the pitch I wanted," the thrilled

Maris said later while sipping a beer, his back to the semicircle of reporters who packed the dressing room. In the other clubhouse, a disconsolate Purkey said, "He homered on a fat, 'slop' slider that broke down. He hit it like he was using a nine-iron."

Maris's 62nd homer of 1961, the season and postseason, tied the record held by Babe Ruth, who had 2 homers in the 1927 World Series. It proved to be the winning run, as Arroyo shut down the Reds in the bottom of the ninth. "It was the key hit of the Series," Hutchinson said later. "We were never the same after that."

Ford left Game 4 after striking his ankle with a foul ball, but not before he threw 5 shutout innings to increase his Series scoreless string to 32 innings. It was a bad year for Babe Ruth, because Ford broke the Series record he had set as a Red Sox pitcher in 1918. Ford, again dueling with O'Toole, left with a 2–0 lead, and the Yankees increased it to 7–0 by scoring 5 runs off Brosnan. The big blow was a single by Hector Lopez in the seventh that scored Richardson and Maris, who had received his first intentional walk of 1961. Lopez had pinch-run for Mantle in the fourth inning after he'd singled. Houk knew he had to take out Mantle and end his Series play when he saw blood seeping through his uniform as he hobbled to first base.

"During the Series," recalls Joe De Maestri, "they had to open up that abscess on his leg because it was draining. Every night, he came into the clubhouse so they could rebandage it. But you know Mickey; he'd say, 'Hey, come look at this.' Then they'd open it up and flip back the skin, and it was so deep you could see the tendons, and he would wiggle his feet and you could see the tendons move up in his hip. The pain when it was touched had to be unbearable. When he tried to play, his pants were full of blood."

Joey Jay wondered why the other Reds pitchers weren't doing as well as he had in Game 2. He found out quickly in Game 5 when the Yankees sent 9 batters to the plate in the first inning and scored 5 runs. The big blows were Blanchard's 2-run homer and Lopez's RBI triple. Jay lasted only two-thirds of an inning. The Yankees went up 6–0 in the second when Maris doubled in Kubek from first base. Terry gave half those runs back in the third on a home run by Robinson. But Bud Daley gave up no earned runs the rest of the way, and the Yankees scored five times in the fifth and twice more in the seventh. Making up for a horrible season, Lopez drove in 4 more runs with a squeeze bunt and 3-run homer.

In Maris's final official at-bat in the Series, he expected Brosnan to throw him a slider and struck out on a changeup. "And he stared at me because he thought I showed him up," recalls Brosnan. "He never forgot that pitch."

Daley was ecstatic to be on the mound for the last out of the Yankees' title-clinching 13–5 victory. "At the end of the '64 season," he remembers, "I was traded to Cleveland and told Ralph Houk that I was sorry I didn't pitch better.' He said, 'Hey! That afternoon in Cincinnati in 1961 was worth everything.' "

The Yankees won the title in just five games although Mantle batted .167 in limited playing time, and Maris had just 2 hits and batted .105. Everyone else picked up their game. Ford was voted the Series MVP for setting the scoreless-innings record.

"The Yankees weren't cocky and didn't do anything to show us up," said a respectful O'Toole in *We Played the Game.* "They just went about their business and kicked the shit out of us. The 1961 Yankees were the greatest team of the era."

The Yankees enjoyed steak and champagne on the train to New York. The official championship party was held at the Savoy Hilton, where the year before Casey Stengel had said farewell and Ralph Houk was introduced as the new manager. Everyone was thrilled for Houk, the third manager to win a world title in his first year on the job. He'd be rewarded with a two-year, $100,000 contract.

Roger's long, torturous season was over. In *Roger Maris At Bat,* he wrote about forgoing the Yankee party because he had to race to the airport in Cincinnati and fly with Pat and Rudy Jr. to Kansas City, where 200 people and the mayor greeted him at the airport. However, a few months before his death in 2009, broadcaster Merle Harmon contended, "Roger didn't fly to Kansas City. He was on the field when he sought me out and said, 'I must go to North Carolina to be in a home-run contest, and Pat's going to go back to Kansas City. Would you look after her at the airport and sit next to her on the plane?' That's what I did."

During the season, Maris had committed to a traveling, postseason home-run-derby exhibition that also featured Harmon Killebrew (46 homers and 122 RBIs) and Jim Gentile (141 RBIs, 46 homers, including a record-tying 5 grand slams, 2 coming on consecutive at-bats in the same game). At the time it sounded like an easy way to pick up some extra money, but that was before the home-run race took a toll on him. Despite enjoying being with Gentile and Killebrew, he had a miserable experience, which he didn't even mention in his book. Again, the press was at the heart of his problems. Gentile recalls:

> We went to Wilson, Raleigh-Durham, Greensboro, and a couple of other places, and everywhere he was badgered by reporters. After spending a whole season being given a hard time by hostile reporters in New York, having a bunch of new writers on his back was tough for him. He told them, "If I had known that you were going to ask me the same old questions, I would have brought a tape with me." In Wilson we had a real nice crowd, but then what Roger said wound up in the papers and it cut us down a little. They didn't write anything nice about us after that. Killer and I usually saw Roger only at the ballpark. I didn't blame him for not hanging out with us because poor Roger couldn't go anywhere. He'd step out of the hotel and people were chasing him all over the place. I thought of Roger when I saw what happened to the Beatles.

The home-run derby petered out, and Maris finally was free to spend time with his family in Raytown. But in late October he flew to Sacramento to make sure Sal Durante received $5,000 for the home-run ball. Durante and Rosemarie Calabrese got married quickly to take advantage of Sam Gordon's offer of an expenses-paid honeymoon that included San Francisco, Las Vegas, Reno, Palm Springs, and Sacramento. "My parents weren't happy about it, but we got married three weeks after Sal caught the ball," says Rosemarie Durante, who almost fifty years later is the mother of three kids and the grandmother of six. "I met Roger in Sacramento, before our honeymoon. He was very friendly, a wonderful man."

Sal Durante recalls:

> Roger was nice enough to come on my behalf to make sure I got the money. He came with his brother, Rudy, and they had trouble landing because the wheels of the plane wouldn't come down. And then Roger walked in and the metal casing of a light fixture fell right on his forehead. It could have killed him. But he didn't say anything about it. He and Sam were cordial during the presentation. We were all smiling. Rosemarie was there, too. There really

wasn't much conversation. We made the switch. I gave Sam the ball and he gave me the check. He handed Roger the baseball and congratulated him.

For some reason Maris had believed Gordon's promise that nobody from the media was going to be at an event meant to publicize his restaurant. Roger told the reporters who surrounded him, "I don't think much of this promotion." Even a surefire heart-warmer went awry. Attending the event in a wheelchair was Kenny Bing, a twelve-year-old with muscular dystrophy. After Roger gave him an autographed baseball, the boy said, "Next time you come here, bring Mickey Mantle with you."

When the Durantes returned to Brooklyn, they found that Roger and Pat had sent them a silver serving bowl as a wedding present, "a nice surprise." The Yankees' present to them was two 1962 season tickets for so-so seats in the second tier behind third base—they went once and gave away their tickets.

That was more than the Yankees gave to Maris for his unprecedented feat. There was not even a day in his honor. "You know what I got?" he'd ask over the years, opening an old wound. "Absolutely nothing."

Maris did receive his second consecutive MVP award from the Baseball Writers' Association of America. He again beat out Mantle in a suspiciously close election, 202–198. They were followed by Gentile (157 votes), Cash (151), Ford (102), who won the Cy Young Award for both leagues, and Arroyo (95). Those who begrudgingly voted for Maris despite his .269 average couldn't ignore that he'd hit a record 61 homers, led the league in runs and RBIs, and had countless clutch hits. But to get their votes again, he'd have to hit 62 home runs.

When Roger Maris was finally able to slow down and contemplate what had transpired in the 1961 season, what did he think? Perhaps the answer can be found in his 1963 novel, *Slugger in Right*. After his counterpart, Billy Mack, has won a championship with the Yankees, his brother Bob and their father enter the clubhouse, tears streaming down their cheeks. Bob's words to Billy conclude the book: "At last you've put down the ghost. Now there's nothing that can stop you. You're really a Yankee and Babe Ruth would be proud of you."

CHAPTER TWENTY-SIX

THE BURDEN OF CELEBRITY

ROGER MARIS OFTEN SAID that his life would have been easier if he'd never hit 61 home runs. But he was tremendously proud of everything he accomplished in 1961, and as Roger Jr. emphasized years later, he "cherished his record." His disenchantment came from the press never giving him credit for his great deed, but punishing him, particularly in 1962. In place of the acknowledgment he felt he deserved, Roger received the kind of attention he could have done without.

"In Roger's romantic view of the world," contends Maury Allen, "he would hit 61 home runs every year and nobody would talk to him except his teammates. But it didn't work that way in New York."

Deirdre Budge spent a good amount of time at the Maris home during the off-season so she could ghostwrite Pat's lengthy "My Husband" article for the *Look* issue that came out in time for the 1962 baseball season. After interviewing both Pat and a hospitable Roger, her foremost conclusion about the couple in the spotlight was "their biggest fear is losing their identity as private citizens."

Roger and Pat didn't think they'd change because of Roger's celebrity and financial success, but worried that other people assumed they would. Pat wrote in her article, "When I say that being in the limelight has been hard for us to face, I hope it doesn't sound as though we're not grateful for the incredible good fortune that has come our way. But the truth is, we're an *average* small-town American family and proud to be just that. The fact that Roger is not just an average baseball player hasn't changed the way we think or the way we like to live."

Roger relished the familiar and mundane: being with his family and friends, hunting, bowling, barbecuing, dabbling in carpentry, eating Pat's home cooking, making his kidney stew, watching television until he and Pat dozed off, and having his kids wake him in the morning and accompany him on his daily excursions. He was bothered by intrusions on his life that reminded him of his job and his 61 home runs. That included receiving more than two hundred pieces of mail a week from well-wishers, angry Ruth fanatics, fake relatives, a woman who claimed they were married when he was a fledgling tennis player, and autograph seekers who expected him to cash their checks and purchase baseball items for him to sign and send to them.

Maris also hated being recognized in public. "We went out to the zoo in San Francisco once," recalls his uncle Don O'Neil, "and there was an ape in his cage that always had a crowd peering at him, and Roger said, 'That's how I feel.' He'd tell me that when people recognized him, they'd run toward him and he'd have to get up and leave."

Walt Seeba recalls when the Maris family spent a week at his home in Sioux City: "It was relaxing for him because people weren't on his back all the time. The neighbors hadn't known Roger was related to us, yet when they found out, they didn't bother him. Roger and I played a little golf, and on the last night I got tickets for Roger, Pat, Mary Jo, and me to go to a nice dance hall where the Les Elgart Band was playing. We would dance to the music and then sit and have drinks. It was a great night and we all enjoyed ourselves."

Roger's version of the story was that he was recognized immediately and they had to leave. When they attended church, the self-conscious luminary noticed that "after only a few minutes, I could feel everyone looking in my direction. I . . . told my wife that we had better leave early." He so detested anyone making a fuss over him that he rejected Frank Scott's proposal that he do a cross-country tour that would earn him $50,000. He explained, "It's worth $50,000 to sit home and play with my kids."

Roger was visited by Jim Ogle and they relived the 1961 season for the memoir *Roger Maris At Bat*, which needed to be written quickly to be published during spring training. But Maris couldn't stay put for long because in January he was committed to attend a series of award banquets. Arriving in Milwaukee to receive the Associated Press's Man of the Year Award, he revealed his level of enthusiasm by saying, "The banquet circuit is okay except for four things—speeches, newspapermen, cameramen, and traveling."

Despite his cynicism, Roger enjoyed his night at the Eagles Club. Maris, with a flower in his lapel, and the remarkable sprinter Wilma Rudolph (Ward), the Female Athlete of the Year recipient, posed for pictures, then sat on a stage and answered questions from local sports journalists. Afterward, they signed autographs. The event ran smoothly, so Roger was extremely upset when a wire-service story alleged that after he received his award, he went into a back room and played pool. He was beginning to suspect that there was a concerted effort to destroy his reputation by hook or by crook.

The next attack on Roger followed the annual B'nai B'rith awards dinner in New York. Again he was accused of receiving his award and then rushing off before the program was over. Maris posed for pictures with Joe DiMaggio and Hank Greenberg and planned to stick around all evening, although he had to catch a morning plane to Rochester, where he was going to be an honored guest at the Hickok Award Dinner. However, a Hickok representative told him that he had to catch a 10:30 train that night because inclement weather was expected the next morning. Roger left early so that he could check out of his hotel in time to catch the train.

On January 22, as Mickey Mantle, Whitey Ford, and Elston Howard looked on, Maris was handed the $10,000 S. Rae Hickok belt at the twelfth annual Rochester Press and Radio Club's charities dinner. This signified that he was the Professional Athlete of the Year, succeeding Arnold Palmer. Maris was asked by a reporter the question that would dog him for the next several months: "Will you hit 62 homers in 1962?" He gave a reasonable response: "I don't believe in miracles."

How he really felt about the possibility of threatening the record again was evident in an article he wrote for *Look* that came out a week before Pat's: "As a ballplayer, I would be delighted to do it again. As an individual, I doubt I could possibly go through it again." Another time he was more adamant: "This was the first time in thirty-four years that someone hit 60 home runs. Anybody who expects me to do it again must have rocks in his head."

The next day Maris was in Boston to receive his MVP Award from the Baseball Writers' Association of America. The other featured guest was Claire Ruth, and her comments during a press conference put Roger on the spot. "Somehow or other, the record belongs to the Babe," she said. "I don't believe Roger broke it. Commissioner Frick doesn't, either." On his best behavior, Roger said, "I would expect my wife to speak in the same manner."

The four Yankees planned on flying back to New York the next day, but the airport remained closed into the night because of a raging snowstorm. So the impatient and, by this time, inebriated teammates decided to rent a car. "We let Ellie drive," wrote Ford in *Slick*, "because he'd drunk less than the rest of us and all the way home Mickey and I kept putting our hands in front of Ellie's eyes as he was trying to drive through the blizzard." After a death-defying six-hour trip, they hung out until 4 a.m. at Ford's old neighborhood bar, McCormick's, in Astoria, Queens.

At the end of the banquet season, Roger said he was proudest of being the Catholic Athlete of the Year, but he also was appreciative of receiving his second Sultan of Swat Award in Baltimore, Babe Ruth's hometown. It was more meaningful than in 1960 because he'd now broken Ruth's record. He was in a good mood, which was fortunate because during dinner "Maris, by actual count," reported the *Baltimore News-Post*, "was interrupted 97 times from the moment he started his fruit cup and worked his way through dessert. There was an endless parade of greeters, hand-shakers and autograph-seekers. . . . His patience was tested to the breaking point, but he acted the perfect guest."

In Maris's acceptance speech, he expressed that he was "enjoying Baltimore more in the winter than the summer." The guests laughed, but a reporter at the event contended, "As a public speaker, Roger Maris is much better as a home-run hitter." Maris posed while playfully trying to balance the expensive, jeweled Sultan of Swat crown on his head. The humorous picture that made the papers showed the crown at a perilous angle.

Next, Maris was in New York to receive the Van Heusen Outstanding Achievement Award, after being selected by a panel of sports broadcasters, sportswriters, and ballplayers. While in town, Roger talked to Frank Scott about his endorsements, including a new mini-pinball game. The television commercial for it began with a clip of the 61st homer, followed by a close-up of Roger in uniform saying, "Hi, kids. That sure was a big day for me. Part of the thrill of baseball, the kind of real excitement I put into my great new game by Pressman, *Action Baseball*."

Also upcoming was a family movie for the M&M Boys called *Safe at Home!* Scott snagged $25,000 for each client without a prerequisite that they take much-needed acting lessons. They needed only to play themselves. Ralph Houk had a couple of scenes in the movie, and Whitey Ford had, literally, a walk-on. Veteran character actor William Frawley played Houk's coach, Bill, but the real star was a nine-year-old named Bryan Russell, who played Hutch Lawton, a young boy who sneaks off to Fort Lauderdale to convince Maris and Mantle to appear at a Little League banquet, as he'd promised the other kids. The low-budget curio, which isn't as bad as its reputation, was filmed on location in Pompano Beach and Fort Lauderdale while the Yankees held their first spring training there.

Mantle's sons Mickey Jr. and David were among the kids in the movie. An adult extra was rookie first baseman Mike Hegan, the son of Jim Hegan, who was the Indians catcher in Maris's rookie year and a Yankee coach in 1961. Mike Hegan recalls, "I was one of the young players in the background when Mickey and Roger were doing their stand-up bits at Fort Lauderdale Stadium. We had to be out there at seven a.m. We made something like fifty bucks and were thrilled doing it. I'd met Roger when I was fourteen and he was a rookie on Cleveland, and he'd been nice to me. My parents also really liked him and his wife, Pat, who gave Roger his strength, if you will. During the two or three weeks we were doing that shoot, Roger and Mickey were always together joking around."

The two stars seem to be joined at the hip in the movie and took turns delivering single lines. Roger got the funnier ones. For instance:

> MANTLE: Take it easy, Bill.
> MARIS: Yeah, Bill, remember your lumbago.

Also:

> MANTLE: A kid—where did he come from?
> MARIS: Did I tell you what I found in my room last week?

Maris had come to spring training without a contract. In early January, Roy Hamey offered him $60,000, an approximate $22,000 raise. Having hit more home runs than anyone else in history and brought to the Yankees a lot of revenue, Maris asked for $100,000. Hamey insisted that was Mantle's salary and nobody else could make what he did. Meanwhile, Hamey told the press that Mantle had signed for $85,000. He raised his "final offer" to Maris to $67,000.

As he had done earlier in his career, Maris threatened to quit baseball and go home. Even when Joe DiMaggio threatened to hold out rather than sign for an insufficient salary, the Yankees organization leaked to the press that he was making impossible demands. This was a tried-and-true tactic for turning fans against their rich heroes. Now Maris read in the papers how he was ungrateful and greedy and should be happy with the Yankees' offer. In late February, he finally signed for what the Yankees said was $72,000. "I'm not saying what Roger made in '62," says Bob Cerv. "But it was more than they said, and Houk promised us he'd get the same the next year, too."

Maris had his fill of bad press during the off-season, so he was disappointed that the reporters in spring training treated him as if Frick's * had been stamped on his forehead like a scarlet letter, the mark of the unworthy. In truth the proposed asterisk had never been implemented. In the two official record books, the *Sporting News's One for the Book* and the Elias Sports Bureau's *Little Red Book*, both Ruth, for 154 games, and Maris, for 162 games, were listed as home-run champions in the new annuals. Maris's 61 homers had no asterisk beside it, but as long as Ruth's name was present, reporters treated him as if one existed.

Maris didn't make nice with the New York reporters who had turned the fans against him during his pursuit of the home-run record and his subsequent salary negotiations. The reporters had convinced the fans that he was a surly, money-hungry ingrate. Roger believed some were out to get him because when he was looking for a collaborator for his book about the 1961 season, he had bypassed the city's vast talent pool. Instead he selected the lesser-known New Jersey sportswriter Jim Ogle, although that meant he'd have to settle for a minor publisher and a smaller advance. "Ogle," recalls Maury Allen, "was very straight and very protective of Roger and the Yankees organization, which he wanted to be part of and eventually was. He hated the Chipmunks and we didn't like him. He hated us talking in the press box. He hated that if Roger wore a funny shirt, we'd write a whole story about it."

One incident that got Maris into hot water with reporters involved

Rogers Hornsby, whose lifetime average of .358 was the highest ever by a right-handed hitter and second best to Ty Cobb's .367. Cobb passed away in 1961, leaving the ornery Hornsby as the least popular old-time ballplayer. He was now making enemies as a coach for the New York Mets, telling the players that no current major leaguer could hold a candle to the stars of his day. When the Yankees traveled to St. Petersburg to play an exhibition game against the new National League franchise, an enterprising photographer suggested that he and Maris pose together, linking Rajahs from past and present. Hornsby agreed.

Maris said absolutely not. He remembered Hornsby telling the press in '61 that he wasn't a good enough hitter to replace Ruth as the home-run champion. The two-time Triple Crown winner was shocked that a young player showed him such disrespect and called him a punk and a bush leaguer. Hornsby's sportswriter contacts relayed his message in their columns.

The press also attacked Maris for an incident involving someone almost sixty years younger than Hornsby. Roger and other Yankees were signing autographs at a function when a young boy handed him a ball. Roger winked at his teammates and signed with an X rather than his name. It was a common trick bored ballplayers played on occasion, as when they followed exact instructions if an adult asked for their "John Hancock" on a ball or picture. He watched the boy wander a few feet away, then stop cold when he looked at the ball. Roger signaled for him to come back. "I took the ball again, signed the autograph, and the kid went away happy."

Several reporters wrote a distorted view of what happened, including Oscar Fraley of UPI, who had cachet as the writer of the television hit *The Untouchables*. Fraley logged great mileage at the 1960 Olympics writing pitiless reports about the failures of elite U.S. athletes, including high jumper John Thomas and sprinter Ray Norton. Now he saw the opportunity to knock the home-run champion to the ground. With self-righteous indignation, Fraley wrote an article that was published in papers around the country that criticized Maris's discourteous treatment of everyone from kids to reporters. His final words were humiliating: "If either of my sons has a hero, I hope it's a modest fellow named John Glenn who went for the circuit when it really counted. Because guys like Maris bat around zero with me."

This stung Maris, a worthy hero to his own sons. A couple of days later, he confronted Fraley at the ballpark. Ralph Terry was a witness:

I heard Roger say to him, "Who are you, you no-good, rotten, little son of a bitch? What rock did you crawl out from under? How could you write that garbage about me when you never even talked to me?" Oscar, who looked like Don Knotts, was a little bit scared he might get punched. He should have been, but Roger told him he was too old and just walked away. After his run-in with Roger, I had dinner with Oscar, who I played golf with, Milt Richman of UPI, and Leo Peterson, their editor. And Leo said, "Oscar, you were wrong. You never talked to Maris. You just teed off on him." Unfortunately a lot of other writers picked up on what Oscar wrote and made up their own stories.

After walking away in a huff from Fraley, Maris immediately clashed with Jimmy Cannon, the esteemed writer for the *New York Journal-American*. They'd got along in the past, but Maris spurned his interview request, saying he would talk to him later. Cannon's response was "Go to hell." Johnny Blanchard remembered:

Roger was out there running while wearing one of those rubber suits, which they later realized were dangerous. Roger wasn't fat, but I guess he was trying to lose a few pounds. When he finished, it was important that he get in the clubhouse, get the rubber suit off, and get some fluids into his body. As he was coming off the field, Jimmy Cannon was sitting there. He asked Roger for a few minutes to talk, but Roger was ready to pass out and said, "I can't do it now." Cannon came unglued. He said, "I interviewed Jack Dempsey and Gene Tunney and a hell of a lot bigger people than you," and Roger just said, "Sorry, I'll see you later," and walked away. Cannon was one of those writers who thought that anytime they wanted to talk to you, you were supposed to run to them.

"Cannon was a crusty, spiteful man," says Maury Allen, "and if you didn't play up to him, he would get back at you because he was pretty powerful. Roger didn't care about him one way or another, and that upset Cannon."

Two days after Cannon felt slighted by Maris, he wrote the first of two scathing articles about him. It was titled "Maris 'The Whiner'—A Threat to the Pennant" and began with two lies: "Success has made Roger Maris the most unpopular player on the Yankees. Their boredom with him has assumed aspects which conceivably could place the team's pennant chances in jeopardy."

Then he spouted nonsense: "The group of sports historians who tagged along last season with Maris and Mickey Mantle were lenient in their appraisal of his character. They believed some of his more noticeable defects of personality were produced by pressure. Their compassion was accepted by Maris as a just tribute." And: "Maris violates all the laws of protocol established by Joe DiMaggio and Babe Ruth." Cannon concluded his essay about the most modest man in baseball by writing, "The absence of stress does not diminish his capacity of self-worship."

The next day, Cannon's equally vicious follow-up essay was printed. Its title, "Maris Envies Mantle's Prestige Among Yankees," discounted the reality that "envy" was anathema to Maris. It also implied that Maris had *no* prestige among the players, when the truth was, as Ralph Terry told Tony Kubek in *Sixty-One*, "To us Roger was a great guy, a real hero . . . the way John Glenn was a hero." (Comparing Maris to the U.S. astronaut who had orbited the earth three times that February was the ultimate compliment.) While praising Mantle, Cannon wrote spitefully about Maris's poor standing in the baseball community and on the Yankees: "They consider Maris a thrilling freak who batted .269. . . . His reputation is demolished when they compare him to Mantle. This apparently irritates Maris, who gives the impression that he inhabits a league filled with enemies. Obviously Maris considers Mantle a competitor instead of a partner on a team."

Cannon's baseless tirade against Maris was syndicated, so baseball fans around the country read it and, because it was in the newspaper, believed it. Worse, since Cannon was an influential figure in sports journalism, his articles brought about an open season on Maris. Others in the media followed his mean-spirited lead, figuring they, too, could target Maris with impunity.

It got so bad that Ralph Houk called what Til Ferdenzi in the *Sporting News* termed "an emergency press conference." Ferdenzi wrote:

> The Yankee manager prefaced his remarks by saying he had not at first intended to dignify the feud by commenting on it. He changed his mind after a couple of days of receiving phone calls at such sobering hours as 5 and 6 a.m. from newsmen in far flung places who wanted the scoop on what Maris' popoffs with writers were doing to the morale in the clubhouse.

Houk warmed up to his oration by describing Maris as "A-1 to me and to the players. . . . He's a good family man and pretty good to most writers I've seen around. . . . Roger is a helluva guy and a very good team man. Every man on this team will tell you that too. . . . We're 100 percent for him. There is no disharmony here, and we don't expect any."

Maris declared that he was no longer speaking to reporters. In this major public-relations blunder, he alienated the very people he needed to project a positive image of him to fans demanding a 62-homer season. New York was tough enough to play in without the media having a lynch-mob mentality toward him.

"In '62, the New York press tried to destroy him," says Joe De Maestri, who retired before the season but still kept an eye on New York. "That was when reporting changed, and it was based on Roger Maris. He was the first guy they really went after."

"I don't think that anybody ever sat down and said, 'Let's hurt him,' " says Maury Allen, "but there was a lot of criticism of Roger, including by myself, for not being open with the media. We made our living by having guys talk to us. If everybody shuts down, it's pretty hard to write an interesting story. At that time all I cared about was writing stories that I could sell and whatever money I could make off Roger. And when he wasn't terribly cooperative, I was pissed off. We all were."

CHAPTER TWENTY-SEVEN

THE UNAPPRECIATED SUPERSTAR

M ARIS HAD TO WONDER what impact all the negative press about him was having on baseball fans. In the Yankees' second game, on April 13, Opening Day in Detroit, the right fielder was struck on the arm by a soda bottle thrown from the stands and was also the target of a broken glass. An apologetic John Fetzer, owner of the Tigers, promised extra police for the rest of the series. Maris summed up his predicament in Detroit and elsewhere: "They created an image of me and the fans bought it."

Early in the season, few fans were openly hostile to Maris at Yankee Stadium. They were expecting to be entertained by another Maris-Mantle home-run race and wanted to see if Maris could beat his own record, which they didn't hold in the same regard as Ruth's. But the tired Maris got off to another slow start. "He was paying the price of the winter he spent," said Houk. After 11 games, he was batting only .152 with 1 home run. He heard the boos—first from a few spectators, then a chorus.

Maris broke out of his slump on the road. In a four-game series in Washington that closed out April, he went 10 for 19 and slugged 3 homers. However, the highlight of Maris's visit wasn't at D.C. Stadium but at the White House. He and a cordial President Kennedy posed for pictures as they autographed a baseball for the National Multiple Sclerosis Society, of which Jacqueline Kennedy was an honorary chairperson. The unique collector's item went to the highest contributor in the society's campaign drive.

Maris met another famous figure a few weeks later. Julie Isaacson was managing heavyweight boxer Billy Daniels, who had just been TKO'd by a young boxer from Kentucky with fast hands and feet who'd won a light-heavyweight gold medal at the 1960 Olympics. Cassius Clay asked Julie if he could get a picture with the "most famous athlete in America." Isaacson arranged for a photographer to be present when Maris met the future Muhammad Ali, the most media-savvy heavyweight champion of the television age.

Mantle was batting .315 with 7 home runs and 17 RBIs. But against the Senators he tore his right hamstring trying to beat out a grounder and was taken to Lenox Hill Hospital, where he and Cerv had resided the previous September. His injury was so severe that he'd miss 28 games, and talk of a home-run race receded.

Maris had lifted his average above .300, but with Mantle not hitting behind him, he saw fewer good pitches. Against the visiting Angels on May 22, he was walked 5 times, a feat that wouldn't be duplicated by a Yankee until Mark Teixeira in 2009. After recording no intentional walks in the entire 1961 season, Maris received a record-tying 4 in the Yankees' twelve-inning, 2–1 victory, one each from Dean Chance, Ryne Duren, Jack Spring, and Tom Morgan. What made the game even more memorable was that Whitey Ford, who never threw a no-hitter, gave up a run but no hits in his 7 innings of work, before leaving with a muscle strain in his pitching arm.

Batting fourth, Maris's average was down to .275 heading into a month-ending doubleheader in Minnesota. As always, his proud parents came from Fargo to watch him play. But this time it was different. "They were split up," recalls Cerv, who in June was sold to the expansion Houston Colt .45s and retired after 19 appearances. "His father came up to the room for a couple of hours and I stayed. Then his mother came up and I left the room so Roger could talk to her."

"You always knew Rudy was around in Fargo because he got permission to have a license plate with the number 9," recalls Rob Johnson. "Roger's mother still lived across from me, and I'd go see her. I enjoyed visiting both his parents because they were common, nice people. They were both very proud of Roger."

Roger was told about the festivities in Fargo that month to honor him. Three of an eventual seven billboards with his image had gone up outside the city to attract tourists:

WELCOME TO . . .
FARGO
POPULATION 50,000
HOME TOWN OF—
ROGER MARIS "The Home Run King"
SEE THE MARIS DISPLAY SHOW CASE
CHAMBER OF COMMERCE BLDG.—CIVIC CENTER

The display showcase at the Fargo Civic Center contained a mannequin wearing a Maris uniform, bats, gloves, balls, photographs, the Hickok belt he'd been given in January, and both his Sultan of Swat crowns.

Maris hit his 8th homer and drove in his 25th and 26th runs against Camilo Pascual in the second game of the twinbill. The next time he played against Minnesota, on July 6, his average was below .250, but he upped his home run total to 21 and RBI total to 52 with shots off Pascual and reliever Lee Stange. The still-hurting Mantle homered twice off Pascual to give him 17 for the year. This homer display came after a big four-game series for the M&M Boys in Kansas City. In the first game, both homered against one of Maris's Raytown friends, Ed Rakow. In the second game, they went deep against both Jerry Walker and Gordon Jones. Then in the second game of the July 4 doubleheader, Mantle hit 2 homers and Maris 1. So in the span of 5 games over four days, Mantle had three 2-homer games and a 1-homer game, and Maris had two 2-homer games and two 1-homer games. Briefly, it was 1961 all over again.

Maris and Mantle's stats were down from 1961, but they again were All-Star starters. Maris batted third and played center field, and Mantle played right as Ralph Houk's American Leaguers lost to Fred Hutchinson's National League squad, 3–1, on July 10. President Kennedy threw out the ceremonial first pitch, and the Dodgers' Maury Wills, who was on his way to breaking Ty Cobb's single-season stolen-base record with 104—for which there was no talk of an asterisk—dazzled on the basepaths to earn the MVP award. Maris drove in his team's lone run with a sixth-inning sacrifice fly off Bob Purkey.

In the second All-Star Game, on July 30, at Wrigley Field in Chicago, the American League prevailed, 9–4, as MVP Leon Wagner, Rocky Colavito, and Pete Runnels homered. Maris started in center again and had a double in four at-bats, with 2 runs and an RBI. A reinjured Mantle was unable to play.

Tom Tresh was on the AL team as a reserve in both games. The switch-hitting son of former major league catcher Mike Tresh became an outfielder but beat out another rookie, Phil Linz, as the Yankees' interim shortstop while Tony Kubek completed a stint in the army. Tresh drilled 20 homers and drove in 93 runs as he put together a Rookie of the Year season. Other rookies making contributions to the Yankees in 1962 were left-handed outfielder/first baseman Joe Pepitone, whose desire for attention and a wild nightlife made him the opposite of Maris, utility infielder Linz, and pitcher Jim Bouton. They played with great competitiveness but believed baseball should be just a single part of an enjoyable life. They respected the veterans—and idolized Mantle—but didn't listen when rookies were told to observe and keep their mouths shut. They changed the tone of the clubhouse.

It would have made sense if Bouton, an intellectual with great empathy for players who didn't toe the line with management, tried to befriend Maris, a nonconformist who had sacrificed a good reputation by doing battle with general managers, managers, and the Fourth Estate. However, Bouton, who got along with all the other Yankees, became the only teammate with whom Maris had personality clashes in his entire career. When Bouton arrived in New York with a shabby old glove, he was touched when Maris gave him a brand-new one, but their relationship went downhill from there.

According to Ralph Terry, they had a falling out during a game Bouton was pitching. Maris had a pulled hamstring, so Houk instructed him not to run hard to first base. Maris did as he was told, and when the second baseman juggled the ball, he failed to beat out the grounder. Terry recalls Bouton yelling at Maris and that "Roger never talked to Bouton again the rest of the time they were together on the Yankees." In future years, Maris ripped down Bouton's posters when he ran for player rep and also made it clear that Bouton wasn't welcome to do his pregame running in right field.

Because there was no homer race in 1962, little electricity was in the air at Yankee Stadium during the season. It was the opposite across the river at the Polo Grounds, where Casey Stengel's and George Weiss's expansion New York Mets set records for losing but were taken to heart by fans starved for National League baseball. Although they were having All-Star seasons, Maris and Mantle, because of his injury, weren't stirring the nation as they'd done in 1961. Of those who played key roles in both seasons, only Richardson, Boyer, Lopez, and Terry, who would win 23 games, were doing better in '62. Stafford finished with an identical 14-9 record but his ERA went up by a full run; Howard hit the same number of homers and drove in 14 more runs, but his average dropped 69 points. The biggest disappointment was Arroyo, who hurt his arm in April and missed two months, then was ineffective when he returned. Fortunately, Marshall "Sheriff" Bridges, a hard-throwing left-hander who had been acquired from Cincinnati during the off-season, picked up some of the slack, winning 8 games and saving 18.

After 81 games on July 13, the Yankees had a record of 46-35 and were percentage points ahead of the Indians, ½ game ahead of the surprising Angels, and 3½ games in front of the Twins. Usually the Yankees waited until September to make their pennant run, but as if Houk rang a bell, they reeled off 9 straight victories. The M&M Boys led the way, as Maris went 9 for 33 with 9 runs, 8 RBIs, and 3 homers, and Mantle, who had a hit in every game, went 10 for 32, with 8 runs, 8 RBIs, and 2 homers. The Yankees extended their lead to 6 games by the end of July, then coasted to the flag, finishing with a 96-66 record, 5 games ahead of Minnesota.

After hitting 21 homers and 14 doubles in the first half of '62, Maris hit 12 homers and 20 doubles in the second half, while raising his average from .252 to .256. He contended that he hit the ball harder than in 1961 but without the loft. At the end of August he had 31 homers and seemed like a lock to reach 40, which would have put him in second place behind Harmon Killebrew's 48, but he homered only twice more and tied for fifth place with Jim Gentile, behind Norm Cash's 39 and Rocky Colavito's and Leon Wagner's 37.

Still, Maris led the Yankees with his 33 homers and 100 RBIs. But the fans weren't pleased by those stats after his 1961 season and let him know that every game when he left the dugout. Mantle wrote in *The Mick* that "in 1962 the fans gave him the worst beating any ballplayer ever took. From April straight through September they stayed on his back."

Maris's minor league roommate Dan Osinski, who finally made it to the majors in 1962 as an effective reliever for the Angels, remembers, "He was getting bad press and was being booed in his own park, which upset me because he was the nicest guy and best player who was my teammate. Everybody was criticizing him for not hitting 62 home runs, but he didn't want to go through that again. He told me that in '61 they were threatening his life, his wife, his kids, his family. There were enough nuts around to make him worry."

"Roger didn't hit 61 home runs again, so everybody was saying it had been a fluke, when that wasn't the case," says Al Downing. "They tried to define him by that one moment. He was much more than that. He contributed every day he walked on the field."

At times, Maris lifted his self-imposed ban on talking to the press, especially when he wanted to vent about the fans. "After Maris said he didn't want to talk to any reporters, I still was able to talk to him," remembers George Vecsey. "He was available when he had to be available, if you know what I mean. When something happened, he would talk. He might not give you much in depth, but sometimes after a game he'd sit with you. On rare occasions he would open up."

"Big Julie Isaacson," recalls Maury Allen, "had a relationship with my sports editor, Ike Gellis, at the *Post* because Julie had contacts with the bookies. So through Gellis and Julie, Roger talked to me when he wouldn't talk to a lot of other people. Even in '62, I had more access than most of the Chipmunks, but he wasn't a joyous person and a fun guy to interview. It was classic pulling teeth. I defended him, but I never could crack through."

The *Post*'s Leonard Shecter was upset by Maris's situation with the fans. "Sixty-one home runs didn't change Maris, they changed everybody else," he wrote in *The Jocks*. "Maris was accumulating enemies at a far faster rate than he had hit home runs the year before. Bedeviled by a low batting average and a high strikeout record, annoyed and hurt at the reviling attention he was getting from fans who resented him as a rival to Super–Mickey Mantle for their affections, stunned by the negative reaction of a fickle nation which had taken him to its heart the year before, Maris was responding the only way he knew how, with anger."

During a doubleheader on July 30 against the White Sox, at Yankee Stadium, spectators in the right-field seats hurled golf balls at him. Maris threw one back and luckily hit no one. The fans retaliated, pelting him with beer cans and other debris. At the top of every inning the umpires had to escort him out to right field. Shecter tried to support Maris by attacking the fans' behavior in print. He quoted what Maris said in the clubhouse about the fans' actions: "Let me put it this way: I don't give a damn." Maris didn't like being misquoted, and apparently he didn't like being quoted correctly, either, because he was furious with Shecter and vowed never to speak to him again.

An article by Milt Gross of UPI on August 12 included many quotes by Maris, who was feeling worn down. Gross reported that Maris remarked to Pete Sheehy, "Only 53 more days to the end of the season." When an "eavesdropper" pointed out that was still a long way to go, Maris responded, "You're telling me. I'm counting the days until the season's over. I can't wait until it ends. Right now I'm ready to write the whole thing off." Of the press and fans, Maris said, "It's the darnedest thing how much harder this year has been than last year. Even after I began to think last year that I had a chance of making it and the pressure was on me, it wasn't as tough as it has been this time."

Gross commented, "This can be accepted as defeatism, if you wish. It can also be interpreted as disappointment and despair. It is all those emotions, but it is so much more because this season for Maris had been a confusing blend of stresses and strains, torments and tantrums, hope and hell."

At the time Roger was having trouble dealing with the hostile fans at Yankee Stadium, he began a lasting friendship with one young fan. Andy Strasberg was a teenager who grew up a "baseball brat" in the Bronx and then in White Plains in Westchester County. When Maris came to New York, Strasberg said, "This is my guy." In 1961, he needed a chaperone to accompany him to games, but in 1962, he was free to hop a train and a subway on his own, and he attended half the Yankees' home games. His favorite player was, more than ever, Roger Maris. He recalls their first meeting:

> For a 1 p.m. game, I got there between 8:30 and 9 a.m. and waited in or near the parking lot. In those days, the players pulled in, and as they'd cross the street to the stadium, I walked with them. That's how I got to meet Roger. You gave the player a postcard with your name and address on it, and then a few days later you'd get it back with an autograph. I handed Roger a note that expressed what a big fan I was of his and what he meant to me.
>
> I had a front-row seat to how he was vilified by many of the fans. I have a distinct memory of sitting in right field in 1962—Roger strikes out with a runner on first base and everyone is booing him and I yell to Roger, "Don't worry, Rog, you'll get them next time," and I was the *only* guy saying some-

thing good to him. Roger noticed that I was feeling stung by the way he was being treated.

One day when there weren't a lot of people around, Roger got out of his car and saw me. He came up to me and I said, "Hi, Rog, how's it going?" And he said, "It's not fun anymore." And the look on his face and the way he said it broke my heart.

CHAPTER TWENTY-EIGHT

A SECOND RING

THE SAN FRANCISCO GIANTS matched up well against the New York Yankees in the 1962 World Series. In fact, the Giants, managed by Alvin Dark, had gone 103-62 and had hit more homers, scored more runs, and had a higher batting average than the Yankees. Future Hall of Famers Willie Mays, Orlando Cepeda, and Willie McCovey spearheaded a frightening lineup that also included former American League batting champion Harvey Kuenn and Felipe Alou. Mays in center, third baseman Jim Davenport, and shortstop Jose Pagan were marvelous fielders. The starting rotation of Jack Sanford (24-7), Billy O'Dell (19-14), Juan Marichal (18-11), and Billy Pierce (16-6) was as strong as the Yankees' Ralph Terry (23-12), Whitey Ford (17-8), and Bill Stafford (14-9), and their bullpen, with Stu Miller and Don Larsen, was better.

What the Yankees had going for them were World Series experience and the Giants' being drained, having just finished a tense three-game playoff with the Dodgers. "We started the World Series without really having thought about the Yankees," remembers O'Dell. "Everything had happened so fast. We were 6 games behind with 7 to play, and suddenly we're in a playoff game with the Dodgers. Nobody thought we were going to win it. There weren't even any television cameras in our clubhouse, they were all in the Dodgers' clubhouse. We were down 4–2 in the ninth inning with two outs, but we pulled out a 6–4 victory, and the Series started the next day. We were in L.A. and had to return to San Francisco for the Series."

In a battle of lefties in Game 1, O'Dell went up against Whitey Ford and came out on the short end, 6–2. Ford, perhaps the greatest World Series pitcher ever, recorded the last of his ten Series victories, though his scoreless streak ended at 33⅔ innings. Batting fifth, Maris ripped a double that drove in New York's first 2 runs in the first inning, and the Yankees didn't look back.

In Game 2, Sanford 3-hit the Yankees, 2–0. Against Ralph Terry, the Giants scored their first run on a groundout in the first inning and the second on a home run by Willie McCovey, far over the right-field fence.

In San Francisco, Don O'Neil recalls, "Roger would come back to the hotel on the team bus, and Jean would be there by our car, and he'd come out to our house and stay. Like Connie, Jean was very attractive and looked twenty years younger than her age. Some fellow accused Roger of having an affair with the girl that was picking him up. Roger told him to think whatever he wanted. He always wanted Jean to make him a special soup. Once he told Mantle to wait for him while he ate it. Mantle said, 'Good God. You are never like anybody else. Why don't you take all your money and order some soup?' Roger just kept eating and said, 'Nobody makes soup like this.'"

The teams flew to New York. Bill Stafford opposed Billy Pierce in Game 3, and it was scoreless going into the bottom of the seventh. Tresh led off with a single to center, and Mantle followed with a single to left. Felipe Alou bobbled the ball, and suddenly the Yankees had men on second and third with nobody out. Dark might have lifted Pierce if he knew how well Maris had hit him when he had been the ace of the White Sox. But Dark went with his lefty against the left-handed Maris, and his strategy backfired. Maris foiled the shift by singling over the infielders' heads, and both runners scored to give the Yankees a 2–0 lead. Maris moved to second when McCovey booted the ball in right. Then with Larsen on the mound, Maris caught Mays napping on Elston Howard's fly to deep center and hustled to third. It was the key play of the game. He made it 3–0 when he came home on a force at second base. That insurance run proved to be the winning run because with two outs in the ninth inning, Giants catcher Ed Bailey hit a 2-run homer off Stafford.

The Giants evened the series 2–2 with a big 7–3 victory. Marichal started against Ford, but the win went to Larsen, the save to O'Dell, and the loss to Coates. Bridges gave up the key blow, an improbable seventh-inning grand slam by left-handed-hitting second baseman Chuck Hiller, who had 3 homers in 602 at-bats during the season.

Many fans anticipated seeing baseball's two best center fielders, Mickey

Mantle and Willie Mays, competing against each other in the Fall Classic for the first time since their rookie year, 1951. They'd both had great seasons: Mantle had batted .321, with 30 homers and 89 RBIs despite missing 39 games; Mays had batted .304, with a major league high 49 homers and a career-high 141 RBIs, while playing every game. But in the Series, Mantle hit .120 with no homers or RBIs, and Mays hit a weak .250 with no homers and 1 RBI.

In Game 5, on October 10, Terry and Sanford locked up in another pitching duel. The Yankees eked out 2 runs on a wild pitch and a passed ball and were tied with the Giants going into the bottom of the eighth. Then Tresh followed singles by Kubek and Richardson with a 3-run blast into the lower right-field stands that sealed what would be a 5–3 victory. "It's the hit that always was my biggest individual thrill," said Tresh a few weeks before his death in 2008. "It was a pivotal game, and we got to go back to San Francisco ahead, not trailing, 3 games to 2."

San Francisco was being drenched by Typhoon Frieda, and that meant no baseball until October 15. Because of the long layoff, Houk could start Ford again in Game 6. Dark countered with Pierce, setting up a matchup of longtime rivals. The Giants knocked out Ford by scoring 3 runs in the fourth and 2 more in the fifth, with Felipe Alou and Orlando Cepeda getting key hits in both rallies. Pierce pitched a brilliant complete game, yielding only 3 hits—a solo homer to Maris in the fifth and a double to Boyer and RBI single to Kubek in the ninth. With their 5–2 victory, the Giants set up a seventh game on their own turf.

A well-rested Sanford and Terry, who had won 47 games between them during the season, squared off for a third time in the decisive game. Terry had led the league in starts and wins; his 23 victories were the most by a Yankees right-hander since 1928; he had logged 299⅓ innings before the Series began; he was third in the league in strikeouts and had even saved 2 games. He had the credentials, but the pundits wondered if he had the mental toughness to put behind him Bill Mazeroski's Series-winning home run off him in the seventh game of the 1960 World Series.

Again, Sanford and Terry held the hitters in check. The Yankees broke through in the fifth on singles by Skowron and Boyer, a walk to Terry, and a double-play grounder by Kubek that scored Skowron. In the bottom of the seventh, Tresh robbed Mays of an extra-base hit with a terrific running catch in the left-field corner. That was a huge play because the following batter, Willie McCovey, tripled over Mantle's head in center field. Cepeda struck out to end the inning, and the Giants felt the frustration settling in. In the top of the eighth, still down only 1–0, Dark pulled Sanford with the bases loaded and nobody out, sending in Billy O'Dell. "I got Maris to hit into a force play at home and Howard to hit into a double play," says O'Dell. "Then I got them out in the ninth inning and thought we were going to win in the bottom of the ninth."

Terry was pitching the game of his life. He had allowed only two base runners through eight innings and hadn't even thrown two consecutive balls. But the bottom of the ninth got off to a shaky start when crafty pinch hitter Matty Alou led off with a bunt single. Terry bore down and struck out Felipe Alou and Chuck Hiller. But on a 2–0 count, Mays slashed the ball down the right-field line. That is when Maris made the defensive play of the Series. Terry recalls, "Roger was running toward the foul line. The field was soft, and because of his momentum he couldn't really plant and throw back to second. He made a great play cutting off the ball before it went to the fence and hit Richardson with an accurate relay. I was behind home plate because Alou had rounded second and was heading to third, hoping to come all the way if Maris didn't get to the ball quickly and make the play. He was held at third."

Matty Alou, the tying run, stood at third base, and Mays, representing the go-ahead run, was on second. First base was open. Striding up to the plate was 6'4" Willie McCovey. He'd homered off Terry in Game 2, singled in his last at-bat against him in Game 5, and tripled to deep center only two innings earlier in Game 7. He batted left-handed, while on-deck hitter Orlando Cepeda was right-handed and was hitless in the game. Terry recalls:

Ralph Houk comes out and says, "I don't know what the hell I'm doing out here." It was kind of funny. Meanwhile Kubek was kidding Richardson, "Well, I hope he doesn't hit it to you, you've already made two errors in this Series." Mays overheard that and cracked up. So Houk says, "Would you rather pitch to McCovey or put him on and pitch to Cepeda and set up a force play?" I scanned my memory banks, and the reason the Dodgers weren't in the playoffs was because Walter Alston had Stan Williams walk a guy to load the bases and then he walked in the winning run. I said, "National League ballpark, National League umpire, bases loaded seventh game, anything close I'm probably not going to get the call." I didn't want to fall behind with the bases loaded to Cepeda, who had 3 hits the previous game. So let me go after McCovey. High and tight, low and away. Don't let him extend his arms. Throw him some good stuff. Go for some good spots. And if I fall behind in the count, we'll put him on.

Terry's cutter, which went in to left-handed batters, had been working all afternoon, but he threw McCovey an off-speed pitch low and away. McCovey caught it on the end of his bat. It headed out to right field. Maris was on the run. Many of the 43,948 fans thought, *Home run.* But the swirling Candlestick Park winds blew it foul.

Terry threw one more pitch:

This time I came up and in, a fastball inside. And McCovey did a good job. He leaned back and he got on that pitch. But he had to use his hands and it had a little topspin on it. I didn't worry about a home run. A single was going to beat us, too. It was whacked. But Richardson was playing deep in the hole, where he used to play Ted Williams. Bobby caught it in front of his chest. He had him played perfectly. They carried me off the field. I had lost the seventh and final game of the 1960 World Series and been the goat. But a couple of years later, I was in the same situation and a higher power smiled on me. It just made it all the sweeter.

The thrilling 1962 World Series ended with heads held high on both teams. Maris had contributed to all 4 Yankees wins with his bat, leading them with 5 RBIs, defense, and legs.

With two consecutive world titles, he didn't probably care that the Baseball Writers' Association ignored him in the MVP balloting, giving him no votes despite his leading the pennant-winning Yankees in homers and runs batted in. "If before the '62 season started," said Blanchard, "someone said Roger's going to hit 33 homers and drive in 100 runs, I'd have been the happiest guy on Broadway. People didn't understand that it ain't easy to hit 33 homers."

The MVP choice of the writers was Mickey Mantle for a record-tying third time. Undeniably, he was exceptional when he was in the lineup, but he played in only 123 games, and his 30 home runs, down by 24 from 1961, was his lowest total since 1954; his 96 runs his lowest since 1952; and his 89 RBIs his second-lowest since 1952. The suspicion was that voters were trying to make it up to the popular Mantle for placing him second the previous two years to someone they didn't like.

Maris didn't get even a tenth-place vote on a ballot, although his stats weren't much worse than in his 1960 MVP season. Further proof of how the press went out of its way to discredit him came when the UPI conducted a poll just for his benefit. "I remember being in the dining room in my house in Spring Valley," recalls Marty Appel, "and the *Journal-News,* which ran only wire-service stories, had the headline 'Maris Named Flop of Year in Poll.' A flop? He'd hit 33 homers and driven in 100 RBIs! Even as a kid I thought, 'UPI doesn't do this poll every year. Who ever heard of this? Show me the list of previous winners!' Obviously that poll was designed just to demean Maris."

UPI's Flop of the Year for 1962 had been on three pennant winners and two world-title teams in his three years in New York, after joining a third-place team. He had hit 133 home runs—more than Hank Aaron, Mel Ott, Hack Wilson, Hank Greenberg, Ted Williams, and even Mickey Mantle ever did in a three-year period. He'd driven in 354 runs. He'd won two MVPs.

According to A's broadcaster Merle Harmon, "If you had called every general manager in the league after the 1962 season and asked if they wanted Roger, they would have said, 'How fast can he get here?' " Yet Yankees general manager Roy Hamey was considering trading him.

CHAPTER TWENTY-NINE

THE VILLAIN

R OY HAMEY ALWAYS DEFERRED to Ralph Houk, so when Houk insisted Maris be on his team in 1963, Hamey took him off the trading block. The Yankees' general manager and vice president felt Houk had the right to pick his personnel because of a secret they shared. At the conclusion of the 1963 season, Hamey planned to step down and hand over his job to Houk. A bout of hepatitis may have influenced his decision, but it's probable that Dan Topping and Del Webb wanted to ease him out the door because the farm system had been in decline since George Weiss's departure.

With Houk moving upstairs, the Yankee brass settled on Yogi Berra as the manager. It's likely they chose the popular icon to counter Casey Stengel, whose lovable last-place Mets were siphoning fans from the champions. Attendance at Yankee Stadium was more than 200,000 less in 1962 than in 1961 despite another world title. Berra was informed of the decision and instructed not to say a word about it. In 1963, he was expected to catch a bit, coach first base, and learn managing from Houk, who had once played behind him. It was the rare secret in baseball that remained one.

Maris spent a leisurely winter in Missouri, paying little attention to the trade rumors swirling back East. He thought he didn't receive enough credit for a solid 1962 season, but was relieved not to be in demand on "the rubber-chicken circuit." "After the World Series," Maris told Til Ferdenzi, "I made up my mind to spend all the time I could with my family and stop this running around to banquets. All I did this winter was bowl a little."

Roger's growing family had moved into a much larger house in Independence, hometown of Harry Truman. At the suggestion of Merle Harmon, they built it in a fashionable area called Manor Oaks, where the Harmons and Cosentinos lived and which would be home to Whitey Herzog and Norm Siebern. The house even had special quarters for Pat's mother and could accommodate frequent visits by relatives and friends from Fargo. Roger's parents vacationed there separately—on Christmas, Rudy came to Roger's house, and Connie visited Rudy Jr., who had married a woman also named Connie and was busy raising a family.

"Nobody made a big deal of Roger Maris living in the neighborhood," says Merle's son Reid Harmon, who was fifteen in 1963. "That was one of the reasons they moved there. Even the kids accepted them as we would anyone else. I remember their house was always one of the targets on Halloween because they gave out good candy."

While Roger and Pat socialized with ballplayers and their wives in the area, they probably spent more time with Jim and Frances Cosentino, new friends Dale Gosser, who manufactured lawn mowers, and his wife, Joy, and George Surprise, a dentist, and his wife, Margaret. The four families became close and took vacations together.

George Surprise remembers:

Roger was very different than your typical professional athletes. They bounce around pretty good, but Roger was a real family man. One time we were sitting in a bar having a drink and probably talking about golf, fishing, and our families. A guy came over and wanted his autograph. Roger gave it to him. Then he said, "George, why did he want my autograph?" I said, "Aw, jeez, Roger, he wants to tell his grandsons he met you." He was just so pure. He didn't understand why what he did as a ballplayer was special to anyone. He said, "I'm playing ball to make a living and wouldn't do it if I could do something else that was better."

During the winter, Maris found time to work with Jim Ogle on *Slugger in Right*, which was published in early 1963. Interestingly, the minibio on the flap jacket said, "His total of 61 homers now stands as the record for the 162-game season." Surely Roger approved the text, so it's curious that he, too, differentiated his accomplishment from Babe Ruth's and was still reluctant to lay sole claim to baseball's biggest record.

An hour before Maris signed his 1963 contract for $75,000, Mantle, in front of reporters and Joe DiMaggio at the Yankee Clipper Hotel in Fort

Lauderdale, put his name on a contract for $100,000. DiMaggio had been the only other Yankee to get six figures. The previous spring, Hamey had told Maris that Mantle was going to get that salary in 1962, but in *All My Octobers* Mantle confirmed he didn't get $100,000 until 1963. If Willie Mays received $100,000 from the Giants, then the Yankees would have looked liked skinflints if they didn't give Mantle the same.

For the first time since Hank Bauer was traded for Maris, a key Yankee had been sent packing. With Joe Pepitone penciled in at first base, New York had sent the heartbroken Bill Skowron to the Dodgers for imposing 6'4" right-hander Stan Williams. The nine-year Yankee learned of his exile at three in the morning in a telegram that said, in effect, "Your services are no longer needed." The Yankees didn't know that Williams, who had won 43 games since 1960, was damaged goods and was going to be throwing more sidearm sinkers than high-and-tight fastballs.

With Rollie Sheldon out for the season with an arm injury, Williams was handed the fourth spot in a strong rotation with Ford, Terry, and Stafford. Bouton was slated to be a middle reliever and spot starter. The big question mark was the closer role, after Marshall Bridges was shot by his girlfriend during spring training. She shot the "Sheriff" in the leg in a bar, and not realizing he'd been wounded, he kept on drinking. With Bridges out of the picture, Houk hoped Arroyo could return to his '61 form. If not, Hal Reniff, not a Houk favorite, waited in the wings.

The well-rested Maris had a good spring as reporters ignored him and the Florida fans were surprisingly civil. One newspaper account stated, "Maybe the fans are willing to forgive and forget—if spring training is any omen. It was noticed at the Yankees training site that Roger Maris no longer is the target of the boo-birds and there is even some applause now when the reluctant hero steps up to the plate."

The Yankees had an epidemic of injuries in Florida. The walking wounded included Kubek, Tresh, Boyer, and Ford. On April 1, Maris joined the parade. In a meaningless exhibition game against the Tigers, he tore his left hamstring while trying to make a diving, game-saving catch. He'd miss Opening Day for the first time in his major league career and six more games. What made it worse is that the first two games were in Kansas City. At least while the Yankees won both games behind Terry and Stafford (who,

along with Daley, hurt his arm that game in the cold weather), Roger convalesced at home with Pat, who was pregnant again.

Maris also missed Opening Day at Yankee Stadium on April 11 versus
Baltimore, when Milt Pappas outpitched Whitey Ford, 4–1. However, Maris
took outfield practice and discovered that the Yankee fans hadn't changed.
Milt Gross wrote that "the jeering and catcalling began even before he turned
his back to the stands. 'What the hell,' Maris said. 'As long as I play in
New York . . . they're never going to get off [my back], but . . . I can shut it
out of my mind.' " Maris, who hoped to clout 30 homers despite trying to
hit more pitches to left field, told Gross that he had a more relaxed attitude
than in 1962. "They called me the Flop of the Year last year," he said. "They
can't do it again for this season after doing it for the last one. So I figure
there's no pressure on me now."

Roger's first appearance in 1963 was on the road against Washington on
April 19. With the Yankees up 4–3 in the ninth behind Williams, Maris de-
posited Jim Duckworth's pitch into the stands, a "Ballantine blast," as Mel
Allen called Yankee homers to plug the team's beer sponsor. The Yankees
scored 3 more runs in the inning and won 8–4. Maris slammed another
ninth-inning homer in the next game to spoil winner Dave Stenhouse's shutout bid.

Maris beat out an infield hit in his only at-bat against Chicago's Juan
Pizarro, but aggravated his left hamstring and had to leave the game. He
missed the two-game series in Cleveland. He played all three games in Los
Angeles, and though he didn't homer, he upped his average to .304, third
best on the team to Mantle's .308 and Boyer's .306. His hamstring was still
bothering him, so when the Yankees came into Minnesota for a three-game
weekend series, May 3–5, Houk instructed him to ease up on running to
first on sure outs. Though this was against his style of play, Maris agreed.

The night game on May 3 was broadcast on Channel 11 in New York.
Against left-handed Minnesota native Dick Stigman, his friend in the Indians system, Maris had a particularly frustrating game. In his first three
at-bats, he flew out to deep center field, struck out with men on first and
third and nobody out, and grounded to third baseman Rich Rollins. Leading off the ninth with the score knotted, 3–3, he knew one big hit would
make up for his early failures. Instead he grounded to second base, an easy

play for Bernie Allen. Heeding Houk's words, Maris jogged toward first base and veered off toward the dugout before reaching the bag. Allen bobbled the ball, and if Maris had run it out, he might have beaten the throw.

The Minnesota fans didn't know about Maris's bad leg and assumed he was just being lethargic. Fans usually boo nonhustling players only on the *home* team, but they made an exception in Roger's case. They didn't like what they read about him in the papers, and they resented that he didn't always acknowledge he was born in Minnesota.

As Roger neared the dugout, the booing was thunderous and the catcalls pervasive. "It was easy to see that Roger couldn't run at full speed," Stigman recalls, "but the fans didn't care about that. I was hearing them react and asking myself, 'What is that?' I just thought, 'Fans can really be cruel.' "

One heckler behind the dugout said something especially nasty, and Maris reflexively gave him the finger as he entered the dugout. His gesture was caught on camera. "I just winced," recalls former Fargo broadcaster Jim Adelson, who saw the game. "I said to myself, 'Oh, God, Roger, *please* don't do that.' "

By the time Clete Boyer's homer won the game in the 10th inning, the switchboard had lit up at Channel 11, as furious callers declared Roger's act had gone far beyond the boundaries of common decency. Maris's gesture became a national story. The *Sporting News* printed a letter from a New Yorker who had "witnessed a disgraceful exhibition of physical obscenity performed by that great 'idol of American children,' Roger Maris. . . . I wonder how many wives were watching the game with their husbands, as mine was. How would Maris feel if someone did the same thing he did in front of his wife and children?" (To view real obscenities, he could have read Maris's fan mail.)

Ralph Houk said that what Maris had done was wrong, but many players had done worse. Commissioner Ford Frick, who knew Maris wasn't the first ballplayer in history to make that gesture, actually defended Maris to a degree by saying TV cameras shouldn't follow players into the dugout.

Roger tried to deal with negative fan reaction as he always had, with his bat. He rebounded with a double and homer off Camilo Pascual in the Sunday finale before the Yankees headed for Detroit. However, his reputation had taken another blow. A few weeks later, Robert W. Creamer wrote an article for *Sports Illustrated* with the fitting title "A Gift for Making a Bad Situation Worse." He wrote of the fans' favorite villain:

> What is it about Roger Maris that makes small boys who don't know him say they hate him? Why is he booed every time he comes to bat in every ballpark he plays in? Why do sportswriters who cover the Yankees shake their heads when you mention Maris and say, "Forget it. He's nothing"? The famous "gesture" that Maris directed toward a fan in Minnesota a couple of weeks ago—a vulgar signal whose meaning no one could mistake—was a bad thing to do, but it was not in itself enough to arouse the rush of criticism that followed. Other ballplayers have done worse, and protests have been minor. With Maris, it became a national issue. When the Yankees return to Minnesota in July, Maris will be booed and reviled all over again. But not for the gesture. Maris will be booed because the crowd despises him. It resents him. It dislikes him. Mostly, though, he is disliked because he has proved to be such an unsatisfactory hero.

If Maris was an "unsatisfactory hero" by 1963, it was only after being rejected by the fans and press when he was a worthy hero in 1960 and 1961. Maris made no overtures to win their favor because he wanted nothing more to do with them. But the anti-Maris faction wasn't finished with him. With relentless negativity, they drove him into becoming exactly what they wanted him to be: a bitter person whom anyone would have difficulty calling a hero. Not content, the most spiteful set out to demean his career and wreck his reputation, thereby ruining his Cooperstown chances. When Maris made the obscene gesture, he helped their cause and added to his discontent.

Milt Gross wrote, "Roger is so emotionally overwrought about how the season is going for him, what with injury, the antagonism of the fans and his own despair, that he's beginning to look at everything with a jaundiced eye. Maris has reached the stage where he firmly believes that nothing he ever does in baseball again will bring him anything but censure and disfavor with the customers. The obscene gesture was a sorry thing, but sadder still is Maris's attitude. You get the feeling he'll never have fun again playing a game that's supposed to be fun for so many."

Roger was only twenty-eight years old but he was losing his enthusiasm for the sport he had loved with a passion. After the 1961 season, he thought he'd play another ten years, but now it was difficult getting through even one season.

"I definitely saw he was not enjoying baseball," recalls Don Mossi, who held him hitless May 7 in Detroit. "When we talked, it was clear that for him the game was now work. The stress had gotten to him."

And there was physical pain, too. In *Roger Maris*: A Title to Fame*, Harvey Rosenfeld claimed "ten injuries pockmarked Roger's 1963 season." "Roger got hurt trying to make diving catches and running into walls and breaking up double plays," said Merle Harmon, "but the fans booed him for not hustling. He hustled. If he hobbled, he hobbled fast."

An amusing sidebar to the Minnesota incident was that soon after the team returned to New York, reporters noticed that Roger had placed a prop on a footstool next to him in the training room. The training room was off-limits to them, but they could look in and clearly see a hand with a middle finger extended. "I think it was made of plaster of paris," says Stan Williams, "though it might have been plaster of Omaha. I'm sure he had bought it at a gimmick store. He wrote at the bottom of it, 'For Press Only.' "

CHAPTER THIRTY

BREAKING DOWN

WHILE MARIS CONTINUED HIS semi-boycott of reporters in 1963, he was more lax about it because he was no longer in such demand. But his cooperation was at best inconsistent. Maury Allen recalls, "With Roger, I never had a 'Get the hell out of here' situation, whereas I had dozens with Mantle. Roger would just say, 'I don't want to talk,' or he'd walk away and you'd feel cheated. I might make an appointment: 'Roger, can I see you when you get dressed tomorrow?' 'Yeah, okay, okay.' And then I'd come in at ten the next morning and go to his locker and some other player would say, 'Don't talk to any of those so-and-sos,' and he'd walk away. It was not easy covering those guys."

"I wish he hadn't said to hell with all the press," says Stan Williams. "The bad ones would have been enough, because then some of the other reporters took offense and really got on him. Roger wasn't an easy guy to know, but once you were his friend, that was for life. He was honest and too humble to ever talk about his accomplishments, and funny enough to say that every time he flew over Missouri, his wife got pregnant. He was one of the few teammates I ever loved, and it was hard to witness what he had to endure from the press and the fans who believed what was written about him."

Roger's injuries mounted. Just as his hamstring started to feel better, he strained a back muscle and missed several games. He continued to play despite suffering a contusion of the left big toe in early June in Detroit. He figured he had no choice with Mantle out at a crucial time of the season.

Justifying his big contract, Mantle overcame some nagging injuries and hit for average and with power in the early part of the season. His highlight came in a home game on May 22, when he crushed a pitch off the A's Bill

Fischer that slammed into the facade on the right-field roof. It came within a few feet of being the only ball ever hit out of Yankee Stadium in major league history. Mantle said it was "as hard a ball as I ever hit in my life." The A's third-base coach, Jimmy Dykes, who had played against Babe Ruth, told reporters after the game, "We have witnessed the hardest ball that has ever been hit with a baseball bat. No one else I've ever seen could hit a ball that hard, not even Ruth."

As Maris continued to fall from grace in the eyes of baseball fans, the deifying of Mantle continued. "Something was going on that season," he wrote in *All My Octobers*, "maybe sympathy for the injuries, or just a reaction to my having been around for thirteen seasons. I was getting applauded and cheered in rival ballparks. In Yankee Stadium, I was getting ovations."

Unfortunately, in Baltimore on June 5, Mantle suffered one of the worst injuries of his career. In the top of the sixth inning, with the second-place Yankees trailing the first-place Orioles, 2–1, Mantle doubled and Maris followed with a clutch homer against Milt Pappas. It was the 200th home run of Maris's career. It seemed that the M&M Boys were back to doing their thing, but in the bottom of the sixth, Mantle raced back on a ball Brooks Robinson smoked over the seven-foot-high center-field fence. There was no warning track and he crashed into the fence. Mantle's spike caught on the wire mesh, causing his foot to bend backward. He was carried on a stretcher to the Yankee dressing room, where Maris, Richardson, and Terry sneaked in between innings to see their friend. He missed 61 games.

Predictably, Maris picked up the slack. He hit his share of homers to right but spread his other hits all over the field to defy managers who implemented the shift against him. He even bunted home a runner to beat Boston with the league's most intimidating reliever, Dick Radatz, on the mound. In one 12-game span he batted .444 with 5 homers and 13 RBIs. On June 29, the Yankees had a record of 42-28 and were in first place to stay. On July 6, Maris was hitting .294 with 19 homers and 42 RBIs. "Maris is playing as good a brand of ball as I've seen him play," Houk raved to reporters.

Batting fourth, Maris led the way, but he had help from Elston Howard, who was being heralded as the league's best all-around catcher, and Joe Pepitone, who was 1 RBI ahead of Roger. Bench players such as Johnny Blanchard, who hit 16 homers in '63, Hector Lopez, Phil Linz, Harry Bright, and even Yogi Berra were coming through when called upon. Defense was a big factor, too. "There wasn't the Yankee power of the past," says Williams. "But with Boyer at third, Kubek at short, Richardson at second, and Pepitone at first, there was no way you could drive a ball through that infield. Pitching for a club like that, especially with a sinker, was fantastic."

Ford's record stood at 13-3, and Bouton, who replaced Stafford in the rotation, was a real surprise at 10-4. Reniff took over as the closer with Arroyo finished and had 8 saves in 9 opportunities. Six-foot-six-inch string bean Steve Hamilton, who came to the Yankees from the Senators in April for Jim Coates, contributed as both a setup man and occasional closer. Al Downing came out of nowhere on June 10 to throw a 2-hitter and best Washington left-hander Don Rudolph (who was the envy of many ballplayers because his wife, Patti Wiggin, was an exotic dancer). On July 2, the twenty-two-year-old lefty from Trenton, New Jersey, 1-hit the White Sox. A victory over the Indians on July 6 gave him a 4-1 record and solidified his place in the rotation.

The Yankees' record improved to 49–30 and they were 5½ games ahead of Boston, Minnesota, and Chicago, 6½ ahead of Baltimore. The emergence of Pepitone, Bouton, Downing, and Reniff meant that the team had the talent to stay on top until Mantle's return. Maris was on track to hit 40 homers and finally bat .300. But after the July 6 game, he underwent what was described only as "rectal surgery." He missed fifteen games and didn't play in the All-Star Game on July 9 after seven consecutive appearances over four years.

Again Roger had to sit out a series in Kansas City. At least he was able to check on Pat, who was due in four months. Margaret Surprise recalls, "They were a very close couple. Roger tried to get in when he could, a few times a year, and she would visit him. It was hard for her to travel because she had too many kids too fast. But she did have a lot of support from friends here in Kansas City. And Mrs. Carvell helped with the kids and that let Pat get away. She was a very good grandmother."

In New York, Maris lived with Dale Long in a Queens apartment rented for them by Big Julie. Long, forever known for homering in eight consecutive games with Pittsburgh in 1956, quickly learned of Roger's eating prowess. Long told Tony Kubek, "Every Monday we had off after a doubleheader, I would go home to Massachusetts. I had a friend up there who would pick up corn in the morning and give me a couple of bushels at noon to take back to the players. One day [Roger] ate twenty-eight ears of corn. He put them in a pound of butter, salted them, and ate them."

Stan Williams recalls:

> I felt sorry for Roger because it was hard for him to go out in public to eat because there were always people around who tried to agitate him. One night we were having dinner with Clete Boyer, Hector Lopez, and Hal Reniff at a little second-floor restaurant in Chicago. Some guy started bad-mouthing Roger. Roger told him to let us eat now that he had his say. But the guy was just looking for trouble. We got on an elevator and the guy followed us down and kept taunting him. I hadn't pitched well and wasn't in a great mood, so I grabbed the guy by the throat and slammed him against the wall and told him not to say another word. And he didn't.

Maris returned to action in late July but immediately suffered a bruised left heel and had muscle spasms in his back. Two days later he strained his left hand. He was in and out of the lineup. After three seasons when he had been relatively free of injuries, Roger was now feeling injury-prone. By the time Mantle returned, Maris's average was down to .278 and he was stuck on the 19 home runs he had on July 6.

Mantle made a dramatic return on August 4 against the Orioles at Yankee Stadium, when he tied the game with a seventh-inning pinch homer off George Brunet into the left-field stands. The fans roared and chanted his name as he rounded the bases. He tipped his cap before entering the dugout, where he was surrounded by emotional teammates. Equally memorable was a homer on September 1, in Baltimore. The night before, Mantle, Ford, and Long had gone to a friend's farm and stayed up most of the night drinking. The next afternoon Mantle had a brutal hangover, and Houk let him sleep it off on the bench. Hank Bauer, now a coach with the Orioles, passed the word that they didn't have to worry about Mantle that day. But in the top of the eighth, with the Yanks down 4–1 and Boyer on base, Houk woke up Mantle and told him to pinch-hit.

Ford, who had been sitting on the Mick's hat, told his groggy friend to just swing at the first pitch and stagger back to the bench. Because of Mantle's sorry condition, lefty Mike McCormick threw a straight fastball. Mantle swung and, miraculously, connected on what he said was "the middle ball." The ball landed in the left-field seats and the legend of Mickey Mantle, who barely made it around the bases, grew. The Yankees prevailed when Tom Tresh hit a 2-run homer off Dick Hall later in the inning. In 2008, Tresh said, "The headlines were 'Mantle Homers as Yanks Win.' But if you read the article, you'd discover where it said, 'Tom Tresh hit 2 home runs from opposite sides of the plate to tie the record.' "

During the rest of August, the reigning MVP batted only 7 times. Both he and Maris struggled to stay in the lineup in August and September. Maris's latest problem was his back, which he strained in late August. He fully realized then what he'd suspected since 1961: a double standard was at work. When Mantle was out with an injury or a hangover, the Yankees told the press that his missing games was justified. But when Maris didn't play, the word around town and in the papers was that he was a malingerer. The Yankees and members of the press knew Maris wasn't able to take the field, but they didn't tell the public the true story, and he was booed. Maris had no jealousy of Mantle, but he resented that he wasn't accorded the same protection. This would be a major issue with him for the rest of his time in New York.

In 1963, Maris played in only 90 games and had only 312 at-bats. He finished with only 23 home runs, with 4 coming after July 6, 53 runs, and 53 RBIs. Mantle played in only 65 games and in 172 at-bats had only 15 home runs, 40 runs, and 35 RBIs. Mantle's slugging percentage was higher than that of league leader Harmon Killebrew, and Maris was right behind the Twins slugger, which indicates that barring the injuries that hampered them even when they did play, both would probably have had outstanding seasons. Together, the M&M Boys had a decent season for one player: 484 at-bats, 38 homers, 88 RBIs.

Remarkably, the Yankees won their fourth consecutive American League crown by 10 games over the White Sox, their largest margin of victory in sixteen years. They won 104 games, had a winning record against every American League team, and never lost more than 4 games in a row, despite not leading the league in any offensive category. Howard was selected the American League MVP for taking charge of the team during the long absences of Maris and Mantle. "The MVP made both of us very happy and proud," says Arlene Howard. "It was like the Pulitzer Prize."

In a pitching-rich season in which only four American League batters had averages over .300 and only two had more than 100 RBIs, Howard was a good choice. Solid on offense and peerless on defense, he also did a tremendous job of handling the pitching staff of veterans and youngsters. Ford went 24-7, giving him a three-year record under Johnny Sain of 66-19, and Bouton surprised by going 21-7. Terry finished at 17-15, Downing at 13-5 with 4 shutouts and 171 strikeouts in 175⅔ innings, and Williams at 9-8. Reniff saved 18 games. The Yankees' 3.07 ERA, bolstered by tremendous defense, was second in the league to that of the White Sox.

Still the pitchers on their World Series opponents, the Los Angeles Dodgers, were superior. The Dodgers' staff led the majors with a 2.85 ERA, 24 shutouts, and 1,095 strikeouts. Offensively, the Dodgers featured stolen-base king Maury Wills, the 1962 National League MVP; ideal second-place hitter Jim Gilliam; speed merchant Willie Davis; two-time batting champion Tommy Davis, who drove in 153 runs in '62 (the most in the National League since 1937); big Frank Howard, who slammed 28 homers; and a strong first-base platoon with Ron Fairly and Bill Skowron. However, the team was only fifth in the league in runs scored. It was the pitching that struck fear in opponents.

Sandy Koufax had harnessed the wildness that plagued him in the 1950s and could throw his 98 mph fastball and incomparable curve for strikes. He threw only those two pitches, but batters couldn't hit either. "Your only hope was that his first pitch was a ball," recalls former Cardinals catcher Tim McCarver. "If he got ahead in the count, you were toast." In a season that would earn him the major leagues' one Cy Young Award, over Ford—his first of three in four years—Koufax led the majors with 25 wins, against only 5 losses, 11 shutouts, a 1.88 ERA, and 306 strikeouts. The twenty-seven-year-old left-hander from Brooklyn was the most dominant pitcher in anyone's memory.

Also set to start against the Yankees were the intimidating Don Drysdale, who had won 25 games in his 1962 Cy Young season and 19 in 1963, and 14-game winner Johnny Podres, still remembered by the Yankees for shutting them out in the seventh game of the 1955 World Series to give the Brooklyn Dodgers their only world title. The bullpen ace was Ron Perranoski. A lefty with a tailing fastball, he won 16 games and saved 21 others while posting a 1.67 ERA.

Ford started Game 1 at Yankee Stadium and blanked the Dodgers in the first inning. Koufax responded by striking out Richardson, Kubek, and Tresh, and the Yankees knew they were in big trouble. When the Dodgers scored 4 runs in the second inning on an RBI single by Skowron and 3-run home run by catcher John Roseboro, it was all over. Ten years to the day after Carl Erskine set the Series record by striking out 14 Yankees, Koufax fanned 15 in throwing a 6-hitter, and the Dodgers won 5–2. His fifteenth victim was pinch hitter Harry Bright, who said, "I waited seventeen years to bat in a World Series, and when it finally happened, everyone was rooting for me to strike out!" Maris went 0 for 5, fanning once. "I can see how he won 25 games," said Berra of Koufax. "What I don't understand is how he lost 5."

In the second game Downing almost wriggled out of trouble in the first inning. Then with two outs, Maris misjudged a fly that allowed Willie Davis to pull into second with a 2-run double. That was enough for Podres, whose circle change baffled Yankee hitters. He and Perranoski held the Yankees to 7 hits and only an insignificant run in the ninth. Still wishing he were a Yankee, Skowron, who drove in 2 runs against Ford in Game 1, hit a solo homer and Tommy Davis tripled in a run as the Dodgers won 4–1.

Davis had another triple in the game, to right-center. Maris galloped after it and struck the outfield railing. His knees buckled but he chased after the ball and got it back to the infield. He was too banged up to stay in the game or play again in the Series.

In Game 3, at two-year-old Dodger Stadium, Bouton pitched a brilliant 4-hitter, giving up only 1 run in the first inning on a walk, wild pitch, and single by Tommy Davis off Richardson's glove. The bad news was that Drysdale pitched a 3-hit shutout. The Dodgers' 1–0 victory put them up 3 games to 0.

Prior to Game 4, in which Koufax faced Ford again, Houk told his team, "No matter what happens out there today, we've had a great season." Despite a cut on his finger, Ford gutted out 7 innings of 2-hit ball. Frank Howard got both hits, a harmless single in the second inning and a blast that sailed over the 450-foot sign in left in the fifth inning. The Yankees managed 6 hits off Koufax but only 1 run—Mantle's fifteenth World Series homer briefly tied the score in the top of the seventh inning.

The Series' most memorable play occurred in the bottom of the seventh, when Gilliam grounded to Boyer. Pepitone had told Ford earlier not to throw to first base to hold on runners because he couldn't see the ball in all the white shirts behind third base. Now he lost Boyer's throw. The ball caromed off his wrist and bounced toward the stands. Gilliam raced all the way to third and scored what proved to be the winning run on Willie Davis's sacrifice fly. In the ninth inning Koufax chalked up his 8th and 9th strikeout victims, Tresh and Mantle. Then, with two men on, he got Hector Lopez to ground to Wills for the final out in the Dodgers' 2–1 victory.

The Yankees had been swept in the World Series for the first time since 1922 against John McGraw's Giants, the year before there was a Yankee Stadium. They hit .171 as a team, scored only 4 runs, and struck out 37 times against the vaunted Dodgers pitchers. "Humiliation may be too harsh a word," wrote Mantle in *All My Octobers*, "but I can't express how embarrassed we were."

During the Series, callous reporters accused Maris of lazily going after Tommy Davis's triple in Game 2, feigning an injury to cover up his bad play, then sitting out the final two games by claiming he hadn't healed. Not until the official 1963 World Series film was released was he exonerated. "The movies show Maris's action was truly stoic," Dick Young said. "He hit with full force, grabbed his left biceps as his knees buckled, but disregarded his pain for the second to pursue the ball."

A week after the Series ended, Roy Hamey retired, Ralph Houk moved upstairs, and Yogi Berra was introduced as the new Yankee manager. By this time Maris was home in Independence. He was still nursing his leg, but when he had an abscessed tooth pulled, the back pain he'd been dealing with since August suddenly disappeared. When Pat gave birth in November to his fourth son, Richard, he had no problem holding him.

CHAPTER THIRTY-ONE

THE YANKEES' LAST HURRAH

A PICTURE OF ROGER Maris putting a bauble on the family Christmas tree in Independence circulated in newspapers in late December. Maris was not smiling, which was probably why this image was chosen to go above a caption that stated he had signed a contract for the 1964 season calling for an estimated $10,000 salary cut. This estimate was $2,500 too high, but it still seemed out of character for Maris, who had threatened holdouts and to quit entirely when he didn't get fair salary offers, to readily accept a cut. Returning from baseball's winter meetings in California, Ralph Houk had stopped in Kansas City to see his own family as well as Maris. Houk had praised him when he was his manager in 1963, but now he was the latest stingy Yankee GM. Afterward, Maris explained to reporters, "After the year I had, I couldn't see how I could ask for a raise or even the same salary." He failed to state the obvious, which was that he would have had solid stats if injuries hadn't limited the number of games he played. Mickey Mantle, who played only 65 games, saw his salary remain at $100,000.

The nation was in mourning after the assassination of President Kennedy on November 22. Certainly it was devastating for Roger, who had been thrilled to meet him, and for others in the Catholic communities in Independence and Fargo, particularly Pat's mother, a staunch Democrat. Shock and sadness permeated the air from coast to coast. Two events signaled optimistic renewal. In February, the Beatles arrived from London to appear on *The Ed Sullivan Show* and brought about a glorious musical, cultural, and societal upheaval that breathed life into America's damaged psyche. And at spring-training camps in Florida and Arizona, there was the welcome cry of "Play Ball!"

Roger had gone to only one ceremony in the off-season and was over-joyed to attend. On January 4, in Fargo, he was the fourth recipient of the Theodore Roosevelt Rough Rider Award in recognition of his achievements and "reflecting credit and honor upon North Dakota and its citizens." Maris followed entertainer Lawrence Welk, actress Dorothy Stickney, and artist Ivan Dmitri. Future honorees would include journalist Eric Sevareid, writer Louis L'Amour, entertainer Peggy Lee, actress Angie Dickinson, and record-ing artist Bobby Vee. It was one of the proudest moments of his life and re-inforced his bond to North Dakota.

Again Roger's family joined him in Florida for spring training. When he wasn't playing ball, he was usually with his children. In ESPN's *Roger Maris: Reluctant Hero*, Robert W. Creamer remembered seeing him "in the coffee shop of the hotel where I guess he had come down earlier with two or three of his sons. I was so impressed with the way he handled those kids. This young father. Didn't yell. Didn't scold. Didn't let them run around. He just said, 'Sit here. Come here.' And they obeyed what he said. Good kids. Bouncy and lively but they were obedient."

At spring training, Roger agreed to appear in an organizational film titled *Baseball—The Yankee Way*. It was one of the few times that he dis-cussed his hitting. Curiously, he did not describe himself as the disciplined contact hitter that most pitchers thought him to be, but as a Berra-like free swinger who didn't take many pitches and work counts: "If the ball's close to the plate, I'll swing at it. It's got to be pretty bad if I don't." He con-cluded wryly, "I've got a theory on hitting that will set baseball back twenty years."

Maris expected that he'd have an easier season than the last one. He stated, "I'm out to lead the league in enjoying myself this year. . . . I've made up my mind not to get mad at newspapermen and I'm not going to let the fans' booing bother me."

He didn't react when the fans jeered him the first time he stepped into the batter's box, and since nobody was going to ask him if he'd hit 64 hom-ers in '64, he made himself available to some reporters. They queried him and Mantle about their physical conditions. Assured that both players were convinced they had fully healed, the reporters moved on to what was the big story of 1964, Yogi Berra's becoming the first Yankee to go directly from the lineup to the manager's office. The assumption was that if Berra's former teammates challenged the chummy ex-catcher's authority, the Yankees wouldn't win their fifth consecutive American League pennant.

"The truth was that the Yankees had made a serious miscalculation if they hired Berra because he was good with the media," wrote David Halberstam in *October 1964*. "Rather, the media was good with him—inventing a cuddly, wise, witty figure who did not, in fact, exist. . . . His new assignment would be difficult: he was replacing a popular manager who was still close to the players and who was now his boss. Moreover, he was going to be managing his former teammates, who respected him as a player but who had frequently joked about him."

"The whole situation was unfair to him," said Tresh in 2008. "He played with all of us, so it was hard to suddenly be the one calling the shots. Particularly since Yogi was not a talker. He believed that if everybody did their jobs, we'd win. Which we did, so I'd say he was a good manager."

"I think the players accepted him as the boss," says Stan Williams, "because they all liked him and wanted him to succeed. I thought Yogi did a hell of a job in the circumstances he came under."

Berra hoped the Yankees started quickly so his managerial style and relationship to his former teammates wouldn't be issues. But they lost the first three games of the season in extra innings, earning them comparison with the crosstown-rival Mets. Fortunately, the Bronx Bombers then won four of five games and stayed above .500 for the rest of the season. But this wasn't going to be an easy year for Berra. When his team's record was 7–6, they'd lost five games by 1 run. Berra accepted the criticism for losing so many heartbreakers. He didn't point out that the Yankee offense hadn't yet scored more than 5 runs in a game and that he didn't have a lights-out reliever to close games. Berra and his pitching coach, Whitey Ford, who picked up extra money by replacing Johnny Sain, had to figure out how to utilize relievers Hal Reniff, Steve Hamilton, and rookie Pete Mikkelsen.

At two different times in May, the Yankees were tied for first place, but each time they tumbled into fourth. In early June they found themselves in fifth. They soon moved up to third and wouldn't fall lower again, but on June 10 they were 6 games behind Al Lopez's pitching-rich White Sox and 3½ behind Hank Bauer's Orioles, who had strong pitching and two early MVP candidates in Brooks Robinson and slugging first baseman John "Boog" Powell.

Maris and Mantle were in and out of the lineup, and Kubek's back was so painful that Linz was getting most of the work at short, but Berra made no excuses for the Yankees' struggles. He was more patient than his players. Several reportedly complained to Houk about Berra's dugout skills and failure to exercise discipline. They had admired Houk for letting them police themselves, but suddenly Berra was at fault for doing the same thing. The managerial job had gone to Berra primarily to boost attendance, but since that wasn't happening, Houk made up his mind to find someone with more experience for 1965. Berra never suspected a thing.

Without much fanfare, the Yankees came to life and played .667 ball from mid-June into early August. On August 6, their record was 64-40 and they were in first place, percentage points ahead of the Orioles and 1½ games ahead of the White Sox. But if Houk was having second thoughts about replacing Berra, they vanished when New York lost three of four to Baltimore and split a four-game series with Chicago at Yankee Stadium to drop back into third place, 3½ games behind the Orioles. The Yankees showed resilience by taking two of three from Baltimore, but they scored only 6 runs as they were swept in a four-games series in Chicago.

New York was now 4½ games behind the first-place White Sox and 4 behind the Orioles, and its title chances seemed remote to the fans and New York press. They were already thinking about next season because the big news was that Dan Topping and Del Webb were considering selling the club to CBS. No one knew what that would mean to the storied franchise in future years. But, in fact, the 1964 pennant race wasn't over.

The most memorable event of the Yankees' peculiar season took place not on the field but on the bus following the team's dismal showing in Comiskey Park in Chicago. To pass time while the team bus inched its way through heavy traffic to the airport, Linz pulled out his Hohner harmonica and practiced "Mary Had a Little Lamb," a tune for beginners. There had already been tension between the younger players and Berra and coach Frank Crosetti. As Jim Bouton later wrote, "Every once in a while Phil Linz, Joe Pepitone and I would giggle about something after a losing game and we got some pretty nasty stares from the old guard."

In a foul mood, Berra shouted for Linz to stop playing. Linz asked the players around him what Berra had said, and Mantle told him, "He said to play it louder." Linz did. Enraged, Berra charged down the aisle and suggested, "Why don't you stick that up your ass!" Linz exchanged words with his manager, then tossed his harmonica at him. Berra slapped it away. It struck Pepitone, who wailed, "My knee—get me a corpsman!" Most of the players cracked up. The next day Linz smoothed things over with Berra at the cost of $200 (though Crosetti never spoke to Linz again). With so much publicity about the harmonica incident, Linz received a $10,000+ endorsement deal from Hohner.

According to Mantle and other Yankees, as well as many sportswriters, Berra's standing firm against one of the team's young free spirits was the pivotal moment in the season. From then on, Berra had the respect of his players and got them to play as a determined unit.

In 1963 the Yankees went 11-5 in extra-inning games and 36-17 in 1-run decisions. In 1964, they were just 11-15 in extra-inning games and 27-24 in 1-run games. Al Downing had the same 13 victories he had in 1963, but Bouton (18-13), Ford (17-6), Terry (7-11), and Williams (1-5) had a combined 28 fewer wins. Considering that the '64 Yankees still won only 5 fewer games than the '63 team, Berra had to pull victories out of his hat. Though criticized for how he used his pitchers, he coaxed 30 wins in 42 decisions from swingman Rollie Sheldon (5-2) and relievers Bill Stafford (5-0), Pete Mikkelsen (7-4), Hal Reniff (6-4), and Steve Hamilton (7-2); got saves from ten pitchers, including Mikkelsen, with 12, and Reniff, with 9; and deftly used as many as six relievers in a game. He also used two late-season additions to perfection.

Right-hander Mel Stottlemyre was brought up from Richmond in August and made it clear that he was Ford's heir apparent. Berra threw him into the fire, and he calmly walked through the flames. The confident twenty-two-year-old sinkerballer won his first game on August 12, besting Ray Herbert of the White Sox, 7–3, to end the reeling Yankees' 3-game losing streak. In his next start, he outdueled Baltimore's Steve Barber for a 3–1 victory to pull the Yankees to within 2½ games. Next was an 8–0 shutout of Boston in the second game of an August 22 doubleheader that ended the Yankees' season-high 6-game losing streak and set the stage for their pennant drive. Stottlemyre won 6 of 9 decisions from then on to finish at 9-3. In his final win, on September 26, he tossed a 2-hit shutout against the Senators and became the last pitcher of the century to have 5 hits in a game.

Pedro Ramos was acquired from Birdie Tebbetts's doghouse in Cleveland in September for Bud Daley and $75,000. The flashy right-hander, who threw a fastball and a mysterious "Cuban palm ball," spent the late fifties pitching well but losing a truckload of games with the awful Washington Senators. Berra used him to finish games, and he was spectacular, with a 1–0 record, 7 saves, and a 1.25 ERA in 13 appearances. He credited Berra and Ford for convincing him to change his approach and use the sinker as his out pitch: "If I got ahead on my fastball or rinky-dink curve, then I used the sinker. I didn't try for the strikeout with the high and hard fastball anymore. I threw from the belt down and was happy if the batter just made bad contact."

In his 2003 book *Ten Rings*, Berra wrote, "Normally, you win a pennant when all your players have good years. We won it with almost everybody having bad years together." He exaggerated a little. While several players in the lineup had years similar to their subpar 1963 seasons, a few were extremely productive down the stretch. Though slowed by injuries, Mantle appeared in 143 games and had his final superseason, with 35 homers, 111 RBIs, and a .303 average (.422 right-handed, .244 left-handed). Howard's solid stats (15 homers/84 RBIs/.313) compared to those in his 1963 MVP season (28/85/.287). And Pepitone shook off a slow start to hit 28 homers and become only the fourth Yankee since DiMaggio retired to drive in 100 runs. All three had excellent Septembers, as did Richardson, who went 39 for 90, and Kubek, until his season suddenly ended when he uncharacteristically slammed his fist into a door and sprained his wrist. But if an MVP trophy had been awarded for the pennant run, then Maris, for his bat and his glove, would have been the prime candidate.

On August 21, Maris, who in his previous three full seasons drove in 112, 142, and 100 runs, had just 47 RBIs through 122 games. He'd missed a lot of time because of injuries, but that was still a low number. It was, however, misleading. Of Maris's first 10 homers, 9 were in Yankee victories, with the other coming in the ninth inning off Dick Radatz. His 11th and 12th homers were in losses, but his 13th homer was a game-winner on June 30 off the Angels' Fred Newman. Although Maris vanished when he had one of his slumps, he emerged at key times throughout the season. When Stottlemyre defeated the White Sox, 7–3, in his debut on August 12, Maris broke a 2–2 tie with a 2-run shot in the sixth inning to greet reliever Don Mossi. Maris's next homer came three games later, when he connected off Baltimore's Dave McNally with a runner on first to pave the way for an 8–1 victory for Bouton.

In the pivotal game of the Yankees' season, on August 22, when Stottlemyre shut out Boston, 8–0, to halt the Yankees' 6-game losing streak, Maris, Mantle, and Blanchard all homered off Jack Lamabe. It was Maris's 20th homer, and his 3 RBIs gave him 50 on the year.

"Mickey used to kid that Roger was stealing all his 'fans,' " Stottlemyre told Maury Allen in the *New York Post* in 1984. "They used to boo Mickey, and then they turned to booing Roger and Mickey became a hero. Everybody on the team got along well with Roger. I stayed in his apartment in Queens that first year. He was great to me. What I remember most is how the press and fans treated him. It got so that he once said he hated to do well because the fans were on him so much."

It wasn't just the press in New York that aggravated Maris. He remembered bad incidents almost everywhere but Kansas City, particularly Detroit and Minneapolis. His first cousin Jim LaFreniere Jr. remembers, "He got tickets for my wife and me to see a game in Minneapolis and invited us to his hotel afterward because it was his daughter Susan's birthday. . . . Shortly before we got there, the media had gotten hold of his little daughter and tried to bully a story out of her. Roger had just bought her a brand-new red-and-white dress for her birthday, and one photographer grabbed her and tore the dress. She felt so bad and Roger got so damned mad."

While it's not accurate that Maris single-handedly carried the Yankees in their final 40 games, as many of his teammates contend, Tom Tresh believed, "Roger Maris was the best player in the league during the last month of the season."

"If there was a key player, both offensively and defensively, in that stretch for the Yankees, it was Roger Maris," wrote David Halberstam in *October 1964*. "When the Yankees seemed on the verge of falling out of contention . . . Roger Maris caught fire and played some of the best baseball of his life."

Berra wasn't surprised Maris still had it in him. "Roger was still a team guy and great all-around player," he remembers. "I didn't think he'd gone downhill."

In a doubleheader sweep of Boston on August 29, Maris went 3 for 4 with 3 runs in the first game and 3 for 4 with 3 RBIs in the second. On September 7 against Minnesota, he went 4 for 5 and drove in 3 runs, homering and dropping a 2-run double down the right-field line to score Kubek with the winning run with two outs in the 11th inning. The next day, he doubled in the seventh inning off Camilo Pascual and came around to score on Howard's single, giving the Yankees and Stottlemyre a 2–1 victory.

On September 16, after getting only 1 hit over the previous six games, he went 2 for 4 with 3 RBIs against the Angels, with his 22nd homer putting the Yankees ahead 5–3 in an eventual 9–4 victory. This win pulled the 85–59 Yankees to within half a game of both Chicago and Baltimore, which was struggling even with Boog Powell back from an injury. The next game Maris went 3 for 4 with 2 runs as Stottlemyre outpitched Fred Newman, 6–2, and the Yankees moved into a tie for first place. Two games later, he hit his 23rd homer off A's reliever John Wyatt in an 8–3 victory that put the Yankees into sole possession of first place, where they would remain. Two games after that, on September 22, Maris went 4 for 5 and ripped his 24th homer off Sonny Siebert, as Stottlemyre and Ramos combined to beat the Indians, 5–3, and move the Yankees 2½ games up in the race.

On September 25, the Yankees won their next-to-last game of an 11-game winning streak, beating Washington, 6–5. Maris went 3 for 5. With the Yankees trailing 5–2, he hit his 25th homer, a 2-run blast off rookie Buster Narum. Then, after Pepitone's homer tied the score, Maris drilled his 26th homer to give the Yankees a 6–5 victory and keep them 4 games in front of the Sox and Orioles. He had one more big offensive game after that, when he had 3 hits and 3 RBIs in an 11–8 victory over Detroit on September 30.

Maris also contributed in the field. Mantle's legs were so painful that he could play only a corner spot in the outfield. Berra smartly shifted Maris to center field beginning on his thirtieth birthday, September 10. Maris made no errors in twenty-three games, displaying, as Til Ferdenzi raved, "a unique style of playing the position." Berra told reporters, "I needed a center fielder, so I went to Roger. . . . He did it and he played great. I really appreciate what he did for the club."

With Maris producing runs with his bat and taking away runs with his glove, the Yankees won 30 of their last 41 games, including 22 of 28 in September, erasing a 6-game deficit. They clinched their fifth consecutive American League title on October 3 with an 8–3 victory over Cleveland at Yankee

Stadium. They finished 99–63, 1 game ahead of Chicago and 2 ahead of Baltimore.

Berra won the pennant despite unrealistic expectations by a front office that didn't recognize the Yankees were in decline due to aging, ailing stars, the lack of talented minor leaguers to take their places, and the slow integration of their roster. In *We Played the Game*, 1964 MVP Brooks Robinson said, "This was the first year the Yankees really could be had. . . . Either they had come back to the pack or the rest of the teams had caught up to them."

The Yankees clinched the American League pennant with one day to spare. Their opponents in the World Series, the St. Louis Cardinals, captured the National League flag on the final day, a game ahead of Philadelphia and Cincinnati. While the Redbirds won 8 in a row, they benefited from a monumental collapse by Gene Mauch's Phillies, who lost 10 straight to blow a 6½-game lead with only 12 games left.

In retrospect, the Cardinals were the best team all along and a formidable foe for the Yankees. They hit 59 fewer homers than the Bronx Bombers' 162, but they scored only 15 fewer runs because they had a higher number of doubles, triples, and stolen bases, a higher slugging percentage, and a .272 batting average that dwarfed the Yankees' .253. They had three .300 hitters in left fielder Lou Brock (.348), center fielder Curt Flood (.311), and first baseman Bill White (.303) to two for the Yankees, Howard (.311) and Mantle (.303); and they had three more hitters above .285 in third baseman Ken Boyer (.295), shortstop Dick Groat (.292), and catcher Tim McCarver (.288). Maris's .281 was third best in the Yankees' lineup. Boyer would be voted the 1964 National League MVP after hitting 24 homers and driving in a league-high 119 runs.

The Cardinals had a strong defense led by Boyer, Flood, White, McCarver, Dal Maxvill, who was subbing for injured second baseman Julian Javier, and strong-armed rookie right fielder Mike Shannon. They also had three exceptional starters to go against the Yankees: 20-game winner Ray Sadecki; veteran Curt Simmons, who won 18 games; and, particularly, the imposing Bob Gibson, a 19-game winner whose fastball and slider exploded in the strike zone. In relief were setup men Roger Craig and Ron Taylor and closer Barney Schultz, the possessor of a dancing knuckler.

The Cardinals also had two intangibles, a fierce and visible competitiveness, which was personified by batterymates Gibson and McCarver, and strong chemistry between all players. Unlike those on the Yankees, the African Americans on the Cardinals—particularly Gibson, White, and Flood—were outspoken and took their places as leaders on the team without having to ask. They inspired in the clubhouse and, with the aggressive Brock, showed the way on the field. According to Halberstam in *October 1964*, this was a major reason that the Cardinals were potentially a perennial contender while the staid, station-to-station Yankees were on their last legs.

The Cardinals' manager was Johnny Keane, who had been in their system for thirty-five years. Like Berra, he was admired by most of his players—the team's black stars appreciated that he gave them their first real chance to play after taking over from Solly Hemus in July of 1961. But Cardinals owner Gussie Busch and consultant Branch Rickey didn't think the team could win with him as skipper. They had negotiated surreptitiously with Dodgers coach Leo Durocher to manage the team in 1965, not expecting the Cardinals to come out of nowhere and win the pennant under Keane.

Of the Cardinals players, only Groat was at all familiar with the Yankees, having played against them in the 1960 World Series as a Pittsburgh Pirate. "They weren't as strong as the 1960 team," he recalls, "because Mantle's shoulder was killing him. But they were still the Yankees. I thought Maris was an excellent hitter in 1960, and I didn't see him as a different player in 1964. But Mantle was still the guy. The Yankees felt better just knowing he was in the lineup."

"Mantle was the guy we feared over everybody," says McCarver. "It wasn't that we didn't think about Maris, but Mantle's presence was just overwhelming. I remember the scouting reports said you could crowd Mantle. We were told Maris was a pull hitter and that we should 'stay out of the middle of the plate,' which covers a lot of hitters. He was not your prototypical left-handed hitter in that he could handle a high pitch well. I remember that we tried to stay away and stay down. He still pulled the ball."

In the first inning of Game 1 in St. Louis, against Whitey Ford, the Cardinals displayed their brand of baseball. Brock singled to right, Groat moved him to third on a hit-and-run, and Ken Boyer hit an opposite-field fly ball to right, knowing Mantle's bad shoulder meant the speedy Brock could walk home after the catch. The Yankees displayed what they were known for in the second inning, as Tom Tresh hit a 2-run homer off of Sadecki for a 2–1 lead.

Going into the bottom of the sixth, Ford held a 4–2 lead despite discomfort in his hand. He recorded only one out. Ken Boyer singled, Shannon hit a towering homer to tie the game, and McCarver doubled to send Ford to the showers. After only 5⅓ innings, Ford was out for the rest of the Series because of the circulatory problems in his shoulder. It was a terrible blow for the Yankees to lose their number one starter, especially since their top reliever, Pedro Ramos, was declared ineligible for the Series because he was acquired after September 1. Ford, who had World Series records in almost every pitching category, would never again take the mound in the postseason. The Cardinals went on to win 9–5 for a 1–0 lead in the Series. Maris reached base twice, on a walk and an infield hit.

The Yankees tied the Series with an 8–3 victory in Game 2, as Stottlemyre threw a complete-game 7-hitter. Gibson dominated early, striking out the side in the first inning and two more batters in the second, but he gave up single runs in the fourth and sixth innings and 2 runs in the seventh when Linz singled and went to third on a wild pitch, Richardson delivered an RBI single, Maris singled Richardson to third, and Mantle grounded to second to bring in Richardson for a 4–2 Yankee lead. The Yankees tacked on 4 runs in the ninth against Schultz and Gordon Richardson, with Maris singling and scoring on Mantle's double.

Game 3 in New York was tense from the beginning as Bouton and Simmons hooked up in a pitcher's duel. For Simmons, who began his major league career in 1947, this was his World Series debut. The tough left-hander's methodology was, simply, to make batters feel uncomfortable, and that's how the Yankees felt facing him. Maris popped out, grounded out, flew out, and struck out. The Yankees got only 4 hits off Simmons, but two came in the second inning—a single by Howard and double by Boyer—which put them ahead 1–0. Their other hits came in the seventh—a single by Richardson and double by Mantle—but they failed to score.

Meanwhile, Bouton lived up to his nickname, Bulldog, by throwing 123 pitches in going the distance, allowing only 6 hits and 1 unearned run after Mantle misplayed a ball. That was probably on Mantle's mind when he led off the bottom of the ninth against Schultz. As he left the on-deck circle, he told Howard, "You might as well go on back to the clubhouse because I'm going to hit the first pitch out of here." Indeed, he smashed a knuckleball into the third tier in right. Everyone in Yankee Stadium, including the Cardinals, stared in awe at Mantle's record 16th World Series homer.

With momentum on their side following their 2–1 victory the previous day, the confident Yankees ripped into Cardinals starter Ray Sadecki in the first inning of Game 4. Linz doubled, Richardson singled him home, Maris singled Richardson to third, and Mantle singled home Richardson and sent Maris to third. But in what turned out to be a key play, Mantle tried for a double and was gunned down by Shannon, a star quarterback in college. Keane brought in veteran Roger Craig. Howard singled home Maris to put the Yankees up 3–0, but Craig then pitched 4⅔ scoreless innings, giving up only 1 more hit. Ron "Twitchy" Taylor, who had been so excited about winning the pennant that he'd hyperventilated and passed out in the clubhouse, relieved Craig and coolly threw hitless ball for the final 4 innings. Craig and Taylor saved the World Series for the Cardinals by allowing them the opportunity to come back and win Game 4, which they did, 4–3, on Ken Boyer's grand slam off Downing in the sixth inning. The Redbirds evened the Series.

Stottlemyre hooked up again with Gibson in the pivotal Game 5. The Cardinals snapped a scoreless tie in the fifth inning, going ahead 2–0 on singles by Gibson and Flood and some shoddy fielding by Richardson and Linz. Gibson sailed along, pitching 5-hit shutout ball with 11 strikeouts through 8 innings. But with one out in the bottom of the ninth, Mantle reached base on a Groat error. Then with two outs, Tresh tied the game with a homer into the right-center-field bleachers.

It was a devastating blow, but the Cardinals rebounded quickly. McCarver remembers, "In the top of the tenth, we got runners on first and third with one out against Pete Mikkelsen and I came up to hit. Mikkelsen's best pitches were his palm ball and sinkerball, but on a 3–2 count he threw me a fat fastball up in the strike zone. I didn't think I hit it that good, but in Yankee Stadium you didn't have to hit it that hard to get it out in right. I remember touching first, but after that I could no longer feel my legs as I circled the diamond. I had to look down to make sure my feet were touching the bases."

Staked to a 5–2 lead, Gibson came back strong in the bottom of the 10th inning. He recorded his 13th strikeout against pinch hitter Mike Hegan, a September call-up who forty-four years later recalled, "I don't know if I took my bat off my shoulder. My knees were buckling." Linz popped up for the second out, but Richardson, who had a record 13 hits and batted .406 in the Series, stroked a single to center. But there was no rally. Maris, hitless for the day, made the final out when Boyer made a nice play on a foul ball by reaching into the box seats behind third. The Cardinals took a 3–2 lead.

The Yankees weren't finished. In Game 6, in St. Louis, the Cardinals scored a run in the first inning off Bouton, but the hurler tied it with an RBI single in the fifth inning. The gutsy right-hander went 8⅔ before being relieved by Hamilton, allowing only meaningless single runs in the eighth and ninth innings. By that time, the Yankees had posted 8 runs on the scoreboard. Maris had broken the 1–1 tie in the sixth inning with a long homer to right off Simmons, and Mantle followed with a shot that was even farther. The Yankees got 5 more runs in the eighth inning, the big blow being a grand slam by Pepitone.

In Game 7, Berra rolled the dice and started Stottlemyre for the third time against Gibson. Both pitchers were working on two days' rest. Berra's gamble worked only until the fourth inning, when the Cardinals rallied for 3 runs. They scored 3 more runs in the fifth inning off Downing for a 6–0 lead. With a well-rested Gibson on the mound, the lead would have been insurmountable, but his arm was worn out. The Yankees cut the lead in half in the sixth, when Richardson beat out a grounder, Maris singled, and Mantle smashed a 3-run homer into the left-center-field bleachers. It was his 18th and final World Series homer. Ken Boyer homered in the eighth inning to give Gibson a 7–3 lead, which he took into the bottom of the ninth. Instructed by Keane to throw the ball down the middle, Gibson gave up solo homers to Linz and Clete Boyer to cut the lead to 7–5 with Bobby Richardson at the plate. "I would look in the dugout," Gibson recalled in the 2008 book *Tim McCarver's Diamond Gems*, "and Johnny would be leaning over the watercooler with his back to the mound because he was afraid to make eye contact with me. Luckily, Richardson popped up."

The St. Louis Cardinals had won a memorable World Series in seven games. The next day, Yogi Berra was fired as the Yankees manager.

"I was surprised," says Berra forty-five years later. And heartbroken. He thought that he was due a two-year contract.

"I think that was the biggest mistake the Yankees ever made," Richardson stated in Dom Forker's 1990 book *Sweet Seasons*, about Berra. "First, it wasn't right. Yogi did a great job under adverse circumstances. Second, it was a public-relations blunder. Look at all the fans that switched their allegiance to the Mets after Yogi got fired." One reason they switched is that Berra accepted Casey Stengel's offer to be a Mets coach. Another blow to the fans was the firing, without explanation, of Mel Allen, the voice of the Yankees' post–World War II dynasty.

Houk said he hadn't decided on Berra's replacement. Meanwhile, the Cardinals held a press conference that many reporters skipped because they were sure it was just going to be a photo op for Cardinals management and Keane as he accepted a new multiyear contract. However, Keane, irate after learning of the Cardinals' overtures to Leo Durocher, made the shocking announcement that he was quitting. His future plans? "I'm going fishing," he said. In fact, in a bizarre turn of events, he was going to New York to see Houk. Although Houk denied it to reporters, he had spoken to Keane on the sly about managing the Yankees.

Maris returned to Missouri, disappointed in the World Series loss but satisfied with his own season and that the Yankees had won their fifth consecutive pennant since he joined the team. If he were one to compare his and Mantle's statistics over those five years, he would have discovered that his production was remarkably similar to that of the man considered the best player in the American League. From 1960 to 1964, Mantle appeared in 637 games, scored 479 runs, drove in 457 runs, and slugged 174 homers. In 685 games, Maris scored 461 runs, drove in 478 runs, and had 182 homers. Mantle's average was much higher for the five years; Maris was the superior fielder. "I thought of Maris and Mantle as equals," says Roy Sievers, a former home-run champion and All-Star who finished his sixteenth season in 1964. "Roger was much underrated by the press, but not the players. To me, Roger was a perfect ballplayer."

CHAPTER THIRTY-TWO

THE BETRAYAL

O N NOVEMBER 2, 1964, the Columbia Broadcasting Company became the first corporate owner of a major league baseball team when it offi-cially purchased 80 percent of the New York Yankees for $11.2 million. Dan Topping and Del Webb, who sensed that the instigation of an amateur-player draft would prevent the Yankees from maintaining their supremacy over poorer franchises, were eager to sell. Each retained 10 percent of the team, though Webb would sell his share to CBS during the 1965 season. Topping kept the title of president of the Yankees, and Ralph Houk, in the second year of a four-year contact, remained general manager, but the new vice president, Michael Burke, took over most baseball operations.

Following a brief stint on the Philadelphia Eagles, the suave, dynamic Burke spent time in the OSS in World War II, winning the Navy Cross and the Silver Star. His exploits behind enemy lines were filmed in Hollywood as *Cloak and Dagger*, starring Gary Cooper, who played Lou Gehrig in *Pride of the Yankees*. After managing the Ringling Bros. and Barnum & Bailey Cir-cus, he came to CBS with instructions to expand operations, which he did by convincing the network to underwrite the smash Broadway musical *My Fair Lady*. It was Burke who advised CBS to buy the Yankees. "The trouble was," the erudite Burke later admitted, "we didn't go in and feel the goods. We bought a pig in a poke."

Maris arrived in Fort Lauderdale with his usual optimism, unconcerned about the ownership change and the hiring of the fourth Yankee manager in his six years with the team. His immediate goal was to have an injury-free spring and prepare to help New York win another title. When spring train-ing began, he quickly impressed Johnny Keane, who told *Christian Science*

Monitor columnist Ed Rumill that Maris was even better than the Cardinals'
scouts asserted prior to the 1964 World Series: "You can't fully appreciate
Maris until you've seen him every day, making the plays and throws in the
outfield, and giving you a power effort at the plate. Roger is one of the most
underrated ballplayers I've ever seen."

Maris was encouraged about the upcoming season because not only did
he feel physically sound, but also Mantle ("I really do feel as though this
might be one of those real big years for me") and Ford were feeling sprightly.
The strong starting lineup was back intact, Stottlemyre and Ramos were
going to be on the team for a full season, and a few promising youngsters
were in camp, including switch-hitting outfielder Roy White and eighteen-
year-old shortstop Bobby Murcer.

"I knew my place and spoke only when spoken to," remembers White.
"But when shagging flies or just being around him, Roger was a gentleman
to me, treating me with respect and kindness. He was a great person."

Murcer, a powerful left-handed batter from Oklahoma, was billed as "the
next Mickey Mantle." He, too, was signed by Tom Greenwade, and the
famed scout asked Mantle to look after the youngster and make him feel accepted. In his 2008 autobiography *Yankee for Life*, Murcer remembered,
"Another thing that made me feel accepted, made me feel like part of the
team that first spring training, was when Clete Boyer and Roger Maris took
me out to dinner one night to this famous, fancy Polynesian restaurant in
Fort Lauderdale named Mai Kai—my first introduction to Polynesian food,
and, more importantly, my first introduction to mai tais." As veterans, Maris
and Boyer felt obligated to give Murcer (the Yankees' future center fielder)
the same welcome that Mantle and Ford accorded them when they arrived
in New York. They were fully aware that the rookie had to go to the park the
next morning with double vision and nausea and try to hit live pitching. It
was part of his initiation.

Another night out for Maris and Boyer prevented Roger from spending
spring training under the radar. They had dinner with Hal Reniff and Joe
DiMaggio at Nick's Cocktail Lounge in Fort Lauderdale. A male model
named Jerome Modzelewski was leaving the restaurant around midnight
with a twenty-one-year-old redhead named Angela Della Vedova when he
spotted the quartet at a table. He interrupted their meal and asked for auto-

graphs or, as he later testified, merely said hello to an acquaintance sitting with the athletes. Reniff brusquely brushed him off and may have made an indelicate remark about him or his date.

The couple left, but Modzelewski returned and demanded an apology. Boyer told him to get lost and a heated argument ensued. The verbal spat between Boyer and Modzelewski moved out into the parking lot and escalated. Maris intervened but not before Boyer got in a few good blows. The next day, the local papers had pictures of the swollen, bruised face of the male model, who needed eleven stitches in his mouth and a loose tooth removed. He insisted *two* players had assaulted him. "I didn't hit anyone," contended Maris. DiMaggio, who had slipped out the side door and probably saw nothing, informed Houk that Maris was innocent.

Boyer and Maris were arrested and had separate trials. Roger's lasted two hours and forty-three minutes. His lawyer, Bill Leonard, produced two witnesses who said Boyer was the only one to punch Modzelewski. Roger testified on his own behalf. *Newsday's* Joe Donnelly wrote, "You can say this for Maris. In the witness chair he was no more politic than he is in dirty, smelly locker rooms. At one point he told the judge, 'I want to tell the story in my own words.'" Municipal Court judge Arnold Grevior dismissed the case against him because of "a reasonable doubt in my mind." Boyer settled with the model he manhandled.

When the Yankees broke camp, they believed to a man that they were the best team in baseball. They still had a swagger and a sense of entitlement. They were sure they would have won the 1964 World Series if Ford, Kubek, and Ramos could have contributed and assumed that with a full cast of players, they'd roll to their sixth consecutive pennant and make amends in the '65 Series. However, their new manager believed that for the Yankees to reclaim their status as baseball's best team they had to change their style of play and attitude.

"Johnny Keane was absolutely the wrong guy for our club," said Clete Boyer. "He was a hell of a good man, extremely religious, in many ways a beautiful guy. He would have made a hell of a college coach. But he didn't fit our clubhouse. Going outside the organization to replace Yogi, who we had all played with, was a dumb idea. Bringing in the guy who had just kicked our asses in the World Series was even dumber."

"Johnny was very hard for us to take because we weren't used to being treated like kids," said Tom Tresh in 2008. "Our job was to win. We didn't need curfews to do that."

"We were used to Casey and Ralph, who didn't even have a curfew, and Yogi, who didn't really enforce one," wrote Mantle in *The Mick*. "Now, all of a sudden, here's this guy coming in like a drill sergeant."

Keane constantly chastised young players such as Bouton, Linz, and Pepitone—and even the unseasoned Murcer—for not focusing on baseball, but he made a more grievous error by challenging Mantle, making him do a long outfield drill as punishment for a hangover. "I knew he wasn't providing instruction," said Mantle. "He was trying to make me sick, trying to set an example. I didn't like it."

Mantle wasn't upset just for himself, but for his best friend, Whitey Ford. Keane said he expected Ford to have a great season, but clearly he and Jim Turner, who had been rehired as the Yankees' pitching coach, didn't see Ford as the ace of a rotation that also featured the much younger Bouton, Stottlemyre, and Downing. Bouton got the Opening Day assignment, and Stottlemyre pitched the first game at Yankee Stadium.

Keane's starters pitched better than their records early in the season, as the anemic Yankees offense scored more than 5 runs only once in the 12 games played in April, twice in the first 20 games, and seven times in the first 47 games. They were shut out six times between May 2 and June 4, when they lost 2–0 to the White Sox in 15 innings.

Maris went hitless as the Yankees lost their first two games of the year in California. But in their third game, April 15 against the Angels, he went 2 for 3 with a homer and 2 RBIs in support of Stottlemyre's 4-hit, 4–0 victory. In the following game, against the A's, he hit a 2-run homer off Orlando Pena to break a scoreless tie in the sixth inning as Downing won 5–2. Maris became the sixth player to launch a ball over both the inner and outer walls in right field at Municipal Stadium.

For the series in Kansas City, Maris was glad to spend time at home with his family, particularly since Pat was pregnant again, with their sixth child due in early summer. As he had in spring training, Roger reached out to some of the younger players. "That was only my second year up," recalls Jake Gibbs, an All-American quarterback at Mississippi who was Howard's backup at catcher, "and Roger invited me and three or four other guys to his house in Independence to have hamburgers before the game that night. I was very appreciative. I thought he had a good way with people. He was a big star but didn't act like a star at all."

The Yankees came home and lost two midweek games to Minnesota as Pascual and Kaat bested Stottlemyre and Downing. Maris had a hit and an RBI in the two defeats. He went hitless but had an RBI two days later against the visiting Angels on Saturday, as 1964 Cy Young winner Dean Chance handed the Yankees their fourth straight loss, 6–3. The Yankees temporarily silenced their critics by taking a Sunday doubleheader from the Angels. Maris smashed his 3rd homer in the first game, as Ford won, 3–2, with a save from Ramos.

The Yankees next played on Wednesday, April 28, and Downing stymied the A's 5–1 on 5 hits to improve New York's record to 6-6. Maris scored their 4th run and drove in their 5th. He also made the fielding gem of the game, a running, backhanded catch of Bert Campaneris's liner to right-center field with men on second and third. Then he collapsed. Maris had pulled the medial muscle in his right thigh and needed to be helped off the field.

He missed 26 games. When he returned on May 25, the Yankees were 17-21 and mired in eighth place, 8 games behind the White Sox and 6 games behind second-place Minnesota. Nobody was batting over .300. Mantle was at .255, and several players were having trouble hitting their weights, including excellent defensive catcher Doc Edwards, who was acquired in early May from the A's for a tearful Johnny Blanchard and Rollie Sheldon.

Because of the team's shaky start, Keane called meetings to reinforce his unpopular rules, even though that drove a wedge between him and the players. A low point was when Keane fined several players for living it up at the airport bar in Newark. Because they had trouble with Keane personally, the Yankee players, as Tresh said, "didn't play well for him." They bristled when he ordered a bunt or hit-and-run with a power hitter at the plate or gave Mantle a "take" sign and responded with halfhearted efforts. They grumbled that the Bronx Bombers were always feared for hitting home runs but Keane was managing them as if they were the Cardinals.

Keane was relieved Maris returned before the team was out of contention. But he managed only 2 hits in his first four games, all losses, as the

Yankees dropped to 17-25 and fell 10 games behind Chicago. It was promising that one hit was a homer, but over the next six games he had only 3 hits and 1 RBI as his average fell to .177.

Maris finally found his rhythm in back-to-back victories over Chicago and Kansas City, going 3 for 6 with 5 RBIs. He went hitless in a loss to the A's, but then had an 11-game hitting streak. On June 18, he drilled his 6th homer of the year off Baltimore's Robin Roberts, but the Yankees lost their fourth consecutive game, 2–1, in 16 innings. The next day, Maris clouted his 7th homer off Jim Perry as the Yankees defeated first-place Minnesota, 10–2. He went 1 for 3 with a run as the Yankees won again the next day when Ford outpitched Mudcat Grant, 5–3. The win cut the Twins' lead over the Yankees to 9 games and set the stage for a big Sunday doubleheader. A fervent crowd of 71,245 packed Yankee Stadium on June 20 to see if the Yankees could get back in the race.

The Yankees jumped on Pascual in the first inning. Richardson doubled to left. Tresh singled to right, with Richardson taking third. Maris took Pascual the other way, grounding a ball through the infield to score Richardson with the first run of the game and move Tresh to second. Howard, batting fourth, singled to left to score Tresh and send Maris to third and reached second himself on an error by Tony Oliva in right. With the Yankees up 2–0 with nobody out, Twins manager Sam Mele moved his infielders onto the grass, risking a big inning in the hope of preventing another run from scoring. He did this although it was just the first inning and the batter was Mantle, who hit the ball harder than anyone else in baseball. His decision had a major effect on Maris's career. Batting left-handed, Mantle grounded sharply to second baseman Rich Rollins (formerly an All-Star third baseman), who threw home and nipped Maris.

"Maris came sliding in," recalls Bill Haller, who was the home-plate umpire. "He extended his right hand and hit my shoe. I didn't know it at the time, but I heard through the grapevine that he broke a finger. It was a shame because I liked Roger. He wasn't the most personable guy with umpires, but he was polite and no complainer."

Not knowing the seriousness of his injury, Maris popped his dislocated ring finger back into place and continued to play. The Twins scored single runs off Stottlemyre in the second, third, and sixth innings to take a 3–2 lead. In the bottom of the seventh, Pascual walked Tresh with one out, prompting Mele to bring in left-hander Jerry Fosnow to face Maris. Although the ring finger and pinkie of his right hand were numb, Maris connected off the rookie with his 8th homer to thrill the crowd and give the Yankees a 4–3 lead. But Harmon Killebrew homered off Ramos in the top of the eighth inning to tie the game. In the ninth inning, the Twins' swift shortstop Zoilo Versalles, who was in the middle of an MVP season, scored on a passed ball and speedy left fielder Sandy Valdespino scored on a wild pitch as the Twins prevailed 6–4. They also won the nightcap, 7–4, as Killebrew's 2-run ninth-inning homer put the game out of reach and the Yankees 11 games back.

Barely able to grip the bat, Maris went 0 for 3 in the second game, then sat out five games. He started in five more games from June 25 to 28, corresponding with the Yankees' season-high 5-game winning streak against the Angels and the Senators. On the final day, the Yankees won a doubleheader from Washington, 3–0 and 4–3. In the first inning of the second game, Maris lost his grip when he swung at the first pitch thrown by Mike McCormick. According to Harvey Rosenfeld's biography *Roger Maris*: *A Title to Fame*, Maris later said, "There was a real sharp pop in my hand, loud enough that I could hear it. It was just like you snap a pencil. The hand swelled up right away, double its size. I ended up taking a pitch right down the middle to strike out."

The Yankees had X-rays taken of Roger's hand, but their doctors reported that nothing was wrong. When the swelling went down, that seemed to confirm their findings. But Maris knew differently because he was in excruciating pain. He couldn't grip a bat, throw a ball, or turn a doorknob. He worried that his slide into Haller's foot had damaged more than his two fingers.

Roger ran in the outfield every day. He shagged flies and shot-put them to the infield. Despite his inability to throw properly, he did not look like an ailing man to onlookers. Keane and Houk kept asking him when he could play again and persuaded him to take batting practice every few days to test his hand. Each time, Maris reported that it was too painful to swing the bat. Houk twice ordered more X-rays, but team physician Dr. Sidney Gaynor repeated that nothing was broken.

If the Yankees wanted to do the wise, considerate thing, they would have taken Maris off the active roster and announced that he was too badly injured to play. It was the best way to protect their valuable property's hand and keep a bull's-eye off his back. But with Maris needed for a pennant drive, the club let it be known that they were waiting day by day for him to say he was ready to be in the lineup. As games passed, innuendos appeared in the papers about how Maris had given up on the team. Fans who were frustrated by the Yankees' lack of offense booed when they caught glimpses of him.

"All the Yankees management cared about was Roger playing," recalls Maury Allen, "not whether he really had a broken bone in his hand. The key to that was Sidney Gaynor, the Yankees' doctor at Lenox Hill Hospital. He was a very nasty man whose job was to get hurt players on the field. His attitude was that they were a bunch of crybabies."

"I love that day-to-day crap," Boyer told Tony Kubek. "That's a terrible thing to do to a ballplayer like Roger. All they did was play games with him, hinting to reporters that the only pain was in Roger's head. How could anyone say that Roger was dogging it? But that's what the front office basically said."

Even some of his younger teammates went along with the inference by management and the press that he was "jaking it." For the first time since he'd arrived in New York, Roger didn't have the full support of his teammates. Two young players who believed Maris, however, were Gibbs and Downing. Gibbs recalls, "He was hurt but he felt nobody believed that. He told me, 'The next time I get hurt I hope there's a visible broken bone and blood gushing.' "

"If you had any kind of injury where the bone wasn't sticking out, they said there wasn't anything wrong with you," remembers Downing. "For three months everybody questioned if Roger was really hurt. That is a long time to be ridiculed. He wanted to play but he just couldn't hit or throw. The sixties was the last decade before there was any kind of sports medicine. Today they'd do an MRI and it would've been taken care of."

Although Mantle was not subjected to the bad press and subsequent negative fan reaction that dogged Maris, he (as did Bouton) had similar experiences with Keane in regard to injuries. "He never seemed to accept the idea that when I couldn't play, I was truly hurting," wrote Mantle in *All My Octobers*. In 1965, Mantle appeared in only 122 games due to a bad shoulder and bad legs. "I never threw the ball back to the infield at all, but would flip it to

Tom Tresh and let him fire it in," he wrote in his 1967 autobiography *The Education of a Baseball Player.* "I did not let this fret me too much. But my wobbly pins, especially my right knee, made it more and more difficult for me to deliver a long blow. . . . 1965 was certainly my low point."

Before Maris's hand injury, the Yankees improved their record to 35-37 and moved into sixth place, trailing Minnesota by 9 games with 90 games to go. At the time, the Twins organization expected Maris to return and the Yankees to make their annual run for the pennant. According to Jim Kaat, the Twins ended the Yankees' slim hopes on Sunday, July 11, when the Yankees needed a victory to cut Minnesota's lead to 12½ games heading into the All-Star Game. "The biggest hit in the history of our franchise at the time," says Kaat, "was the 2-run homer that Harmon Killebrew hit in the bottom of the ninth off Pete Mikkelsen to win that game 6–5. After that you got a sense that their run was over."

"Maybe Keane wasn't the right manager for the Yankees," says Doc Edwards, "but how can any manager lose Elston Howard, Tony Kubek, Mickey Mantle, and Roger Maris and have to replace them with Doc Edwards, Phil Linz, Ross Moschitto, and those type of players? When you're substituting ponies and plow horses for thoroughbreds, it's tough to win a race."

The Yankees' loss to Minnesota on July 11 dropped them into seventh place at the All-Star break. They beat Washington their first game back and again moved into sixth place, which is where they remained for the rest of the year. They finally reached .500 on August 14 in their 118th game and on August 20 and 24 managed to go 2 games over, a season high. Two 7-game losing streaks in September guaranteed them a losing record. The long-mighty Yankees finished 77-85, a humiliating 25 games behind Minnesota.

Many hard-news stories made headlines in 1965—the escalation of the war in Vietnam, the violent civil rights demonstrations in Alabama, the Watts riots in Los Angeles, the passage of the Voting Rights Act and the Social Security Act, the assassination of Malcolm X, the election of liberal Republican John Lindsay as the mayor of New York. New York football fans and a genuflecting press were thrilled that "Broadway Joe" Namath, a media darling, was quarterbacking the Jets. But for baseball fans the biggest story of the year was that the New York Yankees finished in the second division for the first time in forty years.

After his hand injury, Maris traveled with the team and even begrudgingly pinch-hit four times, all in losses. "It wasn't fun to be in the dugout day in and day out and to sit there looking like a jerk," Maris later told *Sports Illustrated*. "It was a long season."

Into September, Yankee management continued to insist Maris was well enough to play, and he repeatedly told them his hand was too tender. Finally, Julie Isaacson arranged for Roger to see a doctor apart from the Yankees, and without their permission. A young technician placed Roger's elbow on the table and stuck his hand straight up in the air and shot the X-ray straight down through the fingertips. It detected that Maris had fractured the hamate bone, a roughly triangular bone at the base of the hand, consisting of two parts, a body and a hook. The hook had detached from the body, or main part of the bone. Finally, the source of Maris's continuous pain had been revealed.

With about two weeks to go in the season Maris went to see Houk to tell him about the X-ray and inform him he was going back to Independence. Faced with Roger's evidence, Houk said, "Rog, I might as well level with you. You need an operation on that hand." The words "I might as well level with you" etched themselves in Maris's brain. He would quote them often over the years to convey his sense of betrayal by Houk and a Yankees organization that had known the severity of his injury but kept it from the press, the fans, and him.

"Roger wasn't happy with the entire organization when he found out that he really did have something broken in his hand," recalls Houk. "But I was never aware of any bad feelings toward me."

Their ruse uncovered, the Yankees quickly held a press conference. Dr. Gaynor explained the injury and stated Maris would undergo surgery to fix it. He then said, "We had hoped that nature would reunite the hamate bone, which often happens. We had hoped surgery wouldn't be necessary, but when we saw that the hook was not going to rejoin the main bone, we decided to operate." His self-incriminating words made it seem that the Yankees had been monitoring Maris's injury since June 28, not denying its existence.

At first Maris balked at surgery, worrying that it might cause nerve damage. He agreed only after Isaacson got Houk to guarantee Maris would receive a full salary in 1966 even if he couldn't play, and that the only team he could be traded to was Kansas City. On September 28, Maris underwent successful reparative surgery by Dr. J. William Littler.

The worst year of Maris's career ended with his clearing out his locker before the season ended. His stats were those of a scrub. He played in 46 games and had 155 at-bats. He batted .239 with 22 runs, 27 RBIs, 8 homers, 7 doubles, 29 walks, and 29 strikeouts.

The only Yankees to have really good seasons were the few pitchers who overcame a conspicuous lack of run support. The offense scored only 611 runs, down 119 runs from 1964, but the strong Yankee staff yielded 7 fewer runs than that. Somehow Stottlemyre went 20-9. Ford had his last good season, going 16-13. Downing went 12-14, Steve Hamilton had a 1.39 ERA, and Pedro Ramos chalked up 19 saves.

Nobody in the Yankee lineup had a particularly good year. Tresh led the team in average, homers, and RBIs, but he batted only a modest .279, with 26 homers and 74 RBIs. It was worrisome that Howard batted .233, Pepitone and Richardson hit only .247, and Pepitone's RBIs decreased from 100 to 62. Kubek hit .218 and vowed retirement because X-rays revealed he'd broken his neck playing touch football in the army.

In 361 at-bats, Mantle hit a lowly .255 with 19 homers and 46 RBIs. If he hadn't been given a "Mickey Mantle Day" by the organization on September 18 and lavished with presents and kudos, he might have retired. However, he had 473 career homers and wanted to hit 500, and it was hard to pass on another $100,000 contract. Houk and Burke coaxed Mantle to keep playing because he still put people in the stands. Mickey Mantle was more popular than ever in New York. It was exactly the opposite for Roger Maris.

CHAPTER THIRTY-THREE

ROCK BOTTOM

AFTER THREE WEEKS, ROGER had the plaster shell on his right hand removed. He told the Yankee front office the following spring that he rehabilitated it in the off-season by playing golf. He played that sport with increasing frequency and skill. He couldn't hit the ball as far as Mantle—only two or three professional golfers could—but he hit it a long way and was less erratic. He played mostly at the Crackerneck Golf Course in Independence but also on frequent trips to Las Vegas that he and Pat took with the Cosentinos, Gossers, and Surprises (with whom they also went to Grossinger's, the famous resort in the Catskills in upstate New York). George Surprise recalls:

> We went to the Flamingo, Caesars, and the Hilton. The men would go one way and the women would go another. People always recognized Roger. We played golf and we also gambled. I taught Roger blackjack. He had never gambled before. He ended up winning several hundred dollars, but I was kind of telling him how to play. After it was over, he said, "That's really easy." I said, "Hey, Rog, you know they couldn't build these big, beautiful hotels if they didn't have an advantage over you." Well, the second time he lost all the money he had won. He got wise real quick and didn't gamble much after that.

Back in Independence, Roger, thirty-one, enjoyed being a full-time father to Susan, Roger Jr., Kevin, Randy, Richard, and Sandra. Like his brother, Rudy Jr., who also had six kids; grandfather Steve, who had five kids; great uncle Paul, who had eight kids; and great-grandfather John Maras, who had six kids, Roger had the large family he and Pat—who was one of five children—always planned. The birth of Sandra meant holiday visits from Roger's parents.

"After the divorce, Rudy spent a lot of the time here and would come into the store," remembers Jerry Cosentino, who along with his older brother, Jim, built the biggest supermarket chain in the Kansas City–Independence area. "I thought it was kind of odd that I never met Roger's mother. She might have been dead for all I knew. I'd think Pat would have mentioned Roger's mother, but she never did."

"Roger's mother and father came here quite a bit and we knew them very well," says Margaret Surprise. "For some reason, Connie wasn't too crazy about her daughters-in-law, Pat and Rudy Jr.'s wife. That was just the way she was."

When Roger visited Fargo, where he played golf with his friends, he saw his parents there, too. After more than thirty years, Rudy still worked for the Great Northern Railroad, as a mechanical supervisor. "Roger's old man was okay, but he was tough and a grouch," Jim Adelson recalls. "When Roger came back, I'd haul a camera crew over to where his dad was living. His dad would growl, 'What the hell are you doing here, Adelson?' I'd go, 'I'm interviewing your kid. Give me a break.' As you can imagine, he was very proud of his son, and Roger loved him without question."

In 1966, Rudy learned of the passing of another of his uncles in Hibbing, ten years after the death of Paul Maras. On Roger's thirty-second birthday his great-uncle Mike Maras, the father of Big Nick Maras and the founder and owner of the Homer Tavern, was found dead at the age of eighty-four, partly submerged in DuPont Lake. His heart was sound and there was no water in his lungs so "the county coroner wanted to have an inquest into my grandfather's death," says Bill Maras. "But our father wouldn't agree to it." The passing of the oldest and least pleasant of the five Maras brothers who immigrated to America in the early 1900s brought an end to an era. Peter Maras, the one surviving brother, lived until 1971; sister Anna passed in 1978.

A press conference was held on January 6, 1966, to announce Maris was signing a new contract. Houk held up Roger's hand for photographers and said he had a clean bill of health from Dr. Littler. Houk beamed, Maris smiled awkwardly. At the press conference Maris came across as an apologist for the organization he could probably have sued, even saying that the Yankees didn't get proper X-rays because "the pain in my hand prevented me from turning it so they could get a shot at the proper angle." In truth, says George Surprise, "He was very upset about hurting his hand and was becoming more disenchanted with baseball."

On this day, Houk cheerfully announced that Maris was going to receive the same $72,000 salary he had in 1965. (Maris later contended it was $75,000.) "We didn't feel he should be cut in salary," Houk explained, "because he was hurt while playing and you can't blame a player for that." Forgotten was that Houk had cut Roger's salary after his injury-plagued 1963 season.

"Public vindication came yesterday to Roger Maris," wrote Dick Young. "Maris was good to the Yankees and the Yankees are being good to Maris."

The reporters at the conference asked Roger about the rectangular adhesive patch on the right side of his face, between the temple and the corner of the eye. Maris said that he'd had occasional rashes in that area for four years and that a sample of skin had been taken for examination. He made no mention of skin cancer, saying that in the past his condition had been attributed to sun poisoning.

Although Keane had let him twist in the wind in '65, Roger was surprisingly supportive of his beleaguered manager, saying, "Keane walked into a situation that he couldn't do anything about last year."

Maris didn't pick up a bat until he reported to training camp in Fort Lauderdale on March 1. He quickly discovered that swinging a golf club at a stationary little white ball wasn't the same as swinging a two-pound bat at a 90 mph fastball. His hand felt fine, but it surely disappointed him that his two numb fingers prevented him from crushing pitches as he'd done in the past. Maris didn't have a good spring as he tried to compensate for his difficulty in gripping the bat through the swing.

Still, he made a positive impression on the young players. Future big league manager Mike Ferraro, who was a rookie third baseman, recalls, "We stayed at the Yankee Clipper Hotel, and in those days you ate at the hotel and signed the check. I'll be damned if every day at dinner Roger didn't sit at the table with us rookies. It was unheard of for a star to hang with a rook, but on a number of occasions after dinner he would offer an invite to go across the street to the Bahia Cabana for an after-dinner drink. Of course you never turn down a star. It even came out in New York papers that Roger was hanging with some rooks."

"I wasn't around him that much," remembers Dooley Womack, an unheralded rookie from South Carolina who became the Yankees' closer in 1966 and arguably their best pitcher. "I admired him. He played hard every game and was an excellent player."

"There's no question that there was an aura around him," says Mike Hegan. "He was very quiet so I don't remember any sit-downs in the dugout when he'd say, 'You know this is what you've got to do, kid,' but we'd talk informally behind the batting cage. I might ask him about my hands or the position of the bat head. I wished I had a swing like his. He had such quick hands, even then."

Maris had learned that it was imprudent to be inhospitable to the media, but he still made no real effort to change his ways, and his relationship with most reporters was prickly at best. He continued to be suspicious of almost all of them, and he held grudges against any who had damaged his image. Ruben Amaro, who had been acquired from Philadelphia for Phil Linz, recalls:

> Roger and I had a lot of fun playing high-low poker with Mickey Mantle and Hector Lopez, for twenty-five cents a hand. He was a great, sentimental, family-oriented guy. I never heard him say anything bad about anybody or lose his temper. But then we went to play the Phillies on the west coast of Florida and were sitting at a bar, when he saw a reporter he didn't like. Evidently the year that Roger broke Babe Ruth's record, he wrote a very derogatory article about him and his family. He confronted the writer and took the article out of his wallet. He told him, "I'm never going to take this out of my wallet because you hurt my children writing it."

Amaro was a "great-field, no-hit" veteran shortstop who was brought in after Tony Kubek retired. His double-play partner, Bobby Richardson, agreed to stay on another year only so the Yankees didn't need to replace both middle infielders at the same time. The Yankees hoped that Richardson and Pepitone would rebound offensively from '65; that Bouton would return to his 1963–64 pitching form; and that Howard's elbow and Mantle's shoulder were sound and they could play 140 games. Keane, Houk, and Burke also wondered if their rookie pitchers—left-handed starter Fritz Peterson and relievers Womack and Jack Cullen—could bolster the staff, particularly if age and injuries caught up to Ford.

However, the biggest question mark that spring was Maris. "I think that it is fairly obvious what a healthy and productive Maris would mean to our attack," said Keane.

"We're counting on Roger to play every day," said Houk. "He's one of our top men, if not the top, without a doubt. I'm expecting his output to be over 100 runs batted in and his home runs somewhere in the 30s."

"[That] may not sound like an ultimatum, but it is," stated Milton Gross, the writer of an April 20 *Sport* magazine article that was ominously titled "Last Chance for Roger Maris." "The time for rationalization is past," wrote Gross. "The time for excuses is past. The memory of Maris hitting 61 home runs in 1961 is growing dim. The urge to say, 'Get with it again or get out,' is growing stronger in the front office. . . . He is now the team's big man and he must either do the job or else his salary will be slashed and/or he'll be traded."

Maris disagreed with those who said he had to prove himself in 1966. "If I have a good year, what's it supposed to mean—that I finally made it after nine years?" he asked. "Or if I have a bad year, is it that I'm through with baseball?" He was cautious about his prospects for the new season. He had learned to play despite sore ribs and knees, but he had no way around the problems with his right hand. Dr. Littler had told him it never would be at full strength again, and the doctor wasn't even taking into account the numbness in Roger's pinkie and ring finger. Roger kept his condition mostly to himself because he wanted his manager to play him every day and did not want opposing pitchers to serve him a steady diet of fastballs.

His friend Dick Stigman, who moved from the Twins to the Red Sox in 1966, recalls, "I don't remember the word going around in '65 and '66 that he had a bad hand and had trouble hitting hard stuff. Usually stuff like that gets around." Bill Monbouquette, who went from Boston to Detroit in 1966, says, "I thought he was the same player."

Assuming their teammates were all fine, every player in camp thought the Yankees would rise again. Even the youngsters felt that way. "Everybody thought '65 was a down year and we'd come back in 1966," recalls Womack.

"Fritz Peterson and I told Mantle that he was going to hit 40 home runs. He told us, 'You guys have come a little bit late.' "

The Yankees had a disastrous start. At Yankee Stadium, they were swept in the three-game opening series by Detroit, as Mickey Lolich, Denny McLain, and Bill Monbouquette outdueled Ford, Stottlemyre, and Bob Friend, who was obtained from Pittsburgh for Pete Mikkelsen. After Peterson beat Baltimore, things were looking up. But in the first inning of the next game, Amaro, while looking up, injured his knee in a collision and was out till September. Amaro's departure prompted Keane to move Boyer to short (after higher-ups told him not to play Murcer), Tresh to third, and Mantle back to center, and to go with a left-field platoon of Roy White and new acquisition Lu Clinton. The realigned Yankees lost their next 7 games.

After 20 games, the Yankees were 4-16 and in last place. They were baseball's biggest joke, having supplanted the Mets, whose seventy-five-year-old manager, Casey Stengel, had retired after four consecutive tenth-place finishes. Maris had 1 homer and 3 RBIs. He had missed a few games, as had Mantle, who had no homers and 1 RBI. Maris's .190 average was still higher than Howard's .180 and Boyer's .149 and not far below Tresh's .200. Mantle and Clinton were the only hitters within sight of .300.

If things were bad for Keane in 1965, they were worse in 1966. Every strategy backfired, no player came through for him. "Johnny Keane started his second year as manager just about the way he ended his first year," Mantle wrote in *The Mick*, "knotting his eyebrows and gnashing his teeth during an April slump that stretched into May."

After a loss to California on May 6, Houk could no longer defend his man. Pressured by Burke, he fired Keane and returned to being the manager.

"Keane was a nice man and the players wanted to play for him," says Womack, "but everyone was injured or getting old and going downhill. No one knew he was on the hot seat."

Nor did anyone realize how much stress Keane had been under, but eight months later, he suffered a fatal heart attack at his home in Houston, Texas. "He was strung too tightly," says Keane's catcher in St. Louis, Tim McCarver, "and eventually the game killed him."

Burke, who became president of the Yankees in September when Dan Topping sold his 10 percent of the team, hired Lee MacPhail to be the

Yankees' general manager. Before being the top aide to Commissioner William Eckert's office, MacPhail, the son of former Yankee co-owner Larry MacPhail, had been the GM at Baltimore. He had acquired Frank Robinson from the Reds for Milt Pappas, and in 1966 Robinson was on his way to taking the Triple Crown, leading the Orioles to their first world title, and being elected the AL MVP. MacPhail wouldn't have such great fortune in New York.

When Houk returned to the dugout, he gave a rah-rah speech, and his inspired team went out and won its next 3 games and 13 out of 16 to move into sixth place on May 27. Downing went 4-0 (on his way to 6 straight victories) and Stottlemyre went 4-1 during this stretch. The Yankees still were 3 games under .500, at 17-20, but Houk had the players convinced they could make up the 9½ games on first-place Cleveland, which had a history of folding, and the mere 5 games they trailed second-place Baltimore. He also made believers of the press.

"I remember Houk saying the Yankees were bound to put it together and make a run for the pennant," says George Vecsey. "He said, 'Well, you know Mantle's going to hit, and you know Maris is going to hit, and you know Tresh, Howard, and Pepitone are going to hit.' Despite 1965, I just assumed the Yankees, whom I hated, were going to win forever, so I agreed they were going to hit. But they didn't. They all fell apart together. The pitchers, too. Ford's and Bouton's arms fell off."

After taking the collar in Houk's first game as manager, Maris batted .433 over the next 9 games. Then he missed time because of an injury that occurred on May 18 in the first inning of a 7–2 victory in Detroit. Maris had a one-out RBI single off tough young southpaw Mickey Lolich and moved to third base on Clinton's single. Boyer grounded to third baseman Don Wert, who came home with the throw instead of trying for an around-the-horn double play. Maris unsuccessfully tried to slide past 6'3" Bill Freehan, and the catcher's shin guard struck him under the left knee. The diagnosis was a "slightly sprained knee." Maris was determined not to sit out after his 1965 experience, so he played a few more games before Houk rested him. He'd return, but his knee bothered him all year.

As Maris cooled off, so did the Yankees. They went 53-69 the rest of the season, never getting closer than three games below .500. Houk was no improvement on Keane. Peterson, Downing, and Fred Talbot (a June 10 addition, in a deal that sent Roger Repoz and Bill Stafford to the A's) pitched respectably—going 29-29 between them—but the rotation had no stopper. Hard-luck Mel Stottlemyre went 7-17 the rest of the way to finish at 12-20. Ford won only 2 games, both coming in relief after blowing saves, July 16 in Kansas City and August 6 in Cleveland. Then he underwent season-ending surgery for a blocked artery in his left arm. The greatest pitcher in Yankee history would win 2 games in 1967 and retire after a brilliant eighteen-year career.

Ford's roommate, Mickey Mantle, had a hot streak in June that reminded fans of his glory days. Two home runs off Boston's Jose Santiago began a remarkable run of 11 homers in 11 days. Late in the season, a round-tripper off Chicago's Bruce Howard gave him 494 career homers, one ahead of Lou Gehrig and second most in Yankee history. He ended the year with 496, with 40 homers still to go in his astounding career.

Unfortunately, Mantle was too banged up to hit with power consistently during the 1966 season. Maris was in worse shape. His knee was painful, he had the two bad fingers and sore ribs, and he suffered hamstring pulls and back strains. He had flashes of brilliance, but his big offensive games were few and far between. Houk grew impatient, and the fans booed.

"Roger came every day prepared to play," remembers Gibbs, "and it bothered him that people didn't think he was giving his all. Roger was hurting but sucked it up and went out on the field. And most of the time he played good."

"Ralph Houk came back to manage, but he had changed," Boyer told Tony Kubek in *Sixty-One*. "I used to think he stood up for us against the front office, but then it turned out he *was* the front office . . . To tell you the truth, I don't think he much liked me and Roger. Ralph's great club was gone. In 1966, everything had gone to hell, and I think Ralph was looking for an excuse to dump me and Roger."

"Roger was unhappy," recalls Dick Schofield, a backup veteran infielder who lived with Maris and Boyer after he was purchased from the Giants on May 11. "When you've got an injury, it's not much fun, especially when the fans are getting on you."

From the dugout of the front-running Orioles, Frank Robinson observed that Maris "looked like a guy who didn't want to play baseball."

By midseason, Maris was seriously contemplating retirement, and he told this to his manager. Houk asked Maris to hold off making an announcement until the following spring. Then if he felt the same way, the Yankees could give him a proper send-off. Maris agreed since that was pretty much his plan anyway. Without Maris's knowledge, Houk spoke to Burke and MacPhail about trading him that winter. Houk told Maury Allen in 1985, "We knew we couldn't get much for him, but if we got a usable ballplayer, it would be better than nothing if he walked away. We had no idea if he would quit once we traded him. That would be the other club's problem."

According to Bing Devine, Maris almost became a New York Met. Devine worked as an assistant to Mets president George Weiss after being fired as the Cardinals GM during the '64 season. He asserted the Yankees placed Maris on waivers and Weiss put in a claim and was prepared to trade for him. The Yankees withdrew Maris's name and never told him what they'd done, or he might have quit on the spot.

Maris missed 43 games during the season, so reporters, particularly those in New York, had plenty of time to ask him about his future plans. But few bothered. Eugene Fitzgerald, the longtime sports columnist for the *Fargo Forum*, was among a small group of reporters who talked to Maris in the Yankee dugout in Minneapolis about whether he planned to return for the 1967 season. Fitzgerald had heard rumors that Maris was exploring business opportunities in Fargo and was considering moving back there. "I know what I want to do, but I haven't told anyone yet," said Maris. But then he revealed that when it was time to report to spring training, he'd choose to go or stay home.

Fitzgerald reported that Roger said Milton Gross's recent characterization of him as being "disappointed, disillusioned, and almost in despair" was inaccurate and that he had no problem playing out the season. However, Maris said his services weren't always required because Houk wanted to take a look at some youngsters—White, Murcer, Horace Clarke (Richardson's replacement), Hegan, Steve Whitaker, Billy Bryan, and Ferraro.

Ferraro, a September call-up, played a part in Maris's final big moment with the Yankees, on September 30. He remembers:

> At the end of the year Roger wasn't playing much, and the writing was on the wall that this was his last year in New York. We were losing a game in Chicago, and Hoyt Wilhelm came in to pitch for the White Sox in the ninth

inning. Richardson said that I'd better hit his first knuckler because I wouldn't come close to the next two. I swung at the first pitch and got a single to left. The next hitter was Roger, pinch-hitting for Dooley Womack. And he hit a two-run homer to give us the lead. After the game he said, "Nice hitting, rook, but the next time I homer, would you mind waiting for me at home plate to shake my hand?" I had been so nervous that after I touched the plate, I ran straight into the dugout.

Maris's clutch home run was a fitting ending to his Yankee career, especially since it came off Wilhelm, the pitcher who denied him his 60th homer in the 154th game of the 1961 season. The Yankees had two more games on their schedule, and Houk wanted Maris to pinch-hit again. Maris said no because he wanted to go out with a homer as had his idol Ted Williams.

Maris's stats in his forgettable final season with the Yankees were not what he hoped for in spring training. In 348 at-bats in 119 games, he batted .233 with 37 runs and 43 RBIs, 13 homers, 9 doubles, and 2 triples. Mantle had 333 at-bats in 108 games and batted a team-high .288, with 40 runs and 56 RBIs, 23 homers, 12 doubles, and 1 triple. Pepitone had Yankee highs with 31 homers and 83 RBIs, with Tresh's 27 homers and only 68 RBIs second best in both categories. As a team, the Yankees batted .235.

For the first time in fifty-five years, the Yankees finished in the cellar, ½ game behind Boston. They fell into last place to stay on September 18, and at the next game, a makeup game with the White Sox on an ugly September 22, only 413 fans in 67,000-seat Yankee Stadium watched them lose 4–1. Red Barber instructed the cameramen to pan the empty seats, saying, "This crowd is the story, not the game." This was the excuse Burke needed to fire the legendary broadcaster.

Roger was almost positive he would retire, but he wanted to make the final decision at home in Independence with Pat's input. In November, he received a call from MacPhail asking him his intentions. "What's the rush?" Maris asked. "We've got until spring training for me to make up my mind. But if you're going to trade me, tell me now and I'll send in my retirement papers to you right away." MacPhail assured him that the club had no intention of trading him.

Maris found out about the end of his Yankee career on December 8, when he came home to find a photographer waiting for him. Pat arrived home with the kids at the same time, and they both were stunned to learn from the photographer and the reporters who showed up that Roger had been traded to the St. Louis Cardinals.

In return the Yankees received third baseman Charley Smith. Maris had never heard of him. The twenty-nine-year-old from Charleston, South Carolina, was labeled a "journeyman," having failed to hook on with the Dodgers, Phillies, White Sox, or Mets before he was swapped to the Cardinals for Ken Boyer a year earlier. Now he was expected to replace Clete Boyer, whom MacPhail had shipped to Atlanta in November. Smith had batted .239 in 6 seasons with 59 career homers, 2 less than Maris hit in 1961.

The New York papers said that Maris's being traded for Smith was the final humiliation the Yankees bestowed on him. After 7 seasons, more than 900 games, and 203 home runs, Roger Maris's Yankee career came to an unceremonious conclusion. No gifts were offered, no thank-yous, no "Roger Maris Day" on East 161st Street. According to Houk, "When Roger left the Yankees, he was pissed off at the world," but in truth, his fury was directed only at the Yankees' front office.

"Ralph Houk and Lee MacPhail had promised not to trade him," said Jim Ogle, who in 1974 became the director of the Yankees' Alumni Association. "They broke that promise, and *that* is the absolute truth of why Roger Maris decided to never again appear at Yankee Stadium for anything."

CHAPTER THIRTY-FOUR

REDEMPTION IN ST. LOUIS

AFTER DEFEATING THE NEW York Yankees in the 1964 World Series, the St. Louis Cardinals succumbed to a heavy dose of injuries, aging, and off years by key players and plunged into the second division. Unlike the Yankees, however, they didn't go into a free fall, and in 1966 the Redbirds finished over .500. The biggest reason for the improvement was the May acquisition of first baseman Orlando Cepeda. After being treated like an outcast in San Francisco, the right-handed slugger was warmly received in St. Louis and became a big run producer. Still, general manager Bob Howsam realized that for the Cardinals to be back on top again they also needed a left-handed power hitter who could bat third, in front of Cepeda. When a trade for the Cubs' Billy Williams fell through, Howsam acquired another sweet-swinging outfielder, Roger Maris, not realizing he was serious about retiring.

The trade caught Maris by surprise, and he found himself in a quandary about what he should do. He needed time to think over his situation, including business offers. Meanwhile, Howsam left for Cincinnati and was replaced as the Cardinals GM by forty-six-year-old Stan Musial, whose extraordinary 22-year playing career in St. Louis ended in 1963. For the Cardinals this was fortuitous because Maris much preferred speaking to a career .331, left-handed hitter than a career executive. He and Pat went to St. Louis and had an enjoyable lunch with the affable Musial and his wife, Lil. The next time Roger heard from Musial was when he received a contract in the mail for $75,000.

Roger put the unsigned contract in a drawer for about a month. He, Pat, and the Surprises went to L.A. to watch the Kansas City Chiefs be demol-

ished by the Green Bay Packers, 35–10, in what later was called the first
Super Bowl. Maris also went hunting. Finally, Musial called to see what he
had decided. Appreciative that he hadn't been pressured to sign the contract,
Maris shrugged and said, "Okay, I'll play another year."

Maris thought his new team was a good fit. St. Louis was about three
and a half hours by car and forty minutes by plane from Independence, so
he could spend a lot of time with Pat and the kids during the season. Being
in the National League, he wouldn't experience the booing he'd been subjected to in American League ballparks. Perhaps the biggest, and strangest,
reason Roger postponed his retirement was that he didn't want fans to have
the impression that he was quitting because he was no longer a Yankee. In
truth he was outraged at the Yankees' deceitful front office and wanted to
show the world that he was happy to go elsewhere.

Then there was beer. Maris often told his Yankee roommate Clete Boyer
that his dream was to own a beer distributorship with his brother, who had a
keen business sense. Although he never associated with his great-uncles Paul
and Mike Maras, he grew up knowing that they made their fortunes running
taverns in Hibbing. As a teenager in Fargo, Roger worked for a beer distributor, Ralph Wood. He lived with Jack Blakely, a wholesale liquor distributor.
His uncle Rudy Marich paid for college in Colorado by working for a beer
distributor. His teammate Joe De Maestri owned a beer distributorship with
his father in California. And in Independence, Roger was close friends with
Mike Roper, a Schlitz distributor.

Carroll Hardy remembers, "I was living in Boulder and Roger visited me
unexpectedly when he came to Colorado to talk to Coors. He was thinking
of buying a distributorship in North or South Dakota, and Rudy Jr. would
run it."

"Roger called me up in Chicago," recalls Dan Osinski, "and he said he
was expecting to get the distributorship for Coors east of the Mississippi,
and I was supposed to get him trucks and find some refrigerated warehouses
and we'd work together. I located some buildings in the stockyards, but
Coors didn't cross the Mississippi and it fell through."

According to Tony Kubek's *Sixty-One*, Julie Isaacson informed the Cardinals that Roger would come to St. Louis only if August Busch agreed to sell
him a beer distributorship. However, Pat Maris asserted, "Roger was never
promised anything when he came to St. Louis. It is true, though, that Roger's

playing in St. Louis made it possible for Mr. Busch to see the type of person that Roger was."

Most likely Roger came to St. Louis without expectations, but with the plan to plant the seed in Busch's mind that he was in the market for a distributorship. He figured playing for Busch was a shrewd move toward a post-baseball career. Of his career as a player, he didn't know that the move to St. Louis would bring him joy, peace, and redemption.

Red Schoendienst, Johnny Keane's replacement as the Cardinals' manager, was glad to get Maris as the team's last puzzle piece. The two had a history. Schoendienst's extraordinary playing career in St. Louis ended when GM Frank Lane dealt him to the Giants in 1956—two years before he traded Maris from Cleveland. He remembers playing in exhibition games against Maris when he was an Indian, including games in Las Vegas, California, and Hawaii that were promoted by tennis player Bobby Riggs.

"I talked to a number of guys about him," recalls Schoendienst, who managed the Cardinals from 1965 to 1976, and again in 1980 and 1990. "Clete Boyer, who was like his brother, said, 'He won't be as great as he was with the Yankees, but he can help you win.' Joe Schultz, one of my coaches, had been in the American League and said, 'Maris can help us.' That was good enough for me. The key was Mike Shannon agreeing to move from right field to third base to accommodate Maris. That meant Shannon had to learn a new position and spend day after day fielding grounders Joe and I hit him on the frozen turf."

At a February 9 press conference Musial introduced a cheerful Maris to St. Louis reporters. Schoendienst was asked how his new player would fare in a spacious ballpark where it was 330 feet down the right-field line. He recalls, "I told the press, 'Now don't expect him to hit as many home runs because our right-field porch is different than in Yankee Stadium. But he's been in the thick of it in the World Series and All-Star Games and he can play. That's why we got him.' Later Maris said, 'Thank you for saying that, Red, so they don't think I'm this or that. All I can promise is that I'll give you 100 percent.' And he did."

In March, Maris reported to his first spring training with the Cardinals in St. Petersburg. It was a stone's throw from the Mets camp, where the Yankees trained during Maris's first two years with the team. Maris had poor numbers but impressed everyone with his aggressive play, work ethic, and personality. One person he won over quickly was instructor George Kissell, who mentored every Cardinal from 1940 until his death in 2008. Kissell was the creator and chief proponent of the "Cardinal Way," which stressed fundamentals and aggressiveness. In 2008, he recalled:

> Here's the home-run champion coming to me, and do you know what he said? He said, 'George, you're talking to an American Leaguer. Consider me a rookie. Whatever you want during spring training, you holler and I'll be there. If I got my brain working, after you help me a bit, you won't have to bother with me anymore.' I was shocked! I said, 'Roger, in my eyes you have always been on a pedestal.' He said, 'I don't want to be up there. I'd rather you just saw me like everybody else around here.' He was so humble that you never would have known who he was. He listened to everything I said and had the memory of an elephant. I taught him the way we played and pitched, and about our defense. I really enjoyed working with him because he understood how to play the right way. And he was a nice young man.

Other than reliever Hal Woodeshick, who was his teammate on the Indians, Maris didn't know anyone on the roster but Cepeda. They'd befriended one another in 1958 when the Indians and the Giants traveled together during spring training. "I was excited we got him because I knew he was a hell of a ballplayer," says Cepeda, "but I had read about him in New York and didn't know if his personality had changed since I knew him."

In his 1968 autobiography, *From Ghetto to Glory*, which was written with Phil Pepe, Bob Gibson said, "We had all read and heard so much about Roger Maris—was he really the brooding, sullen, unapproachable ogre he was made out to be? Now we would see for ourselves just what kind of monster he was. I guess I had a preconceived idea of what he would be like from all the derogatory things I read about him."

"The New York press painted him as being a malcontent," recalls Dal Maxvill, the smooth-fielding, rubber-armed shortstop whom famed St. Louis columnist Bob Broeg dubbed the Silhouette Shadow. "We thought Maris had the talent to help us win a title, but I told Shannon to refuse to switch to third base because we had a great nucleus and I worried Roger wouldn't fit in."

"From his reputation I thought he'd be a bit hostile," recalls Julian Javier, who was known as the Phantom because of his quickness at second base.

"What I expected was somebody who might be stuck on himself because of his accomplishments," says Dick Hughes, a hard-throwing right-hander who would lead the Cardinals with 16 victories in 1967.

Cepeda was the one to break the ice with the shy newcomer. "The Baby Bull" related to Maris on several levels. He, too, was unfavorably compared to a superstar teammate (Willie Mays), and he, too, was criticized whenever he spoke out. The first day of spring training, Maris was standing outside the Outrigger Motel, which the Cardinals purchased in 1962 so that its black and white players could stay together in segregated St. Petersburg. Cepeda recalls:

> Tim McCarver, Curt Flood, and I were driving to the ballpark when we saw him standing there looking for a ride. We told him to get in, and right away we made him feel welcome. When you go to a new team, you don't know what to expect, so you want to feel you belong from the beginning. Tim and Bob Gibson had the skill to make me feel wanted right from the beginning the previous year, and that's what we did with Roger.
>
> I could understand what Roger went through in New York. The press in San Francisco would even tell people close to me that I was faking with my bad knee and that everything was in my mind. I lost my love for the game and didn't want to go to the ballpark. Going to St. Louis made a huge difference for me. I believe that coming to the Cardinals was a new beginning for Roger, too.

Maris's new teammates discovered that he was far more likable than his clippings suggested. Gibson, who like Maris had a thorny relationship with some reporters and a disdain for aggressive autograph seekers, wrote at the end of the year, "I can only say that Roger Maris is one hell of a guy, easy to get along with and a real team player. I think he's great. He was mistreated and abused so badly he became bitter but he was not at all like that with us."

"Roger fit right in," remembers Hughes. "He had a sense of humor and could take it and dish it out."

"I was real surprised," says Javier. "He turned out to be a gentleman and great guy, and it was easy to be his friend."

His teammates discovered that only one subject was off-limits. "Roger had an aura about him because he had the home-run record," recalls Larry Jaster, a left-hander with a 14-5 record in his two years in the majors. "But he wasn't boastful or cocky and never mentioned it. We knew what he did but never said anything."

"I usually talked about family with Roger, not baseball," says Maxvill, "but one time I tried to pry a little and said, 'Tell me what it was like in 1961.' And he said, 'That's behind me, I don't want to talk about it anymore.' I never brought it up again."

"Roger was a humble guy who didn't boast about anything he'd done," remembers McCarver. "The word he hated most was *celebrity*—he just detested it. He talked about how Mantle would have been even better if he had stretched before games; about his hair falling out; and about the time he put crab shells under someone's sheets and a lobster in his toilet. But he never talked about hitting 61 home runs."

In Florida, Roger was relieved to become part of a close-knit unit that was fun and friendly off the field and unselfish on it. He loved how the Cards played the game, manufacturing runs rather than relying on the long ball, and emphasizing pitching and defense. As Schoendienst remembers, "Maybe there were other clubs with more talent, but my guys played hard, were tough, and knew how to win. I had my rules and regulations, but I just let them play. Near the end of spring training I told Pittsburgh manager Danny Murtaugh, 'We're going to win the pennant.'"

Maris's only worry was that fans in St. Louis wouldn't accept him, but teammates assured him that things would be entirely different from New York. Former Cardinal Dick Groat, who played against Roger that spring, recalls, "I was on the Phillies in my last year in baseball. I had almost been traded for him in 1959, but I didn't really know Roger because we'd been in different leagues. Still I went over to him and said, 'I don't know if you are upset by the trade to the Cardinals, but I promise you that when your career is over, you will say that coming to St. Louis was the best thing that ever happened to you because it is a great organization and there are no better fans.' I don't think he believed me then. But I'm sure he did later."

On Opening Day at Busch Stadium, Maris understood what Groat meant. Before the game against the Giants, a motorcade delivered the Cardinal players to home plate as renowned broadcaster Harry Caray made introductions. When Caray announced the name of the Cardinals' new right fielder, 38,117 knowledgeable fans gave him a standing ovation. He surveyed the stands and saw only smiling Midwesterners and heard not boos and vulgarities but cheers and encouraging words. He must have felt that he wasn't just in a different league and a different city after seven years, but in an alternate universe. "I didn't know what to expect," Maris said later. "When they cheered me, though, it surprised the hell out of me."

The Tuesday-afternoon game pitted Gibson, who had gone 21-9 in 1966, against Juan Marichal, who had gone 25-6 but didn't win the Cy Young Award because Sandy Koufax went 27-9, with 317 strikeouts and a 1.73 ERA. Koufax had since retired with a sore arm, so the hard-throwing Gibson and the high-kicking "Dominican Dandy" were vying for recognition as baseball's best pitcher. On this day, Gibson reigned supreme, striking out the first 5 batters and 13 overall, including Willie McCovey 3 times. He yielded only 5 singles as he won 6–0. Maris compared Gibson to Whitey Ford.

Schoendienst's lineup against Marichal was left fielder Lou Brock, center fielder Curt Flood, right fielder Maris, first baseman Cepeda, third baseman Shannon, catcher McCarver, second baseman Javier, shortstop Maxvill, and Gibson. Other than McCarver and Shannon switching positions, this batting order remained the same all year against right-handers. Javier was a switch-hitter; Brock, Maris, and McCarver batted left-handed.

In his first Cardinal at-bat, Maris made the type of out that would have resulted in jeers at Yankee Stadium. Brock had singled and stolen second, and Flood had singled him to third. First and third with nobody out was an ideal situation for a contact hitter like Maris. But he grounded to third base. Brock stayed put as Maris was thrown out, with Flood moving to second. It would be one of the few times all year that he didn't score a runner from third base with less than two outs. Instead of boos, Maris was cheered as he returned to the dugout, and though the Cardinals failed to score, he was cheered again when he jogged out to right field.

He rewarded the supportive fans by hustling a single into a double in his next at-bat. The crowd went wild. They gave him another ovation when he beat out a bunt in the sixth inning. "It's nice to hear cheers like this for a change," he said after the game, still in disbelief. "The reception was far beyond my fondest expectations. I'm sincerely grateful to the fans."

The cheering didn't stop for the rest of the homestand, as the Cardinals swept a two-game series from the Dodgers and a lone game from Houston to improve their record to 4-0. Cepeda went 7 for 12 with a homer and 7 RBIs in the three games, and Brock had back-to-back games in which he went 8 for 11 with 4 homers and 8 RBIs. Yet Maris received equal attention as he went 3 for 4 with a double and a triple, scored 3 runs, and drove in 1 in the 8–4 victory over L.A.; went 2 for 4 in the 13–4 victory over L.A.; and went 1 for 4 with 3 RBIs in the 11–8 victory over Houston. Some delighted fans unfurled banners to salute the .471 hitter.

"He hit line drives all over the place, left and right," remembers Javier. That he had hit no homers, Maris realized, didn't matter. The Cardinals fans were steeped in the tradition of the Gas House Gang, and if a player hustled and dirtied his uniform, he was appreciated.

"The last five years for me were hell—several times I left the ballpark and thought I'd just keep on going to the airport and chuck it all," Maris told AP reporter Will Grimsley in late April, as he looked forward to returning home after the team's first road trip. "It's nice to go out on the field and know people are behind you. It makes you concentrate and want to give your best. I am happy playing baseball again."

"Roger initially told us that baseball was getting old and the game wasn't as much fun, but that quickly changed," says McCarver. "Sometimes he'd be a little withdrawn and I'd have to say, 'Roger, let's go!' After being in a hostile city for seven years, I'm sure he was thinking, 'This is too good to be true.'"

The Cardinals' record went to 6-0, and Maris was already given credit for the team catapulting from being a 12–1 long shot to a legitimate pennant contender. As much as the fans and local press were singing his praises, his biggest champions were his teammates, who saw what a huge difference the ultimate team player was making to the lineup.

"Everybody was surprised by what an unselfish player he was," recalls backup infielder Phil Gagliano. "Who expected the home-run champion to be laying down a drag bunt to get an inning started?"

"What he did was all the little things that had to be done," says Maxvill. "Whenever we needed a ground ball to the right side to move a runner on second to third base with one out, he'd do it. Whenever we needed a sacrifice fly, he'd get it. A typical first inning for us began with a Brock single. Then he'd steal second. Flood then would hit a weak grounder to second base that moved Brock to third. Maris followed with a 300-foot fly to center field to score him. And the Cardinals were up 1–0. Roger was like a machine. It got to the point where if he didn't do it, we were shocked."

"Some of us saw him in the '64 Series," notes McCarver, "but watching him every day, we were surprised by his talent. In New York, he was known as a home-run hitter, and everything else about him was less significant. He was known for something totally different than what he really was. If the beat writers had done their jobs, more of the country would have known that he was an amazing all-around player. He was great in the way that he approached the game, the way he ran the bases, the way he played right field, and the way he relentlessly took out guys to prevent double plays. Nobody wrote about that. He was just a great Hall of Fame–caliber player."

Schoendienst was most excited about Roger's defense: "Maris was as good an outfielder as there was, as far as knowing fundamentals. He knew the speed of all the runners and where to throw the ball in every situation, either to a base or cutoff man. Plus he had a strong, accurate arm. He was great at keeping runners from getting to third base. He never made a mistake."

After getting hits in the Cardinals' first 8 games, Maris went into one of his signature slumps, going hitless in his next 21 at-bats, covering 5 games. In a thirteen-inning loss in Los Angeles, he went 0 for 7. "I was sitting behind home plate doing some advance scouting for the Phillies," says Cal McLish, "and Roger kept fouling fastballs back to the screen. When we talked, I told him, 'Those balls are coming straight back because you're dropping your hands and the ball is hitting the top of the bat.'"

Beginning in Houston, Alex Johnson began playing right field against left-handers, but Roger didn't grow impatient as he tried to regain his stroke. It helped that Brock, Flood, Cepeda, McCarver, Javier, and Shannon were all hitting over .300. Although Maris still squirmed when on the bench, he didn't object to being platooned. "I understand it," he told Bob Broeg. "If the manager thinks that's the way to win, I respect his judgment."

Maris's drought ended with an RBI single on May 2 that drove tough Jim Maloney from the box as Gibson shut down the visiting Reds, 5–0. Ray Washburn shut out the Reds on 2 hits the next day, 2–0, as Maris scored the first run after beating out a bunt against Milt Pappas. "I could see that he was a hell of a lot more relaxed in St. Louis than he'd been in New York," recalls the former Orioles pitcher. "He now smiled and laughed more. Roger didn't change his personality because he never was anything but what he was, but he got rejuvenated."

Maris showed signs that he was getting his swing back when he smacked an RBI double against Vern Law in a 3-run, 10th-inning rally in a 6–5 victory over Pittsburgh. The next night, May 9, Roger's number one fan, to whom he'd talked many times—and given signed bats and balls—over the years at Yankee Stadium, was in attendance. Andy Strasberg, then a student at Akron College, remembers an unusual occurrence:

> My skeptical college buddies convinced me to drive to Pittsburgh so I could introduce them to "your good friend Roger Maris." I was nervous beyond belief because Roger had never seen me outside of Yankee Stadium. We arrived at Forbes Field early enough to see Roger, wearing his familiar number 9, warming up. I called to him. Roger turned and said, "Andy Strasberg, what the hell are you doing in Pittsburgh?" My buddies were surprised that I really knew Roger and lined up as if it was a wedding reception while I introduced them.
>
> We took our seats in right field. I sat in row 9, seat 9. Roger was in the lineup although the Pirates' pitcher, Woodie Fryman, was a lefty. In the 6th inning against Fryman, he hit his first National League home run. And I caught the ball! My friends were witnesses. They were screaming at the top of their lungs as the ball came toward us, and I caught it on the fly bare-handed. I started crying because I was eighteen years old and life was not going to get any better for me. After the half inning, Roger comes out to right field and sees me holding the home-run ball and says, "I don't believe it!"

Maris's first homer as a Cardinal helped Steve Carlton beat the Pirates 3–1.

When the Cardinals came home, he played his first regular-season game against the New York Mets. The Mets had high hopes about their group of young pitchers, and already everybody was raving about Tom Seaver. The hard-throwing right-hander from California would earn 16 of the Mets' 61 victories and be voted the National League's Rookie of the Year. Seaver faced Al Jackson, an original Met, in the Friday opener.

The future 300-game winner knew of Maris's reputation for being a dead fastball hitter. He didn't know, nobody knew, that Maris had turned into an off-speed hitter because of his grip problems. "I had him 1–2 in the first inning and threw a high, lousy changeup," Seaver remembers more than forty years later. "From my perspective he shouldn't have swung, but he was a smart hitter and took what I gave him. He hit the ball up the middle for a single. If I'd known he had a bad hand and could no longer hit a good fastball, I would have approached him differently."

Maris got 2 more hits and scored twice off Mets relievers as the Cardinals overcame a 5–2 deficit and won 7–5 to improve their record to 15-10, 2½ games behind the first-place Reds. Maris was out of his slump. Maury Allen of the *New York Post* was accompanying the Mets on their road trip and noticed a big change in Maris from when they knew each other in New York:

> By the time he was traded, Roger was an angry, bitter man, and I think St. Louis saved him. We had mostly gotten along in New York, but we weren't really friendly until he was no longer in a Yankee uniform. Now he was a terrific interview, open and friendly. I considered Roger an outsider in life and in baseball, but his teammates always loved and respected him on New York and that was certainly true on St. Louis. Mike Shannon loved him to pieces and said, "Moving to third was the greatest thing I ever did because it helped Roger come to the team and be happy." I was glad for Roger and had a warm feeling toward him.

A huge difference was that the St. Louis press didn't turn on Maris when he slumped or treat him like a failure if he didn't homer every game. These reporters appreciated that Roger was still hustling on every play, doing whatever it took to win ball games. It helped that St. Louis had only two dailies, the *Globe* and the *Post-Dispatch*, as opposed to eleven in New York in 1961 and '62, and writers such as Bob Broeg, Bob Burnes, Neal Russo, Ed Wilks, and Jack Herman were friendly, respected men who emphasized the positive in their columns and knew when to leave players alone.

Maris's only memorably awkward moment with a writer came not in St. Louis but in Chicago. Jim Brosnan, reliever-turned-full-time-sportswriter, recalls:

> Roger Maris was the only really great hitter who called me a son of a bitch. About four years after I stopped pitching, I got an assignment from the editor of *Boys' Life* to write a book called *Little League to Big League*. He said, "Why don't you have Roger Maris as one of your chapters?" The last time I'd seen Maris was in the 1961 World Series when I struck him out on a 3-2 changeup. I went to Wrigley Field, and before the game I spotted him at the batting cage. As I walked toward him, he scowled at me. I'm five steps away when he put his bat down and said, "You son of a bitch." I said, "What the hell's wrong with you?" He said, "You embarrassed me before 50,000 people and now you want to interview me for your goddamn book?" I found out later he never said *goddamn* and that wasn't like him at all. Then he started to laugh and said, "Okay, let's go." He walked over to the dugout and I followed. I doubt if the interview lasted ten minutes, but he was surprisingly helpful and gave me enough material to write my chapter. I still don't know if he was serious when he called me an SOB.

A week after the Mets played in St. Louis, the Cardinals played in New York. "We all kidded him on the first flight to New York," recalls Maxvill. "Guys were saying, 'Hey, Rog, only another hour and you'll be right back home with your buddies.' He'd tell us where to go."

Maris felt strange returning to the place where he had experienced several years of grief. He told his teammates that they had to go to his favorite restaurant, the Spindletop, yet, McCarver wrote in *The Perfect Season*, "Roger informed us, 'I'm not going.' 'Why not?' I asked. He answered, 'I never go out in New York anymore.' The sad truth was that Roger's miserable experiences while eating out in public in New York in 1961 and subsequent years would keep him a prisoner in the hotel. He just couldn't bear to relive those moments when fans and reporters saw him dining out in New York."

Roger, who received the most mail of the Cardinal players—and 90 percent was friendly—was reminded of his relationship with New York fans the first time he stepped into the batter's box at Shea Stadium. He almost couldn't hear the insults because the boos were so loud. "I thought you were popular here," Gibson ribbed him.

"When Roger Maris got to the Cardinal dressing room, he was visibly hurt and maybe a little astonished," Dick Young reported in the *Daily News*. "His eyes asked why, but his mouth said nothing."

"In a way, I can't really blame the people," Maris told Ed Wilks. "They just believe what they read in the papers."

Neal Russo wrote, "The Redbird outfielder was disappointed by the booing, even though he expected it, and said, 'The one good thing is I have to put up with it for only nine games.' "

When Maury Allen asked him if he intended to visit Yankee Stadium while in town, Maris bristled, saying, "What for? I'm a Cardinal now." He walked away. "The hurt was still deep," said Allen.

After going 4 for 8 against the Mets in St. Louis, Roger went 5 for 12 against them in New York, lifting his average to .310, as the Cardinals swept the three-games series. In the first game, he drove in the go-ahead run; in the third game he homered off Don Cardwell.

On June 2, Maris faced another young pitcher who, like Seaver, was destined for greatness. Ferguson Jenkins of the Chicago Cubs, who was having the first of six consecutive 20-win seasons, bested Gibson, but no thanks to Maris. "The scouting report said I could throw Maris a slider down and in," he recalls, "so I threw him down-and-in sliders the first game I faced him. The scouts were wrong at my expense." Maris singled to right off Jenkins and lashed a run-scoring triple to left-center in the ninth inning to knock him out of the game.

The Cardinals played only a game above .500 between their 6–0 start and June 7, when their fans had to endure the team's 17–1 humiliation at the hands of the Houston Astros. Then the Cardinals started to roll, winning 15 of their next 17 games. They moved into first place on June 19. The Cubs tied them for first on July 2, July 22, and July 24, but otherwise the Cardinals were alone at the top of the standings for the rest of the season, expanding their lead to double digits by mid-August.

They did this despite Gibson's missing nearly two months after having his leg broken on July 15 on a line drive by Roberto Clemente. Dick Hughes (16-6), Steve Carlton (14-9), Ray Washburn (10-7), and spot starters Al

Jackson (9-4) and Larry Jaster (9-7) all had good seasons. Nelson Briles stepped into Gibson's place in the rotation and was virtually unbeatable. In 1966, his record was 4-15; in 1967 it was 14-5 with a 2.43 ERA. Joe Hoerner, Hal Woodeshick, rookie Ron Willis, who set a Cardinals record with 65 appearances, and new acquisition Jack Lamabe made significant contributions out of the bullpen.

Meanwhile, the offense, led by Cepeda ("I never got so many big hits in my life"), was exceptional. On July 31, three players were batting over .300: Cepeda at .342 (with 79 RBIs), McCarver at .325, and Flood at .315. Not far behind were Maris at .291 and Brock and Javier at .285. The defense, too, was outstanding, particularly up the middle with McCarver, Javier, Maxvill, and Gold Glove–winner Flood, and in right when Maris played. Shannon did a solid job at third base.

The Cardinals' surge on the diamond was fueled by their camaraderie in the clubhouse. Cepeda called this team El Birdos, and after each win he raised his right fist and shouted this name three times. The players responded by shouting, "Yeah!" "Even Roger was part of the El Birdos cheers in the clubhouse," remembers McCarver. "It was so new and novel to him that it was refreshing. He really had a good time."

"Roger participated in everything," says Cepeda. "He was there every day cheering in the clubhouse. He said, 'We aren't the Gas House Gang. We are El Birdos because Cha-Cha named us that.' He called me Cha-Cha or Charley."

"El Birdos was Cepeda's deal, but everybody on the team was part of it," says Hughes. "A lot of people don't understand the importance of togetherness in the clubhouse and when you are on the road. The way we got along was one of the most important things that helped our success in '67. And Roger carried on just like everybody else."

Maris took part in Shannon's Kangaroo Court, when he'd sing the names of the players who were being fined for real offenses (a dollar for leaving a runner on third) or trumped-up charges (an ugly swing). He even took part in the team's charade game, during which players mimicked their teammates' less-than-artistic game moments.

"When someone made a mistake on our ball club it was quite embarrassing," remembers Maxvill, "because you'd have five guys on your ass before you got back to the bench. Roger felt comfortable enough to needle players, too, but he'd do it in an understated manner. If you made an error behind Gibson, he'd remind you that he had to spend extra time on the mound that inning in the hot sun. If a ball went through my legs, Roger might say, 'Dal, I must commend you because I don't know if I ever saw another shortstop do what you did on that play.'"

Roger even had fun on plane trips. He played poker with Javier. He helped devour Katie Brock's lemon-cream pies that Brock credited for his hot streaks. Roger even had crabs delivered to the plane and, according to McCarver, "ate with as much gusto as you could imagine while the rest of us ate airplane fare."

Maris lived in the Executive Apartments, a large complex near the airport where most married Cardinals resided. A few of the wives and children lived in the condominiums year-round; others, like Pat Maris, joined their husbands for homestands and weekends. The Executive was festive with family picnics, frequent barbecues, and kids playing together.

"Five to ten families would get together," recalls Jaster, "and go out for sandwiches and beer or for dinner, or we'd take turns having get-togethers at Tim's place or mine. Everybody loved the barbecues."

"Roger lived above us," recalled Woodeshick a few months before his death in 2009. "Our little boy, John, was always upstairs with the Maris kids because Roger had better pickles than we had. Roger just loved his family, and when they weren't there, he talked about them."

"Roger was kindhearted and down-to-earth," recalls Marianne Woodeshick, "and he and Pat were very close. They were very nice to everybody, but I don't think they had to mix with other people at all because they seemed so happy just being together."

"Pat was a dear person, and what struck me was how comfortable she and Roger were together," says McCarver. "They had a very easy relationship. Their children were friends with my children. They were nice kids who grew up to be nice adults. When Roger told his stories, he had an ear-to-ear, boyish grin—and his children had that same grin. We'd drive them to the park with us and they'd hang around the clubhouse with him, including on game days. The boys loved dressing up for father-and-son games. What impressed me was how well behaved they were. Roger and Pat did a great job with them."

A content Maris was a productive hitter in 1967. Although his final stats—.261, with 9 homers, 107 hits, 64 runs, and 55 RBIs in 410 at-bats—didn't jump off the page, it can be argued that it was one of his finest offensive seasons. With 25 homers, an NL-high 111 RBIs, and a .325 average, Cepeda was the unanimous choice as the league's MVP. He was so vital to the lineup that Gibson wouldn't let the team bus leave the hotel for the ballpark unless Cepeda was aboard. However, Maris led the team with 18 hits that either won games or gave the Cardinals leads that held up. "Don't look at his average," says Cepeda, "He was the best .260-.270 hitter I ever saw. He was such a clutch hitter. He could do everything."

Schoendienst stated that the Cardinals wouldn't have won the pennant without Maris. Curt Flood was more emphatic, saying, "We would have been a second-division club."

Maris was the model of consistency for the first four months of the season, ending April batting .280, May and June batting .297, and July batting .291. As often happened during his career, he lost many points off his average with late-season slumps caused by injuries. "His right shoulder was killing him," remembers McCarver. "He'd tell me about the pain and say, 'Well, I'll just get a cortisone shot and be able to play tonight.' Usually if you got a cortisone shot, you didn't play that night. But Roger never sat out a game after a shot. He played many games when he shouldn't have."

He played in August and September even though the Cardinals had broken open the race. Despite his drop in average, Maris knew he could contribute. "Roger's bat speed had diminished since I pitched to him in the American League," says Jim Bunning, who was then on the Phillies, "but he was still a complete ballplayer."

He also was one of the team's leaders. "He was a quiet leader," says Maxvill. "He never got excited. We would be down 2 runs in the eighth inning, but he wouldn't rant and say, 'Hey, we've got to score 2 runs or we're going to lose!' He would just say, 'Hey, let's go, let's score a couple of runs and win this game.' "

The fiery McCarver, who caught 130 games despite the intense heat in St. Louis and had career highs with a .295 average, 14 homers, and 69 RBIs, was considered a leader on the team. Yet the twenty-five-year-old took valuable advice from the thirty-three-year-old Maris. McCarver remembers, "We were in Pittsburgh and I struck out trying to check my swing in a key situation against Steve Blass. Being hot-tempered, I went up the tunnel to do damage to my bat and a wall. Roger got me to calm down. I'll never forget what he said: 'Do you realize what would happen to this team if you hurt yourself doing that?' He said it with the calmness and directness of a leader, and that's all it took for me to understand my responsibility to the rest of the players. He was Roger Maris, so I listened to him. I'd play thirteen more years and never smashed another bat."

The Cardinals led the majors in attendance, with 2,090,145 tickets sold, but the loyal fans missed out when the team clinched on the road in Philadelphia. Gibson, who won three straight decisions after coming back from his injury, pitched a 3-hitter for 5–1 victory. Maxvill and McCarver searched the town to find a restaurant that would accommodate a party with black players. It was held at the popular Bookbinder's. "We were dancing and singing and drinking, having a wonderful time," remembers Cepeda. "I never saw Roger so happy."

Maris was joyful because for the sixth time in eight years he watched his teammates bathe themselves in champagne after a pennant-clincher. As had happened in New York, he joined a team that was barely over .500 the previous year and helped them capture the flag. After going 83–79 in 1966, the Redbirds finished the season with a 101-60 record, 10½ games ahead of the Giants, and set a team record with 52 road wins. For the first time since 1942, they had over 100 victories. Almost everyone in the lineup did better than in 1966, including the two batters who hit before Maris and two batters who hit after him. With Maris the only addition to the lineup in 1967, the Cardinals scored 694 runs, 123 more than the previous year.

Meanwhile, Ralph Houk's ninth-place Yankees scored a meager 522 runs, less than any team in the majors but the Dodgers. The Cardinals not only outhit the Yankees .263 to .225, but also outhomered them 115 to 100. Mickey Mantle, now a first baseman because his legs were shot, clubbed a team-high 22 homers, with 55 RBIs, the same as Maris, and batted only .245. Charley Smith matched Maris's 9 homers, but hit only .224 with only 38 RBIs. Atlanta third baseman Clete Boyer slugged 26 homers and knocked in 96 runs.

Roger wasn't in top shape heading into the World Series. His shoulder was still hurting, as was the toe he broke during the season but continued to play on. He also was taking antibiotics as he battled a cold. But he asked Schoendienst not to say anything about his weakened condition to the press.

Rather than resting Maris during the Series, Schoendienst announced that the veteran of five World Series would play even against left-handers.

The Boston Red Sox were the Cardinals' unlikely opponent in the 1967 World Series, after becoming the third team to win the American League title since the Yankees' last pennant in 1964. Boston hadn't won a World Series since Babe Ruth pitched for them in 1918. They hadn't even appeared in a Series since 1946, when the Cardinals beat them 4 games to 3, as Enos Slaughter famously dashed all the way home from first base on Harry Walker's short double to win Game 7. Musial and Schoendienst were on that Cardinals team, and Boston's Ted Williams batted .200 with no homers and 1 RBI in his only postseason appearance.

In the spring the oddsmakers gave Boston a 100–1 chance to win the pennant, and their prospects seemed even worse on August 18 when young slugging star Tony Conigliaro was lost for the season after being beaned by the Angels' Jack Hamilton. But the "Impossible Dream" team hung tough, riding the coattails of Cy Young winner Jim Lonborg, who lead the league with 22 victories and 246 strikeouts, and AL MVP Carl Yastrzemski, whose .326 average, 44 homers (tying him with Minnesota's Harmon Killebrew), and 121 RBIs made him the last Triple Crown winner of the twentieth century. Lonborg didn't have much help on a shaky pitching staff—Jose Santiago and Gary Bell each posted 12 victories, Lee Stange had a 2.77 ERA, and closer John Wyatt had 10 victories and 20 saves—but Yastrzemski got decent offensive support from first baseman George Scott (.303, 19 homers, 82 RBIs), shortstop Rico Petrocelli (17 homers, 66 RBIs), and switch-hitting rookie outfielder Reggie Smith (15 homers, 61 RBIs). The Sox also acquired Ken "Hawk" Harrelson to provide power and a past-his-prime Elston Howard from the Yankees to provide experience and stability.

Led by rookie manager Dick Williams, Boston captured the flag by winning their 92nd game on the last day of the season, 5–3 over Minnesota. Lonborg tossed a 7-hitter and Yastrzemski drove in 2 runs to tie the game, then scored the go-ahead run in a 5-run sixth inning. Boston edged the Twins and the Tigers by 1 game and the White Sox, who were in first place earlier in the week, by 3 games in the thrilling race. "There was a fatigue factor and pressure factor," remembers Williams, "and my guys stood up to it."

Before Game 1 at Fenway Park on October 4, Maris posed for pictures and chatted with longtime friends Howard, Bell, Norm Siebern, Dan Osinski, and Williams. "Maris was talked about in our meetings," says Williams. "All year, Roger would bounce the ball to the right side to advance a runner to third with one out. We figured if we kept Brock from getting to first and stealing and Flood off second, then we could pitch Roger a little differently."

In Game 1, Gibson went against Santiago, who was starting rather than the overworked Lonborg. In the top of third, Brock (who batted .299 and led the National League with 113 runs and 52 stolen bases) singled and Flood (a .335 hitter) doubled him to third. Then Maris did his thing, pulling a grounder to first to score Brock with the first run of the Series. The Sox tied the game in the bottom of third, when Santiago slammed a surprise homer. Maris played his part as the Cardinals scored again in the seventh in the manner that had vexed National League opponents all season. Brock, who went 4 for 4, singled and stole second. Flood grounded to first, moving Brock to third. And Maris drove in the winning run by grounding to second base. Maris had done what Williams had feared, knocking in both Cardinal runs without the benefit of a hit. In the 2–1 victory, Gibson tossed a 6-hitter with 10 strikeouts.

In Game 2, Lonborg pitched one of the great games in World Series history, allowing only 2 base runners. He lost his perfect game with one out in the seventh inning when he walked Flood and lost his no-hitter with two outs in the eighth inning when Javier doubled into the left-field corner. Yastrzemski hit a solo homer off starter Dick Hughes and a 3-run homer off Joe Hoerner as the Red Sox evened the Series, 1–1, with a 5–0 victory.

Two days later, the Series resumed in St. Louis, with 54,575 fans passing through the turnstiles. Busch Stadium didn't have that many seats, but the front office persuaded the city fire marshal to allow folding chairs in the aisles. The overflow crowd watched Nelson Briles go against Gary Bell. "It was such a thrill for me to finally be in a World Series," says Bell. "I remember Guy Lombardo and his orchestra playing in center field before the game. Then I pitched against a really strong lineup and the only guy I could get out was Dal Maxvill." Everyone else in the Cardinals batting order had at least 1 hit, with Brock, Maris, and Shannon, who homered, getting 2 each. Briles tossed a 7-hitter, walking none, as the Cardinals won 5–2 to go up 2–1.

Maris's second hit was off Dan Osinski. "Dick Williams and I got into an argument," Osinksi recalls, "because he insisted on pulling around the infield even though when I threw my sinker away, Roger couldn't pull it.

He'd get so mad at me because I was the only pitcher who got him to hit the ball to the third baseman. But Williams moved our third baseman to the shortstop spot, and when Roger hit it down the line, nobody was there."

In Game 4, Gibson remained nearly invincible while Santiago exited in the first inning after giving up 4 runs on 6 hits. The biggest hit was Maris's 2-run double. The Cardinals went on to win 6–0, as Gibson tossed a 5-hitter.

Lonborg came back in Game 5, this time throwing a 3-hitter to best hard-luck loser Steve Carlton, who gave up only 3 hits and an unearned run in six innings. Boston scored 2 insurance runs in the top of the ninth on a clutch bases-loaded single by Howard, and a rare high throw home by Maris. Lonborg's bid for a second straight shutout ended when Maris homered over the right-field fence with two outs in the ninth. Boston won 3–1 and now trailed 3 games to 2.

Back at Fenway Park, St. Louis expected to clinch the Series in Game 6 as Hughes went against untested Gary Waslewski, who had only 2 victories in his rookie season. But Waslewski left after 5⅓ innings with a 4–2 lead, thanks to solo homers by Petrocelli in the second and Yastrzemski, Petrocelli, and Smith in the fourth. The Cardinals tied the game in the seventh when the sizzling Brock socked a 2-run homer off Wyatt. However, Boston shocked St. Louis with 4 runs in the bottom of the inning for an 8–4 victory to tie the Series.

Everyone was abuzz about a seventh-game showdown between Gibson and Lonborg, who had each yielded only 1 run in eighteen innings. Eddie Bressoud, Maxvill's backup and a former Red Sox, recalls, "I thought we would sweep them. After we lost the sixth game, I was really devastated because any team can win one game, especially with Lonborg pitching. I'll never forget Gibson coming by and saying, 'I'll get 'em tomorrow.' I absolutely believed him."

"I'm sitting in the clubhouse next to Gibson," Woodeshick recalled in 2008, "and I'm so nervous that he says, 'What's wrong with you?' I told him, 'All I want to do is see us win this game so I can get my World Series ring and prove I was in one.' He said, 'Don't worry about it. I'll get that ring for you and I'll get the car.'"

In Game 7, Gibson, his competitive juices flowing, not only threw a 3-hitter and struck out 10, but also smashed a home run. Meanwhile, the dead-armed Lonborg was roughed up, giving up 10 hits and 7 runs in six innings. Brock, Maris, and Javier had 2 hits apiece, with Javier's 3-run homer in the seventh putting the game out of reach. Maris contributed a sacrifice fly and a single that sent Flood to third, from where he scored on a wild pitch. The final score was 7–2 as the St. Louis Cardinals won the World Series and were again atop the baseball world. "El Birdos!" "Yeah!"

"Nobody thought we'd even be close with their lineup, but we still took them to seven games," remembers a proud Dick Williams. "Gibson was well rested and beat us three times. He's the best right-hander and the most competitive pitcher I've ever seen."

Gibson deservedly won the MVP for the Series by throwing 3 complete-game victories, in which he gave up only 14 hits and 3 runs and struck out 26. Brock was also outstanding, going 12 for 29 for a .414 average with 8 runs and a Series-record 7 stolen bases. Javier batted .360 with 4 RBIs. Maris had the finest World Series of his career, batting .385 with 7 RBIs, a record for the Cardinals in ten World Series appearances.

The championship was vindication for Maris, who had been written off as a has-been his last few years in New York. "Roger told me that he wanted to prove to the Yankees that he could play on another winner," Woodeshick remembered. "He had a great Series."

The esteemed Shirley Povich, of the *Washington Post*, wrote, "The Series finally returned Roger Maris to the company of gifted athletes he belongs with. The Cardinals had an edge at several positions, but their edge in right field was the widest of all."

The Cardinals' winning the world title would have been an ideal conclusion to Maris's career, but it's not clear if his initial plan was to retire or continue playing and risk finishing on a bad note. McCarver remembers:

I don't think he planned on quitting after the '67 season. He was having too much fun and wanted to play one more year. But he used the possibility of retiring as a negotiation ploy. At our victory celebration at Bookbinder's in Philadelphia after clinching the pennant, John Romano and I were down at the end of the bar and we overheard Roger talking contract with Gussie Busch. It was uncomfortable, but before we could sneak away, we heard Gussie saying, "If you drive in 90 runs and hit 30 homers next year, we'll see about that distributorship." Roger said, "See about it, my ass. It's either going to happen or not. If I come back next year, I get a distributorship; otherwise I'm not playing." Roger was blunt, and that was to his advantage because Gussie loved that. That night, Gussie agreed to give Roger a beer distributorship worth millions of dollars. No player ever did a better negotiation than Roger did that night.

CHAPTER THIRTY-FIVE

THE FINAL SEASON

AUGUST BUSCH MADE GOOD on his promise to offer Roger an Anheuser-Busch beer distributorship. Roger and Pat hoped it would be in Kansas City, but one opened up in Gainesville, Florida, after Busch transferred the previous owner to the lucrative Tampa area. Roger jumped at the opportunity to have a distributorship that was based in a thirsty college town and covered eight counties. Finally, he and Rudy Jr., who was a full partner in the venture, were realizing their dream of going into business together. The news of Maris's return to the team broke in St. Louis on November 2, and the Cardinals and their fans were delighted to have one of their key players back for another run at the title.

The plan was for Rudy Jr. to move to Gainesville to set up and oversee operations of their company. Once Roger's house in Independence was sold, his family would also migrate to Florida, and after the 1968 season, he'd be able to work there full-time. As the *Post-Dispatch*'s Neal Russo cleverly put it, "He and his wife Pat will take along their six-pack, four sons and two daughters."

Roger was delighted by his big break, but couldn't muster even a small grin after coming down with Bell's palsy, a disease that affects the nerves and muscles of the face. When contacted by reporters, Roger said dejectedly, "There is numbness in the right side of my face. My eye gets a little blurry, which is probably due to my not being able to blink. There is nothing to do but wait it out. If it hangs on, I don't think I'll be able to play next season." He didn't suggest that he might then have to return the distributorship.

While Maris waited for the symptoms to subside, he took care of another problem, having a polyp removed from his vocal cords. Apparently, Roger saw this as a yellow flag rather than a red one regarding his future health and he didn't give up his Camels for several years.

On January 2, he was well enough to be in Gainesville, where he and Rudy Jr. officially opened their business at a converted warehouse on Airport Road. They proudly put up a sign:

MARIS

DISTRIBUTING CO.

BUDWEISER BUSCH BAVARIAN

MICHELOB

WHOLESALE ONLY

Less than two weeks later Roger was in St. Peterburg, where at a sales convention of Anheuser-Busch Inc. new Cardinals general manager Bing Devine signed him to another $75,000 contract. Devine had returned from the Mets for his second stint as Cardinals GM because Stan Musial, now listed as a senior vice president, needed more time to devote to his restaurant, Stan and Biggies, following the death of his partner, Biggie Garagnani. Devine arranged a press conference conducted by telephone with writers at Busch Stadium in St. Louis, and team physician Dr. I. C. Middleman was on hand to assure the media that Roger was already 90 percent recovered from the Bell's palsy and would be fit for training camp. Only minimal therapy was needed to correct "some drooping of Roger's lower lip," he stated. "His vision is perfect."

When Maris reported to St. Petersburg, he was in good health but for his weak right hand. Again, he told no one about his inability to grip the bat and turn around a good fastball.

Pat accompanied Roger to Florida for his final spring training and stayed until the exhibition games began. Then he hung out mostly with Dal Maxvill and Mike Shannon. Maxvill recalls, "We'd go to Gene's Lobster House for raw oysters, fish, and beer. My wife, Jenny, would arrive in the middle of spring training and Rog would tell her, 'I'm glad you're back in the fold and Dal's out of here, because he was about to drown me in Budweiser.' I'd say, 'Yeah, like it's all my fault.' We'd go to the dog track and I'd look at him and say, 'Are you crazy coming to the track and not betting? I know you've got the money.' It was the same in New York, when Roger, Shannon, and I went to Aqueduct with Roger's friend Julie Isaacson. Roger didn't care about betting. He just enjoyed being included in the group."

At spring training, Maris was reunited with George Kissell. He didn't need his mentoring again, but Roger still enjoyed chatting with the shrewdest baseball mind in the organization. Roger gave him a memento. Forty years later (and only five months before his death in a car accident), eighty-eight-year-old Kissell recalled, "We were on a road trip and Roger said, 'George, this is going to be my last year and I want to give you something to remember me by.' And would you believe that he took off his sweater and gave it to me? It was a brown sweater with the word *Michelob* on the left side. Roger had big shoulders and it didn't fit me that well, but I was so touched that I wore it anyway. Just today I found it in my closet."

Once again, Roger made himself available to young players in camp. One rookie who was grateful for the attention was Wayne Granger, a skinny reliever from Springfield, Massachusetts:

> I had been up for a cup of coffee in September 1967 and didn't pitch, but I got to meet Roger. He was such a nice guy, just the opposite from what I read in the papers. What really impressed me was that he did something no other ballplayer would do. In December, my wife and I got a Christmas card from Roger and his wife. There were little drawn stick figures of their kids, little pop-ups, with their names. It wasn't a store-bought card, but something personal.
>
> I saw him again in the spring. Roger was a mature leader and I was just a scared rookie. He was calm and unemotional and a steadying influence. He would say, "Wayne, I know you're excited about being here, but just relax and enjoy it. Don't get too excited." I'll always be grateful for how he took the time to calm me down so I could pitch.

Again baseball played an important role in helping a shocked, grieving nation recover from an assassination. The Cardinals opened their season just six days after civil rights leader Dr. Martin Luther King Jr. was gunned down in Memphis.

Their Opening Day roster in 1968 was pretty much the same as the one in 1967, minus the traded Al Jackson and Alex Johnson and the retired John Romano, Eddie Bressoud, and Hal Woodeshick. The Cardinals' front office believed in keeping the roster intact, and only thirty-two players would appear in games in '68, of whom only twenty-seven—as in the previous year—would be in more than ten games.

The Cardinals began the season on April 10 with an exciting 2–1 victory over visiting Atlanta. Gibson, who didn't pick up his first victory until April 24, gave up only 3 hits and 1 unearned run in 7 innings, but the win went to Washburn in relief. Pinch hitter Dave Ricketts's RBI single in the bottom of the ninth got the world champions off to a great start. Maris went 0 for 3. Then, nursing a pulled muscle in his thigh that would bother him all season, he sat out two games as St. Louis improved its record to 3–0.

He was back in the lineup on April 14, against the Cubs' Joe Niekro. In the first inning, he followed singles by Brock and Flood with a 3-run homer, the 271st round-tripper of his career. Dick Hughes, who'd win only 2 games in 1968 because of a career-ending rotator-cuff tear, couldn't hold the lead, and the Cardinals suffered their first loss, 7–6, despite a second homer by Maris. He wouldn't homer again for nearly two months, but he remained productive, as he was the next game when his 2-run double tied Atlanta 3–3 in the eighth inning of an eventual 4–3, ten-inning victory.

Through April 27, Maris was hitting .324 with 7 RBIs for the 11-4 first-place Cardinals. But by May 6 his average had dropped exactly 100 points. He struggled as the Cardinals went 6-13 and slipped into fourth place. The Cardinals stopped their slide when Steve Carlton shut out the Giants 6–0. Then Larry Jaster threw a 2-hitter to beat Mets ace Tom Seaver, 2–0, pulling the Cardinals to within a game of first-place San Francisco. May ended with Maris's average up to .239, but he had only 10 RBIs.

Maris got his 11th RBI the next day against the Mets' young fireballer Nolan Ryan, driving in the Cardinals' first run as they came back from a 3–0 deficit and won 6–5 on a tenth-inning homer by Shannon. Maris wasn't in the lineup against left-hander Al Jackson in the first game of a twinbill against the Mets, but his bat wasn't needed as Gibson broke his 4-game losing streak with a 7-hitter, homering as well in a 6–3 victory. Despite a 1.66 ERA, Gibson's record stood at 4–5.

In the nightcap, Maris went 0 for 4 against Don Cardwell, but with the score tied 2–2 in the seventh inning, he drew a two-out walk. He then showed he could still run by scoring all the way from first on Cepeda's short double into no-man's-land in right field, giving Hughes his first win of the season. The next morning, the player who was compared unfavorably to Babe Ruth by New York writers in 1961 was compared favorably to Enos Slaughter by St. Louis scribes.

Maris's version of Slaughter's "mad dash" put the Cardinals back into sole possession of first place, where they remained for the rest of the season. They built on their lead with a sweep of Houston, with Gibson throwing a 4–0 victory in the finale on June 6. That day presidential candidate Bobby Kennedy, a brother of John Kennedy and a senator from New York, died after being shot twenty-six hours before in Los Angeles. Baseball, however, didn't skip a beat.

The Cardinals' 9th consecutive win gave them a 3½-game lead over four teams. In Gibson's remaining starts before the All-Star break, July 8–10, he would, astoundingly, shut out Atlanta 6–0, shut out Cincinnati 2–0, shut out Chicago 1–0, shut out Pittsburgh 3–0, beat the Dodgers 5–1, and shut out the Giants 3–0, improving his record to 11-5 with a 1.06 ERA. The only run he gave up from June 7 until July 6 came after 49 straight scoreless innings, on a first-inning wild pitch in L.A. That prevented him from challenging losing pitcher Don Drysdale's record of 58⅔ consecutive scoreless innings that he'd set earlier in the year. But Gibson would be just as dominant as the season progressed, accumulating 13 shutouts. McCarver convinced him that he had good enough control to hit the corner with backdoor sliders to left-handed batters. "I started throwing it and I got a little bit more confidence," he said. "That's why I had that good a year."

Though his power was almost gone, Maris still had a flair for the dramatic, as on June 10, when he broke his home-run drought with the 273rd of his career. His 2-run blast against the Braves led to an eventual 4–3 victory. His victim this time was Phil Niekro, Joe's older brother, a knuckleball specialist. Pointing out Maris's value to the team, Bob Broeg reported in the *Post-Dispatch* that the Cardinals had a 19-10 record when Roger played. "I must be dazzling them with my glove," Maris joked, pointing to his .231 average.

Hobbled by injuries, Maris managed only one more start before the All-Star break, on June 23, when he had 2 hits against Pittsburgh. Otherwise he was used as a pinch hitter. He got his only pinch hit in his final at-bat on June 30 before sitting out the next 6 games, all Cardinals victories. His average stood at .235 at the break.

Maris wasn't the only Redbird whose average was down significantly from 1967. Of the regulars, only Shannon at .256 and Maxvill at .239 were hitting higher than in the previous year. Only Flood at .316 was batting over .267. Javier was the only Cardinals position player to make the All-Star team, along with pitchers Gibson and Carlton. The team was scoring far fewer runs and homers were rare—for the season, Cepeda would lead the team with only 16 home runs, and Shannon, with 15, would be the only other player to hit more than 6! But the dearth of long balls didn't seem to matter because before the All-Star Game the Cardinals had 7- and 6-game winning streaks and left for the break with a .638 win-loss percentage (with a record of 53-30) compared to .588 (53-37) at the break in 1967. They were perched 10 games above Atlanta and Cincinnati.

All the other teams in the majors were struggling offensively as well. In what would be called "the Year of the Pitcher," the Yankees batted a feeble .214 yet improved to 83-79; Carl Yastrzemski led the American League with a .301 average; 5 no-hitters were thrown, including a perfect game by the A's Jim "Catfish" Hunter; the Giants' Gaylord Perry and the Cardinals' Ray Washburn tossed no-hitters against each other's team in consecutive games September 17–18; the National League won the All-Star Game, 1–0; Juan Marichal reeled off 26 victories and again *wasn't* voted the Cy Young Award; and Cleveland's Luis Tiant had a 1.60 ERA but didn't lead the majors in that department. Gibson, Drysdale, and the Tigers' Denny McLain, who was on pace to be the first 30-game winner since Dizzy Dean in 1934, were setting records. So dominant was pitching that in December, the Baseball Rules Committee would permanently lower the mound from fifteen inches to ten inches to help batters.

"The Cardinal players were uncommonly proud to be part of those teams," David Halberstam wrote about the 1967–68 squads, "for they won not by dint of pure talent or pure power—San Francisco was far richer in terms of pure talent. Rather, they won through intelligence, playing hard and aggressively, and because they had a sense of purpose that cut across racial lines in a way that was extremely unusual in the world of sports."

"On our club," Schoendienst recalls, "somebody always picked up the other guy if they didn't come through. Nobody moped around or felt sorry for themselves. They wanted to win and they always came up with some way to do it."

"It was the same ball club as in 1967," says Cepeda. "I had an off year and McCarver had an off year, but we still won."

"We still had a really good club," says Maxvill, who was the GM of the Cardinals from 1984 to 1994. "Our clubhouse hadn't changed at all, and that contributed to our success."

"Both years we had a team where everybody ribbed everybody else," says Washburn. "Nobody was immune. Once Cepeda was slumping, so a bunch of us got there early and removed all the clothes from his locker and replaced them with the groundskeeper's tools. Of course, he didn't appreciate it, but everybody else had a good laugh."

Wayne Granger, who had a couple of saves after being called up in early June, was impressed by the friendly clubhouse:

The veterans took away the pressure with their fun and games. I remember the time Tim McCarver brought in an LP and put it on our phonograph player. He said, "You guys gotta hear this song. I love it!" It was "Alice's Restaurant" by Arlo Guthrie. He started to play it while Roger was swinging his bat to get loose. The record was about halfway through when Mike Shannon groaned about it and jerked the record off the phonograph. He said, "Roger, what do you think of this?" and threw it up in the air toward him. And Roger hit it with his bat and smashed it. Tim looked like he was going to cry, but it was a funny thing to do and loosened everybody up.

Maris, too, was teased, often about his new business venture. McCarver recalls, "Roger loved our hitting coach, Dick Sisler, as we all did. Dick had a stuttering problem and wasn't able to say the letter F. So he couldn't say, 'Fuck you!' He'd just say, ' . . . you!' It got so that everybody on the Cardinals would say, ' . . . you!" to each other. We could even do it in public or with our wives around because we were the only ones who knew what ' . . . you' meant. Roger thought that was so funny. He'd particularly laugh when Dick would snap at him, ' . . . you and your eight counties!' "

"Nobody ever said anything negative about Roger getting the distributorship," says Maxvill. "Most of the guys were still young and were going to be playing for several more years, so it didn't cross anybody's mind that 'Gee, I wish I would have got one instead of him.' "

"We loved Roger and didn't resent that he got a distributorship," says

Cepeda. "I could have had one, too. I met with Harry Caray, who was the one who got Roger his distributorship. He mentioned me to Gussie Busch, like he did for Roger. But I wasn't ready. Roger had his brother and Pat to help him, but I didn't have anybody."

Maris again lived at the Executive complex, waiting for school to finish so Pat and the kids could join him for more than weekends. Two of his new neighbors were the off-season acquisitions who contributed most to the 1968 team: catcher Johnny Edwards had come over in a trade from Cincinnati in February; and backup infielder Dick Schofield, Roger's 1966 apartmentmate with the Yankees, was signed as a free agent on April 1.

"We lived next door to each other," recalls Schofield, "and before our wives came to St. Louis, Johnny stayed with me and we'd go with Roger to the store and buy food. You'd think we were three old maids. We'd cook out early in the afternoon and ate pretty good. Roger really could eat."

"I caught with the Reds in the 1961 World Series," remembers Edwards, "and I was a friendly guy who talked to the Yankee hitters. But Roger wouldn't acknowledge me, so I thought, 'What a stuck-up son of a gun.' Until I was his teammate and neighbor, I didn't realize he was just a country boy who was a lot of fun to hang out with. We became close friends. The fans in St. Louis loved him, but we'd run into an occasional loudmouth who still resented him for beating Babe Ruth's record."

In June the Executive Apartments were again transformed into a summer camp full of family activities. "Roger seemed happy in his last year," reminisces Schofield. "Pat was very nice and their kids played with ours in the parking lot every day. My oldest girl was about the same age as their oldest girl, Susan, and my son Dick was around the same age as Kevin and Randy. They were good kids and they thought a lot of their parents."

Off the field Maris was happy; on the field he was frustrated. Not playing because of injuries in the first half of the season made him think increasingly about retirement. Although he had planned on 1968 being his final season, in his mind the door was slightly ajar. Now it was shutting. "Nobody wouldn't be frustrated being on a club that is going to win the pennant and not being part of it," says Maxvill. "But Roger didn't sit around bitching and moaning about it to any of us."

Maris wasn't able to start in either end of a doubleheader against visiting Houston when the Cardinals returned from the All-Star break, but he had pinch singles in both games. The Cardinals salvaged a split in the nightcap, 8–7, when he drove in the tying run in the bottom of the eighth inning, then scored the winning run on Brock's single. He didn't play when Gibson 3-hit the Astros 8–1, but in the following game he drove in the winning run with a pinch single in the eighth inning off Houston's Jim Ray for a 5–4 victory.

Four consecutive pinch hits got Maris ink in the St. Louis papers. In Neal Russo's article "Maris Bounces Off Bench to Hit in Clutch for Cards," Roger said he was content in his new role, particularly since the Cards were winning and Bobby Tolan was playing well. But soon Schoendienst put him back in the lineup against right-handers, with excellent results.

In a victory against the Phillies, he had a 4-RBI game. On July 23, Maris belted the 274th home run of his career. The 2-run shot in the fifth inning came off the Pirates' Steve Blass, as Nelson Briles won his 12th game, 9–1. Maris continued to hit with authority. Even though he went 0 for 4 as Gibson won his 15th game on July 30, Maris batted .359 for the month, going 14 for 39 with 11 RBIs.

Nineteen sixty-eight has always been considered a lost season for Maris because he missed so many games with injuries. But the truth was he was the Cardinals' best hitter in the second half of the season and as valuable as he'd been in 1967. Into mid-September, he accumulated numerous multiple-hit games and, with uncanny, machinelike precision, drove in the first runs in games, tying runs, go-ahead runs, and winning runs. His 31 RBIs in the second half of '68 were the second most on the team, behind Shannon's 40, but coming in 106 fewer at-bats. He had 2 more RBIs than Cepeda in 108 fewer at-bats. For the entire season he excelled in the clutch, batting .299 in victories as opposed to .193 in defeats; .294 with runners on base; and .391 with a runner on third and less than two outs. His defense, too, was still clutch, and on September 3 he leaped high to take away one last home run, from the Reds' Tony Perez.

On September 15, Maris smashed a 2-run homer off Houston's Don Wilson in the third inning of a 7–4 victory. It was the 275th and final homer of his career. Fittingly, it came in the game the Cardinals clinched the pennant for the second straight year. So Maris had extra reason to celebrate in the wild party that followed.

After that monumental moment, Maris didn't play much. When he was in the lineup, he looked drained. "He wasn't up to par," recalls Schoendienst. "He'd pushed himself as much as he could for two years and just couldn't do it anymore, with his bad hamstrings, his foot, his hand, and everything else."

In regard to his hand, Maris told Ed Wilks, "This year they started out giving me off-speed stuff, but then they switched to fastballs. So I've got to assume that they found out about me." Of his final homer, he said, laughing, "That was on an off-speed pitch, too."

Most of the headlines were reserved for Gibson. After 15 consecutive victories, he lost 2 decisions in a row as the Cardinals stumbled to a 4-7 finish—including being no-hit by Gaylord Perry after spending the previous day celebrating their pennant. Then Gibson blanked Houston, 1–0, in his final start. Having given up only 37 earned runs in 304⅔ innings, he ended up with an unfathomable 1.12 ERA, the lowest earned-run average of the modern era. He won 22 games and nobody has ever figured out how he lost 9 times.

On August 5, amid a few hitless games, Maris held a press conference to confirm that he was retiring at the end of the season. "It's getting tougher and tougher for me to play," he said. With Schoendienst and Devine sitting beside him, he told the reporters that the last two years had been much different from playing in New York. "It's like being burned, you never get rid of the scars," he said, adding that playing in St. Louis had been "a pleasure" and "it's too bad that I didn't come here to play a lot sooner." Asked why he was making his announcement in August, he said candidly, "I did not really care to be bothered by the press after the season."

A few weeks later, in New York, Maris gave Maury Allen the true explanation for his retirement: "I'm just tired of baseball. I won't miss it. I'll have a job that will keep me busy, and I'll be able to come home to my family every night." Appropriately, 1968 was also Mickey Mantle's final season, his eighteenth in a Yankee uniform. Mantle was upset that he stuck around too long and his lifetime average dipped just below .300 (.298). But he was proud to have hit 536 home runs, with his last coming on September 19 off Denny McLain, who won his 31st game (against 5 losses), besting 20-game winner Mel Stottlemyre, 6–2, in Detroit.

In Maris's final game in New York City, on September 1, a classy message was posted on the Shea Stadium scoreboard during the third inning: "To

Roger Maris . . . making his last New York appearance as an active player today . . . we express our appreciation of an outstanding career—and wish you and yours the best."

At Busch Stadium, on September 29, Roger received from the Cardinals what the Yankees wouldn't give him: "Roger Maris Day." Pat and their children stood proudly by him. The four boys, miniature Rogers with blond crewcuts, were similarly dressed in white turtlenecks with dark sports jackets. Rudy Sr. was present, having come down from Fargo, as were Roger's good friends Julie Isaacson and Tony Kubek, now an NBC analyst with whom he dined whenever the *Game of the Week* showed the Cardinals.

Kubek read a telegram of congratulations from the Yankees. As Maris stood and fidgeted, speeches were made celebrating his career and the two pennants in two seasons he helped bring to St. Louis. Gifts were bestowed, the most prominent being a Wurlitzer organ that the family had requested. This thrilled the kids. Harry Caray, the master of ceremonies, read off a list of Maris's career accomplishments, then said, "Such records tell only the story of Maris the baseball player. In his relatively brief period in St. Louis, we've also come to know and respect him as Maris the man, a gentleman of warmth and humility, an inspiration to youngsters everywhere, a man who has been genuinely a credit to the game." How would Oscar Fraley or Jimmy Cannon have reacted to hearing these words that exalted Maris's sterling character? Cannon was still writing articles purporting "You're Roger Maris who isn't Babe Ruth."

On that Sunday, before 23,791 fans, Ray Washburn beat Houston 11–1 as the Cardinals finished the season 97–65, 9 games in front of San Francisco. Roger batted only once, as a pinch hitter for Ron Davis in the sixth inning. He grounded into a force play, second to short, in the final regular-season at-bat of his career. At least he pulled the ball. When Maris left his right-field position for the final time, he came trotting toward the dugout. Andy Strasberg, who had to be present at what he called "the end of my childhood," reminisces, "I had positioned myself behind the dugout, and he waved to everybody. He went into the dugout and I didn't think he saw me. Then he popped up out of the dugout and turned his head. He saw me and winked. Then it was over."

The regular season was over, but Maris was still to play in his final World Series. It was his seventh Series in the 1960s, more than anyone else in baseball, and a testament to his career as a winning ballplayer. The Cardinals' opponents were the Detroit Tigers, who hadn't been to a World Series since 1945. The Cardinals' only real advantage was experience. The Tigers won more games (103 to 97), slugged more homers (185 to 73), scored more runs (671 to 583), and even made fewer errors (105 to 140). Detroit led the majors in all those categories. Leading their offense was Al Kaline (.287), who, though past his prime and hurting, was still dangerous, as were Norm Cash (25 homers), Willie Horton (.285, 36 home runs, 85 RBIs), Bill Freehan (25 homers, 84 RBIs), Jim Northrup (21 homers, 90 RBIs), and unorthodox second baseman and leadoff hitter Dick McAuliffe (16 homers, 56 RBIs).

Scarier than all of the hitters was Denny McLain. As he closed in on matching Dizzy Dean's 30 victories in 1934, he was hounded by the press in such a way that the *Detroit Free Press*'s Joe Falls remembered Maris in 1961. In the article "Maris Pressure Reappears in McLain," he wrote:

> It seems to me that the most unpopular ball player of our time has been Roger Maris. Some people still don't forgive him for hitting those 61 home runs in 1961 and . . . [call] him a one-shot wonder, a phony record-breaker and a guy who probably beats up his dog. They make it sound as if Maris used an illegal bat to hit an illegal ball to break Babe Ruth's record. But now, the more I think about it, the more I think Maris' achievement . . . was one of the greatest feats in baseball history. . . . I see it all now, in clearer perspective, because I see what's happening to Denny McLain. I saw Maris only every two or three weeks. . . . I had no idea what kind of strain he was under—day after day after day. I see it all now, and it's not as bad with McLain because Denny works only every four days. Maris was out there every day. Every day was a crisis. If he didn't hit one, they wanted to know why. If he did hit one . . . well, then it got slightly ridiculous.

"All our players were talking about McLain," recalls Maxvill, "and Roger said, 'I'll tell you something, guys. McLain is not the guy we've got to worry about here. We need to worry about the other guy—Mickey Lolich.' And we all looked around and said, 'Oh, yeah? Mickey Lolich?' Only Roger knew that he was a big-time pitcher because he'd faced him when he was a Yankee.

He also said, 'This is not going to be a cakewalk by any means. They are a fine team.' They turned out to be a really fine team."

The Cardinals were confident going into the Series because they had Gibson available for three starts and a whole roster of winners. Plus they believed that Mayo Smith was making a poor decision when he decided to sacrifice defense for offense by moving center fielder Mickey Stanley to shortstop for the weak-hitting Ray Oyler, so he wouldn't have to sit either Kaline or Northrup. Bob Gibson couldn't have cared less. In 1964, he struck out 5 Yankees in the first two innings; in 1967, he struck out 4 Red Sox in the first two innings. Going against McLain in Game 1 in St. Louis, he again put fear in his opponents' eyes as he struck out 6 of the first 7 batters. And he didn't stop there. All game long Tigers were walking back to their dugout shaking their heads.

Smith lifted McLain after 5 innings trailing 3–0, realizing that Gibson wouldn't relinquish that big a lead. Brock's homer off Pat Dobson was an unnecessary insurance run. In the ninth inning, Gibson struck out Kaline for the third time. Then he struck out Cash for the third time to break Sandy Koufax's Series record of 15 strikeouts. He then concluded one of baseball's greatest big-game performances by setting the still-standing record of 17 strikeouts with a called third strike on Willie Horton, who, according to McCarver, "gasped because he thought the ball hit him." Gibson gave up 5 hits while throwing his mind-boggling 14th shutout of 1968, 4–0.

Game 2 was a battle of left-handers as 19-game-winner Briles opposed 17-game-winner Lolich, and it was no contest. Tiger batters battered Briles and Carlton, and Lolich proved Maris prescient, holding the Cardinals to 6 hits and striking out 9 in an 8–1 embarrassment of the defending champions. Lolich even hit the only homer of his sixteen-year career. Maris sat out against the lefty.

The Cardinals came back to win Game 3 in Detroit behind Washburn and Joe Hoerner, an underrated closer who went 8–2 with 17 saves and a 1.47 ERA during the season. The Tigers led 2–0 until the Cardinals scored 4 runs in the fifth off Earl Wilson and Pat Dobson. The big blow off Dobson was a 3-run homer by McCarver, following an RBI double by Brock and walk to Maris. In the seventh inning, Flood singled, Maris doubled, and Cepeda put the game away with a 3-run homer.

Game 4 again matched the year's Cy Young winners, and again Gibson showed his superiority. He yielded a run—a homer by Northrup in the fourth inning—but threw another 5-hitter, striking out 10. Only Maris and Maxvill were hitless for the Cardinals in their 10–1 victory. Brock, who set a record with 13 hits in the Series, had 3 hits and 4 RBIs. He and Gibson homered.

The Cardinals were up 3 games to 1 and expected to close out the Series quickly. And when they scored 3 runs in the first inning of Game 5 against Lolich, 2 on a homer by Cepeda, their confidence was justified. But Lolich shut them out the rest of the way and the Tigers rallied to win 5–3. The pivotal play of the game came in the fifth inning when Javier singled with Brock on second. Brock came home but didn't slide and was tagged out by Freehan.

Needing to win Game 6 in St. Louis, Smith bypassed Wilson and moved McLain up as his starter, figuring he'd do better if he wasn't going against Gibson. McLain gave up 9 hits, including 2 to Maris, but held the Cardinals scoreless until the ninth inning. Maris's single to center field to lead off the ninth inning was the final hit of his major league career. He then scored for the last time on a single by Javier to make the final score 13–1. The Tigers got 2 runs off Washburn in the second inning, then 10 more runs in the third inning off Washburn, Jaster, and Willis. The big hit was a grand slam by Northrup off Jaster. "It wasn't one of my highlights," says Jaster forty years later.

Pitching on two days' rest, Lolich drew the task of opposing Gibson in the decisive Game 7. For six innings, neither pitcher gave up a run. The sense was that the game would turn on one play, and the first team to break through against the seemingly invincible men on the mound would win.

Gibson had 5 strikeouts through the first three innings to break his own 1964 Series record of 31. But he struck out only one batter in the next three innings and didn't look as dominant as he had been. Stanley was his 7th victim leading off the seventh, and Kaline grounded to third for the second out. Then disaster struck.

Cash singled to right and Horton singled him to third. Northrup hit a liner to center field toward Flood. Playing shallow, the brilliant outfielder lost the ball in the shirts behind home plate and moved farther in. He quickly realized the ball was hit better than he'd gauged. He tried to reverse directions but slipped, and the disbelieving fans in the ballpark and watching on television saw the ball sail over his head. By the time Flood tracked it down, 2 runs had scored and Northrup stood on third.

Gibson should have given an intentional pass to Freehan and faced Lolich, but he defiantly went after the Tiger catcher, who lined a double to left to score Detroit's third run. The Tigers added a fourth run in the ninth inning by stringing together 3 singles off the tired pitcher. The Cardinals finally scored a run off Lolich when Shannon homered with two outs in the ninth inning, to make the final score 4–1. McCarver fouled out to Freehan for the final out. In the final at-bats of his career, Maris struck out swinging on a high fastball he couldn't catch up to and popped to short.

The Detroit Tigers, who meant so much to the spirit of a city that had experienced deadly riots in 1967, were the last World Champions before divisional play and playoffs began in 1969. Lolich, who won 3 games, was selected the Most Valuable Player. "We listened when Rog told us about Lolich," says Maxvill, "but our actions didn't show it. What a three-game stretch he had against us."

"Losing that Series still upsets me and everyone on that team," says McCarver, "because we should have won it being up three games to one—and because we never won again. We didn't get a chance because many of us were traded in the next couple of years."

The Cardinals' expected dynasty never happened. Before the Series, *Sports Illustrated* published what became a classic cover of the Cardinals lineup—a Neil Leifer photograph of a racially diverse team that was in striking contrast to the photo taken of the all-white Yankee lineup, including Maris, prior to the 1960 World Series. The corresponding article implied that because of the players' high salaries (which were listed on the cover), they had lost their hunger to win. The charge had no foundation, but it embarrassed the Cardinals front office. Busch and Devine saw that the players were becoming involved in strike talks and other union activities under Marvin Miller and worried that could result in demands for even bigger salaries. So before the 1968 season ended, Devine began making deals that would dismantle the great Cardinals team by 1970. Even Cepeda was traded in the off-season, to Atlanta for Joe Torre. Flood famously challenged the reserve clause by refusing to be part of a trade, with McCarver, to Philadelphia after the 1969 season.

The day after the World Series ended, Roger Maris cleaned out his locker at Busch Stadium and exited the clubhouse with a team photo of the Cardinals under one arm and a bag of gloves and his shaving kit under the other. Unlike the rest of the team (including some players who had already secretly been traded), he would not go on an exhibition tour in Japan after the season. After sixteen years of playing professional baseball, twelve in the major leagues, seven of which concluded in a World Series, his playing days were over.

CHAPTER THIRTY-SIX

FAMILY MAN

ROGER MARIS, CIVILIAN, SHOWED up at the Cardinals' spring training camp in 1969 after it began. His former teammates were delighted to see him, as was his former manager. Schoendienst told the St. Louis reporters that he'd miss "the middle man in our rallies." He was right: the Cardinals would win 10 fewer games and slip to fourth in the National League East.

New York reporters who were in St. Petersburg to cover a Mets team that would startle the sports world by winning the world title in 1969 heard Maris was in town and came to the Redbirds' camp. He was amiable and willing to chat informally, but clearly he wouldn't do interviews. Dick Young's initial impressions of Roger were of how he looked. In his "Young Ideas" column in the *Daily News*, he wrote about the older, retired Maris:

> The tawny hair is crewcut, as before. The smile is a half-smirk, as before (he does not let the world know he is happy). The eyes squint, and penetrate, and he would resemble the young athlete, as before, but the gut gives him away, especially when he is slumped in a chair and it falls over his belt. Roger Maris played ball at 210 pounds and was pudgy at the end. He says he is 220 now. "When will it stop?" "I haven't decided yet," he says, and this time the laugh is full. He has broken out, he is enjoying his freedom.

That spring Jimmy Mann of the *St. Petersburg Times* found Maris seated in the old press box at Al Lang Field watching the Cardinals and the Red Sox play an exhibition game. He asked him point-blank, "Do you miss it?"
"Not one bit."

He did miss the clubhouse camaraderie, but not playing the game because, as he later told sportswriter Marty Ralbovsky for a piece in the *New York Times*, he could no longer withstand the rigors of the sport: "Every day my body tells me I used to be a baseball player. I can't sleep on my stomach because my rib cage is so tender. It got that way because of how I'd bust up double plays. And my knees hurt if I just brush against them; that's from banging into outfield walls. And I still don't have any feel in the ring finger of my right hand. If I had to do it again, I would have been more careful about my health, not to jeopardize it like I did."

He claimed that he thought about his career only when he felt the residual aches and pains. "The 61 homers? I don't think much about that anymore. It's all in the past, and I'm too busy now anyway. Maybe it'll become important to me when I'm 65 or 70. Maybe then I'll think about it more, and even enjoy it."

"Honest to goodness," he said to an AP reporter, "my greatest thrills in life are to work at the plant and then go home to be with my family."

Half a million young people went to Woodstock in 1969. Three astronauts flew to the moon. New president Richard Nixon made an unscheduled visit to Vietnam as the war there and protests in America intensified. Meanwhile Maris was fulfilling his dream of staying home with Pat and watching his children grow up. He was pleased that he could provide them with security, which many retiring players in those days couldn't do for their families. "I'm not making as much money as I did playing ball," Maris told Dick Young. "Not yet, but I will, and more."

Maris's family moved into a large redbrick house that overlooked the seventh green of the Gainesville Golf and Country Club, where Roger and his sons spent many weekends and free afternoons. The man with a large World Series ring on his finger stated he was finished with baseball, but he made no attempt to hide his past. Rather, the staircase banister had baseball bats serving as posts and his two MVP trophies were mounted on each side of the fireplace. In the entranceway of the warehouse was a large glass case containing several large trophies, including the Sultan of Swat crown he received in 1961. Along with pictures of his family, numerous plaques, framed photographs, and mementos adorned his office. Displayed prominently were the photographs of Maris with President Kennedy in the Oval Office and Maris and Mantle with Harry Truman at the ballpark. A framed blowup of a Bill

Gallo cartoon showed Maris in quest of 61 home runs and an inset of a for-
lorn Babe Ruth.

Roger made an appearance at an Old-Timers' Game in St. Louis in '69
and, along with Pat and the Surprises, rooted the Kansas City Chiefs to victory in Super Bowl IV in New Orleans on January 11, 1970. Otherwise he
stayed focused on the beer distributorship, not even reading the papers to
keep up with the Cardinals and the Yankees.

Rudy Jr. took care of the books and made sure orders and deliveries were
running smoothly, while Roger used a newfound personal touch to drum up
business and solidify relationships with clients of the distributorship's previous owner. The competition warned the old clients that they'd never see the
ex-ballplayer who took over, but he made a point of meeting every one of
them. Despite his lifelong bashfulness, he could be found socializing in taverns, buying everyone inside a round of Buds and promoting his beer and
his way of doing business—and even answering baseball questions.

On a typical day in the field, he told sportswriter Ira Berkow, "Rudy and
I drive to the brewery in Jacksonville, we go into the taverns and supermar-
kets and other outlets to see how our Bud stock is, how it's placed on the
shelves. I'm usually out of the house at eight thirty in the morning and
sometimes don't get home until one in the morning."

The hours were longest after the workers at the plant tested the resolve of
the new owners by going on strike. "Now, I'm a union man," Julie Isaacson
told Tony Kubek, "but those guys were trying to hold Roger up." Rather
than give in to their demands when the business was in its infancy, the stubborn Maris brothers let the workers walk. To avoid missing or delaying
scheduled deliveries, they loaded and drove the trucks themselves. "[Even]
the kids were out there throwing cases into the back of trucks," said Isaacson. "It wasn't long before the workers settled."

In the next few years, business boomed for the Maris Distributing Company, a full-time salesman was hired, and Roger's job description changed.
He became heavily involved in public relations, which including attending
golf events around the country. He played in about two weekend tournaments a month. Mostly he golfed for business; other times for pleasure or
charity. He became such a familiar figure on the links that one reporter
quipped that Maris now "confines his swinging to the golf course." He still
went hunting with Mike Shannon, Whitey Herzog, and other ballplayer

friends, but golf was the ideal way to stay in touch with both former team-mates and opponents.

"Anheuser-Busch had a golf tournament at one of the country clubs by me, in Napa," recalls Joe De Maestri. "It was a PGA pro-am celebrity deal, and Roger would come out and we'd play in it. He was so much looser on the golf course than when he was on the Yankees. He was a totally different guy. After hitting 61 home runs, he didn't get nervous trying to make a three-foot putt. There was no pressure and he thoroughly enjoyed playing."

"I finally got to know Roger well when we played golf together," says for-mer AL home-run champion Roy Sievers. "We went on golfing trips to Ari-zona and Harmon Killebrew's charity tournaments for leukemia in Idaho. He seemed so much happier than when he was a ballplayer and was always joking around, pulling pranks, and laughing. He told stories about baseball but not about himself."

"Mickey and Roger probably got even closer in the years after they stopped playing," Whitey Ford told Maury Allen. "Mickey had a golf tour-nament every year in Wildwood, Florida, and Roger would play in it. . . . He was erratic and would shoot 75–76 one day and come back the next day and shoot 88. He was always tougher when there was money on the line." When Roger played for money, the competition level was high, but the stakes were low.

Even with his frequent golf excursions, Roger spent a great deal of time with his kids. He loved that his two girls enjoyed hanging around with their father; the boys, on the other hand, were usually hard to track down. Al-though he refrained from pushing his four sons into sports, they excelled at baseball, basketball, and golf. Pat estimated that she and Roger watched them compete about six times a week, sometimes as many as three times in a single day. "Roger didn't say anything during games," she said. "The thing he hated the most was Little League mothers and fathers. He said they took the fun away from the kids."

Without being pushed by their famous dad to follow in his footsteps, the boys continued to play baseball throughout their youths. At one time the Maris brothers had five boys on the high school team. Kevin would play some minor league ball before becoming a professional golfer, and later he became a high school baseball coach. Randy also coached high school base-ball. The oldest, Roger Jr., who was 6'4", attempted to play professional baseball before accepting a basketball scholarship to a junior college. Roger told Rick Telander of *Sports Illustrated* that he backed his son's decision: "Some of those [baseball] coaches are different, and just because he's Roger Maris Jr., some of them started getting on him. And he thinks he just got tired of it and said the hell with baseball. I'll tell you, if I had it to do all over again, I would never have named him that."

When the boys were still young, Roger took them to Atlanta to watch the Braves. In 1973, they saw Hank Aaron close in on Babe Ruth's record of 714 career home runs. Before a victory against the Mets on July 6, Aaron gazed toward the box seats and recognized Maris, although his kids had convinced him to let his hair grow out to suit the times. (He felt awkward and soon went back to a crewcut.) While Maris and Aaron joked with each other, cameramen took pictures of the two men who shared the experience of chasing a sacred Ruth home-run record. Dick Cecil, then the vice president of the Braves, remembers:

> Roger's kids wanted to see some major league games, so we'd get them tickets. I remember the day Roger and Henry talked, probably about what it was like to chase Babe Ruth. I handled all the stuff going on with Henry, and I can tell you that most of the mail he got were hate letters and letters where the writers demanded that he not break Ruth's record or literally begged him not to do it. I handled all the death threats. I know Roger went through similar things in 1961. I could see that Henry and Roger had a great deal of respect for each other and felt a close bond.

"I thought the pressure on Roger was tougher than the pressure on me," Aaron said a few years later. "He had to get his 61 homers in a set time. I felt it was only a matter of my staying healthy. If I couldn't do it that year, there always was next year."

Maris did agree that Aaron had one distinct advantage over him: "Once he does it, no one will expect him to go out and do it all over again."

Aaron smashed 40 homers in 1973, leaving him 1 shy of tying Ruth. That meant Maris had to endure reporters' phone calls through the winter, asking him to comment on Aaron's feelings as he pursued Ruth. Fortunately, Aaron succeeded early in 1974, dramatically slugging number 714 on Opening Day and his record 715th homer in Atlanta two days later off Roger's former teammate Al Downing, then with the Dodgers. In retirement, Maris got calls anytime anyone had the slightest chance to break his single-season home-run record. Those calls ceased early each season because no real threats occurred during his lifetime. George Foster came closest with 52 home runs for the Reds in 1977.

As a favor, Maris returned to Atlanta Stadium to appear in his second Old-Timers' Game. However, he steadfastly refused to attend any Old-Timers' Day at Yankee Stadium. He didn't even respond to written invitations. Marty Appel recalls:

> I became the PR guy on the Yankees toward the end of '73, but even as Bob Fishel's assistant, the effort to reach out to former players to get them to come to Old-Timers' Day was mine. Our effort with Maris was halfhearted in the sense that we never expected him to come. Everyone was sent the same letter, and I guess we typed each one individually. So it was "Dear Roger" and signed by Bob Fishel and later by me. He was very angry with the organization because it wasn't straight with him about his hand injury in 1965, and when he received our invitations he was of the mind that he was unwelcome by the Yankees and that the fans would boo him.

In spring of 1973, Yankees GM Lee MacPhail drew up plans for Yankee Stadium's 50th anniversary Old-Timers' Day on August 11. Even Bob Meusel of the 1923 team accepted. MacPhail said, "The guy I'd like to have there most is Roger Maris." He assumed Maris was grateful to him for dealing him to St. Louis, where he enjoyed playing and won two pennants and a world title. Apparently, it slipped his mind that Maris detested him for trading him after being told he wanted to retire. It had been seven years, but Maris, like his mother, never got over a grudge. When their paths crossed in Florida, Maris rejected his invitation, snapping, "If the Cardinals have an Old-Timers' Day, I go. If you have one, I don't. Is that plain enough?"

"Okay," MacPhail said, and walked away. MacPhail was still determined to snag Maris so that summer the Yankees' front office promoted a postcard-writing campaign among the fans to persuade him to attend. It didn't work.

Maris had no problem continuing his relationship with the St. Louis organization. "He would come to spring training and we'd go out and have some laughs," Mike Shannon told Tony Kubek. "You could see he really enjoyed his work and being away from the pressures of baseball. His business was very successful and he had no financial worries. He was real proud when the boys started playing golf and winning some of those junior tournaments around home."

"Every now and then he came into St. Louis or where we were on the road if he was there on business," recalls Maxvill. "He had been a very popular guy on the club, so players went out of their way to speak to him. We'd get on him about his beer belly and how he was drinking all his profits. The new guys on the club were excited to introduce themselves to Roger Maris, the home-run king."

In late April 1973, Maris donated the bat he used to hit his 61st homer (which was an ounce lighter than the bat reporters wrote he used) and the ball that Sal Durante caught to the Hall of Fame. A few years earlier, Maris believed he had misplaced the ball or given it to his kids to play with and forgotten about it. He later found the historic ball and was willing to part with it and his 35-inch, 32-ounce Louisville Slugger when museum director Ken Smith, a onetime sportswriter for the defunct *Daily Mirror*, requested they be added to the permanent collection. Maris autographed both items.

The following year, Maris became eligible for induction into the Hall of Fame. Cooperstown took his historic bat and ball but rejected him. Only Roger's former teammates Mickey Mantle, in his first year of eligibility, and Whitey Ford, in his second year, received more than the necessary 75 percent of the votes to be elected by the Baseball Writers' Association of America in 1974. Mantle, with 322 votes, was written down on 88.2 percent of the ballots—the other, shameful 11.8 percent proved that voters had ulterior reasons beyond a player's qualifications for their decisions. Ford just made it with 224 votes, appearing on 77.8 percent of the ballots. Maris finished in sixteenth place with 78 votes, appearing on only 21.4 percent of the ballots.

Maris's low total seemed to indicate that he'd never receive enough votes. Yet of the thirteen also-rans in front of him, who received no more than 61.4 percent of the votes, eleven were eventually accepted—Robin Roberts, Ralph Kiner, Bob Lemon, Enos Slaughter, Pee Wee Reese, Eddie Mathews, Phil Rizzuto, Duke Snider, Red Schoendienst, George Kell, and Nellie Fox, who received only one more vote than Maris. Two players who received fewer votes than Maris, seventeenth-place finisher Hal Newhouser and nineteenth-place finisher Richie Ashburn, who received only 73 and 56 votes, respectively, were eventually selected.

Although the Veterans Committee voted most of them in, their percentages typically increased their last few years on the writers' ballot. Since retired players' statistics never change, the only explanation for dramatic changes in the later vote counts was that lobbying efforts for them increased. Unfortunately, Maris's reputation had been ruined by biased writers, so he knew better than to expect politicking on his behalf. When his vote total remained low the next few years, he assumed getting into Cooperstown was a lost cause. He rarely talked about it. When he did, he tried to be humble, saying, "Maybe I'm not worthy of it." But one time he added a remark that revealed he never expected justice: "But if I am worthy, I've got my doubts I'll make it. I'll just leave it to the *geniuses* who vote on it."

His former teammates on the Yankees and the Cardinals couldn't believe the slight; nor could his friends and family in Fargo, including his father. Rudy Sr. continued to be a supervisor for the railroad—after a merger on March 2, 1970, it was now called the Burlington Northern Railroad—until he'd been there for forty years and retired. Afterward, he divided his time between Gainesville, where Connie also had an apartment, and Fargo, where Roger visited him. According to Roger's first cousin Roger LaFreniere, Roger "bought him a duplex and van and sat by the railroad tracks with him, like he did as a kid." In both places, Rudy Sr. spoke bitterly about how his younger son hadn't properly been recognized for his achievements.

Roger and Pat made it a point to visit Fargo each year. In the summer, they brought their children so they could see the town their parents considered home. Other times they came alone. A favorite stop for both was the second floor of the American Legion building downtown, where Roger played cards and drank beer with his friends. He also spent a lot of time on the links.

"When Roger came in the summer, we'd play every day," recalls Bob Wood. "So Roger, Don Gooselaw, Dick Savageau, and I were together again, just like in high school."

A new friend Maris made in the 1970s while visiting Fargo was John Jensen, who had lost much of his hearing while serving as a loader in the tank corps during World War II. An insurance adjuster, Jensen was eight years older than Maris but they became fast friends. Jensen recalls:

I started the Crew Cut Club of America for charity. I needed a front person, so I tried contacting George Gobel. I told his agent that all the membership fees would go to the Anne Carlsen Crippled Children's School in Jamestown, North Dakota, where I was from. Anne Carlsen had no arms or legs and was well known in the United States then. Gobel's agent wrote me a letter saying, "Be glad to do that. Send us $5,000." I tried somebody else, and then I saw Roger at some function in Fargo. I told him what the deal was for the Crew Cut Club. He picked it up right away and went out and sold $20 memberships for me. Wherever he went, he'd sell them, to Moose Skowron and anybody else who had a crewcut. The school got a lot of money and publicity out of it. It was because of Roger.

In 1976, Roger, Pat, and five of their children arrived in town after having passed through, surprisingly, Hibbing. They surely saw the still-expanding open-pit Hull Rust Mahoning Mine, but they didn't say if they went past the town's other main tourist spots, Bob Dylan's childhood home and high school, or if Roger showed his family where he and Rudy Jr. lived with their parents in Leetonia. Only Susan, who had married, was not with them, although, the *Forum* said, "Plans for a family reunion were crimped a bit when Randy suffered a broken ankle during their Minnesota stay and he will need medical attention here."

In Fargo, Roger went with his father to see the local American Legion team defeat the Alexandria, Minnesota, team 3–1. The game was at Jack Williams Stadium, where baseball was played since Barnett Field was torn down. When asked about his paunch, Roger told his friends that he had quit smoking eight months before. For someone who smoked up to five packs of unfiltered cigarettes a day in 1961, this was quite a change. Their visit over, the family headed west, with Roger telling the *Forum*, "We'll just go where the car takes us."

Back in Fargo the following year, Roger was inducted into the North Dakota American Legion Hall of Fame. One of the other four inductees was the *Forum*'s longtime sportswriter Eugene Fitzgerald. "Fitz," who first covered Roger when he and his brother had been high school football stars, had passed away in 1974.

When Roger played golf or socialized with former Yankee teammates, some would pressure him into joining them at the annual Old-Timers' Day at Yankee Stadium. According to Moose Skowron, "He missed being around the guys after he quit, but he was mad at the Yankees for what they did to him. . . . Anyway, the regime had changed. 'Roger, the guys want to see you, they want to see if you got fat, they want to see if you still have your hair.' He would say, 'They'll boo me.' I told him those fans were all dead."

The Yankees had changed hands on January 3, 1973, when Michael Burke brokered a deal in which CBS sold the team for $12 million to a consortium of private investors led by George Steinbrenner, a Cleveland shipping magnate. Burke was a minority owner and expected to run the team as club president. But when Steinbrenner brought in Gabe Paul to be his right-hand man, a furious Burke stormed off. By the end of the year, MacPhail, who became president of the American League, and Houk, who became manager of the Tigers, were also gone. Steinbrenner established that he was the only boss of the Yankees.

From the beginning, Steinbrenner was criticized for how he wielded his power, fired managers, and arrogantly tried to buy New York another championship by spending huge money on free agents such as former Oakland A's stars Catfish Hunter and Reggie Jackson. But no one doubted that he respected the team's glorious history and players who embodied Yankee pride. Steinbrenner thought Roger Maris was "a true Yankee." He remembers, "I hadn't met him but I'd followed his career and thought he had talent and every quality that I liked. He was a hard worker, he could concentrate immensely, he was all business. He also was clean-cut and honest and not boastful. I thought he was a really good person. I was aware he'd been turning down invitations to Old-Timers' Day at Yankee Stadium since he'd retired, but I wanted to bring him back to where he belonged."

For the first few years of Steinbrenner's reign, Maris told reporters that he had no intention of changing his mind about going to New York. As much as he tried to look forward and forget the unpleasantness he'd experienced there, he couldn't help glimpsing into the rearview mirror. As a player, he'd insisted that the hostility of the fans stopped bothering him, but now he spoke with jarring frankness about being an unpopular Yankee to Art Spander of the *Sporting News*: "You should hear all those boos. They say you should be like a duck and let it run off your back. You can do it for a while, but I couldn't do it for years. . . . If people would have cheered, I think I could have had a much better career."

Steinbrenner kept after Maris to return to Yankee Stadium and be celebrated. In 1977, the Yankees, the defending American League champions, scheduled an exhibition game on March 23 against the University of Florida at Perry Field in Gainesville. They commissioned Maris to supply the beer, assuming he would drop by to say hello because his golf buddy Billy Martin was the Yankee manager, Yogi Berra was a coach, and Mickey Mantle was a special batting instructor. Before the game, Mantle, Martin, and Maris spent time swapping stories at the bar at the Yankees' hotel.

Maris sat with Mantle during the game watching a marvelously talented group of Yankees, including Catfish Hunter, Mickey Rivers, Lou Piniella, Roger's former Yankee teammate Roy White, Ron Guidry, Willie Randolph, Graig Nettles, and the captain, catcher Thurman Munson. "The two men never really knew each other," Tony Kubek said of Maris and Munson, "but they were so alike in that they were portrayed as stubborn and surly, but at the same time they were loved by their teammates."

Maris paid special attention to the Yankees' slugging, left-handed-hitting right fielder, Reggie Jackson, who thrived in the spotlight, loved by Yankee fans and Steinbrenner but disliked by most of his teammates. Rick Telander wrote in the June 20 issue of *Sports Illustrated*, "After the game Jackson sits on a stool in the locker room and explains how he feels about Maris. 'I have so much admiration for the man,' he says solemnly. 'For the mental part almost more than the physical. I mean, can you imagine what it's like to hit 61 home runs in a season? In New York? It's like hitting .400. . . . People don't know what Roger had to go through—he had to act the way he did to maintain his sanity. Believe me, people just don't understand.' "

Roger enjoyed his first meeting with Steinbrenner, who now lived in Tampa, the new home of his American Shipbuilding Company. At a luncheon on the Florida campus, they chatted mostly about business and employee relations. Finally, Steinbrenner made his play: "You know, you're a hard guy to get ahold of, Roger. You're hard to get to New York for just one day. Why don't you come?"

"They might shoot me," Roger said.

"I'm telling you, Roger, you won't ever hear an ovation like the one you'd get if you'd come back to Yankee Stadium."

Looking down, Maris murmured, "Maybe."

Finally, Maris considered returning to New York. All he needed was a little inducement. Maris said he would come back if Steinbrenner donated money to install lights and sod at the ball field at Oak Hall, the private school the Maris children attended. Steinbrenner became a $25,000 contributor to the school, and Roger Maris Field opened for play. Roger agreed to return for Old Timers' Day in 1978. In fact, he came earlier.

In October 1977, the Yankees beat the Dodgers in the World Series, as Jackson slammed 3 homers on consecutive pitches against three Dodgers pitchers in the decisive Game 6. It was the first Yankee world title since 1962, when the M&M Boys led the way, and Steinbrenner thought it would be appropriate if they raised the championship banner on Opening Day, April 13. Maris agreed but stipulated that Steinbrenner promise not to announce his appearance in advance. His game plan was to fly to New York, take his punishment, and hurry back to Gainesville.

On a sunny but chilly afternoon, 44,667 people were at Yankee Stadium anticipating a ceremony for the Yankees first world championship in fifteen years and free "Reggie Bars." Only Steinbrenner, Mantle, and a handful of club officials knew that there would be a special guest that day. Mel Allen, another Steinbrenner reclamation project, was the master of ceremonies. In the dugout Maris stood next to Nettles, waiting to step onto the stadium's grass for the first time since September 1966. The current number 9 asked him, "Are you nervous?" Ever the pragmatist, Roger replied, "I've got nothing to be nervous about. I don't have to face anybody. I'm not going 0-for-5 today."

The video screen in center field showed a grainy film of Roger Maris hitting his 61st home run off Tracy Stallard. As he ran around the bases, emerging from shadows into sunlight, a distinct buzz was in the stands. The Yankee faithful had seen that clip many times, but they wondered why it was played on this day. Could it be . . . ? There was a sudden collective gasp as Allen finished the introductions and two men emerged from the dugout and strode toward home plate. Mantle was immediately recognizable. The other one looked familiar, too, though he was older and heavier than when they'd last seen him. He was wearing a dark tie and open tan suit instead of pinstripes, but that crewcut was unmistakable. The people closest to home plate were the first to shout his name: "Roger! Roger!"

"The plan was for the two of them to be introduced as one, so that the Mantle fans would be cheering so loudly that any residual boos for Maris would get drowned out," recalls Marty Appel. "But there were no boos. There was an ovation and it went on and on. It was a very moving experience for all of us there."

Equally bewildered and delighted, Maris waved to the crowd and smiled, as he had briefly done after his 61st home run. Only this time, he couldn't duck into the dugout for cover. He feigned punching Mantle in the kisser, reminding everyone of their perceived feud, then warmly linked arms with his dear friend. He stood his ground and accepted the unexpected adulation from the crowd. He couldn't stop grinning. Mantle waved, too, but on this day he knew most of the cheers were for the return of the Yankees' prodigal son.

The M&M Men climbed into a golf cart and were driven past the outfield to the flagpole. There, with Mickey's arm around Roger's shoulder, they raised the championship banner. The crowd roared again. Mantle beamed, delighted that his close friend finally felt appreciated by Yankee fans.

"I was glad I was able to bring him back," says Steinbrenner. "It was an enormous upper to see that champion walk onto the field. It was a highlight of my ownership."

The current Yankees watched from the dugout, impressed by the reaction to two men who had accomplished feats that they could only imagine. "Roger was all smiles that day," recalls Roy White, who was about to begin his fourteenth season as a Yankee. "We could tell that he was very moved by the reception he got from the fans."

Jackson stole the next day's headlines by smashing a 3-run homer in the first inning—prompting the crowd to rain his candy bars down on the field—to propel the Yankees to a 4–2 victory over Chicago. He told reporters later about his kinship with Maris: "You bet I relate to . . . what he went through. I appreciate it—the press, the public, the whole pressure." After a pause, he added, "The agony of victory."

After the ceremony on the field was over, Maris and Mantle sat in the stadium's pressroom and took questions from reporters. Asked if he was surprised by the fans' reaction, Roger gave a *Bartlett's*-worthy response: "It's like obituaries—when you die, they always give you good reviews." Not wishing to sound unappreciative, he added, "I've never been in a situation where people cheered for me like that. It was nice." It was nice, too, he said, "to be home."

Maury Allen perfectly summed up Maris's memorable day: "Some seventeen years after that summer of '61, the slate seemed wiped clean. The fans had forgiven Maris for not being Mantle, for driving Ruth from his lofty heights, for not showing more public joy, for surliness under stress, for an obscene finger, for fighting back when he felt he had been abused. On this day, as it should have been in 1961, they cared only that this man had electrified baseball, performed a heroic feat, slugged more homers in one season than any man who ever lived, and did it with determination, grace and pride."

CHAPTER THIRTY-SEVEN

NUMBER 9

ROGER MARIS NEVER ADMITTED that his triumphant return to Yankee Stadium was a pivotal moment in his life, but the proof was that he hung in his office an enormous blowup of himself and Mantle raising the Yankees' championship banner. He also returned without argument to the 1978 Old-Timers' Day and again basked in the glow of an adoring crowd. When in future years he sincerely said that he no longer felt bitterness about what had happened to him in baseball, his change of heart could be traced back to that special day. Afterward he entered what those who knew him best viewed as a welcome period of peace and tranquillity, which was reflected in his buying a second house by a lake thirty miles from Gainesville and spending countless hours on a pier fishing with the equally quiet locals.

He had more leisure time because business had tripled since the Maris brothers had arrived in Gainesville, and the Maris Distributing Company, with fifty people on the payroll, was selling up to 2 million cases of beer each year. Maris was prosperous in his personal life, too. His children were either attending high school or college or finding satisfying work (including at the warehouse). He was working with his brother. His parents, though living apart, were settled, now the grandparents of twelve and great-grandparents of Susan's son. Roger and Pat were happy, seemingly healthy, and grateful as they approached their twenty-fifth wedding anniversary in 1981. Now in their forties, they enjoyed spending time at the lake house and the freedom to visit and travel with family and friends.

"The four of us did a lot of traveling," recalls George Surprise, "and Roger and I played golf around the country. It was great because wherever we went, he opened a lot of doors. When we walked into a pro shop, people would fall all over him. Even on the course, they would yell, 'Roger Maris!' "

"Pat and Roger started visiting Ken and me in California," recalls Sherry Hunt. "At the time, they had five teenagers and a married daughter with a baby going through a divorce. They stayed with Pat's brother in Newport Beach, but we always spent time together. We took them to Angels games, to visit Gene Autry and listen to his funny stories, to Palm Beach and other places they hadn't been, and to restaurants. We were always eating out. They weren't worldly but they were smart and I couldn't get over how warm and friendly they both were. Ken could not believe how relaxed Roger was and how much fun he was to be around. Roger had changed and was no longer bitter toward people."

"He wasn't angry anymore," says Bob Turley, who was, along with Hunt, Mantle, Berra, and Skowron, among the many former Yankees who played golf with Maris in the late seventies and early eighties. Golf even played a part in a commercial Maris did for Southern Bell Yellow Pages. The middle-aged Maris seemed confident in front of the cameras, pretending to inter-rupt his work at his warehouse to show viewers an ad for the Maris Distributing Company that he'd placed in the Yellow Pages. In a final scene on a golf course, Maris, who has free time because of the success of his ad, sinks a long putt. He turns to his playing partner, Mickey Mantle, and says, "Hey, Mick, I hit 61 again. Not bad, huh?" Mantle replies, "Yeah, but we only played nine holes."

Maris and Mantle also revived their Hollywood careers by appearing with Elston Howard, Whitey Ford, Hector Lopez, and many other ballplayers in *It's My Turn*, a romantic comedy that featured Michael Douglas as an ex-ballplayer and Jill Clayburgh as the object of his affections. It was released in 1980.

On December 14 of that year, Howard passed away at the age of fifty-one from a heart ailment. Maris was saddened by the early death of his friend. When a Cardinal, Roger was among those Howard asked to endorse his invention—the "donut," the circular lead weight used by hitters when warming up to make a single bat feel as heavy as several bats.

Long before the HBO movie *61**, Maris received an offer from a produc-tion company that wanted to make a two-hour, made-for-television movie about the 1961 season. Such a film might have swayed public opinion in his favor and improved his chances of being inducted into the Hall of Fame. But he was never a self-promoter and balked. "The offer was pretty good," he told Larry Guest of the *Orlando Sentinel-Star*, "but I'm not sure I'm ready for that. My life is very peaceful right now."

Maris also had no intention of using his free time to write a memoir. As he told *Sports Illustrated*'s Rick Telander, "I personally have no interest in ever doing a book. All the things that happened, it's water down the drain, right? I don't think anybody is interested in what I have to say. I just think you can go to confession without the whole world knowing it." Of Jim Bouton's revealing *Ball Four*, which infuriated many in the baseball establishment, Maris said simply, "In his book he called me the biggest loafer he'd ever seen, which was a compliment compared to what he wrote about the other guys."

Maris became a regular at Old-Timers' Day at Yankee Stadium, beginning in 1978 when he, Mantle, and DiMaggio were the starting outfielders for the home team. Johnny Blanchard said in 2008:

> I was really happy when he came back for the first Old-Timers' Day. He had really mellowed by then, and his resentment about how the Yankees had treated him was gone. He was a little fat, the way most of us were, and we kidded him about that. I said, "Hey, Roger, you really turned out to be a nice guy." He laughed like hell at that.
>
> At the 1980 game, I brought along twelve-year-old John. I introduced Roger to my son, and while I dressed, they talked for about twenty minutes. How can you talk to a twelve-year-old for twenty minutes? After Roger left, Johnny said, "Jeez, that Mr. Maris is a nice man," and I said, "Yeah, he's a really good guy." Twelve years later, my son's wife gives birth to a baby boy. At the hospital I asked him, "What did you name him—John, Bob, or Jim?" And he said, "Maris." He never forgot how Roger was so good to him that day. When we introduced the baby to Pat, the tears flowed.

Ryne Duren and Eli Grba weren't part of the festivities at Yankee Stadium, but Roger kept in touch with the two Yankees who won battles with alcoholism. Duren became the director of alcoholism rehabilitation at Stoughton Hospital in Wisconsin and did drug counseling around the country. Roger was a beer salesman yet when Duren came to Florida, Roger arranged for him to speak at schools and youth organizations about the dangers of alcohol abuse. Grba saw Maris at an Old-Timers' Game in Vancouver, where he was a pitching coach. He recalls, "For the first time in years we talked, and I took a picture of him with Hank Aaron. Later I sent it to him for his signature. He returned it with his autograph and also sent me a picture of him hitting the 61st home run. He wrote, in so many words, 'Eli, I'm so proud of you for breaking the habit of alcohol. You've always been a good friend. Best wishes, Roger Maris.' "

Maris received a number of invitations to ballparks of opponents, as well as teams he played on. In 1980, he went to an Old-Timers' Game at Dodger Stadium, where Andy Strasberg, who was working in the San Diego Padres marketing division, finally got to introduce his father to Maris, the other significant male figure in his life. "Roger and I went out to dinner with my dad, my wife, a couple of people from my office, and Pat," recalls Strasberg, "and Pat showed us a picture of Roger and her when they got married, and Roger told his version of when I caught his first National League home run. I've never forgotten that night."

In October of 1982, Roger was in a wagon being pulled by Clydesdales in a pregame ceremony at Busch Stadium. The Cardinals, managed by Whitey Herzog, returned to the World Series for the first time since 1968 to face the Milwaukee Brewers. "As he rolled by the bullpen, he called to me," recalls Maris's longtime friend Cal McLish, then Milwaukee's pitching coach.

Maris was in Washington, D.C., on July 18, 1983, to play in the annual Cracker Jack All-Star Game. The second Senators team had left for Texas in 1972, and for the first Cracker Jack game in 1982, 29,000 baseball-starved fans had come to RFK Stadium to wax nostalgic over an amazing array of American and National League old-timers. The event, which raised money for the Association of Professional Ball Players of America, garnered national attention when seventy-five-year-old Luke Appling hit a ball into the seats off Warren Spahn.

Maris was on the second-year American League roster with former Indians teammates Rocky Colavito, George Strickland, Early Wynn, Mickey Vernon, and Minnie Minoso and former Yankee teammates Bill Skowron and Bobby Shantz. Also on the team were Joe DiMaggio, Bob Feller, Billy Pierce, Bob Lemon, Camilo Pascual, Bill Dickey, Phil Rizzuto, Brooks Robinson, Harmon Killebrew, Al Kaline, Tommy Henrich, and Hank Bauer. Opponents included a Cardinals contingent: Lou Brock, Red Schoendienst, Tim McCarver, Enos Slaughter, and Stan Musial, who thrilled the crowd by employing his exaggerated crouch. Former Braves executive Dick Cecil, who was the creator and managing director of the nine Cracker Jack games, remembers Maris's participation:

> Roger supported us a great deal because the cause was for ballplayers that needed help—the old guys and minor leaguers who had no money. Roger was very active in a lot of different things, like the alumni association, and was instrumental in getting ballplayers to come. I knew more National Leaguers than American Leaguers, so he worked at convincing those guys to play. He was a real doer. And then during the game he was a real leader. I was very impressed with Roger. He was a very giving family man, a really good person. I looked at him as one of the most closely guarded secrets in baseball.

Maris was often first in line when someone called for help. When Ken Boyer lost his insurance and was unable to pay his medical bills during his fight with cancer, younger brother Clete, then a coach with Oakland, and Billy Martin, the A's manager, organized a benefit dinner, hosted by Joe Garagiola, and a golf tournament in Phoenix. Maris, Mantle, Musial, Mays, and many other players came running. The hope was that the event would raise $10,000, but $100,000 was collected.

"I got to play golf with Roger and Mickey Mantle," recalls Bob Wood, who was visiting from Fargo. "Later we were sitting in a golf cart at the Arizona Biltmore Country Club and Roger was telling me that he was going to play in Mickey's tournament. And I said, 'Why the hell don't we have a Roger Maris tournament up in Fargo?' Naturally Roger said, 'I doubt if you could get anybody to play in it.' But we didn't let go of the idea."

Roger and Pat were back in Fargo in August 1983 as spectators at the American Legion World Series and to attend the banquet at the Holiday Inn. On this nostalgic trip they socialized with friends and attended tournament games. Roger was amused when he heard a boy sitting in front of him tell his friend that Roger was buried on the field at Jack Williams Stadium. At a Legion breakfast, Jim McLaughlin and another official, Bob Smith, a high school classmate of Roger's, suggested that there be a Roger Maris Museum in Fargo. McLaughlin remembers:

> Roger was reluctant because he was very modest. He said, "People in New York still know me, but around here I doubt anybody under twenty-seven knows who I am." Finally, Roger said, "I'll agree only if there is free admission and it's located where a lot of people can see it." At that time I had an ice cream store in West Acres Mall, and the people who ran it said we could place a glass-encased display along a seventy-one-foot-long wall. The American Legion would sponsor it and put up the money to build it. Bob and I went to Gainesville early in 1984 and spent two days inventorying all the things in his house and office so we could later tell him what we hoped he'd send us. His brother had a lawyer draw up papers between the Legion and the Maris family.

Accompanying the museum's two curators was a cameraman from KTHI-TV to conduct a series of interviews with Maris about his career that would play at the museum. In his last filmed interview, Maris was open: "The game was good to me. The good eventually outweighed the bad." Reflecting on his decision to take a day off after hitting his 60th homer near the end of the 1961 season, Maris, for the first time in public, had second thoughts: "I don't know why I did it. Today I look back on it and say how stupid it was. Because for me to have ended up that season having 60 home runs compared to my hitting the 61st—the difference is too much."

Before McLaughlin and Smith returned to Fargo, Maris spoke to them about what Bob Wood had mentioned in Arizona. McLaughlin remembers, "Roger said, 'Shanley High School has talked about having a golf tournament in my name because they need money. If you know anybody who is interested, tell them that when we dedicate the museum, we also should have a golf tournament.' That's how the Roger Maris Celebrity Benefit Golf Tournament got started."

While Maris's Fargo friends formulated the logistics for a tournament, plans went full-steam ahead for a June 23 opening of the Roger Maris Museum. Maris agreed to give the museum 161 items including bats, balls, gloves, trophies, photographs, magazines, newspaper clippings dating back to his childhood, and a large portrait he treasured.

By this time, the entire Maris family was dealing with a potentially dire health crisis. Roger Maris was seriously ill.

According to Joe De Maestri, "Roger suffered from sore throats back when we were teammates on the Yankees. He always was complaining about his throat." De Maestri assumed it was smoking related. Roger gave up smoking in the midseventies, but an asthmatic condition persisted. A few years later, he found himself run-down from frequent headaches and neck pain. Finally, in the fall of 1983, the headaches were so severe that Maris went to a physician for an examination, expecting to be diagnosed with either mononucleosis or a chronic sinus infection.

However, the doctor noticed swollen lymph glands and lumps on the back of Roger's neck and under his armpits. He arranged for further tests. In November, Roger was diagnosed with malignant lymphoma, a cancer of the lymph nodes. The doctor said that Roger could have had it for as long as five years. "The lymph glands were like a horse collar around his neck," said Pat.

Lymphoma is a potentially lethal cancer, but Roger was told that he had the "good type," with an 80 percent survival rate with chemotherapy. Because he was a strong-bodied ex-athlete, he assumed he could beat the disease. So did his family and close friends who rallied around him.

"Every winter," Mike Shannon told Tony Kubek, "Roger and his boys and me and my boys would go hunting. We had some outstanding goose hunts, and Roger liked being outside in the woods. But right after Christmas, Roger called to tell me he couldn't make it."

Maris immediately began a grueling chemotherapy regimen that sapped his energy but not his spirit. "I consider myself lucky," Maris told Jerome Holtzman of the *Chicago Tribune*. "I could have had a heart attack and died. Now at least I have a chance to get well and I feel I am getting well except that I still get tired."

Roger had many brutal days when the chemo kicked in, but by the spring his cancer was in remission. He told the *Tampa Tribune*, "It's not over, but it looks like we're on our way to victory."

Despite his obsession for privacy, Maris did not hide his sickness from the public at a time when cancer was not usually openly discussed. He was surprised by the outpouring of support from fans around the country. "I received hundreds of letters," said Maris, who once dreaded opening the mail. "That was great for my spirits."

He felt well enough to go on ABC's *SportsBeat*. The host was the era's most eminent and controversial sports broadcaster, Howard Cosell, who, Roger joked, was inspired by him to create his "tell it like it is" journalistic persona. Cosell, who was the only reporter aggressive enough to call Maris's hotel room back in 1960, asked him about his health. Roger replied, "I think we've got it pretty much controlled. My last checkup, everything looked very good, so I'm encouraged." Perhaps to give Roger some cheer on the air, Cosell informed him that when he attended that year's Old-Timers' Day in July, the Yankees planned to honor Maris by retiring his number and placing a plaque in Monument Park.

When George Steinbrenner had learned of Maris's illness, he decided that the Yankees should retire Roger's number immediately, at the same time as Elston Howard's. Graig Nettles had been traded, so there was no longer an impediment to retiring number 9. "I was going to surprise Roger," Steinbrenner recalls, "but Cosell spilled the whole bucket of beans."

A startled Maris said to Cosell, "You are serious?" When Cosell confirmed it was happening, Maris's eyes became misty. Then he responded, "I think that's very nice. I would say that was probably the nicest thing that was done to me, if that is true. . . . Because it's been twenty-three years . . . and it's been hard getting any serious recognition for hitting the 61 through baseball."

Now Maris had three things to look forward to in quick succession: the opening of the museum, the golf tournament, and Old-Timers' Day. Life was good.

When the Roger Maris Museum opened in Fargo, about 1,800 people were present to view the impressive collection Bob Smith had brought back from Florida, and to meet Roger and his family. "Roger signed his cards for everybody," recalls McLaughlin. "He was very compatible, very good with people. He said how proud he was to be from Fargo and to have his museum here."

Rudy Sr. was a constant presence at his son's museum. "I got to know Rudy when I put together the museum," says McLaughlin. "Roger was very close to him, although I could detect there was some animosity between him and Pat, especially later on, but I never found out why. Rudy would be there every day. When people came by, he said, 'I'm Roger Maris's father.'"

The Oxbow golf course near Hickson was the site of the first Roger Maris golf tournament. Dick Savageau, Orv Kelly, Dick Wehage, Don Gooselaw, Bob Wood, and Wayne Blanchard had worked for months to organize it. All but Gooselaw had attended the tournament's beneficiary, Shanley High School. In fact, that first year the tournament was called the Roger Maris–Shanley Open. Accompanying it was a fish fry, with everyone sitting on boxes by wooden tables, drinking beer and eating walleyes. A modest number of "celebrities" were present: Mickey Mantle, Moose Skowron, Ken Hunt, Whitey Ford, and former Minnesota star outfielder Bob Allison, who'd befriended Roger in Raytown. John Jensen, the only Protestant of the organizers, recruited 150 other golfers. "Nobody mentioned Roger's illness," says Jensen, who continues to be an organizer. "Instead everyone just told baseball stories, including Mantle, who got a bit tipsy and used colorful language around the bishop."

"You could tell Roger was not as strong as he was before, but he still played eighteen holes," says McLaughlin. "He was very pleased by the number of people who played and looked forward to the next year."

Roger went to New York to be honored by the Yankees on July 21, 1984, coinciding with Old-Timers' Day. He was accompanied by his family and joined by a large number of his fans from Fargo, including Sid Cichy, the Maras brothers' football coach. At a party in the hotel the night before the ceremony, Maris joked around with all the other old-timers. They knew he was battling cancer, and between the laughs some couldn't help shedding a few tears. Roger assured everyone he was doing well and that it was a time for good cheer.

A picture was taken of him the next day hugging and sitting on the lap of an amused Yogi Berra (who was getting his second stint as Yankee manager under Steinbrenner). Roger was truly grinning from ear to ear in the photo but according to Pat Maris in the ESPN *SportsCentury* profile, "Roger was very nervous that day, more so than I've ever seen him. Making his acceptance speech was very hard for him."

Roger received an ovation as he was introduced. Standing at the microphone in his Yankee uniform with his arms crossed, Roger gave a brief but heartfelt speech in which he acknowledged everybody for whom he felt gratitude, including the Fargo friends who sat behind home plate: "This is a big highlight for me. I am very proud, very happy. Ellie and I were good friends, we lockered next to each other, and he was so worthy of everything. I'm really proud for him. And I'm, of course, proud for myself."

"It was great that Roger and Elston had their numbers retired on the same day because they had a special relationship," says Arlene Howard. "George Steinbrenner was very gracious. I thanked the fans for remembering Elston, and I remember that they played Frank Sinatra singing 'My Way.' "

After several tributes, Maris's number 9 and Howard's number 32 were officially retired and added to the wall in Yankee Stadium's Monument Park, following Lou Gehrig's 4 in 1939, Babe Ruth's 3 in 1948, Joe DiMaggio's 5 in 1952, Mickey Mantle's 7 in 1969, Casey Stengel's 37 in 1970, Bill Dickey's and Yogi Berra's 8 in 1972, Whitey Ford's 16 in 1974, and Thurman Munson's 15 in 1979, following his death in a plane crash. The plaques honoring the two stars were placed in front of the numbers. Roger's plaque read:

ROGER EUGENE MARIS. AGAINST ALL ODDS IN 1961 HE BE-
CAME THE ONLY PLAYER TO HIT MORE THAN 60 HOME RUNS
IN A SINGLE SEASON. IN BELATED RECOGNITION OF ONE
OF BASEBALL'S GREATEST ACHIEVEMENTS EVER, HIS 61 IN '61,
THE YANKEES SALUTE HIM AS A GREAT PLAYER AND AUTHOR
OF ONE OF THE MOST REMARKABLE CHAPTERS IN THE HIS-
TORY OF MAJOR LEAGUE BASEBALL. ERECTED BY NEW YORK
YANKEES JULY 21, 1984.

An emotional Maris was especially proud to have his number retired because it was in recognition of his entire career, not just 1961. Still the words on the plaque pleased him because his 61 homers had never received proper acknowledgment before, particularly in New York and from the Yankees. "He walked away," says Dick Savageau, "saying, 'Wonderful. *This* is what it should have been like. *This* was what I was waiting for.' "

There's always a fly in the ointment, as Sid Cichy discovered when he walked to the top level of Yankee Stadium. "There was an austere-looking, elderly gentleman in an usher's uniform," Cichy recalled. "And he said, 'Where are you from?' I said, 'Fargo.' 'Oh? What are you here for?' I said,

'Well, they are honoring Roger Maris, who is one of our boys, this afternoon.' And he just shook his head and said, 'Nobody, nobody should have broken the Babe's record.'" At that moment Cichy really understood what Maris had gone through when he dared challenge the immortal Bambino twenty-three years before.

CHAPTER THIRTY-EIGHT

THE FINAL OUT

*Blessed Are You When They Insult You and Persecute You and
Utter Every Kind of Evil Against You Because of Me. Rejoice
and Be Glad for Your Reward Is Great in Heaven.*

—QUOTE OUTSIDE ST. MARY'S CATHEDRAL,
FARGO, NORTH DAKOTA, MATTHEW 5:11–12

A FTER HE RETURNED TO Florida, Roger's health took a swift turn for
the worse. He began to lose weight. He was put on a ventilator because
he had shortness of breath, and it turned out he had a collapsed lung. Tests
revealed that the cancer was aggressively attacking his system.

For the rest of that year and into 1985 his body gave ground. Still, he
tried to do chores around the house and go to work whenever possible. In
January, Maris spoke about his struggles to Hal Bodley of *USA Today*, explaining, "When I take chemotherapy . . . I can be sitting here feeling perfectly well and it starts to hit me and I break out in a sweat. Until we get it
back in remission, I'm going to have a lot of days I don't feel good. It's something I'm going to have to handle." He added words that would bring solace
to all those who knew him: "I have peace of mind. Life has been good to
me. I can't complain. Other than a few health problems, I feel good about
things, and in the end, that's what counts."

Maury Allen visited Maris in the spring of 1985 while researching his
book *Roger Maris: A Man for All Seasons*. Allen had been getting reports on
Maris from Julie Isaacson and knew the prognosis was not good. He recalls:

Though his face was drawn, he looked pretty normal, and I told him that the treatment was going to work. I was no doctor, so what did I know? Roger was fine with my doing the book, and Pat was sweet and cooperative. I knew Pat from a week I spent with them at Grossinger's after the 1960 season, and she trusted me. Their daughter Susan worked there and was friendly, but Rudy Jr., who had an office next to Roger's, was very tight-lipped. I tried joking around with him, but unlike Roger, who had a dry sense of humor, you couldn't kid with him. There were strange dynamics in the family, a lot of tension surrounding Rudy Jr. and Rudy Sr., who was soon pushed out by the family.

Allen said that Mantle had told him that Maris's home-run record was the greatest achievement he ever saw. Roger was touched, even if he'd heard it firsthand. On cue the phone rang and it was Mantle on the other end. Like Shannon, Clete Boyer, Ken Hunt, and Julie Isaacson, Mantle called Maris with increasing frequency during his ordeal. This time he suggested a vacation together with their wives, though it was hopeful thinking.

Maris saw Mantle next in New York. On the night before Opening Day, Roger received the Lou Gehrig Pride of the Yankees Award at the team's welcome-home dinner. "The *Daily News* always participated in that," recalls the paper's award-winning sports cartoonist Bill Gallo. "I would do a drawing and present it to the recipient. That night I sat next to Roger. I really liked Roger, and my cartoons were always sympathetic toward him, including in 1961. We were talking about this and that and he said, 'Well, I'm not going to make this dinner next year because I'm dying of cancer.' He said it in the same way he might have told me the weather. I almost fell off my chair. I didn't know what the hell to say."

The next day, Maris and Mantle took part in Opening Day ceremonies. Steinbrenner had brought them together with the realization that it might not happen again. Roger Maris received his final ovation in Yankee Stadium.

He returned to Gainesville and again his health deteriorated. He wasn't well enough to travel with his family to the second Roger Maris Celebrity Benefit Golf Tournament on June 24 at Fargo's Edgewood Golf Course. But his spirits were lifted by reports that it was extraordinarily successful thanks to Moose Skowron's recruiting ability. The celebrity golfers included Allison, Berra, Blanchard, Duren, Ford, Herzog, Hunt, Killebrew, Kubek, Larsen,

Shannon, Sievers, Skowron, Slaughter, Spahn, and Terry, all paying tribute to their friend with their presence.

Other Maris friends visited him in Florida. "I saw him in Gainesville when he was sick," recalls Ned Garver, his onetime A's teammate. "He told me that he had it made. He had set it up so that his family was going to be fine. That was comforting to him. But, boy, oh boy, he talked about his dying awfully commonplace. He was at peace with it. I think that was a tribute to his faith."

"I saw Roger that July," recalls Bob Cerv. "He was at the lake house and his dad was there, too, probably taking care of the place. I spent three or four days with him. I think we got two hours' sleep the whole time because we just talked. His frame of mind was good and we had a helluva time. I'd become a metal-detector guy because I needed to walk. We walked on the sand and he put on my detector and I showed him how to do it. He found a few silver coins and said he was going to get one, but he got too sick."

Dan Osinski and his wife also visited Roger that summer. "We pulled into the distributorship and Roger was out there cooking steaks for all his drivers," Osinski remembers. "We had steaks with him, too. Roger was in a good mood. We talked about the cancer, but otherwise he hid it pretty well. I told him that my wife's mother had cancer also and was in such bad shape that she couldn't get out of bed. But we put her on a macrobiotic diet and in ten days she was up and walking around. Roger asked if I could send him the diet when I got back home. I called when I was ready to send it, but Roger was in too bad shape to talk. It was too late for anything to help him."

By his 51st birthday on September 10, Maris was extremely weak and a tragic outcome was inevitable. His body was swollen, and any activity caused him to sweat heavily. "Every few days they were removing fluid from his body," Rudy Sr. told Maury Allen. "One day they had to remove three liters. He was still taking treatments and he was sick most of the time. Roger never complained. He was feeling badly all the time the last few months, but let me tell you this: Roger never wanted to die."

"I heard him complain only one time," recalled Mike Shannon in ESPN's *Roger Maris: Reluctant Hero*. "His wife had a little desk where there was a bay window. He could look out and he could see the golf course and players coming down a fairway. . . . He was looking out and he said, 'Damn.' 'What's the matter?' He said, 'Ah, I just saw a guy coming down the fairway with his kids, his two sons playing golf. You know, I'm not going to be able to do that. I'm going to miss that.' "

Twenty-four years later, Allen says, "It's been said that it's not how you live your life that matters but how you die. To me, Roger was a great hero. He was incredibly courageous, as was his family, who dealt with what was happening as well as anyone possibly could."

Dick Savageau and his wife visited Roger in October. Savageau recalls:

Roger and I were sitting around talking and I said, "Roger, what's going to happen with your business?" And he said, "I don't know whether he is ready yet or not, but I want Roger Jr. to take it over." Roger knew his brother was very smart, but unfortunately Rudy's personality was very different. He could piss off people. Anheuser-Busch dictated how you ran your business, and Rudy would tell them to go jump in the lake. And Roger would say, "Buddy, you can't say that." Anheuser-Busch would call Roger and say, "Tell your brother that you either get with the program or we're going to have to make some moves." There were threats all the way along. Roger would say, "Hey, anytime you've got a problem, just let me know and I'll take care of it."

We stayed with them two nights. I went out to the airport with him to pick up his good friends from Independence, the Surprises. Roger picked up both their suitcases and carried them to his car. I said, "Roger, let me carry them." He said, "No, I can do it."

"Pat called us," remembers Margaret Surprise, "and said, 'Come now. It won't be long.' So we hopped on a plane and spent a week with them. They had a house on the lake and we stayed in their guest cottage."

"We got there," recalls George Surprise, "and Roger said, 'George, I gotta show you something.' He pointed at the game Pac-Man. And, oh hell, we sat down and played it right then, for a long time. He loved that game and was pretty good at it."

"Roger seemed all right," Margaret Surprise says, "but the last day I could see he was failing again. I said, 'Don't bother taking us to the airport, Roger.

Pat can take us.' And he said, 'I want to be with you as long as I can.' So Roger took us to the airport."

There were no more guests as Roger's decline continued. In November, with other treatments not working, he went to Franklin, Tennessee, to see Dr. Robert Oldham, an oncologist who specialized in biological therapy. Roger underwent an experimental treatment in which pieces of a tumor were taken out of him and injected into lab mice. After antibodies were created, they were removed from the mice and injected into Roger. Dr. Oldham explained that some of his patients had gone into remission, but typically that happened after nine months of treatment. Since Roger didn't have that long, he essentially agreed to be a guinea pig to help future lymphoma patients.

When it became clear that the treatment was not helping, Roger was admitted to the M. D. Anderson Hospital and Tumor Institute in Houston. His family traveled from Gainesville to be with him.

Word had spread within baseball circles that Maris was terminally ill. A blood drive in his name was sponsored by the San Diego Padres. "Baseball's winter meetings were held in December in San Diego," recalls Dick Williams. "They had a blood drive there at the hotel. I didn't go to the meetings but I lived in Coronado, so I went over and gave some blood, as did many people." Among the other donors was Hawk Harrelson, who had played against Maris in the 1967 World Series, and Pat Stengel, the former Patricia Blakely, who had married and remained in the San Diego area.

"I got right down to the hotel," says Pat Stengel, "and the lady there said, 'You're the first woman. We've had all of the Padres. Are you with one of the players?' And I said, 'No, Roger is a friend of the family, and he was so kind to call me when my father died.' So I'm lying on the table and there's one other person there, a few beds over. It was Dick Williams, and he asked why I was there. I said, 'Because Roger is such a good man.' "

Twenty-eight pints from the blood drive arrived in Houston. Roger had several transfusions, but nothing reversed his downward spiral. The doctors were out of ideas. He could no longer speak, and only the immediate family was allowed to visit. Yogi Berra, an Astros coach after being fired by Steinbrenner (prompting his own lengthy boycott of Yankee Stadium), drove to the hospital only to be told that Roger was too weak to see him. When Mantle called, the phone had to be held to Roger's ear.

On Saturday, December 14, at 1:45 p.m., with Patricia Ann, his wife of twenty-nine years, by his bedside, Roger Maris passed away. It was on the exact day Elston Howard had died five years before, also at the age of fifty-one.

"Roger died the way he lived—strong, private, and doing what he thought was right," Pat said soon after. "He was at peace with himself and his God."

Mantle broke down when he heard the news. He hadn't been to a funeral since the death of his father because flowers brought back that sad memory, but he would make an exception in Maris's case. "It was like losing a brother," Mantle said on *Sports Innerview with Ann Liguori* in 1989. "Roger gave me a baseball just before he passed away, and it had his picture on one side, and on the other side he wrote, 'To Mickey, the greatest of them all, your friend, Roger Maris.' That's my favorite treasure."

The funeral took place in Fargo. "There was never any question about Fargo," said Pat, when asked why Gainesville wasn't the first choice. "This is our home and these are our people. We moved away in 1957, but our hearts were always here." During a trip there the year before, Roger had bought a plot in Holy Cross Cemetery, on the north side of town.

On December 17, mourners arrived in the bitterly cold town. Maris's Fargo friends volunteered to pick them up at the airport. Don Gooselaw collected Mantle and Ford, who had flown in from Fort Lauderdale, and Skowron, who arrived from Chicago. He drove them to the Holiday Inn, where they were greeted by Pat and the six Maris children, who now ranged in age from twenty to twenty-eight. Also present were Connie and Rudy Sr., who was persona non grata in the family because, friends believed, he had bad-mouthed Pat about her being too lenient with her kids. Other mourners arrived throughout the day by plane or automobile. "It was an emotional time," recalled Richard Maris. "I've never seen so many grown men crying in my life."

On Thursday, December 19, Governor George Sinner proclaimed that all North Dakota flags be flown at half-staff in honor of Roger Maris's noon funeral. He was in attendance with three former governors of the state. St. Mary's Cathedral was overflowing. Each mourner was handed a program that had on the back a photograph of Maris hitting number 61 on October 1, 1961. "More continued to enter the century-old redbrick church, brushing the shoulders of their coats and stomping their feet to bring circulation back, having braved the snow and a temperature of 2 degrees above zero to be here," wrote Ira Berkow in the *New York Times*. "There were about 900 in the main church and another 100 or so in the basement, where they sat on folding chairs and watched the funeral mass on closed-circuit television."

The service began with Roger Jr. and Pat's brother James Carvell reading passages from the Bible. The Reverend John E. Moore delivered the homily, saying how much Fargo loved Roger and that today he had come home. Bobby Richardson delivered the eulogy, declaring that Roger was in "God's Hall of Fame," and "what I think about is Roger as a person, one that was perhaps misunderstood by the outside world, but to those who knew him best it was obvious that his dedication was to his family and to his inner circle of friends." Mantle, who sobbed into a white handkerchief, requested that Richardson someday deliver the eulogy at his funeral.

Then, speaking on behalf of his family, Roger Jr. said, "And a better person he was, for his number one priority out of life was to see that each day his family and friends received as much love and happiness as he could give them in a day's time."

"The funeral was extremely moving," recalls Andy Strasberg. "At the end of the service I paid my respects to Pat Maris. As always, she was extremely gracious and introduced me to her kids, whom I hadn't seen since the last game of the 1968 season. She said to them, 'I want to introduce you to someone very special. This is Andy Strasberg.' And Roger Jr. said, 'You're dad's number one fan.' I said, 'You'll never know how much your dad meant to me growing up.' And he said, 'You'll never know how much you meant to our dad.'"

The twelve pallbearers—Mickey Mantle, Whitey Ford, Mike Shannon, Bill Skowron, Whitey Herzog, Bob Allison, Clete Boyer, George Surprise, Julie Isaacson, Don Gooselaw, Bob Wood, and Dick Savageau—carried the casket to the hearse. The funeral procession wound its way north to Holy Cross Cemetery. According to Herzog in *Roger Maris: Reluctant Hero,* "We were carrying Roger's casket to his grave, and the wind is blowing about twenty miles an hour and it's snowing. And Mickey's behind me and [he] said, 'Roger, you son of a gun. I knew you'd get me one more time. You live in Gainesville, Florida. Why in hell isn't the funeral down there?'"

Pat Maris recalled in the same ESPN documentary, "Somebody said to me, 'Isn't it funny all these reporters are here standing out by the grave-site and it's just freezing?' And someone else said, 'Roger's probably laughing now.' "

The most visibly distraught mourner was Mantle. "Mickey was more broken up about it than the other Yankees," says broadcaster Bob Costas, who grew up as a huge Mantle fan. "He was heard to say, 'Roger was a better person than me. He was a better family man than me. If anyone went early, I should have been the guy.' "

"The funeral was beautiful, if you're Catholic," says Walt Seeba. "I suppose there was relief he'd died because he went through so much. But I never heard anyone say, 'Jesus, it's good that he died.' There was so much sadness in losing a man that young and with a nice wife and six lovely children."

Roger was laid to rest in a less-traveled area of the quiet cemetery. On Memorial Day, when the grass was green, soft, and thick and the nearby tree offered shade and beauty, Pat returned for the installation of a headstone. It was gray-black and diamond-shaped. An engraving of Roger swinging a bat had "61" above it. Below the image, Roger Maris's engraved epitaph read, "Against All Odds."

Six days after the funeral in Fargo, a memorial service was held in New York City at St. Patrick's Cathedral on Fifth Avenue, with mass celebrated by John Cardinal O'Connor. It was organized by George Steinbrenner as a way of showing how much the Yankees and the entire city appreciated Roger Maris as a ballplayer and a person. Among the very few sports figures ever given such a service at the most famous Catholic church in America was Babe Ruth.

Among the 2,500 people in attendance were former president Richard Nixon, New York mayor Ed Koch, baseball commissioner Peter Ueberroth, president of the American League Bobby Brown, former Yankee publicist Bob Fishel, and Steinbrenner. Former players included Yogi Berra, Phil Linz, Sparky Lyle, Ralph Branca, Ed Lopat, Phil Rizzuto, and, significantly, Jim Bouton.

"The church was standing room only," remembered Sandra Maris, "and there were people on the steps outside and it was incredible to think that that many people felt something special for my father."

Among the speakers was Rizzuto, who delivered "A Prayer of the Faith-

ful," and Roger Jr., who gave a talk similar to the one in Fargo. Later Howard Cosell paid tribute:

> Courage, integrity, character, and principle—the perfect equation for guts
> was Roger Maris. I remember January of 1961. Roger had been named the
> American League's Most Valuable Player. He was on the banquet circuit.
> Jamestown, New York. A blizzard. There's always a blizzard there. And Mr.
> Bill Fugazy, who's here, had chartered a plane to take us back. We were all
> tremulous, fearful about the blizzard. Except for one. Roger Maris sat care-
> fully next to the pilot and explained, "I'm sitting next to the pilot so I can
> study his every move, and if anything happens to him, I will land the plane."
> That was Roger Maris.

At the end of the service, Cardinal O'Connor asked "for one last burst of
applause to honor this man." Everyone stood and clapped, an unusual but
fitting ending to what had been a solemn occasion.

"The St. Patrick's Cathedral service moved me immensely and I was quite
emotional," says George Steinbrenner. "Roger was special to the game and
special to the Yankees, and I absolutely would have wanted him to take an
active role in the organization if he hadn't died. There was no doubt in my
mind that he could carry forward the Yankee tradition. I'll never forget him.
He was one of the people who touched my life." At the 1986 Old-Timers'
Day at Yankee Stadium, which celebrated the twenty-fifth anniversary of the
1961 championship team, Steinbrenner would arrange a special tribute to
Maris.

The loss of their youngest son was devastating to his parents. "After
Roger died, I spent a week with Pat in Gainesville," says Margaret Surprise.
"They had set up Connie in an apartment there, and I called and said,
'Grandma, I want to see you.' And Grandma Maris said, 'Well, you'll have
to come over here because I can't go into his house.' I said, 'Listen, Pat and
the children need you. I'm coming over and I'm getting you.' I went and got
her and brought her over and I said, 'This is the way Roger would want it.'
Pat and Rudy Jr.'s wife, Connie, were good to her."

Rudy Sr. wallowed in misery. His son was gone and he was estranged
from Roger's family, who didn't invite him to the St. Patrick's service or
mention his name at the banquet for the annual golf tournament. "Roger's

father was a bitter man," says Sherry Hunt. "He didn't want the tournament to continue because he thought people were making money off Roger,
and that wasn't true. He would come to the tournament and make a scene.
So that caused problems. Connie was there, too. She seemed a little dingy
to me."

CHAPTER THIRTY-NINE

THE LEGACY

IN 1991, THE BASEBALL record books still indicated that Maris's 61 hom-ers was the record for a 162-game season and Ruth's 60 homers in 1927 was the record for a 154-game season. The phantom asterisk still haunted Maris's legacy. Then Fay Vincent, baseball's eighth commissioner, read an article by Roger Angell in the *New Yorker* about the double listing. "The min-ute the issue was raised and focus was put on it," Vincent said, "I felt uncomfortable about not giving Maris his due." He chaired an eight-man committee on statistical accuracy that voted unanimously to drop Ruth's name from the Elias Sports Bureau's official record book, leaving Maris as the only single-season record holder, with 61. "We corrected a wrong done to a good man," Vincent wrote in *The Last Commissioner*.

Elias's Steve Hirdt pointed out the irony: "So thirty years after he broke the record, he broke the record."

At least it happened while Roger's father was still alive, as did Roger's in-duction into both the Ted Williams Museum's Hitters Hall of Fame—along with Cal Ripken Jr., Don Mattingly, Dwight Evans, and Enos Slaughter—and the North Dakota Sports Hall of Fame. On September 12, 1992, two days after what would have been his younger son's 58th birthday, Rudy Maris passed away from natural causes in a Fargo hospital. His obituary stated that he was eighty-one and was survived by a son, two sisters, twelve grandchildren, and five great-grandchildren.

"Rudy Sr. was cremated," says Dick Savageau. "There was no service. The undertaker of the Boulger Funeral Home called my brother and asked him, 'What should I do with these ashes? We can only keep them so long.' So he got ahold of Buddy, in Gainesville, and he came into town. Nobody knew he was here. He went to the funeral home for the ashes. When Buddy picked them up, maybe he went out to Riverside Cemetery. There's a marker in the cemetery for Rudy Sr., but I'm not sure his ashes are down there." Perhaps, as some say, Rudy's ashes were spread over railroad tracks.

In 1995, Mickey Mantle died of liver cancer. He had undergone successful treatment for alcoholism at the Betty Ford Clinic in 1994, but was soon ravaged by illness. He passed away on August 13, leaving behind a country of mourners. Of Maris, his brother-in-arms, Mickey said words for Hall of Fame voters to ponder: "Roger was as good a person and as good a ballplayer as there ever was."

Rudy Jr. continued to run the Maris Distributing Company, which did approximately $50 million a year in business and had over one hundred employees at two locations, including some of his and Roger's children. Roger Jr. had learned the business well and was an effective sales manager. But dealing with Anheuser-Busch had been increasingly difficult since 1974, when August Busch III became the head of the beer business, replacing his father, "Gussie" Busch. Auggie ran a much tighter ship without any sentiment regarding Roger's contribution to the Cardinals' 1967 championship team. In fact, he sold the baseball team in 1996, seven years after Gussie's death.

Initially, Anheuser-Busch attempted to buy out the Marises, offering $12.5 million for the distributorship, which controlled 64 percent of the market in north-central Florida and was valued at four times more. Rudy said no. On March 23, 1997, Anheuser-Busch ceased its deliveries of beer to Maris Distributing. A hand-delivered letter said it was terminating the wholesaler agreement because of "fraudulent conduct" and accused the Marises of repackaging overage beer. With regret, Roger Jr. passed out final paychecks to the shocked employees and told them to stay home until further notice. Rudy, as president of the company, stated, "Allegations of fraudulent conduct and substandard operating procedures are false and we are prepared to prove this in court." Thus began a lengthy David-and-Goliath legal battle between the world's biggest brewery and a stubborn, resilient family that refused to back down.

Roger's single-season home-run record was also in jeopardy. Mark McGwire, a 6'5", 225-pound Bunyanesque slugger with St. Louis, had smashed 52 and 58 home runs in 1996 and 1997, respectively, and in 1998 was homering at a pace well ahead of Maris's in 1961. Moreover, Sammy

Sosa of the Chicago Cubs was ahead of the pace (as was Seattle's Ken Griffey Jr. for a time).

Maris received a great deal of media attention as McGwire and Sosa put on a thrilling back-and-forth home-run race that recalled the one between Maris and Mantle. A major difference was that it was easier for the two participants because the Cardinals and the Cubs limited press access to them, staging only brief press conferences after games. It was also easier because the media didn't manufacture a false feud between the friendly competitors. McGwire, who was much less gregarious than Sosa, became looser with the press as he approached Maris's record.

In late August, a minor controversy erupted when a reporter gazed into McGwire's open locker and spotted androstenedione, a muscle-building hormone that elevates a body's testosterone levels. Equivalent to a steroid, it was banned in other sports. McGwire shrugged it off, saying it was an over-the-counter drug that allowed him to train harder and recover quickly from injuries. McGwire was given a pass despite him and Sosa being a whole lot bigger than they'd been in the recent past. Thus any balls they hit solidly now flew much longer distances. No one wanted to rain on their parade because the fans loved the homers and were coming back to the game after the strike of 1994–1995.

The Maris family became friendly with both players, particularly McGwire, who spoke of Roger and his record with sincere reverence and included the family in the whole experience. "My family doesn't want to see Dad's record broken," stated Roger Jr. "Dad was proud of that record. We definitely want him to keep it. That doesn't mean we'd have ill feeling toward anyone."

Roger Maris's 61-homer record was broken on September 8 in the Cardinals' 145th game when McGwire hit his 62nd barely over the left-field fence at Busch Stadium against the Chicago Cubs. Among those from Roger's days in St. Louis who were on hand to witness the historic blast were Stan Musial, Lou Brock, Red Schoendienst, and Tim McCarver. McCarver, an award-winning baseball analyst since retiring as a player in 1980, was in the Fox broadcast booth with play-by-play man Joe Buck. In *The Perfect Season*, McCarver wrote, "Most of all I was thinking about how receptive the entire Maris family had been to McGwire and Sammy Sosa throughout the season, although it became increasingly clear that their dad would lose the record that kept his name alive. They had not even a trace of spitefulness. That's how Roger would have reacted. . . . He too would have rooted for McGwire to pass him by."

Seated near the Cardinals' dugout were the Maris children, who had followed McGwire as he closed in on the record. Because of exhaustion and the tension surrounding her husband's imperiled record, Pat, the glue to the family, was hospitalized with heart palpitations and stayed away from the ballpark. McGwire, who earlier in the day had gripped the bat Roger used on October 1, 1961—"I touched it, I put it to my heart," he said tearfully—crossed the plate and hugged his batboy son; hugged Sosa, who ran in from right field to congratulate him; blew kisses to the fans; then hopped the railing and went into the stands to hug and whisper to the Maris kids. It was, as Bernie Miklasz of the *St. Louis Post-Dispatch* stated, "McGwire's finest hour."

McGwire ended up with 70 homers in 1998 to establish the new single-season home-run record, and Sosa hit 66 to also pass Maris. Roger Maris remained the American League home-run king.

Like the citizens of Fargo, the Maris family was dejected but moved on. A highlight of 1999 was the U.S. Postal Service issuing a postage stamp of Roger hitting his 61st home run. For the sixteenth consecutive year, the Marises hosted the annual Roger Maris golf tournament, with proceeds going to Shanley High, the Hospice of Red River Valley, and the Roger Maris Cancer Center, which had opened its doors in 1990 as part of St. Luke's Hospital MeritCare in Fargo.

In 1999, the family, which has always spoken with one voice, also made a major move in its dispute with Anheuser-Busch. It sued the beer giant for $49 million in federal court for anticompetitive behavior. In November 2000, a court ruled against the Marises. The following March, the family filed an eight-count lawsuit to the tune of $2.5 billion for breach of contract. In July 2001, a judge threw out four of the eight counts but stated they could still seek $300 million in compensatory damages for the remaining counts. The following month, a jury agreed with the Marises and awarded them $50 million. Unsatisfied, the family filed a $1 billion defamation lawsuit.

The story of Roger Maris's 1961 season came back into national consciousness when entertainer Billy Crystal, a lifelong Yankee and Mickey

Mantle fan, directed *61**, forty years after it happened. Along with baseball scenes, it showed the tremendous pressures Maris endured from a vindictive press and the angry fans of Ruth and Mantle, as well as the strong friendship between Maris and Mantle. Broadcast on HBO in 2001, it was extremely well received. Even those who quibbled about the film's content and language marveled at the spot-on performances by Canadian actor Barry Pepper as Maris and Thomas Jane as Mantle. Pepper, who caught Crystal's eye in Steven Spielberg's *Saving Private Ryan*, recalls:

I knew very little about Maris before Billy sent me the screenplay. Then I researched him and was fascinated by this small-town gentleman and family man who was overwhelmed by the New York press. Being from a small town in Canada and making my living in Los Angeles, I understood his sensibilities.

I spent a lot of time learning how to hit left-handed and emulate his run and the stance. We only had the footage to go on, and we were just trying to perfect these very famous moments. I cut my hair like his right away because the look is really important for me to know how to bring a character to life.

Billy and I were passionate about showing the many faces of Roger Maris. The press was used to more gregarious personalities, and he wasn't willing to mold himself to please it or the public. Ever. I admired that side of him, but I thought it was essential to show him holding, kissing, and playing with his children and the sensitivity in his relationship with Pat. And we also needed to show the heartbreak he felt because he was misunderstood and called awful names without retaliating. He just sucked it up and carried on. But it hurt him far deeper than anyone could ever imagine.

Andy Strasberg was a consultant to Crystal on the film, along with Marty Appel and Julie Isaacson. "When it was done, we brought a rough cut to Gainesville," Strasberg remembers. "I did not sleep because I was so nervous. So we go in, and there had to be fifteen Marises there. I worried that if Roger wasn't portrayed as they saw him, it would break our trust. The movie ended and Roger's mother stood up and said, 'They got it right! This movie tells the story about the person as well as the player!' " Crystal was thrilled when Connie called to tell him, "You got it right—how did you know it so well?"

Roger Maris Jr. said the family "gave it a thumbs-up" because it "shows the human side. Throughout the whole movie, you are fighting back tears." Pat, who was played by the director's daughter Jennifer Crystal, said it was "eerie" seeing an actor who resembled Maris portray her husband, "especially since he really did a good job." Pat and Roger Jr. watched the movie again at the White House with President Bush.

The film apparently did not impress the Veterans Committee, which refused to give Maris the necessary 75 percent of their vote for Hall of Fame induction. Those on the committee who thought Maris deserved consideration were reminded by anti-Maris writers that the Hall's guidelines stipulated that nobody should be voted in who had one great moment or season and an otherwise average career. By "nobody," they meant Maris. That summation of Maris's career was incorrect, but if that tactic didn't work, the writers put pressure on voters or made deals with them regarding other nominees so as to sabotage Maris's election. "I do remember some of the writers, one in particular," says Veterans Committee member Yogi Berra, "who were fairly firm on Roger not being included in the Hall of Fame."

The real culprits were the writers of the 1960s who created a false image of Roger Maris as a player and person and the myopic BBWAA writers, including some from the sixties batch, who believed that reputation and steadfastly rejected him from 1974 to 1988. At his lowest point, in 1982, Maris's name appeared on only 16.6 percent of the ballots with a total of 69 votes; and even after his death, he received only 41.6 percent, 42.6 percent, and 43.1 percent of the vote in his final three years of eligibility. He received more than twice the number of votes in those years than in his first year of eligibility, but it wasn't nearly enough.

Hank Greenberg, who passed away in 1986, grew tired of people saying that Maris didn't deserve to be in the Hall of Fame because hitting 61 home runs was all he ever did. Greenberg's incredulous response was "*All* he ever did?" It was like saying that all Jonas Salk did was develop a polio vaccine, or all Columbus did was discover America. Or all John Glenn did in 1962 was orbit the earth more than any other American in history—that event and its lasting impact on space flight was enough to get him into the Astronauts Hall of Fame in 1990.

Roger Maris's circling the bases more than anyone else in history a little more than four months earlier was the baseball equivalent of Glenn's extraordinary feat, and it has certainly had comparable impact. It would have been enough to earn him entry into many Halls of Fame. But, granted, entry to Baseball's Hall of Fame, to be included among the sport's pantheon of players, demands more. To be worthy of Cooperstown, Maris needed impressive credentials in addition to his greatest achievement.

As Greenberg knew, Maris did much more than hit 61 homers, including winning two MVP awards, being an All-Star, improving almost every team he joined, leading his teams to seven pennants, and being on three World Series champions. The bitter writers of his time didn't recognize Maris's accomplishments or tried to downgrade them. When writers vote that a batter who hits 33 homers and has 100 RBIs is the Flop of the Year, is it the writers or the player who isn't up to standards? The writers didn't sufficiently appreciate what he did on the field because he alienated the press in the clubhouse.

"I never thought a guy's personality should impact on his standing in the game," Maury Allen says today, "but it certainly has in Roger's case. I have always felt Roger Maris was the least appreciated superstar in baseball history. I always argue that he deserves to be in the Hall of Fame."

Hall of Fame voters pointed out that he had only three 30-homer, 100-RBI seasons in New York, but they ignored that his numbers were similar to those of Mickey Mantle in his prime between 1960 and 1964, all championship years; and that from 1957 to 1964, he was the most productive left-handed batter in the American League.

Spiteful New York writers harped on his never hitting .300, but *St. Louis Post-Dispatch* writer Bob Broeg (who always voted for Maris's induction) set the record straight in 1967 by pointing to stats that were never in New York papers:

Although his career batting average for 10 seasons is only .260, the figure is as deceptive as an iceberg, seven-eighths of which doesn't show. Rog is pretty cool himself, especially in the clutch. He muscled up with men on base, especially in late-inning situations. His batting averages there for the last two innings of games, the tying or winning run on base, was .411 in 1961, .375 in 1962, .440 in 1963 and .426 in 1964. Even after he'd suffered the miseries that dipped his season average to .239 and .233 in the last two fragmentary years in New York, Maris batted .333 in the clutch in 1965 and .283 in 1966.

Some influential New York writers unfairly presented Maris as a slugger who most years didn't hit enough home runs. To them and the fans who read them, Maris was a failure as a home-run hitter, and it didn't matter that he did everything else sensationally. As the St. Louis writers quickly realized, Maris was not a slugger at all. He was instead a truly great all-around player who had many superb seasons, regardless of how many homers he hit. In his injury-free seasons, including 1961, he got loft and had a high number of homers.

Maris's contributions weren't always apparent, his numbers weren't always properly interpreted, and he was rarely given due appreciation by the press. But to almost everyone who played with him or against him or managed him—even after his 61-homer season—Roger Maris was a *great* player, a true star. No matter that he played only twelve years and had only 275 homers, as his critics point out. He was a winner. Those who wrote the Hall of Fame's induction rules wouldn't have agreed to only ten years for eligibility if lofty lifetime numbers accumulated over twenty seasons were absolutely necessary for entry. Lifetime stats were always meant to be secondary to greatness and achievement.

However, to later Hall of Fame voters, numbers have always trumped greatness. Hank Aaron, a pretty good judge of baseball talent, said, "What irritates me is the suggestion that Roger was just a fluke who had one good hitting year. Let me tell you, I played against him. He was one of the best all-around outfielders I have ever seen." Unfortunately, the majority of voting writers never took into consideration the glowing praise of Maris from the people who knew best.

In 2004, Maris received more Hall of Fame support because his achievement in 1961 was appreciated as never before. Widespread steroid use in baseball since the late eighties had become a hot-button issue, threatening to leave a black mark on the sport. The chief villain in everyone's eyes was Barry Bonds, whose body and even his head got suspiciously bigger by the time he claimed the single-season home-run record from Mark McGwire in 2001, with 73, and later surpassed Aaron's 755-homer career mark. The retired McGwire and Sammy Sosa were among several big-name ballplayers who testified under oath before a congressional subcommittee about steroids. When asked if they ever took performance enhancers, the two squirmed in their seats and evaded giving straight answers. McGwire repeatedly refused to talk about the past. Their cringe-inducing performances on national television convinced the great majority of viewers that they used performance-enhancing drugs when they broke Maris's single-season home-run record. (In 2010, McGwire confessed to using steroids in 1998.)

The Maris family wasn't happy about McGwire's disgrace because they genuinely liked him—he continues to make an annual $6,200 donation to their charities—but said that Roger Maris should again be declared the single-season home-run champion. "We feel baseball is going to do the right thing in the end," Richard Maris said. "They're going to do their investigation, and they're going to make a correction."

In a *New York Times* article titled "Maris Did Not Need Performance Enhanced," by Selena Roberts, she contended, "Given the current rage over 'roids, what Maris accomplished is even more amazing in 2004 than it was three decades ago." (In 2009, Roberts forced Yankees superstar Alex Rodriguez—who was on pace to break Bonds's career homer record—to admit to three seasons of steroid use by publishing a book about him in which she documented the evidence.)

Not surprisingly, a large contingent of baseball fans want Maris to be given back the title of single-season home-run champion. Some call him "the Natural Home Run King."

In late September 2004, Connie Maris passed away at the age of ninety. She died in Gainesville, but like Roger had her funeral in Fargo. Although she and Rudy had separated in life, they would have a joint marker in Fargo's Riverside Cemetery. Unlike Rudy, who visited his aunts Tilly and Anna in Minnesota after Roger's passing, Connie died without trying to reconnect to the Marases and ending the decades-long feud. Mysteriously, Pat and her children wouldn't extend an olive branch to the Marases either, and continued to avoid contact with them.

The legal wrangling between the Maris family and Anheuser-Busch finally ended in August 2005, on extremely favorable terms for the family. Anheuser-Busch agreed to pay the Marises $120 million in cash—the Maris lawyers said the actual settlement was for a much higher sum. According to the *St. Louis Business Journal*, the huge company's profits plunged 24 percent in the third quarter of that year as a result. The Maris Distributing Company continued to operate in Gainesville as a wholesaler of beer and ale with

Rudy Maras as president. In 2009, the streamlined company had estimated annual sales of $2.3 million.

In 2008, Pat, who decided to sell her big house in Gainesville, donated her husband's two MVP trophies to the Roger Maris Museum, assuring Fargo's top tourist destination of even more traffic in upcoming years. According to Jim McLaughlin, now curator emeritus, "People come from all over the country to see the museum. At the dedication, Roger gave me one hundred signed cards and said, 'You give them to people that know who I am and appreciate what the museum is all about.' There have been a number of instances when I've given a card to someone who came a long way because they were real Roger Maris fans, and they've cried on the spot."

The donation of the MVP trophies was made in conjunction with the 25th anniversary of the Roger Maris Celebrity Benefit Golf Tournament. The tournament was going stronger than ever. "The tournament is a celebration of friendship," said Randy Maris. Among the golfers that year were Barry Pepper, Roy Sievers, Whitey Herzog, Rich Rollins, Bernie Allen, and two ex-Yankees, Tom Tresh and Johnny Blanchard, who passed away unexpectedly within a few months after the event. Andy Strasberg had become a fixture at the tournaments. He and Randy became close friends, and when Randy's wife, Fran, gave birth to a boy in 1990, they named him Andrew and asked Strasberg to be his godfather. "So the grandson of my childhood idol is my godson and my namesake," he says.

At Andrew's christening, Strasberg vowed to take him to Yankee Stadium when he turned thirteen, and on August 6, 2003, he fulfilled his promise. With a baseball glove on his left hand and accompanied by his parents, his other grandfather, and his godfather, Andrew was taken on a tour of the storied ballpark where Roger Maris made history. Their guide was Tony Morante, who began working for the Yankees as an usher in 1958. Andrew was shown Monument Park with his grandfather's "Against All Odds" plaque. He saw his grandfather's retired jersey and one of his bats on the Stadium Club wall. He sat in Roger's locker, which had also been occupied by Thurman Munson. Afterward, Andrew met Sal Durante, and everyone watched the Yankees play the Texas Rangers.

An emotional Randy said, "This is like a circle. Andrew never got to meet my father, but after today it was like he was there with us. I feel Andrew knows him that much better. Dad would be so proud." Asked his favorite Yankee, Andrew said, "My grandpa."

Andrew became a good high school ballplayer at St. Francis Catholic High School, coached by his father. Among their opponents was powerful Oak Hall School, which had a left-handed hitter named Richie Maris and was coached by his father, Kevin Maris. When the teams played for the first time in 2007, in front of Pat and other members of the family, it was on Roger Maris Field.

The unbroken circle Randy Maris spoke about expanded further in 2008 when he had another extraordinarily emotional visit to Yankee Stadium. It came on Sunday, September 21, prior to the Yankees' home finale against Baltimore that evening. This game, won by the Yankees, 7-3, before 54,610 fans, was the last one ever played in the original Yankee Stadium. The house that Babe Ruth and others built in 1923 was going to be replaced by a massive new stadium next to it and eventually torn down. Nostalgic fans arrived twelve hours before the game to tour the field and touch the plaques in Monument Park.

To celebrate eighty-five years and 26 world championships, over 700 Yankee alumni were invited to the special pre-game ceremony. Those who couldn't attend were paid tribute on DiamondVision. Also invited were widows and children of Bronx Bombers who had passed away. Throwing out the ceremonial first pitch was Julia Ruth Stevens, the ninety-two-year-old daughter of the Babe, the first player to hit a Stadium homer on April 18, 1923. (Yankee back-up catcher Jose Molina would be the last.)

Former players and representative family members were introduced, and while the large crowd stood and applauded, they went to the nine positions on the field. Elston Howard's daughter Cheryl and Thurman Munson's son Michael stood at home plate with a tearful Yogi Berra, who would throw out the first pitch in April at the new stadium. Moose Skowron, Chris Chambliss, and Tino Martinez stood at first base. Billy Martin Jr. stood at second with Bobby Richardson and Willie Randolph, who slid into the base one last time. Phil Rizzuto's widow, Cora, was escorted by current Yankees reliever Mariano Rivera (who would record the final out at the stadium) to the shortstop position, where she joined Gene Michael, the ex-shortstop who was the architect of the Yankee dynasty that began in the mid-1990s. Third basemen Graig Nettles, Wade Boggs, and Scott Brosius completed the in-field. On the mound, Catfish Hunter's widow, Helen, was surrounded by Whitey Ford, Don Larsen, Goose Gossage, Ron Guidry, David Wells, and David Cone.

Roy White and Dave Winfield walked out to left field. Mickey Mantle's son David and Bobby Murcer's widow, Kay, and their two children shared the center-field spot with Bernie Williams.

Reggie Jackson was with the son of one of his idols. Wearing the pin-stripes with the number 9 on the back and clearly enjoying the cheers that made his father feel at home beginning in 1978, Randy Maris stood in right field, waving and smiling. Perhaps he exchanged glances with David Mantle in center field, just as their fathers did when they played beside each other and they were the storied M&M Boys.

Surely some of the older fans who saw Randy in right field were trans-ported back to that golden October day in 1961, when his marvelously gifted father, Roger Maris, a twenty-seven-year-old reluctant hero with a sweet and powerful swing, ran out of the darkness and into the light.

POSTSCRIPT

W E CAN TESTIFY THAT it's the plight of biographers to never stop researching their subjects, even after our books are published. Think Sisyphus and his rock. The hardcover of this biography was shipped to bookstores in March 2010, coinciding with the fiftieth anniversary of Roger Maris first playing for the Yankees and the twenty-fifth anniversary year of his death. Yet we continued to gather new items that added to the story we'd told. We knew we'd pass along a few in this paperback, which is being released in the fiftieth anniversary year of Maris breaking Babe Ruth's single-season home-run record.

In the hardcover, we wrote about Maris's love affair with Kansas City, both the town and the team, and his disappointment when he learned he was going to New York for the 1960 season. Still, we didn't know exactly how much he wanted to stay, until we were alerted to a photograph that was taken at an autograph event in Kansas City a few weeks prior to his going to Florida for his first spring training with the Yankees. He had been traded and was property of the Yankees, yet in the photo he's still wearing an Athletics jacket.

His bond with the A's fans was so strong that when he was a Yankee and being booed at Yankee Stadium, he was appreciative that he was still welcome back home. However, we discovered in Larry Moffi's 1996 book, *This Side of Cooperstown*, that while Maris didn't want to play so far away from his family, he anticipated an affable relationship with fans in the Bronx. George Vecsey had told us that when Maris was an A in 1958 and '59, he'd come to Yankee Stadium and the fans in right field good-naturedly chanted "cha-cha" because of how he'd move his feet while anticipating making a play. Moffi remembers that in the bottom of the third inning of a game at the stadium in July 1959, the fans in right "sang out in unison, 'Ma-ris, cha, cha cha.'

And Maris, his back to the stands, punched out the beat in the air with his glove. . . . By the middle innings, Maris had assumed the role of conductor, leading the right field chorus in an up-tempo hymn to himself. In the top half of the seventh inning, Maris doubled off the bullpen fence in right, and the entire right-field choir, probably two or three hundred strong by now, rose up and cheered wildly like some precursor of the dreaded 'wave.' When Kansas City took the field in the bottom of the inning, the chorus reached a magnificent crescendo as Maris took his position. He grinned, doffed his cap, and in one grand and elegant gesture he bowed to us all."

As a Yankee, Maris spent a lot of time at the stadium signing autographs, but this was a playful side of him toward fans that never came across once he donned pinstripes, even in early 1960 when he was only cheered.

Conversely, fans at Yankee Stadium and every other park were familiar with the image of Roger trying to escape one of his annual batting slumps. Perhaps there has never been a player whose fortunes at the plate changed so quickly because of imperceptible changes to his swing. A passage about Maris that we came across in Gil Hodges's 1969 book, *The Game of Baseball*, reminded us of one way he battled to keep a repetitive swing: "To make sure that he didn't get into the habit of overstriding, which can be very bad for a hitter, Maris used to smooth out the dirt in the batter's box after each pitch. When the ball was delivered, Maris would stride. Then he would check the spike marks in the dirt to see if he was striding too far. After checking, he'd smooth out the dirt again before the next pitch." Maris claimed he was a swing-at-anything-within-reach hitter, but in truth he was so serious about hitting theory and mechanics that Clete Boyer wanted him to be his batting instructor if he ever became a manager.

Three stories relating to Maris didn't require us to dig into the past. In fact, they made headlines in 2010. One was about Maris and Jim Gentile, Baltimore's powerful first baseman in 1961. When Maris slugged his 61st home run to break Ruth's record on the last day of the season, he also upped his RBI total to a league-leading 142, one more than Gentile, who achieved his high total in only 486 at-bats (getting 20 of those RBIs on just five swings). We pointed out in our book that some statisticians have insisted for years that Maris and Gentile actually both had 141 RBIs because Maris was incorrectly credited with one RBI when a runner scored on an error. This mistake was pointed out in 1995 by researcher Ron Rakowski, but it took another fifteen years before MLB's official record book made the simple change. We appreciated that the Orioles honored the 76-year-old Gentile at Camden Yards for his belated RBI title and gave him the contractual bonus he should have received in '61.

However, we objected to misleading headlines in *USA Today* and elsewhere that proclaimed "Maris Loses RBI Title" and accompanying articles that purported Maris would have been distressed if he lost the title he got unfairly. As has long been the case, the media slighted Maris's accomplishment and made him sound petty. The truth was that Maris didn't lose the 1961 RBI title, but now shared it. He wouldn't have celebrated the record books reducing Mickey Mantle's runs-scored total in 1961 to 131, making Maris the lone titlist with 132 runs; and he would have been just fine sharing the RBI title with his friend Gentile. Roger was delighted when he thought he won the 1961 RBI crown outright, but when he chose to sit out a game late in the season he did so knowing he might not have enough at-bats left to break Ruth's home-run record *or* beat out Gentile and the Tigers' Rocky Colavito (who finished with 140) in the RBI race.

In New York, a major story during the 2010 season was Alex Rodriguez's countdown to 600 career home runs, which the Yankees' 35-year-old third baseman achieved on August 4. Throughout the year, the Yankee organization worked closely and cleverly with Rodriguez to transform his image from egocentric, steroid-taking villain to hero/great teammate/great guy/humanitarian so that someday, he hopes, he'll become the first admitted steroid user elected to the Hall of Fame. (Meanwhile, they distanced themselves from *former* Yankee pitching hero Roger Clemens when he was indicted on perjury charges for testifying before Congress that he hadn't taken HGH or steroids.)

Ignoring Rodriguez's reluctant admission in 2009 that he slammed 156 homers while taking steroids as a Texas Ranger from 2001 to 2003, the Yankees promoted and then celebrated the 444th homer that he contends (and others dispute) he hit while steroid-free. They also fulfilled their part of his contract by awarding him $6 million for this "milestone" homer. If he maintains his pace, he will pick up another $24 million as he passes Willie Mays (660), Babe Ruth (714), Hank Aaron (755), and Barry Bonds (762) and becomes the all-time career home-run leader. And there will be much celebration. That the Yankees are championing Rodriguez, paying him obscene bonuses, and legitimizing his home-run total—while making a mint selling his jerseys and other merchandise—makes their mistreatment of Maris in 1961 seem even more shameful. There is, of course, new ownership, but this is the same organization that wouldn't even promote Maris in the final eight games of the season (official games 155 to 163) despite his closing in on Ruth's record; and, as he'd always lament, gave him "absolutely nothing" for becoming the new homer champion.

The biggest story in 2010 involving Maris made national headlines and not only in sports sections. On January 11, when Mark McGwire made his long-overdue admission to steroid use during his career, including in 1998 when he broke Roger Maris's single-season home-run record, our hardcover book was at the printer. We had time and space enough only to insert a mention of McGwire's act, but we weren't able to expound on what it meant to Maris's legacy until interviewers brought up the subject when we were publicizing the book's release in the early spring. Our response was that McGwire's teary-eyed confession came across as disingenuous, motivated less by a crisis of conscience than a desire to repair his image so that he could make a smooth return to baseball as the new hitting coach of the St. Louis Cardinals.

We pointed out that McGwire was still in denial because, incredibly, he didn't express sorrow for taking steroids, just for not admitting he took them. He insisted that he used them only to help him overcome career-threatening injuries, not to make Big Mac into Bigger Mac or give him herculean strength. Indeed, he maintained he was able to hit balls into the stratosphere on checked swings and accumulate 9 more homers in '98 than Maris did in '61 because of the ability God gave him. Steroids and God provided him with a lethal one-two punch. McGwire inadvertently made a solid case for steroids being positive performance *enablers* that allow injured athletes to get back on the field rather than performance *enhancers* that provide struggling athletes with the unfair opportunity to become national heroes. It was ironic that he suddenly sounded like admitted-steroid-user Jose Canseco, the former A's teammate he now bashes.

Earlier in a day that culminated with a television interview with Bob Costas, McGwire had called the Maris family and reported back that Pat Maris was "hurt and disappointed." But it's doubtful that he apologized to her for anything other than having never before admitted to steroid use, because he had talked himself into believing that his record was legitimate. Later, Maris's sons, recognizing steroids are enhancers, reiterated their assertion that their father's 61 homers should be reinstated as the major league record, but at the same time they praised McGwire for confessing and emphasized that he was still like a "brother to us."

They didn't seem to comprehend that McGwire was directly responsible for the damage that had been done to their father's legacy. At the same time he was winning them over with his kindness, he was secretly taking steroids as he attempted to replace their father in the record books. Spiteful reporters had ruined Maris's reputation but they could do nothing about the 61 home runs in the record book that kept Maris's name alive and made the curious investigate who he was. But McGwire took care of that. We told our interviewers that Maris deserved to have his baseball identity restored.

We also told them that once the 2010 baseball season began we expected a sideshow atmosphere as McGwire visited National League ballparks with the Cardinals. But instead of fans subjecting him to boos and insults, they treated him with decided indifference. Perhaps they were still grateful for his thrilling home-run race with Sammy Sosa in 1998—a throwback to the Maris-Mantle race in 1961—that made them forget the baseball strike of 1994–1995. So while the majority of baseball fans and the media expressed an off-with-their-heads attitude toward Bonds, Sosa, and Clemens, McGwire got off easy. He was punished only in one way: Mark McGwire Highway, a stretch of I-70 by Busch Stadium in Missouri, reverted back to its old name, Mark Twain Highway. It had been dedicated in 1999, a year after McGwire dethroned Maris as the single-season home-run king. No one is questioning the credentials of the renowned author from Hannibal, Mo., but wouldn't justice be better served if Maris, who finished his career in St. Louis, replaced the scandalized McGwire on the highway signs just as McGwire replaced him in the record books after pilfering his crown?

When the interviewers asked us if we thought McGwire's admission improved Maris's chances of being inducted into the Hall of Fame, we weighed our answer while wondering if we were being baited. The late Maury Allen warned us that interviewers could be cordial *until* the Hall of Fame question came up and then reveal their anti-Maris bias. He recalled that when he published *Roger Maris: A Man for All Seasons* in 1986, months after Maris's death, television and radio hosts were hospitable as he told them about Maris's career. But he was met with hostility and incredulous looks when he advanced the notion—our notion, too—that Maris would be in the Hall of Fame if not for vindictive reporters tarnishing his achievements and name. He singled out Bryant Gumbel, then the host of *Today*, who insisted Maris's lifetime stats didn't warrant induction. But Gumbel was not alone.

Because of Allen's uncomfortable experience, we prepared to debate unreceptive television, radio, newspaper, and online interviewers on the Hall of Fame issue. That included answering the question about whether McGwire's admission should change the minds of those who don't think Maris is qualified for Cooperstown. We said with regret that we didn't believe that if MLB did the impossible and reinstated Maris as the single-season home-run champion that would guarantee him entry into Cooperstown because that hadn't been enough for the BBWAA voters between 1974 and 1988, his years of eligibility. Moreover, if *being* the homer king again would be enough to qualify Maris for induction in the voters' eyes, then that would imply that he should be disqualified if someone legitimately hits 62 home runs. It was his *becoming* the home-run king in 1961, as the only person who ever could supplant Babe Ruth, that is a more convincing credential for Hall of Fame selection. So is his holding the record for 37 years (three years more than Ruth) even before McGwire came along and another 13 years and counting if they quite properly erase McGwire, Sosa, and Bonds from the record books.

McGwire's admission, we pointed out, reinforces how great an achievement was Maris's 61 home runs. Hank Greenberg contended that was enough to get Maris into Cooperstown, and, as we've written, similar major-impact achievements (such as winning Olympic gold medals) get athletes into many sports' Hall of Fames even if they accomplished little else. We told our interviewers that it is baffling how Maris's detractors regard his 61-homer season as nothing more than just one of his "too few great seasons."

Of course, in our Hall of Fame argument we listed many of Maris's credentials that we emphasized in our book, including his back-to-back American League MVPs; seven All-Star game appearances; power stats in his seven years as a Yankee that matched Mantle's; power stats that were the best of any left-handed hitter in the American League during his years in the junior circuit; and playing in seven World Series and winning three world titles in his final nine years, the most for any player of that time. As for Maris's lifetime stats, we reminded our interviewers that those who founded the Hall of Fame asked for only ten years of impressive stats and accomplishments to qualify and he certainly had that—and, significantly, he hit more lifetime homers than Hall of Famer Hack Wilson, the National League's premiere slugger in his day. As for Maris having only three seasons with 100 RBIs, we pointed out that he did that in twelve seasons while Mantle had only four 100 RBI seasons in eighteen years. Hall of Famer Roberto Clemente was a sensational hitter who won four batting titles, but he had only two 100-RBI seasons (and, like Maris, two seasons with more than 100 runs scored). And Hall of Famer Al Kaline, Maris's chief rival as the American League's top right fielder in the sixties, accumulated 3,007 hits but had only three 100-RBI seasons (and two 100-run seasons) in 22 years and none in his final 11. Kaline won many Gold Gloves over Maris (who only received one), but Ernie Harwell, who broadcast much of Kaline's career and shared the booth with him after his retirement, told us that he considered the two equals in the field and at bat.

Harwell passed away in 2010, as well as others we interviewed for the hardcover, among them George Steinbrenner, Ralph Houk, George Strickland, Maury Allen, Ryne Duren, and Bobby Bragan. They each hoped Maris would be inducted into the Hall of Fame someday. (We told them that it's unfortunate that the voting writers have stubbornly ignored all endorsements of Maris by baseball people.) They agreed with us that not all Maris's "stats" appeared in the record book. Two examples: there is no official stat for *never making a mistake* and there is no official stat for coming to two third-place clubs—the Yankees in 1960 and Cardinals in 1967—and leading them to titles. And they agreed with us that Maris's detractors have cherry-picked numbers to obfuscate his achievements, his character, and, most of all, the *greatness* that we all saw through his entire career, including years when his smaller numbers didn't tell the real story.

After we advanced our argument on behalf of Maris's Hall of Fame selection, we waited for the interviewers to launch a swift counterattack. Instead, time and again, the interviews agreed with us! We were startled by their benevolence and for a time believed that the winds had changed and everyone was ready to see Maris for who he was as a player and person and call on the Hall of Fame voters to do the right thing—particularly since the rules for the Veterans Committee have been changed, making it more favorable to bypassed individuals. We were mistaken. It soon dawned on us that we were being invited only on those TV and radio shows with producers and hosts that were already Maris advocates. And the same was true for the reporters who requested interviews with us. Apparently, the people who were turning us down, including in New York, didn't want to read a book about Maris or discuss him. Their minds were made up and to them Maris was the individual whose stats—yes, those numbers again—made him the prime example of a player who wasn't worthy of induction.

From the feedback we have received, we believe that the hardcover delivered our message clearly and the number of fans who think Maris should be in the Hall of Fame has increased. New optimism lies with 2010 inductee Whitey Herzog, who, interestingly, was selected to Cooperstown because of his *greatness* as a manager and not because of his lone world title. Herzog is close to the Maris family and has said that his friend deserves to be in the Hall of Fame more than anyone who has been overlooked. Perhaps he and 2008 inductee Dick Williams (also picked because of his managerial success) will spearhead a campaign that will silence those powerful writers who have held court for too long and get Roger Maris into the Hall of Fame. Meanwhile, we hope this paperback edition of our book will keep the debate alive.

March 2011

ACKNOWLEDGMENTS

D URING THE TWO YEARS that we researched and wrote about the player who gave us the most thrilling baseball season of our youths, we were given tremendous help from old and new friends. Like us, they passionately believed that Roger Maris never received proper recognition from fans and the media for his talent and achievements, his fine character, and his pivotal role in the emerging war between the press and uncooperative celebrities.

Our first expressions of gratitude go to several individuals whose help proved invaluable: Marty Appel, Johnny Blanchard, Sherry Hunt, John Jensen, Bill Maras, Michael Maras, Nick Maras Jr., Tim McCarver, Peggy Sanborn, Dick Savageau, George Steinbrenner, and Andy Strasberg.

We had the good fortune to talk to players, coaches, managers, batboys, umpires, and a trainer who knew Roger Maris in the minor and major leagues: Joe Altobelli, Ruben Amaro Sr., Earl Averill II, Gary Bell, Fred Bengis, Yogi Berra, Bobby Bragan, Eddie Bressoud, Jim Brosnan, Jim Bunning, Joe Camacho, Orlando Cepeda, Bob Cerv, Tex Clevenger, Bud Daley, Joe De Maestri, Art Ditmar, Al Downing, Ryne Duren, Doc Edwards, Chuck Estrada, Elroy Face, Don Ferrarese, Mike Ferraro, Terry Fox, Terry Francona, Phil Gagliano, John Gamble, Joe Garagiola, Ned Garver, Jim Gentile, Jake Gibbs, Wayne Granger, Mudcat Grant, Eli Grba, Dick Groat, Bob Hale, Bill Haller, Carroll Hardy, Billy Harrell, Mike Hegan, Ray Herbert, Clell Hobson, Ralph Houk, Dick Hughes, Larry Jaster, Julian Javier, Ferguson Jenkins, Paul "Cooter" Jones, Jim Kaat, Al Kaline, Ralph Kiner, Bill Kinnamon, George Kissell, Johnny Kucks, Jim Landis, Don Larsen, Frank Lary, Vern Law, Paul Lozito, Jerry Lumpe, Joe Macko, Frank Malzone, Bob Martyn, Dal Maxvill, Cal McLish, Jerry Mehlisch, Bill Monbouquette, Billy Moran, Joe L. Morgan, Joe M. Morgan, Don Mossi, Stan Musial, Hal Naragon, Ray Narleski, Russ Nixon, Billy O'Dell, Dan

Osinski, Jim O'Toole, Milt Pappas, Billy Pierce, Mert Prophet, Rudy Regalado, Rich Rollins, Red Schoendienst, Dick Schofield, Tom Seaver, Ray Seif, Bobby Shantz, Rollie Sheldon, Roy Sievers, Dick Stigman, George Strickland, Tom Sturdivant, Ralph Terry, Wayne Terwilliger, Dick Tomanek, Tom Tresh, Bob Turley, Coot Veal, Preston Ward, Ray Washburn, Roy White, Floyd Wicker, Dick Williams, Stan Williams, Dooley Womack, and Hal Woodeshick. Additionally, we drew from conversations conducted for the 1994 book *We Played the Game* with Chico Carrasquel, Tom Cheney, Harmon Killebrew, Minnie Minoso, Vic Power, Pedro Ramos, Bobby Richardson, Brooks Robinson, Bill Skowron, Al Smith, and Gene Woodling.

We also spoke to members of Roger's family, his friends, and others whose lives were touched by him: Jim Adelson, John Blakely, MarLynn Blakely, Nancy Blanchard, Wayne Blanchard, Dick Cecil, Pat Colliton, Catherine Cortese, Michelle Cortese, Violet Marich Cortese, Jerry Cosentino, Anna Dosen, Sal and Rosemarie Durante, Bill Gallo, Don Gooselaw, Bill Grigsby, Merle Harmon, Reid Harmon, Arlene Howard, Rob Johnson, Orv Kelly, Jim LaFreniere Jr., Roger LaFreniere, Rod Lucier, Anna Marie Maras, Nick Maras Sr., Rudy and Betty Marich, Jim McLaughlin, Jane Oftelie, Don O'Neil, Mike O'Neil, Barry Pepper, Tilly Sanborn, Larry Scott, Walt Seeba, Bill Starcevic, Elizabeth Starcevic, Pat Stengel, George and Margaret Surprise, Larry Sweeney, Gailen Telander, Maureen Tomanek, Bobby Vee, Bob Wood, and Marianne Woodeshick.

We were aided in our research by the National Baseball Hall of Fame, New York Yankees, New York Mets, Fargo Public Library, East Hampton Free Library, New York Public Library, ESPN, Iron Range Research Center, Minnesota Historical Society, Hibbing Recorder's Office, Hibbing High School, Crow Wing County Historical Society, Duluth County Courthouse, North Dakota State Education Office, Roger Maris Museum, Major League Baseball Alumni Association, and in particular Pam Anderson, Janis V. Baker, Betty Birnstihl, Tonya Boltz, Diane Briggs, Helen Dizazenovich, Shane Etter, Bill Francis, Sue Godfrey, John Hallberg, Lorraine Hamilton, Geoff Hixon, Diana Hock, Al Houle, Stephen Hubbard, Gregg Inkpen, Dave Kaplan, Pat Kelly, Lucille Kirkeby, Scott Kuzma, Whitney La Rocca, Brenda Macki, Jessica Oftelie, Rusty Papanek, Beth Pierce, Howard Rubenstein, Gabriel Schecter, Connie Schwabe, Joanne Sher, and Tim Wiles.

We applaud sportswriters Maury Allen, Stan Isaacs, George Vecsey, and

Ralph Wimbish for providing insightful, first-hand recollections of Roger Maris. We also thank all the writers whose articles and books we used as sources.

Extra praise goes to our terrific transcribers Kelly Olsen, Valerie Pillsworth, and Paul Brenner, and our assistant Emily Edahl. We want to make special mention of our much-missed friend and researcher Ruth Simring.

We also want to express our deep appreciation to Sandra Boynton, Greg Christensen, Jeanie Dooha, Ann ffolliott, Isaac Fox, Cory Gann, Barbara and Charlie Haynes, Carol Hopkins, Pamela Jameson, Ryan Jimenez, Jill Susan Joi, Mark Kriegel, Joe Koch, Doris LaFreniere, Shirley LaFreniere, Ann Liguori, Lee Lowenfish, Carol Maras, Alana McElroy, Herman Milligan, Charles Nauen, Elinor Nauen, Nathan Prosser, Amy Rackear, Tom Rock, Melissa Rogers, Steve Rosenbaum, Leo Seif, Caitlin Speed, Rosy Stefanates, and Bill Turk.

We are most grateful to everyone at RLR Associates, particularly those who found a splendid home for this biography—Robert Rosen, Scott Gould, Gary Rosen, and Jennifer Unter. We also thank all the people at that home, Touchstone/S&S, especially our editor Zach Schisgal, who lived the book with us, publisher Stacy Creamer and editor in chief Trish Todd, senior production editors Mara Lurie and John Paul Jones, super editorial assistant Alessandra Preziosi, publicity director Marcia Burch, publicist Jessica Roth, Mark Gompertz, and copyeditor Steve Boldt.

Finally, we thank family and friends who supported us every step of the way. Tom would like to thank Leslie Reingold, Bob Drury, Denise McDonald, and Bob Schaeffer, and his children, Kathryn and Brendan Clavin, who are fourth-generation Yankee fans. Danny thanks his wife Suzanne, daughter Zoë, son-in-law Gene, granddaughter Julianna, brother Gerald, and sister-in-law Amy Geller—none of whom are Yankee fans.

APPENDIX

61 IN 1961

NUMBER	GAME	DATE	PITCHER	TEAM
1	11	04-26	Paul Foytack	Detroit
2	17	05-03	Pedro Ramos	Minnesota
3	20	05-06	Eli Grba	Los Angeles
4	29	05-17	Pete Burnside	Washington
5	30	05-19	Jim Perry	Cleveland
6	31	05-20	Gary Bell	Cleveland
7	32	05-21	Chuck Estrada	Baltimore
8	35	05-24	Gene Conley	Boston
9	38	05-28	Cal McLish	Chicago
10	40	05-30	Gene Conley	Boston
11	40	05-30	Mike Fornieles	Boston
12	41	05-31	Billy Muffett	Boston
13	43	06-02	Cal McLish	Chicago
14	44	06-03	Bob Shaw	Chicago
15	45	06-04	Russ Kemmerer	Chicago
16	48	06-06	Ed Palmquist	Minnesota
17	49	06-07	Pedro Ramos	Minnesota
18	52	06-09	Ray Herbert	Kansas City
19	55	06-11	Eli Grba	Los Angeles
20	55	06-11	Johnny James	Los Angeles
21	57	06-13	Jim Perry	Cleveland
22	58	06-14	Gary Bell	Cleveland
23	61	06-17	Don Mossi	Detroit
24	62	06-18	Jerry Casale	Detroit
25	63	06-19	Jim Archer	Kansas City
26	64	06-20	Joe Nuxhall	Kansas City

27	66	06-22	Norm Bass	Kansas City
28	74	07-01	Dave Sisler	Washington
29	75	07-02	Pete Burnside	Washington
30	75	07-02	Johnny Klippstein	Washington
31	77	07-04	Frank Lary	Detroit
32	78	07-05	Frank Funk	Cleveland
33	82	07-09	Bill Monbouquette	Boston
34	84	07-13	Early Wynn	Chicago
35	86	07-15	Ray Herbert	Chicago
36	92	07-21	Bill Monbouquette	Boston
37	95	07-25	Frank Baumann	Chicago
38	95	07-25	Don Larsen	Chicago
39	96	07-25	Russ Kemmerer	Chicago
40	96	07-25	Warren Hacker	Chicago
41	106	08-04	Camilo Pascual	Minnesota
42	114	08-11	Pete Burnside	Washington
43	115	08-12	Dick Donovan	Washington
44	116	08-13	Bennie Daniels	Washington
45	117	08-13	Marty Kutyna	Washington
46	118	08-15	Juan Pizarro	Chicago
47	119	08-16	Billy Pierce	Chicago
48	119	08-16	Billy Pierce	Chicago
49	124	08-20	Jim Perry	Cleveland
50	125	08-22	Ken McBride	Los Angeles
51	129	08-26	Jerry Walker	Kansas City
52	135	09-02	Frank Lary	Detroit
53	135	09-02	Hank Aguirre	Detroit
54	140	09-06	Tom Cheney	Washington
55	141	09-07	Dick Stigman	Cleveland
56	143	09-09	Mudcat Grant	Cleveland
57	151	09-16	Frank Lary	Detroit
58	152	09-17	Terry Fox	Detroit
59	155	09-20	Milt Pappas	Baltimore
60	159	09-26	Jack Fisher	Baltimore
61	163	10-01	Tracy Stallard	Boston

Career Stats

YR	CLUB	LEAGUE	G	AB	R	H	TB	2B	3B	HR	SG%	RBI	SH	SF	TBB	IBB	HP	SO	SB	CS	GDP	PCT
53	Fargo-Moorhead	Northern	114	418	74	136	207	18	13	9	.495	80	4	–	76	–	3	62	14	–	–	.325
54	Keokuk	Three-I	134	502	105	158	292	26	6	32	.582	111	1	1	80	–	4	53	25	–	–	.315
55	Tulsa	Texas	25	90	9	21	25	1	0	1	.278	9	0	2	15	–	1	18	2	1	–	.233
55	Reading	Eastern	113	374	74	108	186	15	3	19	.497	78	1	4	77	–	4	60	24	–	–	.239
56	Indianapolis	Amer. Assn.	131	433	77	127	214	20	8	17	.494	75	2	5	41	–	4	55	7	–	7	.293
57	Cleveland	American	116	358	61	84	145	9	5	14	.405	51	3	2	60	5	1	79	8	4	6	.235
58	Cleveland	American	51	182	26	41	75	5	1	9	.412	27	0	3	17	2	0	33	4	2	0	.225
58	Kansas City	American	99	401	61	99	176	14	3	19	.439	53	2	2	28	1	2	52	0	0	2	.247
59	Kansas City	American	122	433	69	118	201	21	7	16	.464	72	0	4	58	5	3	53	2	1	4	.273
60	New York	American	136	499	98	141	290	18	7	39	.581	112	1	5	70	4	3	65	2	2	6	.283
61	New York	American	161	590	132	159	366	16	4	61	.620	141	0	7	94	0	7	67	0	0	16	.269
62	New York	American	157	590	92	151	286	34	1	33	.485	100	1	3	87	11	6	78	1	0	7	.256
63	New York	American	90	312	53	84	169	14	1	23	.542	53	1	1	35	3	2	40	1	0	2	.269
64	New York	American	141	513	86	144	238	12	2	26	.464	71	1	2	62	1	6	78	3	0	7	.281
65	New York	American	46	155	22	37	68	7	0	8	.439	27	1	1	29	1	0	29	0	0	4	.239
66	New York	American	119	348	37	81	133	9	2	13	.382	43	0	4	36	3	3	60	0	0	8	.233
67	St. Louis	National	125	410	64	107	166	18	7	9	.405	55	1	5	52	3	4	61	0	0	10	.261
68	St. Louis	National	100	310	25	79	116	18	2	5	.374	45	4	4	24	3	1	38	0	0	3	.255
	12 Major League Seasons		1463	5101	826	1325	2429	195	42	275	.476	851	12	43	652	42	38	733	21	9	75	.260

SELECTED BIBLIOGRAPHY

Adams, Charles J., III. *Baseball in Reading*. Chicago: Arcadia Publishing, 2003.

Allen, Maury. *Roger Maris: A Man for All Seasons*. New York: Donald I. Fine, 1986.

Anderson, Dave, Murray Chass, Robert Lipsyte, Buster Olney, and George Vecsey of the *New York Times*. *The New York Yankees Illustrated History*. New York: St. Martin's Press, 2002.

Appel, Marty. *Now Pitching for the Yankees: Spinning the News for Mickey, Billy, and George*. Kingston, NY: Total Sports Illustrated, 2001.

Barra, Allen. *Yogi Berra: Eternal Yankee*. New York: W. W. Norton, 2009.

Berkow, Ira. *Beyond the Dream: Occasional Heroes of Sports*. New York: Atheneum, 1968.

Berra, Yogi, with Dave Kaplan. *Ten Rings: My Championship Seasons*. New York: William Morrow, 2003.

Berra, Yogi, and Ed Fitzgerald. *Yogi: The Autobiography of a Professional Baseball Player*. Garden City, NY: Doubleday, 1961.

Bouton, Jim. *Ball Four*. Ed. Leonard Shecter. New York: World Publishing, 1970.

———. *I'm Glad You Didn't Take It Personally*. Ed. Leonard Shecter. New York: William Morrow, 1971.

Bragan, Bobby, and Jeff Guinn. *You Can't Hit the Ball with the Bat on Your Shoulder: The Baseball Life and Times of Bobby Bragan*. Fort Worth, TX: Summit Group, 1992.

Broeg, Bob. *Bob Broeg, Memoirs of a Hall of Fame Sportswriter*. Champaign, IL: Sagamore Publishing, 1995.

Brosnan, Jim. *Little League to Big League*. New York: Random House, 1968.

Buck, Jack, with Bob Rains and Bob Broeg. *Jack Buck: "That's a Winner!"* Champaign, IL: Sports Publishing, 2002.

Cannon, Jimmy. *Nobody Asked Me, But . . . : The World of Jimmy Cannon*. Eds. Jack Cannon and Tom Cannon. New York: Holt, Rinehart and Winston, 1978.

Castro, Tony. *Mickey Mantle: America's Prodigal Son*. Dulles, VA: Potomac Books, 2002.

Cepeda, Orlando, with Herb Fagen. *Baby Bull: From Hardball to Hard Time and Back*. Dallas: Taylor Publishing, 1998.

Creamer, Robert W. *Stengel: His Life and Times.* New York: Simon & Schuster, 1984.

———, ed. *Mantle Remembered (Sports Illustrated Presents).* New York: Warner Books, 1995.

Daley, Arthur. *Kings of the Home Run.* New York: G. P. Putnam's Sons, 1962.

Durso, Joseph. *Casey: The Life and Legend of Charles Dillon Stengel.* Englewood Cliffs, NJ: Prentice-Hall, 1967.

Dylan, Bob. *Chronicles, Volume One.* New York: Simon & Schuster, 2004.

Flood, Curt, with Richard Carter. *The Way It Is.* New York: Trident Press, 1971.

Ford, Whitey, with Phil Pepe. *Few and Chosen: Defining Yankee Greatness Across the Eras.* Chicago: Triumph Books, 2001.

———. *Slick: My Life in and Around Baseball.* New York: William Morrow, 1987.

Ford, Whitey, Mickey Mantle, and Joe Durso. *Whitey and Mickey: An Autobiography of the Yankee Years.* New York: Viking Press, 1977.

Forker, Dom. *Sweet Seasons: Recollections of the 1955–64 New York Yankees.* Dallas: Taylor Publishing, 1990.

Frommer, Harvey. *A Yankee Century.* New York: Berkley, 2002.

Gallo, Bill, with Phil Cornell. *Drawing a Crowd: Bill Gallo's Greatest Sports Moments.* Middle Village, NY: Jonathan David Publishers, 2000.

Gibson, Bob, with Phil Pepe. *From Ghetto to Glory: The Story of Bob Gibson.* Englewood Cliffs, NJ: Associated Features, 1968.

Golenbock, Peter. *Dynasty: New York Yankees, 1949–1964.* Englewood Cliffs, NJ: Prentice-Hall, 1975.

Greenberg, Hank. *Hank Greenberg: The Story of My Life.* Ed. Ira Berkow. New York: Times Books, 1989.

Grimes, Tom. *A Stone of the Heart.* Dallas: Southern Methodist University Press, 1990.

Halberstam, David. *October 1964.* New York: Villard Books, 1994.

Harmon, Merle, with Sam Blair. *Merle Harmon Stories.* Arlington, TX: Reid Productions, 1998.

Herskowitz, Mickey. *The Mickey Herskowitz Collection.* Dallas: Taylor Publishing, 1989.

Houk, Ralph, and Charles Dexter. *Ballplayers Are Human, Too.* New York: G. P. Putnam's Sons, 1962.

Houk, Ralph, and Robert W. Creamer. *Season of Glory: The Amazing Saga of the 1961 New York Yankees.* New York: G. P. Putnam's Sons, 1988.

Howard, Arlene, with Ralph Wimbish. *Elston and Me: The Story of the First Black Yankee.* Columbia, MO: University of Missouri Press, 2001.

Izenberg, Jerry. *The Jerry Izenberg Collection.* Dallas: Taylor Publishing, 1989.

Jenson, Brian. *Where Have All Our Yankees Gone?* Lanham, MD: Taylor Trade Publishing, 2004.

Kahn, Roger. *Beyond the Boys of Summer: The Very Best of Roger Kahn.* Ed. Rod Miraldi. New York: McGraw-Hill, 2005.

Katz, Jeff. *The Kansas City A's & the Wrong Half of the Yankees.* Hingham, MA: Maple Street Press, 2007.

Kiersh, Edward. *Where Have You Gone, Vince DiMaggio?* New York: Bantam Books, 1983.

Kiner, Ralph, with Danny Peary. *Baseball Forever: Reflections on 60 Years in the Game.* Chicago: Triumph Books, 2004.

Kriegel, Mark. *Namath: A Biography.* New York: Viking Press, 2004.

Kubek, Tony, and Terry Pluto. *Sixty-One: The Team, the Record, the Men.* New York: Macmillan, 1987.

Mann, Jack. *The Decline and Fall of the New York Yankees.* New York: Simon & Schuster, 1967.

Mantle, Merlyn, Mickey Mantle Jr., David Mantle, and Dan Mantle, with Mickey Herskowitz. *A Hero All His Life: A Memoir by the Mantle Family.* New York: HarperCollins Publishers, 1996.

Mantle, Mickey, with Mickey Herskowitz. *All My Octobers: My Memories of Twelve World Series When the Yankees Ruled Baseball.* New York: HarperCollins, 1994.

Mantle, Mickey, with Herb Gluck. *The Mick.* New York: Doubleday, 1985.

Mantle, Mickey, and Robert W. Creamer. *The Quality of Courage: Heroes In and Out of Baseball.* Garden City, NY: Doubleday, 1964.

Maris, Roger, and Jim Ogle. *Roger Maris At Bat.* Des Moines, IA, and New York: Meredith Press, 1962.

———. *Slugger in Right.* Larchmont, NY: Argonaut Books, 1963.

McCarver, Tim, with Phil Pepe. *Few and Chosen: Defining Cardinal Greatness Across the Eras.* Chicago: Triumph Books, 2003.

McCarver, Tim, with Danny Peary. *The Perfect Season: Why 1998 Was Baseball's Greatest Year.* New York: Villard Books, 1999.

Murcer, Bobby, with Glen Waggoner. *Yankee for Life: My 40-Year Journey in Pinstripes.* New York: HarperCollins Publishers, 2008.

Orr, Jack, ed. *Baseball's Greatest Players Today.* New York: J. Lowell Pratt, 1963.

Peary, Danny, ed. *Cult Baseball Players: The Greats, the Flakes, the Weird and the Wonderful.* New York: Fireside, 1990.

———, ed. *We Played the Game.* New York: Hyperion, 1994.

Pepitone, Joe, with Berry Stainback. *Joe, You Coulda Made Us Proud.* Chicago: Playboy Press, 1975.

Peterson, John E. *The Kansas City Athletics: A Baseball History 1954–1967.* Jefferson, NC: McFarland, 2003.

Richardson, Bobby. *The Bobby Richardson Story.* Westwood, NJ: Fleming H. Revell, 1965.

Robinson, Ray. *The Greatest Yankees of Them All.* New York: G. P. Putnam's Sons, 1969.

———. ed. *Baseball Stars of 1961.* New York: Pyramid Books, 1961.

———. ed. *Baseball Stars of 1962.* New York: Pyramid Books, 1962.

Rosenfeld, Harvey. *Roger Maris*: A Title to Fame.* Fargo, ND: Prairie House, 1991.

Shecter, Leonard. *The Jocks.* Indianapolis: Bobbs-Merrill, 1969.

———. *Roger Maris: Homerun Hero.* New York: Bartholomew House, 1961.

Schoendienst, Red, with Rob Rains. *Red: A Baseball Life.* Champaign, IL: Sports Publishing, 1998.

Skipper, John C., ed. *Umpires: Classic Baseball Stories from the Men Who Made the Calls.* Jefferson, NC: McFarland, 1997.

Smith, Red. *Red Smith on Baseball: The Game's Greatest Writer on the Game's Greatest Years.* Chicago: Ivan R. Dee, 2000.

Smith, Ron. *(The Sporting News Presents) 61*: The Story of Roger Maris, Mickey Mantle, and One Magical Summer.* St. Louis: Sporting News, 2001.

Stout, Glenn, ed. *Top of the Heap: A Yankees Collection.* New York: Houghton Mifflin, 2003.

Swearingen, Randall. *A Great Teammate: The Legend of Mickey Mantle.* Champaign, IL: Sports Publishing, 2007.

Tan, Cecilia. *The 50 Greatest Yankee Games.* Hoboken, NJ: John Wiley & Sons, 2005.

Vincent, Fay. *The Last Commissioner: A Baseball Valentine.* New York: Simon & Schuster, 2002.

Young, Jon M. *Roger Maris Died Yesterday: A Collection of Short Stories.* Boone, NC: Parkway Publishers, 2004.

INDEX